ASSESSMENT IN COUNSELING

THIRD EDITION

A Guide to the Use of Psychological Assessment Procedures

Albert B. Hood
and
Richard W. Johnson

5999 Stevenson Avenue
Alexandria, VA 22304-3300
www.counseling.org

ASSESSMENT IN COUNSELING
Third Edition

Copyright © 2002 by the American Counseling Association. All rights reserved. Printed in the United States of America. Except as permitted under the United States Copyright Act of 1976, no part of this publication may be reproduced or distributed in any form or by any means, or stored in a database or retrieval system, without the prior written permission of the publisher.

10 9 8 7 6 5

American Counseling Association
5999 Stevenson Avenue
Alexandria, VA 22304

Director of Publications
Carolyn C. Baker

Production Manager
Bonny E. Gaston

Copy Editor
Elaine Dunn

Cover design by Brian Gallagher

Library of Congress Cataloging-in-Publication Data
Hood, Albert B. (Albert Bullard), 1929–
    Assessment in counseling: a guide to the use of psychological
assessment procedures / Albert B. Hood, Richard W. Johnson.—3rd
ed.
        p.   cm.
    Includes bibliographical references and index.
    ISBN 1-55620-187-7
    1. Psychological tests.   2. Counseling.   I. Johnson, Richard W.,
1934–   II. Title.
BF176.H66   2001
150′.28′7—dc21   2001045823

CONTENTS

I

SECTION
Basic Concepts of Psychological Assessment

CONTENTS

II

SECTION
Cognitive Assessment

CONTENTS

III

SECTION

Career and Life Planning Assessment

CONTENTS

IV

SECTION
Personality Assessment

V

SECTION

Professional Practices and Considerations

VI

SECTION

Appendices

CONTENTS

FOREWORD
Written for 1st Edition

PSYCHOLOGICAL TESTS first became available in the United States during the early part of the century. Lewis Terman's Stanford–Binet Intelligence Test, a carefully standardized and individually administered intelligence test that initiated the famous $MA/CA = IQ$, became public in 1916. This remained a basic test for the next 7 decades and beyond. In 1921 Arthur Otis, a former student of Terman's, published the first Group Intelligence Test, a paper-and-pencil test using the extensive research performed on the Army Alpha and the Army Beta tests of World War I. E. K. Strong, Jr., opened another area when the Vocational Interest Blank was published in 1927. This test, with major revisions and additions, has become one of the most widely used tests of the century. Robert Woodworth's Rating Scale appeared early in the 1920s. Around 1930 personality tests began to make their appearance, with pioneering productions by Robert Bernreuter and Hugh Bell. All but one of these early productions originated at Stanford University. They became part of my life because I did my graduate work at Stanford at about that time (1928–1932) with Terman and Strong as my MA and PhD advisors. I did my bit in these early ventures by bringing out the first edition of the Study Habits Inventory in 1935.

Let me add to the personal note of these years by recalling that during my first year at Stanford I was given an appointment as what we would now call a student personnel assistant—Stanford's first. This involved counseling in the registrar's office and giving admissions tests for the university. Stanford had pioneered in those early days by giving what we would now call scholastic aptitude tests as part of the admissions process. I made trips each spring throughout the state giving the Thorndike Intelligence Test to prospective students at Stanford testing centers. Kathleen, my wife, accompanied me and scored the tests as we moved along—at 25¢ an hour!

After 8 years at Stanford, I accepted an appointment at the University of Minnesota (1936–1964) and again moved into another center of intense test activity. Over these past 75 years, I have seen an accelerating development of psychological tests and other types of assessment, tests for many purposes. During World War II, tests were used in selecting millions of war workers, in assigning other millions in the Armed Forces, and in diagnosing the mental and social health problems of men and women under stress. Today also, tests are used to make decisions for or against a client. This is not a counselor's use of tests; a counselor uses tests or other assessment measures to help clients understand themselves. The authors of this book state this very clearly in words that should appear in large black type: "*In the counseling setting . . . psychological tests are used to help clients to understand themselves. . . . [They are] used primarily to assist individuals in developing their potential to the fullest and to their own satisfaction*" (italics mine) from "Final Statement," Chapter 18, p. 394.

This is a significant book in my experience, a book written by two professionals whose scholarship, depth of experience with assessment in counseling, and sheer desire to be helpful to the reader are apparent on every page. It is a pragmatic book, focusing on what has been useful to others and using a simple problem-solving model. The authors clearly indicate how tests are used differently in different counseling settings: schools, university counseling centers, hospitals and mental health centers, banks, business, government, and private practice.

The first four chapters (Chapters 1–4) introduce the reader to basic concepts in psychological assessment and to the statistical understandings necessary in the selection and interpretation of tests, not in their construction. The last three chapters (Chapters 16–18) deal with special populations, communications, and ethics in the use of tests.

Chapters 5–15 treat with care and skill the use of more than 100 tests, inventories, and other assessment measures in each of 11 categories. Numerous tables, figures, appendices, and reference citations provide a great deal of information in compact bundles. The treatment of the literature is admirable—no long quotations in varying styles of writing, but interpretations and applications all in the same simple, consistent wording of the two authors.

By this time, the reader may begin to suspect that I like this book. I do indeed! I commend it to counselors and psychologists without reservation. I wish that it had been available to me during my lifetime of service. I would have been a better counselor.

—*C. Gilbert Wrenn*

PREFACE

A
S WITH PREVIOUS EDITIONS, the purpose of this book is to provide information about the various psychological assessment procedures that are specifically relevant for practicing counselors. The book deals with the use of these assessment procedures in the counseling process and includes illustrative case studies. It emphasizes the selection, interpretation, and communication of psychological test results and highlights the basic principles of psychological assessment. It also emphasizes the importance of integrating test results with other information about the client.

The book is not designed to be a comprehensive textbook or desk manual on the various tests themselves. There are a number of excellent books that describe psychological tests and other assessment procedures in detail (such as Kapes & Whitfield, 2001, and the *Mental Measurements Yearbooks*). It is expected that counselors will make use of such publications along with other resources, including the test manuals themselves, which deal with the construction, reliability, and validity of the various assessment instruments. This book assumes that the reader possesses basic knowledge of statistics often required in the evaluation and use of psychological tests.

Since the first two editions of this book, a number of assessment instruments often used in counseling have been revised. Major revisions include the Beck Depression Inventory–Second Edition (BDI-II); Myers–Briggs Type Indicator (MBTI, Form M); Wechsler Adult Intelligence Scale–Third Edition (WAIS-III); new editions of the Stanford, Iowa, and Metropolitan achievement tests; Otis–Lennon School Ability Test–7th edition (OLSAT7); Kuhlmann Anderson Tests (KA); Career Maturity Inventory; Career Orientation Placement and Evaluation Survey (COPES); California Psychological Inventory–3rd edition (CPI); Jackson Vocational Interest Survey (JVIS); Tennessee Self-Concept Scale–2 (TSCS:2); Jackson Personality Inventory–Revised (JPI-R); Marital Satisfaction Inventory–Revised (MSI-R); State–Trait Anger Expression Inventory–2 (STAXI-2); and Multidimensional

Aptitude Battery–II (MAB-II). The material in this book has been updated for each of these tests.

Several new tests have been developed to replace old tests. The General Aptitude Test Battery and U.S. Employment Service Interest Inventory have been replaced by the O*NET Career Exploration Tools. The ACT Career Planning Survey supplants the ACT Career Planning Program. The TerraNova achievement and basic skill batteries supersede the California Achievement Tests.

In addition to the changes found in established tests, a number of promising new instruments are discussed. New tests that have special interest for counselors include the Kuder Career Search With Person Match, the Skills Confidence Inventory (which has been developed for use with the Strong Interest Inventory), ACT WorkKeys, Quality of Life Inventory, Career Decision-Making Self-Efficacy Scale, Hogan Development Survey, Personality Assessment Screener, Naglieri Nonverbal Ability Test, and Clinical Assessment Scales for the Elderly. Each of these new instruments is described in this edition.

This edition contains information on changes in professional guidelines for the use of tests, on the profound transformations concerning computer use in testing, and on research pertaining to the use of various tests with minority populations. The implications of the newly revised *Standards for Educational and Psychological Testing* for use of assessment procedures in counseling are discussed. The development of computerized adaptive tests, such as those used for the Graduate Record Examination (GRE), Graduate Management Admission Test (GMAT), and Test of English as a Foreign Language (TOEFL), are discussed. A number of Web sites that provide information related to assessment procedures are identified. Other topics that receive increased attention include the rights and responsibilities of test takers, assessment of attention-deficit/hyperactivity disorder, structured interviews, mental status exams, and the use of assessment instruments with elderly individuals.

As with the previous editions, this volume is again organized into five sections. Section I presents basic concepts of psychological assessment. It includes an introduction to the nature and use of psychological assessment procedures in counseling, briefly describes certain important measurement concepts, and discusses initial assessment procedures. This section provides an overview of the commonly used descriptive statistical concepts but is not intended as a substitute for a basic knowledge of psychological statistics. Section II covers cognitive assessment and the various tests that assess intelligence, academic aptitude, and academic achievement. Section III deals with assessment procedures used by counselors to assist clients in making decisions regarding careers and life plans. In Section IV, personality assessment is considered, including the use of personality inventories and other personality measures in counseling. This section also reviews instruments used for assessment of interpersonal relationships, various aspects of mental health, and certain mental disorders. Finally, Section V deals with professional practices and considerations. It includes assessment of ethnic and special populations; guidelines for the communication of test results, both in interviews and in case reports; and a discussion of the significant ethical and social issues that arise with psychological assessment procedures used in counseling.

Appendices A, B, and C provide excerpts from the ethical codes and test standards of professional organizations that are particularly appropriate for counselors. Appendix D lists the names, addresses, and Web sites of publishers of tests commonly used by counselors, along with the names of the instruments that may be ordered from these publishers.

In graduate courses that cover the use of tests and other appraisal procedures in counseling, information about the various instruments is typically covered, but the actual use of psychological assessment procedures in counseling often must be learned through trial and error. This volume should remedy that situation by providing information to assist the counselor in choosing, administering, and interpreting psychological assessment procedures as part of the counseling process.

ACKNOWLEDGMENTS

Albert B. Hood wishes to acknowledge the contributions of many colleagues at various institutions who, at formal presentations as well as informal conversations at lunches and social gatherings, have helped him stay abreast of developments in the psychological testing field. He also expresses his thanks to Ginny Travis and Reta Litton for the word processing of numerous manuscript drafts as rough notes were transformed into finished chapters for this and previous editions. He is also grateful for the collections of the Paul Blommers Measurement Resources Laboratory as a valuable resource of test information.

Richard W. Johnson would like to acknowledge the influence of his mentors at the University of Minnesota who first taught him to appreciate the importance of assessment in counseling. He is thankful to his colleagues, graduate students, and clients at the University of Wisconsin–Madison who have contributed to his knowledge and understanding of the use of psychological assessment in counseling.

Both authors are grateful to the following people for their help in reviewing portions of the manuscript or for providing information that aided in the preparation of the manuscript: David P. Campbell, Jerome T. Kapes, Lisa Munro, Dale J. Prediger, Angela Schmidt, Jeannie P. Stroupe, Ann White, and Donald Zytowski.

Both authors continue to be grateful to their wives—Jean and Adelle—for their patience with curtailed social activities and deferred home maintenance schedules during the time that this volume was being written and revised.

—Albert B. Hood
Iowa City, Iowa
—Richard W. Johnson
Madison, Wisconsin
May 2001

ABOUT THE AUTHORS

Albert B. Hood is emeritus professor of education and former chair of the Division of Counselor Education at the University of Iowa. He received his BA degree (1951) from the University of New Hampshire in psychology and his EdD degree (1957) from Cornell University in counseling and student personnel administration.

He has been the assistant director of the Student Counseling Service at Princeton University and a counseling psychologist in the Student Counseling Bureau at the University of Minnesota. In addition to using psychological tests regularly in his counseling practice, he worked with several colleagues at the Educational Testing Service in Princeton and consulted with various test authors as he conducted research studies on academic aptitudes (with Ralph Berdie; the Minnesota Scholastic Aptitude Test), interest inventories (with David Campbell; the Strong Vocational Interest Blank), and personality measures (with Starke Hathaway; the Minnesota Multiphasic Personality Inventory). Now at the University of Iowa, he has coauthored several student development inventories and has consulted with staff members of the American College Testing Program. He held a research fellowship in Kyoto, Japan, and a Fulbright lectureship in the Soviet Union, and he has been a visiting faculty member at the University of Utah, at San Francisco State University, and at IKIP Yojyakarta, Indonesia.

Author of more than 100 books, monographs, and professional articles, Dr. Hood received the Contribution to Knowledge Award of the American College Personnel Association (ACPA) in 1985 and the American Counseling Association's Extended Research Award in 1994. He was the editor of ACPA's *Journal of College Student Personnel* from 1970 to 1976 and is a fellow in the American Psychological Association's Division 17 (Counseling) and in the American Psychological Society. Dr. Hood's scholarly work has dealt primarily with research on the psychological, educational, and vocational development of college students, and a large proportion of the over 60 PhD dissertations he has directed have dealt with psychological assessment.

His e-mail address is albert-hood@uiowa.edu.

Richard W. Johnson is former director of training for Counseling and Consultation Services, a unit of University Health Services, at the University of Wisconsin–Madison, where he also served as adjunct professor of counseling psychology until his retirement in 1997. He obtained his PhD degree in counseling psychology at the University of Minnesota in 1961, after graduating with honors in psychology from Princeton University in 1956. Prior to joining the staff at the University of Wisconsin–Madison in 1968, he taught and counseled at the University of Massachusetts–Amherst and at the University of North Dakota.

Dr. Johnson has served on the editorial boards for three journals of the American Counseling Association: *Journal of College Student Development, Measurement and Evaluation in Counseling and Development,* and *The Career Development Quarterly.* He has been a frequent contributor to scholarly journals in the field of counseling psychology. His professional interests include psychological assessment, career development, cognitive–behavioral counseling, and individual differences. He was the recipient of the Exemplary Practices Award from the Association for Assessment in Counseling in 1998.

His e-mail address is rwjohnso@facstaff.wisc.edu.

I

Basic Concepts of Psychological Assessment

1

USE OF ASSESSMENT PROCEDURES IN COUNSELING

ASSESSMENT HAS ALWAYS PLAYED an important part in counseling. During the early days, counseling and testing were virtually synonymous. Many of the counseling centers established during the 1930s and 1940s were called Counseling and Testing Centers. At that time, counseling typically involved helping students to make educational or vocational plans on the basis of test results.

In recent years, the role of counseling has broadened to include many issues beyond academic and career planning. Counselors help clients address a variety of concerns, such as self-esteem, shyness, personal growth, family and couple relationships, sexual identity, sexual abuse, cross-cultural communication, substance abuse, eating disorders, depression, anxiety, and suicidal ideation. Many counselors now work in community mental health settings, private practices, hospitals, and businesses as well as in educational institutions. During the same time, the nature of psychological assessment has expanded to assist counselors and clients in all of these areas.

Psychological assessment, which includes the use of a wide variety of evaluation methods, enables counselors to identify the nature of a client's concern and to consider possible treatment approaches. Counselors also rely on assessment data for program planning and evaluation. Clients use the results of assessment to understand themselves better and to make plans for the future.

The assessment process can be therapeutic in itself by helping clients to clarify goals and to gain a sense of perspective. Research indicates that clients benefit significantly from personality assessment (Finn & Tonsager, 1992), vocational interest assessment (Randahl, Hansen, & Haverkamp, 1993), and relationship assessment (Worthington et al., 1995) when the assessment is accompanied by a feedback session.

For most purposes, assessment can be conceptualized in terms of problem solving (Lovitt, 1998; Nezu & Nezu, 1993; Walsh & Betz, 2000). This chapter begins with a discussion of the purpose of assessment within the framework of a problem-solving model. Principles of psychological assessment are then considered, followed by a discussion of attitudes toward psychological assessment. Finally, results of surveys of psychological test usage by counselors are presented.

PURPOSE OF PSYCHOLOGICAL ASSESSMENT

The problem-solving model often used by counselors provides a convenient means for summarizing the purposes of psychological assessment in counseling. Each of the five steps discussed below in the standard problem-solving model entails the need for information that can be gained through psychological assessment (D'Zurilla & Goldfried, 1971).

Problem Orientation

The first step requires the client to recognize and accept the problem. If the client denies the problem, it cannot be dealt with adequately. Almost any assessment procedure can be used to increase sensitivity to potential problems. Instruments that promote self-awareness and

4

self-exploration can stimulate clients to cope with developmental issues before they become actual problems.

Surveys of groups or classes can help counselors to identify common problems or concerns that can be taken into account in planning programs for clients. A number of needs assessment instruments (e.g., alcohol screening inventories and sexual behavior questionnaires) have been developed for this purpose.

Both client and counselor need to recognize the problem. As soon as a problematic situation is recognized, the client and counselor can begin to approach it in a systematic fashion as indicated by the problem-solving model. The problem-solving model helps to normalize a client's concerns. It implies an acceptance of problems as a normal part of life. The counselor provides support and perspective for the client as the client begins to address the problem. Recognition of the problem, together with a means of addressing it, helps the counselor to establish rapport with the client.

Problem Identification

In the second step, the counselor and the client attempt to identify the problem in as much detail as possible. Assessment procedures can help clarify the nature of the client's problem. For example, problem or symptom checklists can be used to assess the type and the extent of a client's concerns. Personal diaries or logs can also be used to identify situations in which the problem occurs. Personality inventories can help counselors and clients to understand personality dynamics underlying certain situations. Information gained during the course of identifying client problems can be used to specify counseling goals.

Problem identification improves communication with the client. A client is more likely to continue in counseling if the counselor and client agree on the nature of the problem (Epperson, Bushway, & Warman, 1983; Pekarik, 1988). Identification of the problem also aids in communication with others, such as referral sources, family, and friends.

Problem identification includes diagnosis, a term that is anathema to some counselors because of its medical connotations; however, diagnosis can be broadly defined to pertain to any classification system used in assessment (Hohenshil, 1996). For example, counselors often distinguish between developmental and pathological problems.

An increasing number of counselors now work in mental health settings where they need to become familiar with the *Diagnostic and Statistical Manual of Mental Disorders* (4th ed., *DSM–IV*; American Psychiatric Association, 1994), the system most often used to classify mental disorders.

Generation of Alternatives

In the third step, the counselor and client generate alternatives to help resolve the problem. Assessment procedures enable counselors and clients to identify alternative solutions for client problems. For example, an interest inventory can suggest alternative career choices for a client. An assessment interview can be used to determine what techniques have worked for the client in the past when faced with a similar problem. Checklists (such as a study skills inventory or work skills survey) yield data that can be used to generate alternatives.

Test results can help clients to view problems from different angles. For example, instruments that measure personality styles provide clients with alternative ways of looking at their behavior or the behavior of others. Assessment exercises can identify positive self-statements of clients, which can open up alternatives for clients (Parks & Hollon, 1988). Counselors use assessment procedures to assist clients in discovering strengths on which they can build to overcome difficulties or enhance development (Duckworth, 1990).

Assessment instruments can also be used to stimulate new learning (Krumboltz & Worthington, 1999). For example, the profile report for the Campbell Interest and Skill Survey encourages clients to explore career fields in which their skills are high but their interests are relatively low. Similarly, clients are encouraged to develop skills in those areas in which they have interests but lack skills.

Decision Making

In deciding on a solution to a problem, clients need to anticipate the consequences of the various alternatives. According to classical decision theory, choice is a function of the probability of success and the desirability of the outcome (Horan, 1979). This equation emphasizes the importance of assessing both the likelihood of success of various alternatives and the attractiveness of those alternatives for the client.

Clients will usually want to consider those alternatives that maximize the likelihood of a favorable outcome.

In the fourth step, counselors use assessment materials to help clients weigh the attractiveness of each alternative and the likelihood of achieving each alternative. For example, the attractiveness of various alternatives can be assessed by values clarification exercises. The likelihood of achieving different alternatives can be evaluated by expectancy (or experience) tables that show the success rate for people with different types of test scores or characteristics (Anastasi & Urbina, 1997). Balance sheets or decision-making grids enable clients to compare the desirability and feasibility of various alternatives (Cochran, 1983).

Counselors can use assessment data to help determine the appropriate treatment for clients. For example, achievement test scores can be used to guide a student's course selections. Scores on the Minnesota Multiphasic Personality Inventory (MMPI) can be used to help decide which type of treatment program to use for a client (Butcher, 1997). *DSM–IV* diagnoses can provide a basis for treatment planning (Seligman, 1998).

Verification

Counselors need to evaluate the effectiveness of their counseling (Steenbarger & Smith, 1996). They need to verify that the client's problem has been resolved or reduced. The counselor should discuss with the client how the client would know when the problem has been solved. This fifth step requires that goals be clearly specified, that they be translated into specific behavioral objectives, and that the possibility for progress in accomplishing these goals be realistically viewed. Assessment procedures for this purpose include goal attainment scaling (Kiresuk, Smith, & Cardillo, 1994), self-monitoring techniques (Korotitsch & Nelson-Gray, 1999), the readministration of tests that the client completed earlier in counseling, client satisfaction surveys, and the use of outcome questionnaires (M. G. Wells, Burlingame, Lambert, & Hoag, 1996).

Besides serving as a guide for the counseling process, verification efforts also provide a means of accountability for the counseling agency. Positive feedback from clients can be used to gain support for counseling practices, especially in managed-care settings. Negative feedback can be used to help revise programs to make them more effective.

PRINCIPLES OF PSYCHOLOGICAL ASSESSMENT

According to the *Standards for Educational and Psychological Testing,* the term *assessment* refers to "any systematic method of obtaining information from tests and other sources, used to draw inferences about characteristics of people, objects, or programs" (American Educational Research Association, American Psychological Association, & National Council on Measurement in Education, 1999, p. 172). The first part of this definition ("any systematic method of obtaining information from tests and other sources") indicates that a broad range of evaluation methods, such as standardized tests, interviews, and rating scales, may be used as a means of obtaining data about clients. Different methods of assessment used by counselors are discussed in Chapter 2.

The second part of the definition ("used to draw inferences about characteristics of people, objects, or programs") emphasizes the use of the assessment data to help counselors to understand their clients and the situations in which the clients find themselves. Psychological assessment is a more comprehensive activity than testing by itself because it includes the integration and interpretation of the results of the tests and other evaluation methods. The data provide a basis for forming and testing hypotheses regarding the nature of a client's issues and possible treatment approaches.

The process of psychological assessment can be described as both a science and an art. Many of the instruments used in psychological assessment have been developed by means of empirical research; however, the process of interpreting the assessment data often depends on the counselor's best judgment. In addition to learning about different evaluation procedures, counselors need to consider how they can improve the judgments they make in the assessment process.

Basic principles for conducting psychological assessments are listed below. Counselors should be able to improve their psychological assessments by adhering to these principles.

1. Consider the purpose of the assessment. As noted in the previous section, a problem-solving model can often be used as a means of

identifying the purpose of assessment in counseling. Focusing on the purpose of the assessment will aid counselors both in selecting assessment instruments and in interpreting their results.

2. Include the client as a collaborator in selecting topics for assessment and in interpreting the results of assessment instruments.

3. Use several methods of assessment. A multimodal assessment method provides a broader view of the issue and can also serve as a means of corroborating the results of any one assessment method. For example, interview impressions may be compared with the results from standardized tests and reports from those who know the client.

4. Assess more than a single variable at a time. A multidimensional approach enriches the assessment process by providing additional information that can be helpful in forming assessments. For example, career counselors may wish to assess such variables as career planning readiness, personal values, interests, and abilities in helping a client with a career planning concern.

5. Use instruments with validity checks, such as "fake good," "fake bad," and "random responding" scales. Make sure that a client's test responses are valid before attempting to interpret the test results.

6. Consider the possibility of multiple problems, such as depression coupled with substance abuse, anxiety, or physical problems. Clients with mental disorders often meet the criteria for more than one disorder at the same time (Kessler et al., 1994).

7. Assess the situation as well as the client. Avoid *attribution bias*, which indicates a predisposition to attribute the cause of problems to the individual rather than to the situation. Environmental factors interact with individual characteristics in affecting one's behavior in a particular situation (Galassi & Perot, 1992).

8. When possible, combine the different assessment data by means of a systematic approach that has been studied and verified. In general, statistical (objective) means of combining data have proved to be superior to clinical (subjective) means of combining data (Grove, Zald, Lebow, Snitz, & Nelson, 2000).

9. Consider alternative hypotheses. Counselors need to be watchful for *confirmatory bias*, that is, a tendency to look only for evidence that will support a favorite hypothesis (Spengler, Strohmer, Dixon, & Shivy, 1995). Seek data that may support an alternative hypothesis as

well as data that may prove a preestablished hypothesis. For example, a counselor who believes that a student is failing in school because of lack of ability should also consider other factors, such as health, personal or family problems, and study skills, which may be affecting academic performance.

10. Treat all assessments as tentative. As additional data become available, the counselor should be ready to revise the assessment. Information obtained over an extended time period is likely to be more valid and reliable than information obtained at one point in time (Garb, 1998). Clients' viewpoints change, and clients' memories of past events are often inaccurate.

11. Keep in mind the *regression effect* when interpreting very high or very low scores, all of which are influenced to some extent by chance factors. On retesting, a client's scores tend to regress toward the mean of the population that the client represents. "Less likely states tend to be followed by more likely states" (Tracey & Rounds, 1999, p. 126). For this reason, it is often helpful to test a client more than once.

12. Become familiar with the issue being assessed. Make use of base rates (frequency of occurrence of a particular behavior or diagnosis within a given population) in undertaking and forming an assessment. For example, because of the frequency of problem drinking among college students, counselors should routinely assess college clients for alcohol abuse (H. Wechsler, Davenport, Dowdall, Moeykens, & Castillo, 1994).

13. Be aware of common cultural or personal biases that may influence assessment decisions. For example, studies show that race bias, social class bias, and gender bias may affect clinical judgment (Garb, 1997).

14. Identify, interpret, and incorporate cultural data as part of the assessment process (Ridley, Li, & Hill, 1998). Use a measure of acculturation to help determine if a client fits the population on which a test was developed and normed (Comas-Díaz & Grenier, 1998).

15. Consult with other professionals regarding assessment procedures and outcomes.

16. Use the assessment results to provide feedback to clients as part of the therapy process. Clients can use the information gained in a feedback session to improve self-understanding and to make

positive changes in their lives (Finn & Tonsager, 1997). Assessments should include an evaluation of a client's strengths as well as limitations.

ATTITUDES TOWARD PSYCHOLOGICAL ASSESSMENT

Psychological testing, which became very popular during and after World Wars I and II, has also been the subject of criticism throughout the years ("Controversy Follows Psychological Testing," 1999; Lehman, 1999; Samuda, 1998b). Tests have been criticized for their lack of predictive validity, misuse in labeling or judging others, bias in regard to assessment of minority groups, invasion of privacy, and disproportionate influence in "high-stakes" decisions such as selection for college or employment.

Some time ago, Goldman (1972) lamented the shortcomings of standardized tests, particularly ability tests, and the counselor's lack of preparation and skill in the use of such tests. In revisiting this issue years later, he reiterated his reservations regarding standardized testing (Goldman, 1994). He argued that most counselors should rely primarily on qualitative assessment and that quantitative assessment should probably become a specialized field for about 10% of the counselors who are well qualified in its use.

Surveys indicate that most counselors understand and use desirable assessment practices; however, some areas of concern have been detected (Elmore, Ekstrom, & Diamond, 1993; Elmore, Ekstrom, Diamond, & Whittaker, 1993). These areas of concern include inadequate knowledge of test norms, too much reliance on test scores without additional information, and insufficient knowledge of possible test bias and how to use tests fairly.

In response to criticisms of the use of tests in counseling, Zytowski (1994b) pointed out that the qualifications required to enter the counseling profession have become more rigorous throughout the years so that new counselors should be better prepared to deal with psychological assessment. He also noted that new tests such as the Self-Directed Search have been developed, and that old tests such as the MMPI-2 and the Strong Interest Inventory have been improved. Finally, he stressed that tests have been more helpful in counseling when they have been used with clients as measures of similarity to different criterion groups (e.g., occupational groups or diagnostic classifications) rather than as measures of potential success in various endeavors.

A comprehensive review of the research literature based on more than 125 meta-analyses found the evidence for psychological test validity to be "strong and compelling" (G. J. Meyer et al., 2001, p. 128). On the basis of this review, Meyer et al. concluded that the validity of psychological tests was comparable with that of medical tests, which are generally well accepted. They emphasized the use of multimethod assessment procedures by skilled clinicians to maximize the validity of individual evaluations.

Most of the dissatisfaction with tests has its basis in unrealistic expectations for tests or misuse. Tests do not provide an infallible answer; instead, they should be looked on as one additional source of information that may be helpful in problem solving. The tests need to be soundly constructed and responsibly applied (Dahlstrom, 1993). Tests can be especially helpful in counseling if they are designed to stimulate self-exploration and self-development, if they are accompanied by extensive interpretive materials, and if counselors are well schooled in their use (Prediger, 1972, 1994b).

To offset criticisms, counselors need to become aware of the strengths and limitations of the assessment procedures used in their counseling. They need to understand both the psychometric properties of tests and the psychological findings regarding the behavior being assessed (Anastasi, 1992). They need to use tests effectively with clients from diverse backgrounds. For example, test experts suggest the following strategies may help to improve the performance of ethnic minorities in high-stakes testing: (a) supplementing cognitive ability tests with noncognitive predictors such as conscientiousness, interpersonal skills, and situational judgment, (b) offering test preparation or orientation programs, (c) using test materials that are motivating for clients to complete, and (d) providing credit for relevant job or life experiences (P. R. Sackett, Schmitt, Ellingson, & Kabin, 2001).

In general, counselors need to learn effective and appropriate procedures for selecting, administering, and interpreting tests and other evaluation methods that they use with clients. They need to be able to integrate the use of psychological assessment procedures with other aspects of counseling to help clients in self-understanding and self-determination. Principles and procedures to aid counselors in these endeavors are presented throughout this book.

SURVEYS OF TEST USAGE

Despite adverse criticism, psychological tests continue to play an important part in counseling. Recent surveys of test usage in different counseling settings are described below. Although preferences for particular tests have changed somewhat over the years, counselors continue to make extensive use of tests for a variety of purposes.

In a survey of National Certified Counselors, Loesch and Vacc (1993) found that the majority of counselors "frequently" or "routinely" assisted clients in understanding test results. Furthermore, this activity was considered to be "very important" or "critically important" by the majority of the counselors. The counselors who responded to the survey considered psychological assessment procedures to be important in both personal and career counseling. In regard to personal counseling, they emphasized the importance of assessing the client's potential for harm to self and others, the client's movement toward counseling goals, and the extent of a client's psychological dysfunction. In regard to career counseling, the counselors stressed the importance of test results for client decision making.

Community Mental Health Counseling

In a comprehensive survey of counselors employed in community-based work settings, Bubenzer, Zimpfer, and Mahrle (1990) found that the majority of the respondents used standardized testing in their counseling practice. They were most likely to use the MMPI, followed by the Strong Interest Inventory (formerly known as the Strong–Campbell Interest Inventory), the Wechsler Adult Intelligence Scale–Revised (WAIS-R), the Myers–Briggs Type Indicator, and the Wechsler Intelligence Scale for Children (WISC). These tests measure a range of behaviors, including psychopathology, career interests, intellectual abilities, and variations in normal personality.

A recent survey of licensed mental health counselors found that the majority of the respondents used assessment instruments in their work (Frauenhoffer, Ross, Gfeller, Searight, & Piotrowski, 1998). In addition to an assessment interview, counselors were most likely to use the MMPI-2, Beck Depression Inventory, WISC-III, WAIS-R, projective tests (House-Tree-Person Projective Technique, Human Figures Drawing Test, and Sentence Completion Test), and the Wide-Range Achievement Test–3 as assessment procedures. These tests have been designed primarily to measure psychopathology and intellectual status.

In a related study, Camera, Nathan, and Puente (1998) found that clinical psychologists in private practice, with whom community-based counselors often work, were most likely to use measures of personality/psychopathology and intellectual/achievement status. As measures of personality/psychopathology, they most frequently used the MMPI-2, projective tests (Rorschach Inkblot Test, Thematic Apperception Test, and House-Tree-Person Projective Technique), Beck Depression Inventory, and Millon Clinical Multiaxial Inventory (MCMI). To measure intellectual/achievement status, they most often used the WAIS-R, WISC-III, or Wide Range Achievement Test–3.

Many of the instruments identified in these surveys require intensive training in their use, particularly the MMPI-2, MCMI, projective techniques, WAIS-R, and WISC-III. These surveys show the need for advanced training in the use of assessment procedures for the counselors who work in these settings.

Career Counseling

According to a survey conducted by Watkins, Campbell, and Nieberding (1994), counseling psychologists most often used the following instruments for vocational assessment (ranked in descending order of usage): Strong Interest Inventory, Self-Directed Search, Kuder Occupational Interest Survey, Differential Aptitude Tests, and General Aptitude Test Battery. Each of these instruments was used by 25% or more of the respondents.

More than two thirds (461 of 637) of the respondents indicated that they used the Strong Interest Inventory for career assessment. In general, the counselors in this study placed greater emphasis on interest measurement than on aptitude measurement, although both were important. They also made use of other types of career assessment instruments, including values inventories (e.g., Work Values Inventory), vocational card sorts, and career development inventories (e.g., Career Maturity Inventory and Career Decision Scale).

According to the survey respondents, they used the assessment instruments (a) to increase client self-knowledge, (b) to help clients make career choices, and (c) to encourage client participation in career counseling.

School Counseling

A survey of members of the American School Counselor Association found that school counselors often engaged in assessment-related tasks in their work (Schafer, 1998). They most frequently performed the following assessment activities:

- Refer students when appropriate to other professionals for additional assessment
- Interpret test scores and use the information in counseling
- Synthesize and integrate testing and nontesting data to make decisions about individuals
- Communicate and interpret test information to students and help them use it for educational and career planning
- Communicate and interpret test information to parents
- Read about and be aware of ethical issues in assessment
- Communicate and interpret test information to teachers, school administrators, and other professionals

The majority of the counselors in the survey indicated that they believed it was essential for school counselors to know how to perform these activities. School administrators and teachers typically consider school counselors to be "test experts," whom they will consult in test matters such as those listed above (Impara & Plake, 1995).

Table 1-1 shows the results of a national survey of school counselors regarding test usage (Elmore, Ekstrom, Diamond, & Whittaker, 1993). In contrast with community-based counselors and career counselors, school counselors are more likely to use tests of scholastic aptitude and achievement.

Approximately two thirds of the respondents indicated that testing was an "important" or "very important" part of their work. Nearly all of the respondents said that they were responsible for interpreting test results to students.

In addition to the tests noted in Table 1-1, school counselors are also likely to be exposed to behavioral assessment procedures, which

TABLE 1-1. Usage of Psychological Assessment Instruments by School Counselors

Rank	Instrument	Total Mentions[a]
1	Wechsler Intelligence Scale for Children–Revised	78
2	Preliminary Scholastic Aptitude Test	77
3	California Achievement Test	67
4	Differential Aptitude Tests	64
5	Strong–Campbell Interest Inventory	62
6	Scholastic Aptitude Test	60
7	American College Testing Program	55
8	Iowa Tests of Basic Skills	53
9	Armed Services Vocational Aptitude Battery	50

Note. From "School Counselors' Test Use Patterns and Practices," by P. B. Elmore, R. B. Ekstrom, E. E. Diamond, and S. Whittaker, 1993, The School Counselor, 41, p. 75. Copyright 1993 by the American Counseling Association. Reprinted with permission. No further reproduction authorized without written permission of the American Counseling Association.
[a]Based on the responses of 423 members of the American School Counselor Association.

are often used by school psychologists to evaluate students for developmental disorders. A recent survey indicates that school psychologists frequently use the Behavior Assessment System for Children, Achenbach Child Behavior Checklist, or Conner's Behavior Rating System for this purpose (Zaske, Hegstrom, & Smith, 1999). Although school counselors may not administer these instruments themselves, they can work more effectively with students if they are familiar with the instruments, both for referral purposes and for understanding and implementing recommendations based on their use.

Most of the tests identified by means of the test usage surveys are discussed in this book. It is important for counselors to learn about these tests so that they can use them successfully in their own practices and so that they can interpret scores from tests for clients referred to them by other mental health professionals.

SUMMARY

1. Psychological assessment is an integral part of counseling. Assessment provides information that can be used in each step of the problem-solving model. The assessment process can be therapeutic in and of itself.

2. Assessment serves the following functions: (a) to stimulate counselors and clients to consider various issues, (b) to clarify the nature of a problem or issue, (c) to suggest alternative solutions for problems, (d) to provide a method of comparing various alternatives so that a decision can be made or confirmed, and (e) to enable counselors and clients to evaluate the effectiveness of a particular solution.

3. Psychological assessment refers to the process of integrating and interpreting client information from a broad range of evaluation methods. This process can be improved by adhering to the basic principles of psychological assessment outlined in this chapter.

4. Negative attitudes toward psychological tests can be traced to unrealistic expectations regarding tests and to the misuse of tests. Psychological assessment needs to be seen in perspective, and counselors must be trained in the proper use of tests.

5. According to surveys of test usage, counselors often engage in assessment activities in their work. Although there is some overlap in the types of tests used in different settings, community mental health counselors are most likely to use measures of psychopathology and intellectual status, career counselors are most likely to use interest inventories and occupational aptitude tests, and school counselors are most likely to use scholastic aptitude and achievement tests.

2

NATURE OF PSYCHOLOGICAL ASSESSMENT IN COUNSELING

COUNSELORS NEED TO BE INFORMED about the basic characteristics of psychological assessment procedures. They must be able to compare and evaluate different assessment procedures. Information presented in this chapter should aid counselors in these endeavors.

In this chapter, the different criteria that have been used to distinguish among psychological assessment procedures are reviewed and then used to describe six common assessment procedures. These procedures include standardized tests, rating scales, projective techniques, behavioral observations, biographical measures, and physiological measures. The standards that have been established for evaluating tests and test usage are identified, and the chapter concludes with a list of informational sources about assessment procedures.

DISTINCTIONS AMONG PSYCHOLOGICAL ASSESSMENT PROCEDURES

Psychological assessment procedures differ from each other in a variety of ways. As indicated below, these differences can be categorized by six basic questions regarding the nature of the assessment procedure itself.

Who Is Making the Assessment?

Is the person making a self-assessment, or is another person making the assessment? Block (1961) differentiated between "S-data" based on self-reports and "O-data" based on the reports of others. Both types of data are needed to obtain a full appraisal of the individual. O-data can be used to validate self-reports; S-data can provide valuable insights regarding self-perception not available in the reports of others.

What Is Being Assessed?

"What" here refers to the subject of the assessment procedure. Is the *individual* or the *environment* the subject of the assessment? Counselors have usually been interested in individual assessment; however, instruments that evaluate the environment (e.g., classroom atmosphere or residence hall settings) can also provide important information for understanding or treating a problem (Chartrand, 1991; S. L. Friedman & Wachs, 1999). The client's behavior depends on both individual and situational characteristics, so counseling can be most effective when psychological assessment includes both the individual and the environment.

If the individual is being appraised, does the content of the assessment deal primarily with *affective* (feeling), *cognitive* (thinking), or *behavioral* (doing) aspects of the individual? These three aspects of the individual may be further subdivided as discussed below.

Affective characteristics may be subdivided into *temperamental* and *motivational* factors (Guilford, 1959). Temperamental factors include the characteristics assessed by most personality inventories, for example, self-sufficiency, stability, and impulsiveness. Motivational factors refer to interests or values. According to Guilford, temperament governs the manner in which an individual performs, whereas motivation determines what activities or goals the individual will choose to pursue.

Cognitive variables may be based on learning that takes place in a specific course (*course-related*) or learning that is relatively independent of specific coursework (*non-course-related*; Anastasi & Urbina, 1997). This distinction describes a basic difference between achievement and aptitude tests. Achievement tests evaluate past or present performance; aptitude tests predict future performance. Achievement tests measure learning that has taken place in a particular course or series of courses. Aptitude tests assess capacity to learn, based on items that are relatively independent of the classroom or of any type of formal educational experience.

Behavioral measures include responses that are *voluntary* or *involuntary* in nature. Voluntary responses may be assessed either by self-monitoring or by other-monitoring techniques. A systematic record is kept of measurable items such as calories consumed or hours spent in watching television. In the case of involuntary responses (e.g., blood pressure or heart rate), various types of physiological measures are used to assess individual reactivity. Biofeedback devices, often used to teach relaxation methods, are a good example of the latter type of assessment measure.

The question of what is being assessed also pertains to the variables chosen for the assessment process. Individuals can be assessed by *common* variables that apply to all people or by *unique* variables that apply only to the individual. In the first case, sometimes referred to as *nomothetic assessment*, emphasis is placed on variables that show lawful or meaningful distinctions among people. The group provides a frame of reference for determining which variables to assess and how to interpret the results. In the second case, sometimes referred to as *idiographic assessment*, emphasis is placed on those variables that can be most helpful in describing the individual. The individual serves as the reference point both to identify relevant variables and to interpret data.

Most psychological tests, such as interest and personality inventories, use the nomothetic approach. These tests use the same scales to describe all clients. Scores are interpreted in regard to a set of norms. In contrast, many of the informal assessment procedures, such as the interview, case study, or card sorts, use an idiographic approach. A different set of variables is used to describe each client. Nomothetic techniques can be more readily interpreted, but they may not be as relevant or as penetrating as idiographic methods, which have been designed to measure variations in individuality (Neimeyer, 1989).

Where Is the Assessment Taking Place?

The location in which the assessment takes place is important in the sense that it helps to differentiate between test results obtained in *laboratory* settings and those obtained in *natural* settings. Many psychological tests must be administered under standardized conditions so that the test results can be interpreted properly. For these tests, a testing room or laboratory is usually used. If the circumstances of test administration differ from person to person, differences in the testing conditions can influence test results. Some measures such as employee ratings are obtained in natural settings under conditions that may vary considerably for different individuals. Variations in job circumstances can greatly affect the ratings. Interpretations of the results must take into account the setting in which they were obtained.

When Is the Assessment Occurring?

The question of when an assessment takes place is of value in distinguishing between assessments planned in advance (*prospective*) and those based on recall (*retrospective*). Self-monitoring techniques are usually planned in advance. For example, students may be asked to keep track of the number of hours that they studied or the number of pages that they read during a study period. In contrast, biographical measures such as life history forms are recorded to the best of the individual's recollection after the event has occurred.

Why Is the Assessment Being Undertaken?

The question of why pertains to the reason for administering the test rather than to the nature of the test itself. The same test can be used for a variety of purposes, such as counseling, selection, placement, description, and evaluation. As noted in Chapter 1, tests are often used in counseling as part of the problem-solving process.

When tests are used in counseling, all data obtained must be regarded as confidential. Such *private data* may be contrasted with *public data*—data originally obtained for another purpose, such as selection or placement. Examples of public data include academic grades, educational level, or occupational status. Counselors use public as well as private data in helping clients to address certain issues, because the public data can provide a great deal of information about the client's past performance under various circumstances.

How Is the Assessment Conducted?

"How" here refers to the manner in which the test material is presented, how the data are analyzed, and how the score for the assessment procedure is obtained. First, is the type of behavior that is being assessed *disguised* or *undisguised*? Projective techniques (described in Chapter 12) are designed so that the respondent is typically unaware of the true nature of the test or of any "preferred" answer. Because the intent of the test is disguised, it is more difficult for respondents to fake their answers to produce a particular impression.

Second, is the information obtained in the assessment analyzed in a *quantitative* or *qualitative* fashion? Quantitative procedures, which include most psychological tests, yield a specific score on a continuous scale. Qualitative procedures, such as card sorts, work samples, or structured exercises, produce a verbal description of a person's behavior or of a situation that can be placed into one of several categories (e.g., outgoing vs. reserved personality type). By their very nature, quantitative procedures have been more thoroughly studied in terms of reliability and validity. Qualitative procedures, however, are more open-ended and adaptable for use in counseling, especially with a diverse clientele (Goldman, 1992; Okocha, 1998).

Finally, are scores arrived at *objectively,* free of individual judgment, or *subjectively,* based on the scorer's best judgment? Tests that can be scored by means of a scoring stencil are objective. That is, different individuals using the same scoring stencil with an answer sheet should obtain the same score if they are careful in counting the number of correct answers. In contrast, rating scales are subjective—the score assigned will often vary depending on the individual rater.

TYPES OF PSYCHOLOGICAL ASSESSMENT METHODS

The various assessment methods used in counseling may be conveniently classified by using different combinations of the criteria discussed in the previous section. Six popular types of psychological assessment methods are described below.

Standardized Tests

By definition, standardized tests must meet certain standards for test construction, administration, and interpretation (Anastasi & Urbina, 1997). These standards include uniform procedures for test administration, objective scoring, and the use of representative norm groups for test interpretation. Most standardized tests have been studied in terms of their reliability and validity. Many assessment procedures used in counseling fail to meet these standards.

Standardized tests include the following assessment procedures, each of which is discussed in this book: achievement tests, aptitude (or ability) tests, personality inventories, interest inventories, values inventories, and environmental inventories. Strictly speaking, a test refers to a task on which people are asked to try their best, such as an aptitude or achievement test. Tests measure *maximum* performance, in contrast with questionnaires and inventories, which evaluate *typical* performance (Cronbach, 1990). Questionnaires and inventories, such as personality and interest inventories, elicit self-reports of opinions, preferences, and typical reactions to everyday situations. In practice, questionnaires and inventories also are often referred to as tests if they meet the standardization criteria noted above.

Nonstandardized assessment procedures, which are discussed below, include rating scales, projective techniques, behavioral observations, and biographical measures. Nonstandardized techniques produce results that are less dependable (i.e., less reliable and valid) compared with standardized techniques; however, they allow counselors to consider aspects of behavior or the environment not covered by traditional psychological tests. Counselors must be concerned not only about the *dependability* of test results but also about the *exhaustiveness* of the results (Cronbach & Gleser, 1965). Tests that provide highly dependable information often describe only a small part of the information a counselor needs. Assessment procedures such as interviews, projective techniques, or essays, which provide less dependable information, can nonetheless aid counselors in obtaining information on topics that would be missed by formal testing procedures. Exhaustive procedures should be used when counselors need to obtain a large amount of information pertaining to a variety of decisions (e.g., which problems to address or which treatments to consider). Information obtained in this manner can be verified in subsequent assessment with more dependable measures that must be administered and scored according to specified procedures.

Rating Scales

Rating scales, which provide estimates of various behaviors or characteristics based on the rater's observations, are a common method of assessment. In contrast with standardized tests, rating scales are derived from subjective rather than objective data. Rating scales include self-ratings, ratings of others, and ratings of the environment. Interview data are often summarized by means of rating scales.

Because of their subjectivity, rating scales have a number of disadvantages. Three common errors associated with rating scales include (a) halo effect, (b) error of central tendency, and (c) leniency error. In the case of the halo effect, raters show a tendency to generalize from one aspect of the client to all other aspects. For example, if a person is friendly, that person may also be rated highly in unrelated areas such as intelligence, creativity, leadership, and motivation. The error of central tendency describes the tendency to rate all people as "average" or near the middle of the rating scale. The leniency error refers to the tendency to rate the characteristics of people more favorably than they should be rated.

To control for such errors, raters are sometimes asked to rank people on each rating scale. As an alternative, raters may be forced to distribute their ratings across the entire rating scale according to the normal curve or a similar system. When these techniques are applied to a large number of people, they prevent ratings from bunching up in the middle of the distribution or at the top end of the distribution. Kenrick and Funder (1988) offered the following suggestions for improving the validity of ratings: (a) use raters who are thoroughly familiar with the person being rated, (b) require multiple behavioral observations, (c) obtain ratings from more than one observer, (d) use dimensions that are publicly observable, and (e) identify behaviors for observation that are relevant to the dimension in question. These suggestions can help counteract limitations posed by the various sources of invalidity.

Examples of rating techniques include the semantic differential and situational tests. The semantic differential technique requires raters to rate concepts (e.g., "my job") by means of a series of seven-step bipolar scales (e.g., competitive vs. cooperative). This technique can be readily adapted to a variety of situations, including cross-cultural assessment (Osgood & Tzeng, 1990).

Situational tests require the person to perform a task in a situation similar to that for which the person is being evaluated. For example, the *in-basket technique* requires candidates for an administrative position to respond to the daily tasks of an administrator by means of an in-basket (work assignment basket) that simulates the actual work assignments of administrators. Situational tests can often meet the conditions suggested by Kenrick and Funder (1988) noted above. For this reason, they often prove to be beneficial in predicting performance in a situation similar to that of the test. Situational tests are frequently used to assess leadership or management skills.

Projective Techniques

Projective tests use vague or ambiguous stimuli to which people must respond. Because the stimuli (e.g., inkblots, ambiguous pictures, and incomplete sentences) are vague, people tend to make interpretations of the stimuli that reveal more about themselves than they do about the stimuli. They "project" their own personality onto the stimuli. Responses are usually scored subjectively. Common projective techniques include the Rorschach Inkblot Test, Thematic Apperception Test, and Rotter Incomplete Sentences Blank. For many years projective tests dominated the field of personality testing, but during the past few decades objective (standardized) tests have become more popular. The use of projective techniques in counseling is discussed further in Chapter 12.

Behavioral Observations

Behavioral observations refer to behaviors that can be observed and counted. The observations are planned in advance or based on recent events. The behaviors, which usually occur in a natural setting, are monitored by the client, by an observer such as a spouse or parent, or both. The observer usually records the frequency of a discrete behavior, for example, the number of "I" statements made in an interview or the number of conversations initiated. Frequently, the duration of the response and the intensity of the behavior (as rated by the observer) are also recorded.

Behavioral observations have the advantage of pertaining directly to a behavior that a client is concerned about. The behavior can usually be included as part of a goal. The measure is directly related to the client's treatment.

Biographical Measures

Biographical measures refer to one's accomplishments or experiences as reported by the client or as reflected in historical records. For example, an employment resume or college application form usually provides an extensive amount of biographical information. Biographical measures differ from behavioral measures in that the observations are not planned in advance. They differ from rating scales in that the information is usually a matter of fact rather than a matter of judgment. Biographical data (biodata) include information maintained in cumulative records by schools or in personnel records by businesses, such as academic grades, extracurricular achievements, job promotions, hobbies, and volunteer work experiences.

The value of biographical measures in assessment is expressed in the well-established psychological maxim: "The best predictor of future performance is past performance." As a rule, the best single predictor of college grades for an individual is usually that person's high school grades. A person who has functioned well in a particular job in the past will probably perform well in related types of activities in the future.

Biographical data are usually collected by means of a written form or during the course of an initial interview with a client. Although this information is most often used in a qualitative manner, it can also be quantified for assessment purposes (Owens, 1983).

On the one hand, biographical measures are both economical and efficient. They can provide information on topics such as leadership experiences or creative accomplishments that may be difficult to assess by other means. On the other hand, they may be inappropriate or difficult to interpret if the person's experiences have been unusual or severely limited. Biographical measures yield a broad range of information, but the meaning of the information requires additional interaction with the client or others familiar with the situation.

The Quick Job-Hunting Map (QJHM) by Richard Bolles (1990, 1991) represents an example of a biographical measure. The QJHM asks clients to review their accomplishments in terms of the transferable skills that are involved. It provides a systematic means of analyzing one's history in regard to career opportunities. Other examples of biographical measures include career assessment portfolios (McDivitt, 1994) and psychosocial inventories such as the Quickview Social History (Giannetti, 1992).

Physiological Measures

Physiological measures promise to become increasingly important in understanding and monitoring client behavior (Goldfried, 1997; Sturgis & Gramling, 1988). Such measures refer to bodily states or bodily functions that are primarily involuntary in nature, including skin temperature, muscle contractions, and blood pressure. Advances in instrumentation (e.g., biofeedback devices) make it relatively easy to include such variables in the assessment process.

STANDARDS FOR EVALUATING TESTS AND TEST USAGE

Several sets of standards have been published by professional organizations concerning the development and use of psychological assessment procedures. Counselors should be familiar with each set of standards or guidelines for test usage presented in this section.

ACA Code of Ethics and Standards of Practice

The American Counseling Association (ACA) Code of Ethics and Standards of Practice specify principles of ethical conduct and standards of professional behavior for counselors (ACA, 1995). Sections of this document devoted to psychological assessment are reproduced in Appendix A. Other professional organizations have also published ethical codes that address the use of psychological assessment procedures in a similar fashion (American Mental Health Counselors Association, 2001; American Psychological Association, 1993; American Rehabilitation Counseling Association, Commission on Rehabilitation Counselor Certification, & National Rehabilitation Counseling Association, 1995; American School Counselor Association, 1992; National Board of Certified Counselors, 1997). The ACA Code of Ethics is discussed further in Chapter 18 and in other sections of this book.

Responsibilities of Users of Standardized Tests (RUST Statement–Revised)

ACA (formerly known as the American Association for Counseling and Development; AACD) and the Association for Assessment in Counseling (formerly known as the Association for Measurement and Evaluation in Counseling and Development; AMECD), one of the subdivisions of ACA, have prepared a policy statement called "Responsibilities of Users of Standardized Tests," which lists responsibilities of test users in seven categories: test decisions, qualifications of test users, test selection, test administration, test scoring, test interpretation, and communication of test results (AACD & AMECD, 1989). Counselors should be familiar with the recommendations made in this policy statement, frequently referred to as "the RUST Statement." The most significant recommendations for counselors are reproduced in Appendix B.

Competencies in Assessment and Evaluation for School Counselors

The American School Counselor Association and the Association for Assessment in Counseling (1998) listed nine competencies in the area of assessment that school counselors should possess. These competencies, each of which embraces a number of specific skills, include the following topics: selection of assessment strategies, knowledge of appropriate assessment instruments, test administration and scoring, test interpretation and reporting, use of tests in decision making, use of statistical information, evaluation of school counseling programs, use of local assessment instruments, and observance of professional codes and standards. Similar competencies pertain to other types of counseling. The list of competencies can serve as a means for counselors to evaluate their individual professional development and need for continuing education.

Standards for Educational and Psychological Testing

The *Standards for Educational and Psychological Testing* provide criteria for evaluating both the tests themselves and use of the tests. The criteria were prepared by a joint committee of the American Educational Research Association, the American Psychological Association, and the National Council on Measurement in Education (1999). The most recent version of the *Standards* represents the sixth in a series of documents on this issue beginning in 1954. Originally, this publication emphasized technical standards for test construction and evaluation. As the editions evolved, the joint committee placed increased emphasis on the responsibilities of the test user and the need for fairness in testing. Adherence to the *Standards* should help to reduce criticism of tests and test usage. Excerpts from the *Standards* that pertain to the responsibilities of test users (Standards 11.1–11.24) are presented in Appendix C in this book.

Test User Qualifications

The Joint Committee on Testing Practices (JCTP), which presently includes members from the American Counseling Association, American Psychological Association, American Speech-Language-Hearing Association, National Association of School Psychologists, and National Council on Measurement in Education, represents an interdisciplinary effort to improve the use of tests. Members of this committee have identified a total of 86 competencies required for the proper use of different instruments (Eyde, Moreland, Robertson, Primoff, & Most, 1988; Moreland, Eyde, Robertson, Primoff, & Most, 1995). Of the 86 competencies, 12 embody minimum proficiencies for all test users (see Table 2-1).

Factor-analytic research indicates that the 86 competencies can be reduced to seven broad factors: comprehensive assessment, proper test use, psychometric knowledge, integrity of test results, scoring accuracy, appropriate use of norms, and interpretive feedback. On the basis of research regarding test misuse, the relative significance of the seven factors varies with the particular type of test. For example, competencies in comprehensive assessment are more important in using clinical tests, whereas skills in the appropriate use of norms are more important in vocational tests (Moreland et al., 1995).

TABLE 2-1. Twelve Minimum Competencies for Proper Use of Tests

Item No.	Competency
1.	Avoiding errors in scoring and recording
2.	Refraining from labeling people with personally derogatory terms like *dishonest* on the basis of a test score that lacks perfect validity
3.	Keeping scoring keys and test materials secure
4.	Seeing that every examinee follows directions so that test scores are accurate
5.	Using settings for testing that allow for optimum performance by test takers (e.g., adequate room)
6.	Refraining from coaching or training individuals or groups on test items, which results in misrepresentation of the person's abilities and competencies
7.	Being willing to give interpretation and guidance to test takers in counseling situations
8.	Not making photocopies of copyrighted materials
9.	Refraining from using homemade answer sheets that do not align properly with scoring keys
10.	Establishing rapport with examinees to obtain accurate scores
11.	Refraining from answering questions from test takers in greater detail than the test manual permits
12.	Not assuming that a norm for one job applies to a different job (and not assuming that norms for one group automatically apply to other groups)

Note. From "Assessment of Test User Qualifications: A Research-Based Measurement Procedure," by K. L. Moreland, L. D. Eyde, G. J. Robertson, E. S. Primoff, and R. B. Most, 1995, *American Psychologist, 50,* p. 16.

The JCTP has stressed educational efforts, not restriction of access, as a means of ensuring qualified test users. Examples of appropriate and inappropriate test usage based on the 86 competencies and seven broad factors are provided in the casebook, *Responsible Test Use: Case Studies for Assessing Human Behavior,* published under the auspices of the JCTP (Eyde et al., 1993).

Rights and Responsibilities of Test Takers

In one of its efforts to improve testing practices, the JCTP has developed a statement that lists the specific rights and responsibilities of individual test takers (Joint Committee on Testing Practices, 1998). The purpose of the statement is "to inform and to help educate not only test takers, but also others involved in the testing enterprise so that measurements may be most validly and appropriately used"

(JCTP, 1998, p. 10). Each of the 10 rights and 10 matching responsibilities identified by the committee is shown in Table 2-2. For example, test takers have a right to know the purpose of testing, who will have access to their scores, how the tests will be used, and possible consequences of taking or not taking the test. They also have personal responsibilities, such as reading or listening to descriptive test information, informing test administrators of special needs, and asking questions about specific concerns they might have.

This document (which is available on the Internet at www.apa.org/science/jctpweb) also provides detailed guidelines for test administrators to ensure that test takers receive their rights and understand their responsibilities. As test administrators, counselors should clarify

TABLE 2-2. Rights and Responsibilities of Test Takers

As a test taker, you have the *right* to:

1. Be informed of your rights and responsibilities as a test taker.
2. Be treated with courtesy, respect, and impartiality, regardless of your age, disability, ethnicity, gender, national origin, religion, sexual orientation, or other personal characteristics.
3. Be tested with measures that meet professional standards and that are appropriate, given the manner in which the test results will be used.
4. Receive a brief oral or written explanation prior to testing about the purpose(s) for testing, the kind(s) of tests to be used, if the results will be reported to you or to others, and the planned use(s) of the results. If you have a disability, you have the right to inquire and receive information about testing accommodations. If you have difficulty in comprehending the language of the test, you have a right to know in advance of testing whether any accommodations may be available to you.
5. Know in advance of testing when the test will be administered, if and when test results will be available to you, and if there is a fee for testing services that you are expected to pay.
6. Have your test administered and your test results interpreted by appropriately trained individuals who follow professional codes of ethics.
7. Know if a test is optional and learn of the consequences of taking or not taking the test, fully completing the test, or canceling the scores. You may need to ask questions to learn these consequences.
8. Receive a written oral explanation of your test results within a reasonable amount of time after testing and in commonly understood terms.
9. Have your test results kept confidential to the extent allowed by law.
10. Present concerns about the testing process or your results and receive information about procedures that will be used to address such concerns.

(continued)

TABLE 2-2. Rights and Responsibilities (*continued*)

As a test taker, you have the *responsibility* to:

1. Read and/or listen to your rights and responsibilities as a test taker.
2. Treat others with courtesy and respect during the testing process.
3. Ask questions prior to testing if you are uncertain about why the test is being given, how it will be given, what you will be asked to do, or what will be done with the results.
4. Read or listen to descriptive information in advance of testing and listen carefully to all test instructions. You should inform an examiner in advance of testing if you wish to receive a testing accommodation or if you have a physical condition or illness that may interfere with your performance on the test. If you have difficulty comprehending the language of the test, it is your responsibility to inform an examiner.
5. Know when and where the test will be given, pay for the test if required, appear on time with any required materials, and be ready to be tested.
6. Follow the test instructions you are given and represent yourself honestly during the testing.
7. Be familiar with and accept the consequences of not taking the test, should you choose not to take the test.
8. Inform appropriate person(s), as specified to you by the organization responsible for testing, if you believe that testing conditions affected your results.
9. Ask about the confidentiality of your test results, if this aspect concerns you.
10. Present concerns about the testing process or results in a timely, respectful way, if you have any.

Note. From *Rights and Responsibilities of Test Takers: Guidelines and Expectations* [On-line], by the Working Group of the Joint Committee on Testing Practices, 1998. Copyright 1998 by the American Psychological Association. Adapted with permission. The Working Group members included Kurt F. Geisinger, PhD (Co-chair); William D. Schafer, EdD (Co-chair); Gwyneth Boodoo, PhD; Ruth Ekstrom, EdD; Tom Fitzgibbon, PhD; John Fremer, PhD; Sharon Goldsmith, PhD; Joanne Lenke, PhD; Kevin Moreland, PhD; Julie Noble, PhD; James P. Sampson, Jr., PhD; Douglas Smith, PhD; Nicholas Vacc, EdD; Janet Wall, EdD; and staff liasons Heather Fox, PhD, and Lara Frumklin, PhD.

the rights and responsibilities of test takers and obtain informed consent before proceeding with testing. They should be able to offer reasonable accommodations for test takers with disabilities. Counselors should provide appropriate information to clients concerning the testing process, such as suggestions for test preparation, scoring procedures, opportunities to retake the test, provisions for feedback, availability of interpretive materials, and confidentiality safeguards.

Code of Fair Testing Practices in Education

The *Code of Fair Testing Practices in Education* (1988), which was prepared by the JCTP, focuses on the use of educational tests. The code addresses a public as well as a professional audience. It lists standards for educational test users and developers in four areas: developing and selecting tests, interpreting scores, striving for fairness, and informing test takers. The code lists 22 standards that specify the responsibilities of counselors and other test users in each of these areas. Most of the responsibilities described by the code are discussed in appropriate sections of this book.

Test Publisher Requirements

Requirements for test usage depend on the complexity of the test. Test publishers often distinguish between Level A tests (no restrictions), Level B tests (purchaser must have a 4-year college degree and must have completed a college course in tests and measurements), and Level C tests (purchaser must have completed an advanced degree in an appropriate profession, belong to an appropriate professional organization, or be licensed or certified in an appropriate profession). Specific levels and qualifications vary according to the test publisher. Recently, test publishers have begun to give greater emphasis to the competencies required for the use of different types of tests rather than relying strictly on one's professional credentials.

The JCTP has worked with test publishers to prepare qualification forms for potential customers. These forms ask test purchasers to indicate the purpose for which they will use the test, their level of training, their professional credentials, their educational background, the specific training they have received in the use of tests, and their testing competencies (Moreland et al., 1995).

Counselors need to be aware of the qualifications for the specific tests they wish to use. *Counselors should not attempt to use tests for which they lack adequate preparation.*

Multicultural Assessment Standards

The *Multicultural Assessment Standards*, a publication of the Association for Assessment in Counseling (AAC), a division of the ACA, lists 34 standards of test practices that are relevant for clients from

34

multicultural populations (Prediger, 1994a). The booklet lists standards compiled from different sources that should be followed in selecting, administering, scoring, and interpreting instruments for clients from minority cultures. Further information on this topic can be found in Chapter 16 and throughout this book.

SOURCES OF INFORMATION ABOUT ASSESSMENT PROCEDURES

Although there are vast numbers of tests available in the United States, and there is a constant stream of new tests and revisions of old tests on the market, most of the tests are published by a few large publishers, such as the Consulting Psychologists Press, the Psychological Corporation, and Psychological Assessment Resources. These publishers distribute test catalogs from which manuals, scoring keys, and the tests themselves may be ordered. Appendix D shows the names, addresses, Internet Web sites, and related information for the publishers of tests most likely to be used by counselors.

The best general source of information about commercial tests is the *Mental Measurements Yearbook* series. First published in 1938 by Oscar K. Buros at Rutgers University, the series is now published at the Buros Institute of Mental Measurements at the University of Nebraska–Lincoln. The yearbooks provide descriptive information about each test, including the publisher, prices, and persons for whom the test is appropriate, along with critical reviews by test experts and a list of recent publications pertaining to the test. The *Fourteenth Mental Measurements Yearbook* contains information for over 400 new or revised instruments (Plake & Impara, 2001). Critical reviews are not published for each test in each yearbook, as each new volume is designed to add to, rather than replace, information found in prior volumes. A comprehensive listing of all tests currently available for purchase in English-speaking countries is provided in another publication, also initiated by Buros, titled *Tests in Print*. The most recent edition of this publication is *Tests in Print V*, a two-volume set that contains nearly 3,000 test entries (Murphy, Impara, & Plake, 1999). The tests listed in *Tests in Print* are cross-referenced to the test reviews found in all previous editions of the yearbooks.

The publisher plans to issue a new edition of *Tests in Print* every 5 years. The yearbooks are now published every 2 or 3 years. Supplements to the yearbooks are published between editions of the yearbooks.

In addition to the publications of the Buros Institute, counselors can consult similar reference books by the Test Corporation of America. This organization began publishing *Tests* and *Test Critiques* in the mid-1980s. *Tests*, now in its fourth edition, provides updated information on tests available from a total of 221 test publishers (Maddox, 1997). The information includes a description of each test, its cost, scoring procedures, and publisher information. The 10 volumes of *Test Critiques* offer in-depth reviews of psychological assessment instruments (Keyser & Sweetland, 1984–1994). The reviews, which average eight pages in length, provide a discussion of the practical applications of each test as well as its technical aspects. Each volume of *Test Critiques* provides an updated cumulative index of test reviews included in all previous volumes.

The *Test Locator*, an Internet resource sponsored by several organizations with an interest in testing, provides information on tests, test reviews, and test publishers (ERIC Clearinghouse on Assessment and Evaluation, 1999). This resource allows access to the Educational Testing Service Test Collection database, which contains descriptions of over 10,000 tests and research instruments. The *Test Locator* may be used to search for citations to test reviews and for the names and addresses of over 900 test publishers.

Most of the information required for evaluating any particular test should be available in documents provided by the test publisher (American Educational Research Association, American Psychological Association, & National Council on Measurement in Education, 1999). In addition to the test manual, these documents may include a technical manual, user's guide, and supplementary materials. The test manual should contain information regarding the construction of the test together with directions for administering, scoring, and interpreting the test. Norms should be reported, including a comprehensive description of the norm group and the sampling techniques used to obtain the norms. Information regarding the reliabilities of the test scores and the validity evidence for proposed interpretations should be presented in the manual. Examples of comprehensive, well-documented manuals include the *Manual for the Campbell Interest and Skill Survey* (D. P. Campbell, Hyne, & Nilsen, 1992) and the

Strong Interest Inventory Applications and Technical Guide (Harmon, Hansen, Borgen, & Hammer, 1994). For a nominal cost, most test publishers will provide qualified test users with a specimen set of a test that includes the test itself, answer sheets, scoring keys, and a test manual.

Professional books and journals also provide extensive information about tests. *A Counselor's Guide to Career Assessment Instruments* (4th ed.) reviews popular assessment procedures used in career counseling along with a list of sources of information about assessment procedures in general (Kapes & Whitfield, 2001). Copies of selected tests together with brief test reviews can be found in a number of sourcebooks (Corcoran & Fischer, 2000; Fischer & Corcoran, 2000; Nezu, Ronan, Meadows, & McClure, 2000; Robinson, Shaver, & Wrightsman, 1991; Schutte & Malouff, 1995).

Counselors are most likely to find information about assessment procedures pertinent to their work in the following journals: *Measurement and Evaluation in Counseling and Development, Journal of Counseling & Development, Career Development Quarterly, Journal of Counseling Psychology, Psychological Assessment, Journal of Personality Assessment, Journal of Career Assessment*, and *Assessment*. A wide range of test information may also be accessed by means of electronic-mail services (Denzine, 1995).

Information may be difficult to obtain for some proprietary tests that are exclusively owned and used within an organization such as a psychological consulting firm. Counselors should be cautious in relying on the results of a test that has not been submitted for professional review.

SUMMARY

1. Psychological assessment procedures can be distinguished from each other in terms of *who* is making the assessment, *what* is being assessed, *where* the assessment takes place, *when* the assessment occurs, *why* the assessment is undertaken, and *how* the assessment is conducted. These distinctions can be used to classify tests into six broad categories: standardized tests, rating scales, projective tests, behavioral observations, biographical measures, and physiological measures.

2. Standardized tests have been the most thoroughly studied of all psychological assessment procedures in terms of reliability and validity; however, they cover a limited domain of behavior or situations. Counselors need to use a broad range of assessment procedures to obtain information on relevant matters not included in standardized tests.

3. Counselors should be familiar with professional recommendations for evaluating tests and test usage. Important sets of guidelines include the ACA *Code of Ethics and Standards of Practice*, *Responsibilities of Users of Standardized Tests* (The RUST Statement–Revised), and *Standards for Educational and Psychological Testing*.

4. The most important sources of information about psychological tests are the *Mental Measurements Yearbooks*, *Test Critiques*, test manuals, and professional journals.

3

MEASUREMENT CONCEPTS AND TEST INTERPRETATION

T O MAKE EFFECTIVE USE OF TESTS, counselors must understand certain elementary statistical concepts that are used in conjunction with the development and interpretation of tests and test scores. In this chapter, only a few descriptive statistical concepts involved in understanding and interpreting tests are presented. Neither the underlying concepts of statistics nor their calculations, elements commonly found in a basic statistics course, are included. This chapter describes (a) some of the measures used to organize and describe test information, (b) the concepts of test reliability and test validity, and (c) the interpretation of reliability and validity information.

A simple raw score on a psychological test, without any type of comparative information, is a meaningless number. If a graduate student obtains a raw score of 58 on a mid-semester examination in a course called "Theories of Counseling," the student's next question will be about the meaning of that score. A student whose score falls in the top 5% of the class will obviously react very differently from one whose score falls in the bottom 5%.

Some type of interpretive or comparative information is necessary before any information is conveyed by a score. To say that a client obtained a raw score of 37 out of 60 on an anxiety measure conveys no useful information, nor does the fact that this score of 37 meant that the client answered 62% of the anxiety items. To know that the same client obtained a raw score of 48 on a 60-item measure of tolerance does not indicate that he or she is more tolerant than anxious, nor does it yield any other useful information. Some frame of reference is necessary to give a test result meaning (Anastasi & Urbina, 1997).

Scores on tests can be interpreted from three points of view: (a) comparison with scores obtained by other individuals, (b) comparison with an absolute score established by an authority, and (c) comparison with other scores obtained by the same individual. The first type of comparison is usually referred to as a *norm-referenced* interpretation. This type of comparison is used most often in interpreting scores on standardized tests. The second type of comparison is often described as a *criterion-referenced* interpretation. For example, a program administrator may require students to understand 90% of the material in a course before they receive credit for that course. Scores for tests based on this course would then be compared with this 90% passing score, not with the scores of other students.

Both of the first two types of comparisons use an external frame of reference. The third type of comparison, which uses an internal frame of reference, can be best thought of as a *self-referenced* (or ipsative) measure (e.g., At age 35 he weighs substantially more than he did in his late 20s). An article in the local newspaper carried the following headline: "Smith's Is Best for Breakfast." This headline could imply that Smith's restaurant was the best restaurant in the city for breakfast. In the article, however, it was pointed out that Smith's was not a particularly good place to eat, but if one had to choose, it was better for breakfast than it was for lunch or dinner. The reporter was making an internal (self-referenced) rather than an external type of comparison.

In a norm-referenced interpretation, individuals' scores are compared with others so various statistics are used for these interpretations. A frequency distribution is constructed with the scores on the test indicated on a horizontal axis and the number of individuals receiving a particular score shown on the vertical axis. This results in a frequency polygon, which when smoothed for the typical distribution results in the familiar normal or bell-shaped curve shown in Figure 3-1.

MEASURES OF CENTRAL TENDENCY

When examining an individual's score, one will often find it useful to have some indication of the typical or average score. There are three measures of central tendency that are often computed. The *mean* or arithmetic average has algebraic properties that make it the most frequently used measure of central tendency. It is equal to the sum of the scores divided by the number of individuals in the group. The *median* is the middle score below which one half or 50% of the scores will fall and above which the other half will fall. The *mode* is the score that appears the most frequently in a set of scores.

In a perfectly normal frequency distribution, such as that shown in Figure 3-1, all three measures have the same value. When larger numbers of individuals score at one of the ends of the distribution, the distribution is not symmetrical and becomes *skewed* (pulled) in one direction or the other (Figure 3-2). Differences that result between these measures of central tendency indicate the magnitude and direction of this skewness. If the mean is higher than the median, the distribution is positively skewed; if the mean is lower than the median, the distribution is negatively skewed. In a skewed distribution, the median becomes the better measure because it is not affected by extreme scores.

NORMS

Standardized tests by nature are norm-referenced. Norms are established by administering the instrument to a standardization group and then referencing an individual's score to the distribution of scores obtained in the standardization sample. The individual's raw score is converted into some type of derived score, which indicates the indi-

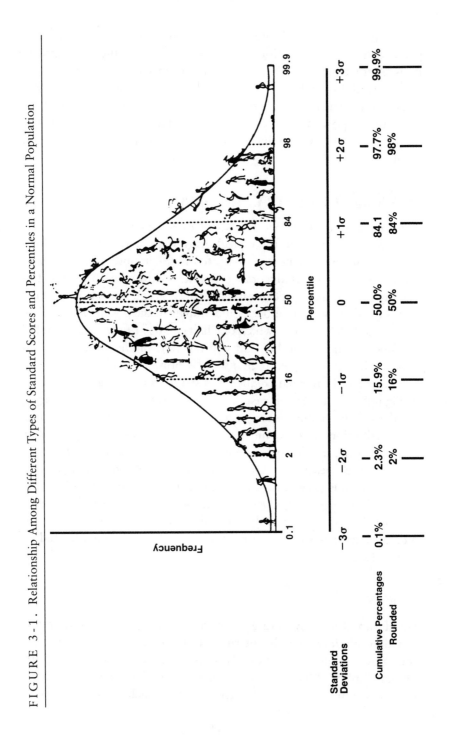

FIGURE 3-1. Relationship Among Different Types of Standard Scores and Percentiles in a Normal Population

Percentile Equivalents	1	5	10	20	30 (Q₁)	40	50 (Md)	60	70 (Q₃)	80	90	95	99

Typical Standard Scores

z-scores	-3.0	-2.0	-1.0	0	$+1.0$	$+2.0$	$+3.0$
T-scores	20	30	40	50	60	70	80
ACT scores	1	6	12	18	24	30	36
CEEB/GRE scores	200	300	400	500	600	700	800
GATB scores	40	60	80	100	120	140	160

Stanines

Stanines	1	2	3	4	5	6	7	8	9
Percent in stanine	4%	7%	12%	17%	20%	17%	12%	7%	4%

Wechsler Scales

Subtests	1	4	7	10	13	16	19
Deviation IQs	55	70	85	100	115	130	145

FIGURE 3-2. Examples of Skewed Distributions

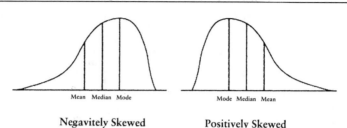

Negavitely Skewed   Positively Skewed

vidual's relative standing to the normative sample. This then provides a comparative measure of the individual's performance on whatever characteristic that instrument is assumed to measure.

Rank

A person's rank or standing within a group is the simplest norm-referenced statistic, with its interpretation based on the size and composition of the group. It is used extensively for grades—for example, a high school student who ranks 12th in grade point average (GPA) in a graduating class of 140—but it is seldom used in describing psychological test results.

Percentile Rank

Percentile rank is much more often used because it is not dependent on the size of the comparison group. Percentile scores are expressed in terms of the percentage of people in the comparison group who fall below them when the scores are placed in rank order. A percentile rank of 65 indicates a score or rank that is as high as or higher than those made by 65% of those in the comparison group. A percentile can be interpreted as a rank out of 100 persons in the comparison group (see Figure 3-1). Higher scores yield higher percentile ranks, and the lower the percentile, the lower the person's standing. The 50th percentile corresponds to the middle-most score or the median. The 25th percentile is the first quartile point, marking the bottom quarter of the distribution, and the 75th percentile is the third quartile point, above which is found the top one quarter of the scores. The advantage of using percentiles is that they are easily calculated and easily understood by most people (provided it is made clear that a percentile indicates ranking in the comparison group rather than the percentage of correct responses).

The principal disadvantage of percentile ranking is that the distribution of most scores resembles the familiar bell-shaped curve (as in Figure 3-1), whereas the distribution of percentiles is always rectangular in shape. Ten percent of the cases fall between the 40th and 50th percentiles, in the same way that 10% fall between the 80th and 90th percentiles. Because of the pile-up of scores near the center of a distribution, a small difference in middle raw scores can yield a large difference in percentile ranks, as can be seen in Figure 3-1. At the extreme high and low ends of the distribution, however, large raw score differences may yield only small differences in percentile ranks. Percentile ranks are generally intended as a means of conveying information concerning a person's relative rank in a group, but because of the nature of percentiles, they are generally not used in additional statistical computations.

Grade Equivalents

Grade equivalents are often used on educational achievement tests to interpret how a student is progressing in terms of grade level. Grade equivalent scores consist of a number representing a grade followed by a decimal representing the 10 months of the school year from September through June. The grades range from K (kindergarten) to 12. Grades above 12 are occasionally used but are not particularly meaningful. The mean raw score obtained by students in each grade is computed, with fractions of a grade determined either by interpolation or by testing students at different times during the school year.

The principal advantage of grade equivalents is the seeming ease of interpretation to those without any understanding of measurement concepts. Actually, grade equivalents are subject to considerable misinterpretation. A sixth grader obtaining a grade equivalent score of 9.3 in arithmetic could easily be assumed by parents and teachers to have a knowledge of mathematics equivalent to the average student in the ninth grade at that time. A more correct interpretation would be that the student obtained a score on the arithmetic test equivalent to the score the average ninth grader would have obtained on that test in the unlikely event that ninth graders might have a sixth-grade arithmetic test administered to them. It would not mean that the sixth grader would have obtained a score equal to the average ninth-grade student on the ninth-grade test, which would undoubtedly have included algebraic and other mathematical concepts unfamiliar to sixth graders. Such a score would certainly indicate superior performance by a sixth grader but could not be regarded as equivalent to a ninth-grade performance (Anastasi & Urbina, 1997). In addition, because grade equivalents are computed from mean raw scores, students will vary in a bell-shaped curve above or below the mean. Thus, a teacher might attempt to bring each student up to grade level— all students scoring at or above the mean. If national grade equivalents are used, this could perhaps be accomplished in a particular classroom, but if local norms are used, such a feat would obviously be impossible.

Standard Deviation

If a frequency distribution is constructed of a sufficiently large number of measurements of many naturally occurring phenomena, a bell-shaped curve is likely to be produced. Results of most measurements occur close to the average, and relatively few are found at either extreme. For this type of distribution, the most dependable measure of variability is the standard deviation. The larger the standard deviation, the wider the spread of scores away from the mean. The standard deviation is the most widely accepted measure of variability for test users because (a) it is the basis for standard scores, (b) it yields a method of presenting the reliability of an individual test score as described in a later section, and (c) it is used in research studies for statistical tests of significance.

In a normal curve, the numerical value of the standard deviation divides the raw score range into approximately six parts, with three above the mean and three below. Scores occurring above or below the distance of three standard deviations occur only very rarely. In a normal distribution, shown in Figure 3-1, approximately 34% of the sample lies between the median and one standard deviation above it and another 34% within the standard deviation below it. Thus, the distance of one standard deviation in each direction encompasses approximately 68% of the sample. An additional 14% or so of the sample is found within the second standard deviation above the mean and 14% below the mean, and approximately 2% is found in each of

46

the measurements occurring in the third standard deviation above the mean and below the mean.

A person scoring two standard deviations below the mean, therefore, falls at the second percentile, and at one standard deviation below, at the 16th percentile. A person scoring at the median or mean is at the 50th percentile, a person scoring one standard deviation above the mean is at the 84th percentile, and a person scoring two standard deviations above the mean is at the 98th percentile. These percentages and points along the normal curve are shown in Figure 3-1. Because the standard deviation is the basis of standard scores, which are used in reporting the results of most psychological tests used by counselors, these percentages and points along the normal curve should be thoroughly understood and *memorized* by anyone who makes substantial use of psychological test results.

Standard Scores

Because there are several problems related to using percentiles and other measures of variability, many tests make use of standard scores as the most satisfactory method of reporting test results. Standard scores are based on standard deviations and means. A standard score is defined as a score expressed as a distance, in standard deviation units, between a raw score and the mean. The basic standard score is the *z score*. A *z* score of -1.5 on this scale indicates that the raw score falls one and a half standard deviations below the mean of the reference group. A *z* score of 0 means the raw score falls exactly at the mean, and a raw score falling two standard deviations above the mean would yield a *z* score of $+2.0$. Because *z* scores produce both decimals and negative values, they cause difficulties in computations and interpretation, so other types of standard scores have been developed based on a linear transformation of the *z* score.

The most common standard score is the *T score,* which is used on a number of the most widely used educational and psychological tests. By definition, the *T* score has an arbitrary mean of 50 and an arbitrary standard deviation of 10. The *T* score is rounded to the nearest whole number, and because most raw scores do not exceed plus or minus three standard deviations from the mean, *T* score distributions usually range from 20 to 80. The results of many aptitude, interest, and personality measures are profiled in terms of *T* scores. To aid in the interpretation of T scores, half standard deviation units along with their comparable percentiles are shown in Table 3-1. The interpretations commonly given to the different ranges of T scores (along with percentile equivalents) are also given in that table (assuming of course that the norms are appropriate to the individual or group being assessed). It can be seen in Table 3-1 that T scores of 45 to 55, the middle 38% of the distribution, are commonly interpreted as *average*; those above 55 as *high*, and those above 65 as *very high*. T scores below 45 can be interpreted to clients as *low* and those below 35 as *very low*.

Other test publishers have selected different scales using different means and standard deviations, which can be interpreted the same way as z scores or T scores. The College Entrance Examination Board and the Graduate Record Examination (GRE) scores are reported in standard scores that use a mean of 500 and a standard deviation of 100. Thus, a raw score falling one standard deviation above the mean, which would yield a z score of $+1$, produces a standard score of 600. All scores are reported in increments of 10. This produces a scale that is recognizable for these instruments, although the scores may be thought of simply as T scores with an additional zero added. This type of scale can cause a minor problem in that small differences in raw scores may seem to be much larger because of the large-scaled score differences that range through 600 points (200 to 800).

TABLE 3-1. Interpretation (Assuming Appropriate Norms) for Given T Scores and Percentile Ranks

T Score	Percentile Rank	Interpretation
70	98	Very high
66	94	
65	93	High
60	84	
56	70	
55	69	Average
50	50	
45	31	
44	30	Low
40	16	
35	7	
34	6	Very low
30	2	

Until recently, there was considerable confusion concerning the Scholastic Aptitude Test portions of the College Entrance Examination Board (which is discussed further in Chapter 6). A mean of 500 was established many years ago when a smaller proportion of college-bound students took those tests. The typical college-bound student in recent years scored less than 500. In 1995, the scores were "recentered" and 500 again became the college-bound student mean (College Board, 1994a).

The American College Testing Program (ACT) uses standard scores similar to those developed for the Iowa Tests of Educational Development ($M = 15$, $SD = 5$). The ACT has been standardized with a mean of 18 and a standard deviation of 6, yielding a range of standard scores from 1 to 36. Standard scores developed for the General Aptitude Test Battery (GATB) used by the U.S. Employment Service yield a mean of 100 and a standard deviation of 20.

When the first intelligence tests were developed, a ratio of mental age to chronological age was developed and this ratio multiplied by 100. This ratio was later called the Intelligence Quotient, or IQ. The ratio IQ had a number of problems, including the fact that the ratio became invalid beginning in the adolescent years. Deviation IQ standard scores have since been developed to replace ratio IQs. Current results still report the mean at 100, as was the case with ratio IQs, but they report a standard score based on standard deviation units. Therefore, tests such as the Wechsler scales and the Stanford–Binet established a mean of 100 and a standard deviation of 15 or 16 depending on the test. The positions at which these standard scores fall along the normal curve are shown in Figure 3-1. Again it is important in interpreting test results with any of these types of standard scores to have firmly in mind the points along the normal curve where these scores fall and the proportions of the population on which the standard scores are based that fall at various points on the normal curve.

Another type of standard score is the *stanine,* based on the term *standard nine.* Stanines have a range of 1 to 9 and a mean of 5. The stanines of 1 and 9 at the ends of the distribution contain 4% of the cases, and these increase as in the normal curve so that the center stanine of 5 includes 20% of the cases. Test scores can be converted to stanines by referring to the normal curve percentages in Figure 3-1. Stanines are infrequently used because of the difficulty in explaining their meaning. Their chief advantage lies in the single-digit numbers, which do not imply greater accuracy than most tests can deliver. However, single digits can sometimes suggest a significant difference between two individuals where none exists.

CORRELATION

The correlation statistic assesses the degree to which two sets of measures are related—for example, how a tested trait or ability is related to a behavior. If a counselor had a score on a mathematics achievement test and the grades in arithmetic achieved by each student in a class, the counselor might wonder to what extent those students who scored well on the mathematics test also get good grades in arithmetic. To the extent that the rank orders of the students on each of these indices were similar—that is, those who scored high on the test obtained good grades and those with lower scores obtained poorer grades—the counselor would conclude that a relationship existed between the two indices. Such a relationship is expressed through a statistic known as a correlation coefficient. Each correlation coefficient contains two bits of information: The sign of the correlation tells whether the two variables tend to rank individuals in the same order or in their reverse order, and the magnitude of the correlation indicates the strength of this relationship.

Among the several different types of correlation coefficients that can be computed, the Pearson product–moment coefficient (r) is the most common and can range in value from $+1.00$, a perfect positive relationship; through .00, no relationship or a chance relationship; to -1.00, indicating a perfect negative or inverse relationship. For example, the correlation between scores on a college entrance test and the freshman-year GPA of college students might yield a correlation coefficient of .40. Distance of students' homes from the college might yield a random or complete lack of a relationship, .00, with grades, and number of hours that students spend watching television might yield a low negative relationship with grades of $-.20$.

It must be remembered that a substantial correlation between two variables does not imply that either variable causes the other. They both can be under the influence of a third variable. Heights of children could show a significant correlation with their scores on a vocabulary test, but both of these variables could be related to the children's ages and maturational growth.

RELIABILITY

Reliability and validity are two technical subjects that may not be of great interest to most people-oriented counselors, but they are extremely important for those who use psychological tests. They are concepts that need to be well understood when selecting, administering, and interpreting psychological tests.

Inherent in the concept of reliability of psychological tests is the recognition that none of these instruments measure perfectly. Educators and behavioral scientists are interested in measuring much more complicated human characteristics than people's physical aspects. Anxiety, intelligence, depression, and potential to become a substance abuser are complex qualities that are difficult both to define precisely and to measure.

Reliability refers to how consistently a test measures and the extent to which it eliminates chance and other extraneous factors in its results. Synonyms for reliability include dependability, reproducibility, stability, and consistency. A score that a person receives on a test is made up of two elements: the person's true score and an error score that may add to or subtract from the true score. A test with perfect reliability would be one on which everyone's scores remained in the same relative position on each administration (although they would not necessarily receive the exact same scores each time). Although we refer to the reliability of a test, reliability is actually the property of the test scores for the particular group on which it was administered—not of the test itself. In computing a correlation coefficient for a group of people on two sets of scores, the perfect relationship would yield a correlation of 1.00. If the test scores were completely unreliable, the relationship between the two would be a chance relationship, and the correlation would be approximately 0.

Reliability is concerned both with the natural variation in human performance and with the technical aspects of psychological measurement. The stability of the trait or variable being measured obviously influences the amount of variation expected or considered normal when measured at different times. On the one hand, it would be expected that ability variables would have less variation than psychological states, but changes in ability measures can still occur as a result of growth and development. On the other hand, measures of personality variables, such as a state of depression, a state of anxiety, or a state of stress, could be expected to vary considerably at different times and under different circumstances.

Factors that are irrelevant to the purpose for which the test is designed represent error variance. Attempts to maintain uniform test conditions by controlling the instructions, time limits, and the testing environment are undertaken to reduce error variance and make test scores more reliable. No test is perfectly reliable, and because psychological measurement is often imprecise, it is important to check the accuracy and consistency of the instrument constantly to ensure that the unreliability is kept within reasonable limits. The current *Standards for Educational and Psychological Testing* (American Educational Research Association, American Psychological Association, & National Council on Measurement in Education, 1999) emphasize that test developers should provide test users with substantial amounts of information on test reliability and standard errors of measurement. This includes reporting in test manuals specific details about populations on which reliability data were obtained, standard errors of measurement for all types of scores reported, and intervals between retests and interrater consistency where appropriate.

Reliability coefficients usually run within the range of .80 to .95, but what is considered to be acceptable reliability varies substantially depending on both the testing circumstances and the type of reliability. For national testing programs such as the GRE or the Iowa Tests of Educational Development, reliability coefficients are expected to be above .90. For certain other types of psychological tests, this type of reliability is substantially lower. A score on the Depression scale of the Minnesota Multiphasic Personality Inventory (MMPI), for example, is an indication of the person's mood at the time the inventory was administered. Because people's moods change, a very high test–retest reliability would be neither expected nor desired. Thus, for personality measures, interest measures, and attitudinal measures, test–retest reliability coefficients often fall below .90, although if they fall below .70, the consistency of the instrument becomes suspect (Cicchetti, 1994).

Types of Reliability

Reliability can be measured in several different ways, so there is not a single reliability for a test but different coefficients depending on how they are determined. Test scores can vary in their consistency in terms of time, test forms, or test items. Traditionally, there are three basic methods of estimating the reliability of an instrument based on these variables: test–retest, alternate forms, and internal consistency. The proportion of test error attributable to each of these sources of unreliability can be calculated by analysis of variance procedures with an approach to reliability measurement known as generalizability theory (American Educational Research Association, American Psychological Association, & National Council on Measurement in Education, 1999).

Test–Retest Reliability. Test–retest reliability, which is a common method of estimating traits, measures consistency over time. The correlation coefficient in this case indicates the relationship between scores obtained by individuals within the same group on two administrations of the test. Test–retest correlations tend to decrease as the interval between the test administrations lengthens. If the interval is brief, there are potential problems of practice and memory, which tend to make the reliability estimation spuriously high. If the time interval is too long, variation can be influenced by events that occur to participants between the two test administrations, and spuriously low estimates of reliability may be obtained.

Alternate-Form Reliability. Alternate-form or parallel-form reliability is computed by comparing the consistency of scores of individuals within the same group on two alternate but equivalent forms of the same test. Because the test items are different, the effect of memory and other carryover effects are eliminated. The crucial question remains whether in fact the two alternate forms of the test are actually equivalent.

Two tests that measure the same content or variables and that are equivalent in difficulty level can be administered on the same day or very close to each other without concern about the practice effect. They can be alternated so that Test A is given to one group first and

Test B to the other group first, and the practice effect can thus be controlled.

The problem with this type of test reliability is that it is often difficult enough to come up with one good form of a test, much less two good forms. Therefore, unless there is a national testing program with a staff working on developing test forms, as is the case with some of the national testing programs such as the Medical College Admissions Test or the ACT tests, hope for this form of reliability is unrealistic.

In national testing programs, the problem of developing equivalent forms is met by administering experimental items with each test administration. The people taking the test respond both to items that count and to those that are being tried out. The latter do not count in scoring for that administration but provide data for the construction of future forms of the test. The experimental items do not have to be the same for all those taking the test on a particular date, as item information can be collected from random subsamples. This is how national testing programs are able to produce equivalent forms year after year.

Internal Consistency. Measures of internal consistency provide an estimate of test reliability that indicates the consistency of responses to the different items or parts of a test during a single test and administration (American Educational Research Association, American Psychological Association, & National Council on Measurement in Education, 1999). Two common measures of internal consistency are split-half and interitem consistency.

Split-half reliability is a popular form of establishing reliability because it can be obtained from a single administration by dividing the tests into two comparable halves and comparing the resulting two scores for each individual. It is administered all at once, so no time-to-time fluctuation occurs. From this point of view, it can be thought of as a special case of alternate-form reliability. In most tests, the first half and the second half would not be comparable because of differences in the difficulty of the items, as well as effects of practice and fatigue that are likely to vary from the beginning to the end of the test. Therefore, most tests are split into odd and even items, except when several items deal with a specific problem, in which case the entire group of items is assigned to one or the other half. An important weakness in the split-half approach lies in the general principle of sampling—that is, usually the greater the number of items, the more stable will be the concept being measured. All things being equal, the longer the test, the more reliable its scores will be. The split-half procedure cuts the test length in half, thus decreasing the reliability estimate. To correct the computed reliability based on the shorter length, the Spearman–Brown Prophecy Formula can be used to yield an estimate of what the reliability would be if it were obtained on the test's full length.

Interitem Consistency.   Interitem consistency is a measure of internal consistency that assesses the extent to which the items on a test are related to each other and to the total score. This measure of test reliability provides an estimate of the average intercorrelations among all of the items on a test. Depending on the type of response called for on the instrument, formulas known as the Kuder–Richardson Formula 20 for two-response answers (e.g., *true* or *false*, *yes* or *no*) or Cronbach's *alpha* reliability coefficient for more than two alternatives are computed. These reliability coefficients indicate the consistency with which the items sample the trait being measured.

This method requires that individual item responses for each person in the entire sample be placed in a computer file. This method is simplified when the responses can be read into the computer using mark sensing or optically scannable answer sheets.

Profile Reliability.   For tests that yield a profile of scores on a number of different scales, the concept of profile reliability may be more appropriate than a mean reliability coefficient from a number of different scales of varying reliability. Profile reliability is obtained by computing the overall similarity of two profiles obtained for the same person at two different times. If the profile reliability is greater than .75, there is little difference in the interpretation given to the profile by counselors (Hoyt, 1960).

Considerations in Reliability

The appropriateness of a particular method depends on the nature of the trait being measured, particularly in terms of the stability of the trait. If one is interested in a measure that indicates the degree to which the items in a scale are interrelated, then the interitem consistency technique would be recommended; if the concern is with dependability for predictive purposes, then the test–retest or parallel forms with an increased time interval would be more appropriate.

The interpretation of a reliability coefficient also depends on the nature of the trait being measured. A paper-and-pencil IQ test with a reliability coefficient of .75 would not be acceptable, whereas the same coefficient for a measure of anxiety would be fairly acceptable for use. Reliabilities of tests can be compared with those of other similar instruments, remembering that the lower the reliability, the less confidence is possible in using and interpreting the resulting test data.

Reliability estimates are influenced by the nature of the group on which the reliability measure was computed. In a group that is heterogeneous on the characteristic being measured, there will be a greater range and greater variability and hence a higher reliability coefficient. An introductory course at the undergraduate level is likely to have a relatively heterogeneous group of students, with the result that a relatively poorly constructed final examination may yield a considerably higher reliability coefficient than a carefully constructed final examination in a graduate-level course, which will likely contain a much more homogeneous group of students. Thus, in examining the reliability of a particular instrument, it is necessary to look at the type of sample on which the reliability coefficient was obtained as well as the type of reliability that was obtained. Information on reliability in a test manual should include the means and standard deviations, as well as the demographic characteristics of the sample on which the reliability coefficients were computed (American Educational Research Association, American Psychological Association, & National Council on Measurement in Education, 1999).

An important point to remember regarding reliability is that longer tests are usually more reliable than shorter tests. It is also true that speed tests such as those assessing clerical aptitude or manual dexterity can yield reliability coefficients that are spuriously high. On speed tests, individuals are likely to complete approximately the same number of odd and even items and do not receive credit for items at the end of the test because they did not get that far. This results in a similarity of performance between the two halves and yields a high split-half reliability coefficient. The split-half method takes into account accuracy of performance on the odd versus even items but not the number of items completed, which is usually the most important consideration on the speed test. Another form of test reliability should be used to determine the consistency of speed at which a person works.

Reliabilities of scored essay tests have always been quite poor, a problem when national testing organizations have attempted to use writing samples as criteria for college admissions. Even well-trained raters often vary substantially in the ratings they give to writing samples required by some institutions.

Standard Error of Measurement

The standard error of measurement (*SEM*) yields the same type of information as does the reliability coefficient but is specifically applicable to the interpretation of individual scores. Its most common use is to construct bands of confidence around an individual's obtained score. It represents the theoretical distribution that would be obtained if an individual were repeatedly tested with a large number of exactly equivalent forms of the same test. Such a cluster of repeated scores would form a curve, with a mean and standard deviation of the distribution, and that standard deviation is called the *SEM*. An individual's single score on a test is assumed to be the mean of repeated scores, and the *SEM* can be interpreted in terms of normal curve frequencies. Thus, if a student's true raw score was 40 on a particular test and the *SEM* was 3, then if we repeated the test many times, 68% of the individual's scores would fall between 37 and 43, and we could be 95% confident that the individual's true score would be between 34 and 46—two *SEM* units above or below the obtained score.

The *SEM* is easily computed when the standard deviation and the reliability coefficient of the test are known by using the following formula: The *SEM* equals the standard deviation of the test (*SD*) times the square root of the quantity 1 minus the reliability of the test:

$$SEM = SD \times \sqrt{1 - \text{reliability}}.$$

As an example, the SAT scores of the College Entrance Examination Board have a standard score mean of 500, a standard deviation of 100, and test–retest reliability of approximately .91 for college applicants. The *SEM* is 30 ($100 \times \sqrt{1 - .91} = 100 \times \sqrt{.09} = 100 \times .3 = 30$). If Susan, a college applicant, scores 490 on the test, the odds are high (68% of the time) that her true score falls between 460 and 520 (i.e., plus and minus 1 *SEM* of the obtained score). Similar estimates can be made of the true scores for individuals on the ACT test, which, with a mean of 18, a standard deviation of approximately 6, and reliability coefficients of about .90, has an *SEM* in the vicinity of 2. In the case of the Wechsler intelligence scales with full-scale score standard deviations of 15 ($M = 100$) and reliability coefficients in the vicinity of .96, the *SEM* equals 3.

Although most test manuals interpret *SEM* according to classical test theory in the manner discussed above, item response theory recognizes that the interpretation of *SEM* will vary depending on the degree to which the individual scored above or below the mean. In general, test error is higher for extreme scores because there are fewer items of sufficient difficulty at this level to measure the variable in question (Embertson, 1996). Extreme scores can be expected to change more on retesting than scores in the average range.

VALIDITY

Whereas reliability is concerned with whether the instrument is a consistent measure, validity deals with the extent to which meaningful and appropriate inferences can be made from the instrument. Validity asks the question of whether a test measures what it purports to measure. Does a test that is supposed to measure arithmetic skills really measure arithmetic skills, or is it composed of word problems of such reading difficulty that it is actually measuring reading ability instead? It is possible for a test to have high reliability without validity (but in order to have good validity, high reliability is necessary).

The question "validity for what?" must always be asked, as the validity of a test varies depending on the purpose and the target population. For example, scores on the Strong Interest Inventory have considerable test–retest reliability even when the second test is taken many years later. Validity, however, is much more complicated. Because of the large number of scales and the different types of scales, specific definitions must be developed before they can be applied to a criterion to obtain validity. As will be seen later (Chapter 9), scores on the Strong can be used effectively to predict the occupation that a person is likely to enter in the future. However, it is not particularly valid for predicting success in an occupation. People who enter an occupation for which they get a low score on the Strong may very well not stay in that occupation. People who score high are much more likely to stay in the occupation, but the few low scorers who stay in that field are just as likely to be successful as those who score high. Therefore, a score on a Strong scale may have some validity for predicting whether people will enter an occupation and, if so, how long they will stay in it, but it will have little validity when it comes to predicting success in that occupation.

According to the *Standards* (American Educational Research Association, American Psychological Association, & National Council on Measurement in Education, 1999), test validity should be assessed in terms of the use to which the test is put, such as counseling, selection, or classification. Once the use of the test is clear, the test user should study the evidence of the validity of the test for that particular purpose. It is therefore important that test manuals contain detailed information regarding both theoretical and empirical evidence of validity for the interpretation and use of test scores.

The range of validity coefficients runs much lower than that of reliability. Whereas coefficients of .80 to .95 are common for reliability, validity coefficients seldom run above .65 and are more typically in the range of .30 to .50. Validity coefficients as low as .10 and .20 can still be useful in predicting future behavior (Rosenthal, 1990; Rosnow & Rosenthal, 1988). In predicting grades in college from test scores, coefficients are almost never obtained above .60. Even when other measures of high school achievement, personality, and some type of achievement motivation are all combined, validity coefficients above .60 are seldom achieved for college grades.

We emphasize here that psychological test data provide unique information beyond that obtained from relying only on the interview. In their review of 125 meta-analyses of psychological test validities, G. J. Meyer et al. (2001) concluded that they are comparable with the validity of many medical tests and have "strong and compelling" (p. 128) validity for use in clinical and counseling practice.

Evidence of a test's validity for a particular purpose can be assessed in different ways. Different types of validity evidence are discussed below.

Content Validity

In the case of content validity, the items on a test are examined carefully to determine whether the items measure what the test is supposed to be measuring. If the test is designed to measure achievement in high school physics, a number of high school physics teachers, and perhaps some college physics teachers, examine the items on the test to determine whether these items are in fact measuring knowledge of what is typically taught in high school physics. Content validity involves judgment by people competent in that field.

Content validity should not be confused with face validity, which is not really validity at all, but merely deals with the question of whether the items seem to be relevant to the person taking the test.

Criterion-Related Validity

Criterion-related validity pertains to validity evidence that is obtained by comparing test scores with performance on a criterion measure such as grades or job satisfaction. All criterion-related measures can be described as *empirical* (as contrasted with theoretical) in that they involve the collection of data.

In the case of *concurrent validity*, the test scores and the criterion performance scores are collected at the same time. Correlation coefficients are calculated between the test score and the scores on the criterion variable. For example, a test of mechanical aptitude might be given to a group of working machinists, and then the ratings that they receive by their supervisors might be examined to determine whether the mechanical aptitude scores are related to their current work. Often measures of concurrent validity are obtained because the test is going to be used in the future to predict some type of behavior—such as the ability to do the work of a machinist.

A second type of criterion-related validity is *predictive validity*. In this case, the person's performance or criterion measure is obtained some time after the test score. For a scholastic aptitude test designed to predict college grades, the grades that the students earn in college are examined to determine whether the scholastic aptitude test given in high school has predictive validity. Does it predict what it is supposed to be predicting—in this case, college grades?

One of the problems in measuring either concurrent or predictive validity is that the size of the correlation coefficients will be reduced if the range of scores on either the test or the criterion variable is restricted in any way. Because scholastic aptitude test scores are often used to select students for a particular institution, and many students with low scores are eliminated, the group being studied to measure the test's predictive validity will have a narrower range, with a resulting lower validity coefficient. One way of avoiding this is to administer the instrument before any selection has taken place and to have the selection take place without regard to the criterion being assessed. For example, in one of the validation studies for the GATB of the U.S. Employment Service, the entire battery was given to all applicants for jobs in an industrial plant that was being built in a particular town. Workers were then selected without regard to their GATB results. Performance ratings for the workers were obtained at a later date, and these were then related to the previously obtained GATB results showing substantial predictive validity.

Spuriously high validity coefficients can also be obtained from a form of criterion contamination if, for example, the people doing the rating know the test results. University professors' knowledge of graduate students' GRE test results might (but obviously should not) influence the grades they assign, which could result in a higher relationship between test results and graduate GPAs.

An important concept related to the validity of a test concerns the base rates of the characteristic that is being measured in the population. *Base rates* refer to the proportion of people in a population who represent the particular characteristic or behavior that is being predicted. Base rates are important because they have a marked influence on how useful or valid tests are in making predictions. If the base rates are either very low or very high, the predictions made from the tests are not likely to be useful. If almost every student admitted to medical school graduates, then scores on the Medical College Admission Test (MCAT) are unlikely to differentiate between those who will graduate and those who will not. The best prediction to be obtained would be not to use the test scores but merely to predict that every student admitted will graduate. Suicide rates are examples of low base rates. Although people who obtain high scores on a scale that measures depression are more likely to commit suicide than those with lower scores, most people who obtain high scores on a measure of depression do not commit suicide. Because suicide is relatively rare, the base rate is so low that even with a high score on a depression scale, the most accurate prediction to be made would still be that any individual is not likely to commit suicide.

The purpose of tests is, of course, to provide more information than could be obtained by chance or other unreliable means. Validity of tests is evaluated in terms of how much they contribute beyond what could be predicted without them. *Incremental* validity refers to the extent to which a particular assessment instrument adds to the accuracy of predictions obtained from other tests or other less-extensive methods of assessment. The real value of the MCAT would be if the correct prediction rate could be increased beyond that available without the use of the test. Incremental validity should be taken into account in deciding whether to use an additional assessment instrument.

When a test is used to make a dichotomous, either/or decision (e.g., acceptable or unacceptable, successful or unsuccessful, positive diagnosis or negative diagnosis), cutoff scores are usually used. The point at which the cutoff score is established is often a matter of relative cost. In some cases, a miss can be very costly, for example, concluding that someone is not suicidal because he or she is below a cutoff score on a suicide potential scale when in fact the person is suicidal. The cost of this type of miss could be that a suicide takes place that might have been preventable. This type of case is called a *false negative*. The person fell below the cutting score and was therefore predicted *not* to be suicidal when in fact he or she was suicidal. A *false positive* occurs when a person obtains a score above the cutting score and, for example, is predicted to be successful on the job but in fact fails and is discharged. Again, the time and money invested in training the person are likely to influence where the cutting score is placed and therefore to influence the proportion of false positives.

The accuracy of classification of individuals into different diagnostic categories or related groups based on a particular cutoff score can be expressed in terms of sensitivity and specificity. *Sensitivity* refers to the accuracy of a cutoff score in detecting those people who belong in a particular category. By definition, testing procedures that are sensitive produce few false negatives. *Specificity* indicates the accuracy of a cutoff score in excluding those without that condition. Testing procedures that possess specificity yield few false positives. Sensitivity and specificity will vary depending on the particular cutoff score used to select individuals considered to be meeting the condition. Generally, if sensitivity is increased, specificity say will be reduced and vice versa.

For example, most clients who commit suicide or have seriously considered suicide obtain an elevated score (T score > 65) on the Depression scale of the MMPI. However, a large number of individuals who are not suicidal also obtain elevated scores on this scale. When the MMPI Depression scale is used in this manner, it can be said to possess sensitivity in identifying potentially suicidal individuals but to lack specificity in ruling out individuals who are not suicidal (Cicchetti, 1994). If a higher cutoff were used (e.g., T score > 75), specificity would be increased, but sensitivity would be lessened (there would be more false negatives).

The amount of variability in a criterion that a correlation coefficient is considered to account for is determined by the square of the correlation. Thus, a correlation coefficient of .30 means that the predictor accounts for 9% of the variance. In using a correlation coefficient for prediction, however, Rosnow and Rosenthal (1988) showed that the correlation coefficient can be taken to indicate the improvement in success of prediction over chance or over the base rate by the percentage indicated by that correlation. Thus, a correlation of .30 means that using that variable in prediction improves the prediction by approximately 30%. When considered in this way, a moderate correlation can be seen to have considerable usefulness in counseling over that which would have been obtained had that test not been taken into consideration.

Where a test has been shown to possess considerable validity for predictive purposes, counselors are encouraged to produce materials adapted for local needs (American School Counselor Association & Association for Assessment in Counseling, 1998). An example is the expectancy table shown in Table 3-2, in which ACT Math scores are related to success in a university mathematics course typically taken by freshmen. Such a table would be useful not only for determining a cutoff score for placement into this particular mathematics course but also as a valuable counseling tool. We could say to a student who

TABLE 3-2. A Locally Produced Expectancy Table

ACT Mathematics Score	Percentage Obtaining a B or Better	Percentage Obtaining a C or Better
33+	88	98
31–32	81	96
28–30	67	93
25–27	44	85
21–23	18	64
18–20	9	43
15–17	3	23
12–13	1	9
11–	1	6

Note. From *Using the ACT in Advising and Course Placement 1999–2000,* by the American College Testing Program, 1999c. Copyright by ACT Research Services. Adapted with permission.

scored a 20 on the ACT Math, "Of those who achieved your ACT score, 9 students out of 100 got a B or higher, 43 got a C or higher, and therefore 57 did not get a passing C grade. Now we don't know whether you will be 1 of the 9 who gets at least a B, 1 of the 43 with a C, or 1 of the 57 falling below—but this gives you a chance to see what the odds are if you decide to take it."

Construct Validity

A third type of evidence pertaining to the validity of a test for a particular use has been referred to as construct validity. This type of validity asks the following questions: Do the test results make psychological sense? What is the underlying "construct" (or factor or characteristic)? Are the test results related to variables that they ought to be related to and not related to variables that they ought not be? For example, do results on the test change according to what we know about developmental changes? Do older students do better on the test than younger students; for example, do sixth graders do better on arithmetic tests than third graders?

Two aspects of construct validity are those of *convergent validity* and *discriminant validity.* On the one hand, tests should be expected to show a substantial correlation with other tests and assessments that measure similar characteristics. Measures of mathematical aptitude ought to be related to grades in mathematics. Most validation studies report convergent validity. On the other hand, tests should not be substantially correlated with other tests from which they are supposed to differ; that is, they should show discriminant validity. A test of mathematical ability probably should not show a strong correlation with a test of clerical speed and accuracy. A measure of sociability should be negatively related to the score on a schizophrenic scale and positively related to the score on a scale of extraversion.

If an instrument is related to a particular psychological theory, then the results should fit that theory. Factor analysis is used to determine whether the test items fall together in different factors the way that the theory suggests they should. If a test is constructed along the lines of Jungian theory, such as the Myers–Briggs Type Indicator, the resulting factors from a factor analysis should be related to such Jungian concepts as introversion versus extraversion, sensing versus intuition, and thinking versus feeling.

An additional component of construct validity is *internal consistency*. Measures of internal consistency, which are used primarily to indicate reliability, show the extent to which the items in the test are related to each other and to the total score on the test. High internal consistency is therefore one indication of construct validity. When test scales are internally consistent, they are easier for the counselor to interpret because all of the items are measuring the same construct.

Treatment Validity

There is yet another type of validity that may be considered by counselors and clinicians. It has been termed *treatment validity*: "Do the results obtained from the test make a difference in the treatment?" (Barrios, 1988; Holland, 1997). If the test results are useful, if they make a difference in the counseling process, then the test could be said to have treatment validity. For example, Finn and Tonsager (1992) found that clients who had their MMPI scores interpreted to them showed significant improvement on several treatment variables. In a similar fashion, Randahl, Hansen, and Haverkamp (1993) found that clients who had their Strong Interest Inventory profile interpreted to them made significant progress on their career planning.

The question, then, is not simply "Is the test valid?" but "What is the validity evidence to support the planned use of the test?" Criterion-related validity is important, for example, if the test is to be used for selection, whereas content validity is important if it is to be used as a measure of achievement. In the overall construction and development of a test, various validation procedures are applied throughout the developmental stages. All the types of validity can be conceived as contributing to the construct validity of a test, which may also include the social value consequences of its use (Messick, 1995). Measures of internal consistency are built into the early stages of development; criterion-related validation typically occurs in some of the latter stages. Validation continues long after the test has been published and distributed for use.

TEST DEVELOPMENT

To produce a well-designed standardized psychological test or inventory, the test developer generates a large amount of data. First, test items are written, usually by specialists or experts in the field according to the objectives and purpose of the test (Drummond, 1996). They are then checked for cultural, sexual, or regional bias, and items that might be unfair or offensive to any group are eliminated. They are then tried out on sample populations similar to the targeted group, and the results are analyzed to determine those items that are of appropriate difficulty and discriminating power. The items must differentiate between people who represent more and less of the behaviors or the domain that is being measured using item response theory models. After the resulting items have been assembled into a test and scored, the scores must be converted into a continuous scale, norms must be developed that are applicable to the groups for which the test is designed, and reliability estimates must be calculated. Correlations of the test with other similar variables, with background variables, and with predicted criteria must then be determined. All of these analyses are facilitated by computers.

SUMMARY

1. Test scores may be interpreted in terms of a comparison group (norm-referenced), a preestablished standard (criterion-referenced), or one's earlier performance on the same measure (self-referenced).

2. Correlational coefficients indicate the degree and direction of a relationship between two measures or variables.
3. Reliability refers to the consistency or generalizability of test scores over time (test–retest reliability), forms (alternate-form reliability), and items (internal consistency).
4. The standard error of measurement indicates the amount of variation that can be expected in an individual's score on retesting because of test unreliability.
5. Validity refers to the degree to which accumulated evidence supports the proposed interpretation of test scores.
6. Different procedures for obtaining validity evidence include content validity ("Is the content appropriate for the intended use?"), criterion-related validity ("Are the test scores significantly correlated with relevant criteria?"), and construct validity ("What is the psychological meaning of the test scores?").

4

INITIAL ASSESSMENT IN COUNSELING

W HAT ASSESSMENT PROCEDURES should counselors pursue at the beginning of counseling? What steps should be taken to ensure that assessment procedures are appropriately selected and administered? This chapter addresses these questions.

First, the counselor needs to determine the client's orientation toward problem solving. Next, the counselor needs to assess the nature and severity of the client's problems. Assessment procedures that can aid in these endeavors are described in the first parts of this chapter, and the chapter concludes with a consideration of the principles of test selection, administration, and scoring.

CLIENT ORIENTATION TOWARD PROBLEM SOLVING

Clients differ in their readiness for counseling, their expectations of counseling, and their problem-solving styles. Counselors can be more effective with clients if they take these differences into account.

Readiness for Counseling

In their work with individuals with addictive behaviors, Prochaska, DiClemente, and Norcross (1992) noted five stages of change experienced by their clients: precontemplation, contemplation, preparation, action, and maintenance. These same stages of change pertain to clients with a wide variety of problems.

In the *precontemplative* stage, individuals are not especially aware of their problem and have no plans to change their behavior in the foreseeable future. Individuals who seek counseling while in the precontemplative stage usually do so at the insistence of someone else who is concerned about their problems.

Clients in the *contemplative* stage are aware of their problem but have not yet made a serious commitment to do anything about it. Individuals in this state are considering making changes in their behavior sometime within the next 6 months; however, it may be much longer than this amount of time before they actually do make changes.

In the *preparation* stage, clients have begun to make small changes in their problematic behaviors with the intention of making more complete changes within 1 month. The *action* stage is reached when clients successfully change their behavior for short periods of time. If the changes persist for longer than 6 months, the client enters the *maintenance* stage, in which the goal is to maintain the behavioral and attitudinal changes that have occurred.

Assessment of the client's stage of change is crucial for determining the most effective treatment technique. As noted by Prochaska et al. (1992), different approaches should be used for clients in different stages. For example, individuals in the precontemplative and contemplative stages can be helped most by early intervention techniques such as consciousness raising and dramatic relief, whereas individuals in the action and maintenance stages can benefit most from later intervention techniques such as reinforcement management and support groups.

It is important to note that most clients recycle through some or all of the stages several times before successfully achieving long-term changes. Although recycling is the norm, most clients learn from their previous attempts so that they make faster progress through the cycle in subsequent attempts to resolve their problems.

Expectations of Counseling: Models of Helping and Coping

Client expectations for counseling will vary depending on their view of the problematic situation. Clients differ in the extent to which they accept responsibility for the problem or its solution. This distinction is important because it makes it possible to separate *blame* for the problem from *control* of its solution. Brickman et al. (1982) identified four different orientations toward counseling based on the client's views. As indicated below, clients may subscribe to any one of these four models.

which client would you like to work with?

Moral Model. People are responsible for their problems and solutions. Clients who fit this model look on counselors as consultants who can help direct them to resources, such as self-help books and personal growth groups, that they can implement on their own. They perceive themselves as lazy people who must work harder. Clients seek stimulation from counselors to do what they know they must do.

Compensatory Model. People are not responsible for their problems but are responsible for solutions. Clients with this point of view perceive counselors as advocates who can help them to overcome a problem that they did not cause (e.g., poor education, which can be helped by tutorial programs). They think of themselves as deprived individuals who must assert themselves. Clients look to counselors for empowerment to help them correct situations that cause problems.

Enlightenment Model. People are responsible for their problems but not for solutions to the problems. Clients who endorse this model look on counselors as saviors who can provide long-term care for them by means of ongoing support groups or other methods. They see themselves as guilty individuals who must submit to a higher authority. Clients expect counselors to help provide them with discipline they lack themselves.

Medical Model. People are not responsible for problems or solutions. Clients who fit this model view counselors as experts who will be able to remedy their problems by external means (e.g., by prescribing a treatment program). They regard themselves as ill people who must accept advice or treatment from the proper authority. Clients expect counselors to prescribe the solution, which they will then follow.

The problem-solving process can be aided by taking into account the orientation of the client and that of the counselor. Clients report more satisfaction and work more effectively with counselors who agree with them regarding responsibility for the problem and its solution (Hayes, Wall, & Shea, 1998). Clients who accept responsibility for causing or solving their problem respond better to insight-focused counseling; those who attribute their problem or its solution to outside forces show greater improvement with symptom-focused interventions (Beutler, 2000).

Counselors can usually determine the client's orientation by means of an interview. They can ask clients who (or what) is to blame for their problem and who (or what) is in control of solving the problem. They can use the distinctions among the models indicated in the preceding paragraphs to help frame questions for clients. Internal versus external locus of control scales may also be helpful in this regard (Corcoran & Fischer, 2000). Clients who believe that they are in control of their destiny (internal locus of control) fit the moral or compensatory models; clients who believe that they are the victims of chance or their environment (external locus of control) conform to the enlightenment or medical models.

The compensatory model produces the best results for counselors in many situations (Brickman et al., 1982). It has the advantage of absolving clients of blame for the problem, thus justifying their request for assistance, at the same time that it places them in control of removing or reducing the problem. As indicated in a number of studies reviewed by Brickman et al., changes that occur as a result of counseling are most likely to persist when clients feel that they are responsible for the change. If change is attributed to the counselor's efforts, the change in client behavior is less likely to endure. Counselors can help clients to reattribute solutions for their problems to factors that they can control (Dorn, 1988).

Problem-Solving Style

Individuals differ in how they define the problem, how they solve the problem, and which part of the problem-solving process they tend to emphasize (defining the problem or solving the problem). The Myers–Briggs Type Indicator (MBTI) can be used as a means of analyzing one's problem-solving style. As indicated in Chapter 11, the MBTI includes four bipolar dimensions. Each of these dimensions can be used to describe an important aspect of the client's problem-solving style.

First, the Extroverted versus Introverted dimension indicates the extent to which the person chooses to solve problems as part of a group or individually. Second, the Sensing versus Intuition dimension offers insight into the manner in which the client defines a problem. Does the client give predominant consideration to facts (Sensing type) or possibilities (Intuitive type)? Third, the Thinking versus Feeling dimension indicates the extent to which the person solves the problem by logic (Thinking type) or values (Feeling type). Finally, the Judging versus Perceiving dimension shows which function (problem definition or problem solving) the client will emphasize. Judging types place greater importance on solving the problem, whereas Perceiving types give primary consideration to defining the problem.

These same personality variables are also included as part of the Millon Index of Personality Styles (MIPS; Millon, 1995). Counselors can use the MBTI or the MIPS to help clients to identify their problem-solving style. They can help clients to recognize both strengths and weaknesses in their preferred styles. Counselors can teach clients to "stretch" their styles when necessary to include some of the advantages of the other personality styles.

Problem-solving style can also be assessed by means of several instruments specifically designed to measure the manner in which individuals cope with difficult situations. For example, the Problem-Focused Style of Coping inventory measures reflective, suppressive, and reactive styles of coping (P. P. Heppner, Cook, Wright, & Johnson, 1995). Individuals who score high on the Reflective factor emphasize rational techniques in solving problems, those who score high on the Suppressive factor are likely to deny or avoid the problem, and those who score high on the Reactive factor will most likely exhibit strong emotional responses and impulsivity when faced with a major life event. Other instruments of this sort include the Ways of Coping Questionnaire (Folkman & Lazarus, 1988), the Problem-Solving Inventory (P. P. Heppner, 1988), and the Coping Inventory for Stressful Situations (Endler & Parker, 1994).

DEFINING THE PROBLEM

What is the nature of the client's problem? How severe is it? How does it affect the client's life? Answers to these questions can help counselors to plan and to evaluate treatment for their clients. In this section, a number of systematic procedures for addressing these questions are considered.

Counselors can gather significant information from clients in a short period of time by means of an intake (initial contact) questionnaire, a problem checklist, and an interview. The intake counselor uses this information in arranging counseling for the client or in making a referral.

Intake Form

An intake form contains questions about client status and presenting issues that can help guide the first counseling session. Common questions include name, address, sex, age, ethnicity, educational and work history, presenting problem (or problems), previous counseling, and urgency of request for counseling. Intake forms vary somewhat from agency to agency depending on the particular type of services offered by the agency.

In general, the intake form should be kept relatively short so that it does not become an imposition in counseling. The form can be supplemented with additional questionnaires designed for particular issues, such as career planning, study skills, or relationships, as counseling progresses.

If desired, an agency's intake questionnaire can be supplemented with a standardized questionnaire to obtain more complete information regarding a client's background. As an example, the Quickview Social History contains 130 questions pertaining to the client's developmental history, family of origin, educational history, marital history, occupational history/financial status, and legal history, together with 105 additional questions that address psychological and medical issues (Giannetti, 1992). The client's answers are processed by computer to provide a four- to five-page narrative report plus a follow-up section that highlights client problems and areas that the counselor may wish to explore further with the client.

Information obtained from the intake form orients the counselor toward the client's problem, serves as a checklist to make sure that important points are covered, and provides a record for future counseling contacts. This information can also be compiled and used to describe the nature of the clientele served by a counseling center during a given time period. These data can be helpful in budget and program planning.

Problem Checklists

Counselors often use problem checklists or screening instruments to obtain a quick, comprehensive, and systematic evaluation of a client's concerns. These instruments usually ask clients to check which ones of a variety of problems or symptoms may have been troubling them during the past week or two. Two checklists that have proved to be particularly valuable for use in counseling are described below. In addition to these instruments, other popular or promising checklists or screening inventories include the College Adjustment Scales (Anton & Reed, 1991), Holden Psychological Screening Inventory (Holden, 1996), Psychological Distress Inventory (Lustman, Sowa, & O'Hara, 1984), Personal Problems Checklist–Adult (Schinka, 1984), Personal Problems Checklist–Adolescent (Schinka, 1985), and Psychological Screening Inventory (Lanyon, 1978).

Inventory of Common Problems (ICP). The ICP was developed by Jeffrey Hoffman and Bahr Weiss (1986) for use as a screening instrument in college counseling centers. It lists 24 specific problems that college students may confront (see Figure 4-1). These items represent six major types of problems as follows:

- Depression: Items 1–4
- Anxiety: Items 5–8

75

- Academic problems: Items 9–12
- Interpersonal problems: Items 13–16
- Physical health problems: Items 17–20
- Substance-use problems: Items 21–24

Clients must indicate to what extent each of the 24 problems has distressed, worried, or bothered them in the past few weeks. Answers

FIGURE 4-1. Inventory of Common Problems

Instructions: The following items represent common problems of college students. How much has each problem distressed, worried, or bothered you in the past few weeks? Please circle the answer that is most nearly correct for you.

Not at all	A little bit	Moderately	Quite a bit	Very much
1	2	3	4	5

1. Feeling depressed, sad, dejected?		1 2 3 4 5
2. Blaming, criticizing, or condemning myself?		1 2 3 4 5
3. Feeling discouraged or like a failure?		1 2 3 4 5
4. Suicidal thoughts or concerns?		1 2 3 4 5
5. Feeling irritable, tense, or nervous?		1 2 3 4 5
6. Feeling fearful?		1 2 3 4 5
7. Spells of terror or panic?		1 2 3 4 5
8. Feeling like I'm "going to pieces"?		1 2 3 4 5
9. Academic problems?		1 2 3 4 5
10. Difficulty caring about or concentrating on studies?		1 2 3 4 5
11. Indecision or concern about choice of career or major?	1 2 3 4 5
12. Feeling like I'm not doing as well in school as I should?	1 2 3 4 5
13. Problems with romantic or sexual relationships?		1 2 3 4 5
14. Family problems?		1 2 3 4 5
15. Difficulty getting along with others?		1 2 3 4 5
16. Feeling lonely or isolated?		1 2 3 4 5
17. Physical health problems?		1 2 3 4 5
18. Headaches, faintness, or dizziness?		1 2 3 4 5
19. Trouble sleeping?		1 2 3 4 5
20. Eating, appetite, or weight problems?		1 2 3 4 5
21. My use of alcohol?		1 2 3 4 5
22. My use of marijuana?		1 2 3 4 5
23. How many psychoactive drugs I use?		1 2 3 4 5
24. How many prescribed drugs I use?		1 2 3 4 5
If so, what? _____		

Note. From "A New System for Conceptualizing College Students' Problems: Types of Crises and the Inventory of Common Problems," by J. A. Hoffman and B. Weiss, 1986, *Journal of American College Health, 34,* p. 262. Copyright 1986 by the Helen Dwight Reid Educational Foundation. Published by Heldref Publications, 4000 Albermarle Street, NW, Washington, DC 20016. Reprinted with permission.

range from 1 (*not at all*) to 5 (*very much*). Scores for each scale can vary from 4 to 20; total scores can vary from 24 to 120.

Normative data for a sample of college students collected by Hoffman and Weiss (1986) showed no significant sex differences. Thus, the same set of norms may be used with both male and female clients. The highest mean score (11 points) was obtained on the Academic Problems scale, whereas the lowest mean score (5 points) was recorded for the Substance Use scale. The mean total score for college students was approximately 45 points with a standard deviation of about 10 (Hoffman & Weiss, 1986).

The ICP possesses sufficient reliability and validity evidence for its use as a screening instrument with most college students, but it should not be regarded as a diagnostic instrument (Hoffman & Weiss, 1986). The results should be used primarily to suggest topics for further exploration in counseling. Counselors can easily readminister the ICP to clients to obtain a rough measure of progress during the course of counseling. If administered to all clients as part of the intake process, it can also be used to provide a comprehensive picture of the types of psychological problems presented at the agency (Keutzer et al., 1998).

From a practical point of view, the ICP offers several advantages for the counselor. It can be completed by most clients within 5 to 10 minutes, it represents most of the problems that clients are likely to encounter, and it can be reproduced for little cost if the original source of the instrument is acknowledged (J. A. Hoffman, personal communication, April 18, 1988).

The ICP has been designed so that it can be used together with the Therapist Rating Form, which asks therapists to classify the type of crisis encountered by the client as psychopathological, developmental, or situational (Hoffman & Weiss, 1986). A case example based on the use of the ICP with a college student is presented below.

CASE EXAMPLE

Linda came to the university counseling center as a senior because of dissatisfaction with her major. She felt particularly uneasy because most of her peers were participating in job interviews for the next year. She was majoring in banking but was not happy with it. She did not like the competitiveness of the students in her field. According to the intake form that she completed at the same time as the ICP, she wanted help in "choosing a major" and "career planning." She marked all of the items except one in the first three categories (Depression, Anxiety, and Academic Problems) of the ICP as 4 or 5. She was feeling very distressed by her career indecision.

On the Therapist Rating Form, the intake counselor attributed Linda's problems primarily to developmental issues, not psychopathological or situational factors. Based on the counselor's judgment, short-term counseling was arranged. Linda needed help in dealing with developmental tasks, especially in resolving her career choice, not in making fundamental changes in her personality.

Linda met with a counselor for six sessions for help in acquiring decision-making and assertiveness skills and for assistance in working through conflicted feelings about her career choice. She decided to add personnel management as a second major to that of banking. This combination was supported by the tests (including the Strong Interest Inventory) that she had taken and by the information that she had gained in her career exploration.

The ICP was readministered at the conclusion of counseling. Linda marked no 4 or 5 responses the second time she completed the inventory. Her total score, which dropped from 66 to 34, and all of her subscores fell well within the normal range compared with other college students. The ICP was helpful with Linda both in determining the nature and the severity of her initial complaints and in evaluating the progress that she showed in counseling. Linda's rapid progress in counseling supported the perception of the intake counselor that her problems were developmental, not psychopathological, in nature.

Symptom Check List–90–Revised (SCL-90-R). The SCL-90-R has been widely used for research and clinical purposes in a variety of medical and mental health settings (Derogatis, 1994). As indicated by its name, the SCL-90-R contains a list of 90 symptoms such as "headaches," "feeling critical of others," and "feeling tense or keyed up." Clients respond to items in terms of how much they were distressed by that symptom during the past week. Each item is answered on a five-step scale ranging from 0 (*not at all*) through 4 (*extremely*). Most clients complete the SCL-90-R within 15 minutes. With practice, it can be easily hand-scored.

The SCL-90-R provides scores for the following nine scales: Somatization, Obsessive–Compulsive, Interpersonal Sensitivity, Depression, Anxiety, Hostility, Phobic Anxiety, Paranoid Ideation, and Psychoticism. Scores for each scale show the mean response for the items in that scale. It also yields three total scores: Global Severity Index (GSI), Positive Symptom Total (PST), and Positive Symptom

Distress Index (PSDI). The GSI, the best single index of psychological disturbance, shows the mean response to all 90 items. The PST indicates the number of symptoms reported (all items marked 1 or higher). The PSDI, which shows the mean response to all items included in the PST, reflects the severity of the client's symptoms.

Scores on the SCL-90-R vary depending on age and sex. Adolescent nonpatients report more symptomatology than do adult nonpatients. Women acknowledge more symptoms than do men. The SCL-90-R manual provides separate-sex norms for adolescent nonpatients, adult nonpatients, adult psychiatric inpatients, and adult psychiatric outpatients.

The SCL-90-R scales show adequate internal consistency and test–retest reliability over short time periods for psychiatric patients. It appears to be most valid as a broad measure of psychological disturbance. The test scores have demonstrated sensitivity to many forms of treatment (Derogatis & Savitz, 2000; Vonk & Thyer, 1999).

The SCL-90-R is particularly valuable as a screening instrument to detect cases that need additional assessment. As a general rule, Derogatis (1994, p. 58) suggested that counselors should refer clients for psychiatric evaluation if their scores on the GSI or any two of the individual scales equal or exceed the 90th percentile (T score = 63) compared with adult nonpatients.

Several abbreviated versions of the SCL-90-R have been developed. The Brief Symptom Inventory (BSI) contains 53 of the 90 items on the SCL-90-R (Derogatis & Melisaratos, 1983). Administration time for the BSI is approximately 10 minutes, compared with 15 minutes for the SCL-90-R. Intercorrelations between the two sets of scales range from .92 to .99. According to its authors, the BSI has become a more popular instrument for research and clinical use than the SCL-90-R. The BSI can also be administered as an 18-item form (Derogatis & Savitz, 2000).

In addition to the self-report forms (SCL-90-R and BSI), Derogatis has constructed matching rating scales for use by clinicians familiar with the client. The Derogatis Psychiatric Rating Scale and the SCL-90-Analogue can be used to obtain clinician ratings on the same symptom constructs included in the SCL-90-R. Counselors can obtain a more thorough and accurate assessment of a client's status by using both self- and clinician rating scales.

The SCL-90-R and BSI have been used extensively in different cultures throughout the world. The instruments have been translated into more than two dozen languages (Derogatis & Savitz, 1999).

Suggestions for Using Problem Checklists in Counseling

1. Identify critical items on the problem checklist (e.g., items that refer to thoughts of suicide or violent behavior) that can be used to help determine if the client is in a state of crisis. Be sure to make a suicide risk assessment (see Chapter 14) if the client shows signs of suicidal thinking.

2. Examine general level of responses. If a client marks a large number of extreme responses, consider the need for immediate counseling and possible psychiatric referral. Ask clients to discuss each of these responses, especially ones that they perceive to be most crucial.

3. Note the client's responses for substance abuse and health items. These problems may be overlooked in the counseling interview if the counselor does not bring them up with the client.

4. Readminister the problem checklist at the conclusion of counseling or after a significant time period has elapsed to evaluate changes that have taken place during the course of counseling. Clients who have shown little improvement may need to be referred.

5. Use problem checklist scores to consult with supervisors or colleagues regarding treatment of case. Problem checklist scores can be used to communicate the nature and severity of the client's issues within a few minutes.

6. Add items to standard problem checklists to assess matters of importance to your agency. For example, one agency added the following items to the ICP to identify potentially dangerous situations: "urge to harm myself," "plan to harm myself," "urge to harm someone else," "plan to harm someone else," and "concern that someone else may harm me."

7. Administer problem checklists or screening inventories for specific topics (e.g., Michigan Alcohol Screening Test, My Vocational Situation, or Eating Attitudes Tests) when these seem to be appropriate. Ask clients to identify any issues that they might be experiencing that are not represented on the problem checklist.

8. Consider the possibility that clients could be minimizing or exaggerating their problems. Use both number and intensity of symptoms to help gauge possible distortion. If clients mark most items at a low level of intensity, they could be minimizing their problems. Similarly, if they mark a large number of problems at a high level of intensity, they could be exaggerating their concerns.

9. Problem checklists should be used in conjunction with other assessment methods. Use individual scales and items primarily as a means of identifying significant subject matter for discussion and further assessment.

10. Use problem checklists to monitor the caseload in your agency. What types of clients are receiving treatment at the agency? How many of the clients express suicidal ideation? How many of the clients indicate problems with substance abuse? Use these data to develop local norms to help interpret problem checklist responses. The data may also be used to help decide which types of services to emphasize in the agency.

Intake Interview

The purpose of the intake (or assessment) interview is to assess the nature and severity of the client's problems and to determine possible treatment programs. The interview, which provides more flexibility than most other assessment procedures, enables the counselor to clarify the client's responses on the intake forms and to explore the client's concerns in some depth.

Most intake interviews cover the following topics: (a) general appearance and behavior; (b) presenting problem; (c) history of current problem and related problems; (d) present level of functioning in work, relationships, and leisure activities; (e) use of alcohol or other drugs, including medications; (f) family history of mental illness; (g) history of physical, sexual, or emotional abuse; (h) risk factors, including urge to harm self or others; (i) previous counseling; and (j) attitude of client toward the counseling process. The interviewer should explain the policies of the agency, such as session limits, rules of confidentiality, and referral options. The intake interview should help the counselor to decide the immediacy of the need for counseling, the type of expertise required, and the type of service (e.g., individual counseling, couples counseling, group counseling, or consultation and referral).

Interview Guidelines.   Initial interviews usually progress on a continuum from minimal structure to more structure. As the interview proceeds, the client may need help or direction in continuing to respond. Questions that probe or clarify can be used to obtain a clearer understanding of what the client feels or means. Statements like "Can you tell me more about . . ." or "Tell me more about how you felt when . . ." or "I don't think I understand what you mean by . . ." provide relevant information from the client's point of view and help to maintain rapport. Rephrasing of questions can sometimes help to clarify client responses if other techniques have not been effective. In general, it is best not to ask "why" questions because they may cause the client to become defensive.

It is important to determine what factors led the client to seek help at this particular time. Has the problem recently become worse? Have other people become concerned about the person? Has the problem begun to interfere with the client's functioning at work or home? Answers to such questions can help clarify the nature of the client's problem and assess the client's motivation for participating in counseling.

As part of the intake interview, counselors should also seek information about behaviors or events that have been helpful in the past or that the client expects might be helpful in the future. For example, when has the problem been least likely to occur in the past? What has kept the problem from getting worse? What is one small step the client could take to improve the situation? Answers to such questions can be useful in considering possible solutions for the client's problem (Dejong & Berg, 1998).

The counselor should pay attention to the client's nonverbal behavior, such as eye contact, facial expression, and activity level. Observations of the client's nonverbal behavior can be particularly important for clients who may have difficulty in communicating with the counselor.

The information obtained in the initial interview needs to be organized systematically to help identify significant patterns of behavior. Fong (1993) suggested that counselors sort observations of client functioning into four broad areas: cognition, affect, behavior, and physiological functioning. Figure 4-2 shows an example of a worksheet based on this system for a client named "Charles." Each of the items represents an observation that can be helpful in diagnosing Charles's mental condition.

In preparing such a worksheet, the counselor's observations should be described in an objective manner, for example, "moved slowly" or "didn't smile," instead of in the form of an interpretation such as "seemed sad." Interpretations of behavior, which may vary greatly from counselor to counselor for the same behavior, should be reserved until sufficient data have been collected to formulate hypotheses regarding the client's problem and possible interventions. In the case of Charles, the worksheet reveals a pattern of anxiety symptoms that merits further examination, especially in regard to a possible anxiety disorder (see Fong & Silien, 1999).

FIGURE 4-2. Observation of Client Functioning Worksheet: Charles

Cognitions
> Oriented to person, place, and time
> Goal directed, precise speech
> Worried about "experiences" of intense anxiety and impact on him
> Thinks job is stressful, but proud of success at sales

Affect
> Controlled, somewhat limited range of affect

Behaviors
> Well groomed, expensive suit and watch
> Insomnia several nights per week
> Divorced, now engaged to be married
> Good working relationships, but prefers not to socialize outside
> Intense anxiety attacks without warning
> Has started to drive only in right hand lane, avoids crowds
> Separation anxiety and shyness as child
> Denies drug use, infrequent drink with client

Physiological Functioning
> Heart palpitations, sweating hands, difficulty breathing, and weakness
>   during intense anxiety attacks
> Diagnosed irritable bowel syndrome
> Frequent headaches, "tight band around my head"

Note. From "Teaching Assessment and Diagnosis Within a DSM-III-R Framework," by M. L. Fong, 1993, *Counselor Education and Supervision, 32,* p. 286. Copyright 1993 by the American Counseling Association. Adapted with permission. No further reproduction authorized without written permission of the American Counseling Association.

The intake counselor should also be aware of the possibility that the client's psychological symptoms may be caused by physical illness, particularly if (a) the client has not responded well to counseling or psychotherapy, (b) the symptoms have not occurred previously, (c) the client reports physical as well as psychological symptoms, (d) the client is disoriented, or (e) psychosocial stressors are absent or minor (Diamond, 1989; Pollak, Levy, & Breitholtz, 1999). If the client is on medications, possible side effects of these medications should be checked in the current edition of the *Physicians' Desk Reference* (published annually by Medical Economics Company, Inc., Montvale, NJ 07645).

Although interviews can serve as a rich source of information, observations based on interviews are frequently biased or subject to misinterpretation. Common errors of judgment based on interview assessments include the following (Spengler, Strohmer, Dixon, & Shivy, 1995):

- Anchoring: placing too much emphasis on information obtained early in the interview
- Availability: relying too much on one's favorite theory or on popular diagnoses such as borderline personality disorder or adult child of dysfunctional family
- Diagnostic overshadowing: ignoring or minimizing problems because they are less noticeable or are of less interest to the counselor
- Attribution: attributing the problem primarily to the client without giving sufficient consideration to the environment.

Counselors may combat these errors by adhering to the principles of assessment listed in Chapter 1. In particular, it is important to keep an open mind and to use a multimethod, multifactor approach to assessment. Multimethod assessments include a variety of assessment methods such as interview schedules, objective instruments, and observations by the client and others. Multifactor assessments provide data concerning a range of individual and environmental factors. A multimethod, multifactor approach enables counselors to see issues from different viewpoints and to consider alternative explanations of client problems.

Mental Status Exam (MSE). In some mental health settings, counselors routinely administer a mental status exam (MSE) during the intake interview. In other settings, counselors may perform an MSE if they perceive the client to be disoriented, confused, or out of touch with reality. Information obtained by means of an MSE can be especially important when the counselor does not have access to psychological test data (Groth-Marnat, 1997).

The MSE consists of a series of questions and observations designed to evaluate the client's current level of functioning (Polanski & Hinkle, 2000; Waldinger, 1986). It provides a format for organizing information provided by clients (referred to as *subjective* data) and information based on observations of clients (referred to as *objective* data) that has been collected in a scattered fashion throughout the interview. It usually includes a consideration of the client's general appearance and behavior, speech, emotions, thoughts, perception, and cognition. The cognitive section of the MSE is the only part that involves the use of specific tests (e.g., counting backward by 7s or 3s from 100 to test concentration).

The MSE is usually administered informally. Interviewers ask questions only in those areas in which they have concerns. Information is picked up naturally during the course of interviewing the client. Anything that seems unusual should be explored in depth. Vague or puzzling matters should always be clarified.

The results of the MSE can usually be reported in one or two paragraphs. Attention is drawn to any usual features of the client that may demand further attention. The MSE should not be used by itself to make a diagnosis, but it can be helpful in suggesting areas in which further assessments should be made.

Structured Interviews. The reliability and validity of psychiatric diagnoses based on interview data can be improved by the use of structured interviews, especially if the interviewer adheres to diagnostic criteria such as those provided in the *Diagnostic and Statistical Manual of Mental Disorders* (4th ed.; American Psychiatric Association, 1994; Garb, 1998). In general, structured interviews follow a standardized format in regard to the content, presentation, recording, and scoring of questions. Some flexibility may be permitted in the conduct of the interview depending on the particular interview schedule. When used in a counseling setting, structured interviews can improve rapport with clients, reduce errors of clinical judgment, ensure comprehensive coverage of symptoms, and increase commitment to counseling (Vacc & Juhnke, 1997).

In a review of structured interviews most likely to be used by counselors, Vacc and Juhnke (1997) noted the Composite International Diagnostic Interview, the Diagnostic Interview Schedule, the Psychiatric Research Interview for Substance and Mental Disorders, and the Structured Clinical Interview for *DSM-IV* Disorders for adults. For children, they found the Diagnostic Interview for Children and Adolescents and the Diagnostic Interview Schedule for Children to be most noteworthy. All of these interview schedules can be used to assess the broad spectrum of mental disorders. Most counselors probably would not use one of these instruments in an initial interview; however, they may find such an approach beneficial as part of an extended intake process.

In addition to the general interview schedules listed above, specialty interview schedules have been constructed to evaluate specific disorders or concerns. Specialty interview schedules can be useful for counselors who wish to focus on a particular issue, such as substance abuse or suicide risk (Vacc & Juhnke, 1997). Intake interview schedules that emphasize multicultural factors include the Person-in-Culture Interview and the Career-in-Culture Interview (Ponterotto, Rivera, & Sueyoshi, 2000).

TEST SELECTION, ADMINISTRATION, AND SCORING

Test Selection

Testing should be seen as a part of the counseling process and not as an interruption of it. People often approach tests with some anxiety. This is particularly true of aptitude and achievement tests because of fear of failure. Anxiety regarding testing can influence the entire counseling process. Even interest and personality tests can reveal aspects of a person's character that may indicate weaknesses or undesirable features. To reduce the threatening aspects of tests, the counselor should make clear to clients that the purpose of testing is to provide self-understanding, not evaluation of the client by the counselor. The counselor needs to convey to clients the feeling that they will be accepted whatever the test results happen to be.

If at all possible, clients should actively participate in the selection of tests that will be used in counseling (Duckworth, 1990; Healy, 1990). By learning about the purpose and nature of particular tests, clients can profit more from the test results. If convinced of the usefulness of the tests, clients will be more motivated to do their best on ability tests and to be accurate and truthful in responding to items on interest and personality inventories. By having participated in the decisions to use the tests, clients are also more likely to accept the results and their interpretations with less defensiveness. They can be more objective in their perception of the results of the tests.

In the case of academic or career counseling, clients often feel dependent on tests. They perceive the counselor as an expert who will select tests that will tell them what to do. Active participation by clients in test selection helps to counteract overreliance on the counselor.

Generally, the client does not select specific tests. That is a technical matter that counselors must decide on the basis of their knowledge of tests. Instead, the client helps to decide the types of tests that can provide the information most useful for whatever actions or decisions are going to be made. Clients are not nearly as interested in specific characteristics of tests as they are in the implications the results will have for them. The types of tests are therefore described in a general fashion. For example, a counselor should describe the Strong Interest Inventory to a client simply as "an interest inventory that enables you to compare your likes and dislikes with those of people in different occupations." The counselor should not overwhelm the client with a detailed description of the instrument itself.

After the client and counselor have agreed on the type of test, the counselor must decide which specific test would be best to use. In particular, the counselor needs to consider the test's reliability, validity, normative data, and practicality for its intended purpose. Does the test possess sufficient reliability and validity to answer the questions posed by the client and his or her situation? Does the test provide appropriate normative data for the client? Is the test easy to administer and score? How expensive is it? Is the reading level appropriate?

The counselor can best answer these questions, which require specialized knowledge regarding the technical quality of different tests.

A client's statement of need for tests should not necessarily be taken at face value. An initial request for a personality test should result in an effort to explore the meaning of the request, not simply acceptance of it. The client may be experiencing a significant problem such as anxiety or depression that should be explored before tests are assigned. The client may be asking for help regarding a particular problem but having difficulty revealing the problem or asking for help directly. The request for tests serves as an avenue to get at the major problem.

Tests should not be used unnecessarily. Other sources of data in addition to tests should also be explored. In a college counseling center, little is gained by selecting scholastic aptitude tests when records of college entrance tests, high school grades, and college grades are readily available. Other counseling agencies, of course, often start with no previous information. Nevertheless, counselors can first attempt to explore with the client previous experiences that may provide relevant information and self-descriptions. Recall of previous experiences can provide a great deal of information either to supplement test results or to eliminate the need for particular tests.

Test Administration

Standardized tests must be administered in a specified manner under controlled conditions with uniform instructions and materials. The person who administers the test must be familiar with the instructions and other aspects of the administration. The knowledge necessary for administering the test differs greatly depending on the test. On the one hand, standardized scholastic aptitude tests can be administered with relatively little training. On the other hand, the knowledge and skill needed to administer individual intelligence tests requires extensive coursework and practicum experience.

Inexperienced test administrators often do not fully appreciate the importance of the test administrator's role. Irregularities identified in test administrations in school settings include inaccurate timing, altering answer sheets, coaching, teaching the test, scoring errors, recording errors, and student cheating (Gay, 1990). Most test manuals provide detailed instructions for the administration of a particular test, which should be followed exactly. It is the standardization of instructions that makes it possible to compare one person's scores with those of another or with different groups.

In administering tests, the examiner must elicit the interest and cooperation of the test taker. In obtaining rapport, the examiner should attempt to convince test takers that the results will be useful and that they are not wasting their time in a task that will be of little consequence or value to them. Usually clients are cooperative if they have voluntarily sought counseling. If they are being tested against their will, perhaps because of a court order or because they feel that the test information is not important, good rapport may be difficult to establish.

On performance or aptitude tests, the test administrator must encourage examinees to follow instructions carefully and to perform as well as they can. With small children, tests may be presented as a game. For interest or personality inventories, examinees should be encouraged to answer honestly and frankly to preclude invalid results.

The administrator should be familiar with the test being administered so that clients do not doubt the administrator's competence. Self-confidence should be exhibited together with a warm and friendly manner.

The testing environment should be suitable for test administration, with adequate seating, lighting, ventilation, and temperature. It should be free from noise, interruptions, and other distractions. Time limits should be followed exactly and measures taken to prevent cheating. Factors, even minor ones, that can alter test performance should be recognized and minimized. These factors contribute to the error variance in test scores. Any problems in administering the test should be noted and taken into account when interpreting the test results.

At times, the test administration procedures may need to be altered to take into account such matters as a client's disability or language problems (American Educational Research Association, American Psychological Association, & National Council on Measurement in Education, 1999). Accommodations in test administration, such as additional time or the use of an interpreter, should be made if they can improve the opportunity for the client to demonstrate his or her abilities, but not if they provide that client with an advantage over other test takers. Sometimes it is difficult to make this distinction, but the test administrator must make the best decision possible. Any alterations in administration procedures should be noted and included in the report of test results.

Individual Versus Group Tests.   Some tests are designed to be administered to one individual at a time by a trained examiner; other tests can be administered to a group of people. Group tests allow information to be obtained from many people within a short period of time at relatively little cost, whereas individual tests allow the examiner to adapt the test administration to the needs of the client. Individual tests must be used with certain populations such as very small children and those with particular handicaps. Individual tests permit observational data, such as the client's language proficiency and level of cooperation, to be obtained in addition to the test scores.

Speed Versus Power Tests.   Some ability tests place a heavy emphasis on speed of response. These tests often consist of a large number of easy items that a person must complete quickly. Examples of speed tests with relatively short time limits include finger and manual dexterity tests and clerical speed and accuracy tests.

In contrast, power tests contain items of varying difficulty, most of which the person is expected to complete within the time limits. If 90% of the people for whom the test is designed can complete the test within the time limits, the test can be described as a power test. Although speed can still be a factor for some students on power tests, speed would not have much influence on the total score for most students. Most intelligence tests, scholastic aptitude tests, and achievement tests are basically power tests.

Computer-Based Test Administration.   Test administration by means of computers has become widespread in recent years with the availability of low-cost personal computers. Computer-based testing offers a number of advantages compared with traditional paper-and-pencil methods. These advantages include (a) reduced amount of time required for test administration, (b) immediate feedback concerning client performance, (c) improved standardization of test administration procedures, (d) use of new types of items that use movement or sequential presentations, and (e) use of adaptive (or tailored) testing procedures that take into account the client's previous responses (S. L. Wise & Plake, 1990).

The computer has been used to create new types of tests, such as the Test of Variables of Attention (TOVA; Greenberg, 1994). TOVA is a gamelike computer test that uses continuous movement in the form of a target stimulus as a means of assessing clients for attention deficit disorder. It yields scores for several variables, including reaction time, errors of omission (inattention), errors of commission (impulsivity), and anticipatory and multiple responses, that would be difficult to obtain with paper-and-pencil testing.

The computer can be used to reduce testing time by as much as one half. By the use of item response theory, the computer is able to analyze an individual's responses as he or she progresses through the test and to eliminate items that would be too difficult or too easy. Adaptive versions of the Graduate Record Exam and the Minnesota Multiphasic Personality Inventory (MMPI) represent examples of the use of the computer to administer individualized tests based on the examinee's pattern of test responses (Handel, Ben-Porath, & Watt, 1999). Scores obtained in this manner are just as reliable and valid as scores based on the complete test.

Most research supports the use of computer-based test administration. Counselors are more likely to use assessment instruments as part of the counseling process when the computer can administer them (Flowers, Booream, & Schwartz, 1993). Students have reported positive attitudes toward computer-based test administration and interpretation (J. C. Hansen, Neuman, Haverkamp, & Lubinski, 1997). The computer and booklet forms of tests have produced comparable means and standard deviations (Finger & Ones, 1999; Vansickle & Kapes, 1993).

Tests administered by means of a computer have been shown to yield results that are more reliable than paper-and-pencil tests (Kapes & Vansickle, 1992; Vansickle & Kapes, 1993). Clients are generally more honest and often prefer computer-administered tests instead of clinician-administered tests when responding to sensitive matters such as suicide, alcohol or drug abuse, sexual behavior, or HIV-related symptoms (Kobak, Greist, Jefferson, & Katzelnick, 1996).

In the use of computer-based tests, counselors should make certain that clients are familiar and comfortable with the computer equipment. The computer equipment should be checked routinely to ensure that it is functioning properly.

Test Scoring

Tests can be scored by hand or by computer. Tests that are scored by hand usually involve the use of a scoring template that can be placed over the answer sheet to identify incorrect responses. In some cases, clients score their own tests by the use of "self-scorable" answer sheets that reveal the correct answers behind a seal on the reverse side of the answer sheet. Examples of measures that use self-scorable answer sheets include the MBTI and the Kuder General Interest Survey. If more than a few tests or scales are involved, hand scoring can become time consuming, tedious, and subject to error. If at all possible, another person should also score tests that are scored by hand to ensure accuracy of results.

Compared with hand scoring, computer scoring is more rapid, more accurate, and more thorough (S. L. Wise & Plake, 1990). The computer makes it possible to undertake elaborate test scoring programs such as those required for the Strong Interest Inventory and the Campbell Interest and Skill Survey that would be virtually impossible to do by hand. In addition to specific scores, computers can also generate test interpretations by means of scoring rules, or algorithms, stored in the computer's memory.

Computer-based test interpretations (CBTIs), such as those that have been developed for the MMPI, provide a "second opinion" that counselors can use both to create and to test hypotheses about clients. Compared with counselor interpretations, CBTIs tend to be more comprehensive, more objective, and less subject to interpreter bias (Sampson, 2000). CBTI reports should be interpreted for clients with the aid of a counselor unless the report has been specifically validated as "self-interpreting" (National Career Development Association, 1997).

Despite their popularity, the validity of CBTIs has not been well studied (Butcher, Perry, & Atlis, 2000). The scoring rules on which the interpretations are based are often a "trade secret" so that it is difficult to evaluate how adequately they have been developed. In fact, the publishers of the *Mental Measurements Yearbooks* abandoned an effort to provide a separate volume of reviews of CBTIs because of the difficulty they encountered in obtaining information from the test publishers regarding the computer programs and their algorithms (Kramer & Conoley, 1992).

Counselors should examine CBTIs in light of other information that they have been able to collect about the client. They should use their best professional judgment to take into account any individual or situational factors that could alter the CBTI for a particular client. As with any test data, the results should be viewed as hypotheses that need to be confirmed or revised on the basis of other information that is collected regarding the particular client.

SUMMARY

1. A client's readiness for counseling can be assessed in terms of the five stages of change: precontemplative, contemplative, preparation, action, and maintenance.
2. Counselors can use Brickman's "models of helping and coping" to clarify a client's expectations of counseling. Clients differ in their expectations of counseling based on the degree to which they see themselves as responsible for causing or solving their problems.
3. The MBTI can be used to help clients identify their orientation toward problem solving. Clients should be helped to recognize the advantages and disadvantages of their particular problem-solving style.
4. The nature and severity of a client's problems can best be determined by means of an intake form, a problem checklist or screening inventory, and an intake interview used in combination. Both the ICP and the SCL-90-R contain comprehensive lists of client problems or symptoms that can be used systematically to clarify a client's concerns.
5. The intake interview provides a flexible format for assessing a broad range of topics as needed. The client's psychological well-being can be assessed systematically by means of a mental status examination or a structured interview.
6. The client should be integrally involved in all aspects of test selection. A variety of assessment procedures should be considered for this purpose.

7. The counselor should be careful to establish rapport with the client and to follow the prescribed procedures for test administration.

8. Computer-based test interpretations, which have become increasingly popular, require thorough knowledge and understanding of the test itself, the testing circumstances, and characteristics of the client to ensure proper use. Computer-based test interpretations do not replace the need for counselor training and experience in psychological assessment.

Cognitive Assessment

5

ASSESSMENT OF INTELLIGENCE

COUNSELORS WHO WORK in certain settings, such as schools, or who are involved in employment or vocational counseling make considerable use of the results of intelligence tests. Others, working in colleges and secondary schools, constantly make use of a particular type of intelligence measure (a scholastic aptitude test), whereas marriage counselors and those working with substance abusers, for example, may only occasionally use such instruments. Some general knowledge of intelligence assessment is important, and test results influence many decisions clients make. All counselors are expected to have some knowledge of intelligence assessment and the ability to make use of test results in assisting clients to make decisions. In this chapter, some of the most often-used instruments are described along with considerations regarding their use. Scholastic aptitude measures are discussed in the next chapter.

Assessment instruments designed for special populations are described in Chapter 16.

Intelligence has been one of the most thoroughly studied fields throughout the history of psychology. It was Alfred Binet in France who, in the early 1900s, conceptualized intelligence as a general ability to judge, to comprehend, and to reason well. With this definition, he then developed a series of measures by which he could identify children for whom it was necessary to provide special educational programs. The measures he used showed that mental processes increase as a child grows older. Three-year-olds could be expected to be able to point to their nose, eyes, and mouth and repeat two digits. The typical 7-year-old could distinguish right from left and name various colors, and the typical 12-year-old could define various abstract words and make sense of a disarranged sentence.

In 1916, Lewis Terman, at Stanford University, revised and standardized Binet's test for use in the United States. It became known as the Stanford–Binet Intelligence Scale. Making use of the concept of mental age developed by Binet, Terman devised the concept of the now-outdated intelligence quotient (IQ). This IQ score is a ratio calculated between one's mental age and chronological age. A child's mental age is divided by the child's chronological age and multiplied by 100. A child exactly 10 years of age with a mental age of 12 will obtain an IQ score of 120. A mental age substantially below a child's chronological age was considered evidence of mental retardation. This type of an IQ score has a number of problems connected with it. In the first place, answering all of the items correctly on the original Stanford–Binet yielded a maximum mental age of less than 20. Thus, anyone 20 or older automatically received an IQ score of less than 100. The usefulness of the ratio score therefore disappears during the teen years. In addition, the concept of a person's IQ has been erroneously viewed by the public as a fixed measure, similar to the color of a person's eyes, rather than as a particular score on a particular test at a particular time. The ratio IQ has therefore been replaced by a derived IQ standard score (known as the deviation IQ) to circumvent some of these problems.

The question of what it is that actually makes up intelligence and what it is that intelligence tests actually measure has long been the subject of much controversy. One conceptualization divides intelligence into two types: crystallized and fluid. Crystallized intelligence deals with an individual's ability to solve problems and make decisions on the basis of acquired knowledge, experiences, and verbal conceptualizations. Fluid intelligence is an individual's ability to be adaptable and flexible in solving new problems (Carroll, 1993a). Most of the tests in the content areas of verbal reasoning and quantitative reasoning would be considered crystallized intelligence and those in the abstract/visual reasoning area fluid intelligence.

POPULAR INDIVIDUAL INTELLIGENCE TESTS

The Stanford–Binet

The Stanford–Binet became the best-known intelligence test in the world and was used as the "gold standard" against which all other intelligence tests being developed were validated. The 1916 Stanford–Binet Intelligence Scale had a number of weaknesses and was therefore revised to produce the 1937 scale, in two parallel forms (L and M). The ratio IQ score was eliminated, and standard scores were calculated to provide each age with a mean of 100 and a standard deviation of 16. A 1960 revision was developed and was restandardized in 1972 to provide more adequate norms intended to be representative of the entire U.S. population.

The 1986 revision (Thorndike, Hagen, & Sattler, 1986a, 1986b) is the fourth edition of the Stanford–Binet Intelligence Scale. The authors attempted to provide a continuity with the previous editions by retaining the advantages of the early editions as an individually administered intelligence test and still take advantage of the more recent theoretical developments and new research in cognitive psychology. A wider variety of tests, particularly those of a nonverbal nature, are included.

The fourth edition includes 15 separate tests that cover four different content areas: (a) verbal reasoning, (b) abstract/visual reasoning, (c) quantitative reasoning, and (d) short-term memory. Whereas certain of the 15 subtests are administered to subjects of all ages, others have more restricted age ranges.

In the administration of the 1986 revision, as in the case of the previous editions, individuals are administered a range of tasks suited to their abilities. A level is established at which it is expected that they would have answered all of the previous lower level items correctly, and testing continues to a point at a ceiling level. Answers on the vocabulary test along with the individual's chronological age provide a method by which the entry level is determined to begin testing on the remaining tests. Testing then proceeds on each test until at least three out of four items are missed, which determines a ceiling level on that test at which further items can be expected to be answered incorrectly.

On most of the tests, each item has only one correct answer, and the raw score on each test is converted into a standard age score with a mean of 50 and a standard deviation of 8. Standard scores are also provided for each of the four cognitive areas along with a total composite score that reflects general mental ability. Each has a mean of 100 and a standard deviation of 16. The total testing time for the fourth edition takes approximately 1 hour and 15 minutes. No individual is administered all 15 tests; a complete battery includes 8 to 13 tests depending on the individual's entry level.

The fourth edition was standardized on more than 5,000 individuals from throughout the United States and included representative samples based on gender, age, ethnic group, and community size. Internal consistency reliabilities tend to be very high for the composite (above .95) and for each of the cognitive areas (above .93). In general, test–retest reliabilities on both the individual tests and the composites are higher for older than for younger age levels. The authors have provided validity data on the fourth edition by using (a) constructs based on current research in the field of cognitive intelligence, (b) internal consistency and factor-analytic methods, and (c) correlations with other intelligence tests.

The Wechsler Scales

The Stanford–Binet was originally developed for children, with some more difficult items added for adults. David Wechsler, working at Bellevue Hospital in New York, believed that there was a need for an intelligence test more suitable for adults, and he therefore developed the Wechsler Bellevue Intelligence Scale in 1939. In addition, believing that the Stanford–Binet placed too much emphasis on language and verbal skills, he developed a totally different performance scale measuring nonverbal intelligence. The Wechsler scales were reported to be among the five most widely used instruments by school counselors (the Wechsler Intelligence Scale for Children [WISC]) and community mental health counselors (both the WISC and the Wechsler Adult Intelligence Scale [WAIS]; Bubenzer, Zimpfer, & Mahrle, 1990; Elmore, Ekstrom, Diamond, & Whittaker, 1993).

The Wechsler Adult Intelligence Scale–Third Edition (WAIS-III). The 1939 scale was revised in 1955 to correct a number of deficiencies that had been found in the earlier form and became the WAIS. The WAIS was revised in 1981 to produce the WAIS-R and standardized on a sample selected to match the proportions of the U.S. population in regard to race, occupational level, education, and residence (D. Wechsler, 1981). During the 1990s, it was expanded by adding three new optional subtest scores on four factor-analysis-based indexes and was restandardized to yield more comprehensive and updated norms as the WAIS-III (Kaufman & Lichtenberger, 1999; D. Wechsler, 1997).

There is a core of nine subtests with two added to obtain IQ scores and a different two added to get index scores. Thirteen are administered to obtain both, and there is an optional Object Assembly subtest that may be substituted for a "spoiled" performance subtest. IQ scores are derived from norms on 13 age bands 16–89 and can range from 45 to 155 (Hess, 2001).

The Wechsler tests yield a profile of scores (such as that of the case example for the WAIS-III, some of which are displayed in Figure 5-1) showing the scale score for each of the 13 subtests along with verbal IQ, performance IQ, and the full-scale IQ scores. The mean and standard deviation for each of the 14 subtests are 10 and 3, respectively. For the performance, verbal, and full-scale IQ scores, the mean is 100 with a standard deviation of 15 (as compared with 16 for the Stanford–Binet). Standard error of measurement for the three IQ scores is reported to be approximately 2.5 for the full-scale IQ, 2.7 for the verbal IQ, and 4.1 for the performance IQ. A client's true full-scale score could thus be assumed at a 95% level of confidence to fall within 5 points in one direction or the other from the client's obtained full-scale IQ score. Here is a case example of a WAIS-III administered at the time of admission to a residential alcoholism treatment facility.

FIGURE 5-1. Wechsler Adult Intelligence Scale–III Summary

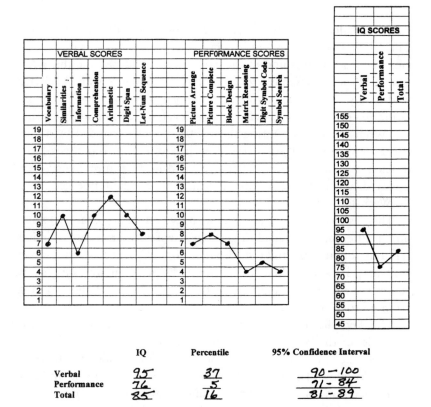

Name __Peter__ Gender __Male__ Age __24__

Education __10th grade__ Occupation __Unemployed__

Age Group Norm __20-24__

	IQ	Percentile	95% Confidence Interval
Verbal	95	37	90-100
Performance	76	5	71-84
Total	85	16	81-89

CASE EXAMPLE

Peter, 24 years old and single, had the WAIS-III administered to him while undergoing treatment for alcoholism in a residential alcohol detoxification center. He had been treated twice before for alcoholism, but, being single and without family or other support systems, he found it easy to drift back into alcoholism upon discharge. He suffered from mild depression and antisocial tendencies and had been in trouble with the law in addition to his problems with alcohol. In the center, however, he was a model client and cooperated fully with the treatment and testing he received. His verbal score on the WAIS-III fell in the normal range although he scored substantially lower on the performance subtests, giving him a total score that would place him in the dull-normal range. The large difference between the verbal and performance portions of the WAIS-III may very likely have been caused by the effects of continued alcohol abuse.

Wechsler Intelligence Scale for Children (WISC-III). The WISC was originally developed as a downward extension of the Wechsler Bellevue Intelligence Scale for use with children ages 6 to 16 years. It was revised in 1974 (WISC-R) to contain more child-oriented items, to include more African American and female figures, and to provide a normative sample more representative of children in the U.S. population (D. Wechsler, 1974). A third revised and updated edition, standardized on a census-based normative sample of 2,200 children, was published in 1991 as the WISC-III (D. Wechsler, 1991).

The WISC-III contains 13 subtests, 3 of which are supplementary, to be used if needed. The subtests generally parallel those in the WAIS-III and provide verbal, performance, and full-scale IQ scores similar to the WAIS-III. The three supplementary tests provided are the digit span subtest, which may be substituted for a verbal test, and the maze and symbol search subtests, which may be substituted for tests in the performance battery, if the examiner meets with difficulty in administering one of the regular subtests to a particular child. As with the WAIS-III, the subtests are administered by alternating the verbal and performance subtests.

The subtests, the two partial IQ scores, and the full-scale IQ scores have means and standard deviations similar to those of the WAIS-III. Norms are provided for each 4-month age group between 6 and 16 years. The WISC has been found to be a useful instrument for the diagnosis of learning disabilities and mental retardation.

Both split-half and test–retest reliabilities for all three IQ scores fall within the range of .90 to .96. The standard error of measurement for the full-scale IQ test is approximately 3 points. Thus, a child's true WISC-III IQ score would be estimated to be no more than 6 points above or below the obtained score at a 95% level of confidence.

The Wechsler Preschool and Primary Scale of Intelligence (WPPSI-R).
In 1967, a downward extension of the WISC was developed for use with children 4 to $6\frac{1}{2}$ years of age, called the Wechsler Preschool and Primary Scale of Intelligence (WPPSI), which was revised in 1989 to become the WPPSI-R (D. Wechsler, 1989). It includes 11 subtests, of which 10 are used in obtaining the IQ scores. Eight of the subtests represent downward extensions of those from the WISC, and 3 unique subtests were added. Normalized standard scores for subtests and IQs are similar to those on the other Wechsler tests.

The Wechsler Abbreviated Scale of Intelligence.   There is also a short-form Wechsler instrument, the Wechsler Abbreviated Scale of Intelligence (WASI; D. Wechsler, 1999). Taking only 15 to 30 minutes to administer, the WASI yields a brief measure tied to both the WISC-III and the WAIS-III. It is appropriate for individuals ages 6 to 89.

The Kaufman Batteries

More recently, several tests have been developed that make use of Luria's (1980) Planning-Attention-Successive-Simultaneous (PASS) model of intelligence. These include the Kaufman tests and the Das Naglieri system. The Kaufmans have developed several intelligence test batteries, including the Kaufman Assessment Battery for Children (K-ABC) and the Kaufman Adolescent and Adult Intelligence Test (KAIT). The K-ABC is composed of 16 subtests of which 13 are administered for any one child (Cohen, Swerdlik, & Smith, 1992; Kaufman & Kaufman, 1983). It is designed for children $2\frac{1}{2}$ to $12\frac{1}{2}$ years old and contains sets of both mental processing and achievement subscores. The K-ABC is considered to be more cross-culturally fair than most comparable tests of intelligence, in part because it separates processing scores from achievement scores (Samuda, 1998a).

The KAIT consists of six core subtests and four additional subtests in an expanded battery and is normed for ages 11 to 85 years (Kaufman & Kaufman, 1993). It yields scores on both crystallized and fluid intelligence and a composite IQ score, each with reliability coefficients above .90. A short form, the Kaufman Brief Intelligence Test (K-BIT; Kaufman & Kaufman, 1990), which can be administered in

15–30 minutes, consists of a vocabulary (through pictures) portion and a matrices portion using pictures and abstract designs. It is useful when time constraints preclude the use of a longer measure (Naugle, Chelune, & Tucker, 1993).

The Cognitive Assessment System

An instrument developed to provide a broader measure of children's cognitive abilities is the Das Naglieri Cognitive Assessment System (CAS; Naglieri, 1999). Based on Luria's (1980) cognitive-processing theory of intelligence, it contains 13 subtests (only 12 are used in any administration) yielding four scales labeled *Planning, Attention, Simultaneous processing,* and *Successive processing* (PASS) and a full-scale score ($M = 100$, $SD = 15$). Internal consistency and test–retest reliabilities are in the vicinity of .90, and the planning and attention scales assess concepts not found on traditional intelligence tests.

Other Individual Intelligence Tests

There are several individually administered intelligence tests designed to provide brief assessments of cognitive abilities for individuals of widely varying ages. The Peabody Picture Vocabulary Test–Third Edition (PPVT-III; L. M. Dunn & Dunn, 1997) is a brief (10–15 minutes) screening test of listening comprehension and verbal ability. A word is given, and the examinee is told to point to the appropriate one picture out of four on a card.

The Slosson Intelligence Test–Revised (SIT-R) is an individual screening test of verbal intelligence made up of items similar to those found on the verbal subtests of the Wechsler scales (C. A. Campbell & Ashmore, 1995; Nicholson & Hibpshman, 1998). It requires 10–25 minutes to administer and was renormed in 1998. Both of these instruments can be administered to individuals of widely varying ages from 3 or 4 years to 65 and older, both report reliability coefficients of above .9, and both show substantial concurrent validities with the verbal portions of other instruments such as the Wechsler and Kaufman batteries. They yield deviation IQs with a mean of 100 and standard deviations of 15 for the PPVT-III and 16 for the SIT-R.

Advantages and Disadvantages
of Individual Intelligence Tests

Each of these intelligence tests is individually administered and requires a highly trained examiner. Considerable training and practice in administering each test are necessary for a competent administration that produces reliable results. An experienced examiner has the opportunity to observe and judge a variety of behaviors and aspects of the individual's personality. Thus, for the competent examiner, these tests provide aspects of a clinical interview as well as a standardized test.

Because these individual intelligence tests provide several different types of IQ scores, the counselor has the opportunity to pay particular attention to those clients for whom the difference between the scores is substantial. In such cases, an exploration is warranted to attempt to discern factors that might account for the differences. The different subtest scores also provide an opportunity to examine the pattern of scores that appear as a profile on the report form, such as that shown for the WAIS-III case example of Peter in Figure 5-1.

There have been a number of hypotheses advanced regarding emotional, neurological, and pathological problems that yield differential subtest scores. Considerable research has shown differential diagnoses resulting from patterns on such profiles to be questionable. Because the different subtests vary in reliability, difference scores obtained among the subtests can be particularly unreliable. Nevertheless, most sophisticated users of the Stanford–Binet and the Wechsler tests regard differential patterns as suggesting certain types of dysfunction. For example, higher scores on various verbal scales and lower scores on certain of the performance scales are suggestive of such problems as brain damage, drug abuse (as in the case example), or, in an older person, Alzheimer's dementia. Verbal subtest scores falling well below performance scores may suggest poor reading ability or lack of motivation for academic achievement.

The primary disadvantages of individual intelligence tests are their costs, both in terms of time and money, and the extensive training required for them to be properly administered and interpreted. Counselors often lack both the resources and the training to use these instruments themselves. Instead, they refer clients in need of individual testing to competent examiners and receive the results from them.

Counselors should encourage such examiners to report their observations and any other information that can assist counselors in interpreting the results, particularly in regard to information that can help to explain any discrepancies. In place of individual intelligence tests, counselors are more likely to use group intelligence tests to assess the cognitive abilities of their clients.

GROUP INTELLIGENCE TESTS

Group intelligence tests are considerably more cost-efficient than individual tests in the time and expense required for administration and scoring. They require simpler materials; typically only a printed booklet, a multiple-choice answer sheet, a pencil, and a scoring key are needed. They also usually offer more normative information as this type of data is easier to collect for group tests.

The development of group tests was stimulated by the need to classify almost 2 million U.S. Army recruits during World War I. The Army Alpha and the nonreading companion test, the Army Beta (now in its current revision, Beta III), were developed for military use. Group intelligence tests designed for educational and personnel uses were developed shortly thereafter, with these two tests as models. Such group-administered tests are now used at every educational level from kindergarten through graduate school. They are also used extensively by industry, by the military, and in research studies. To avoid the term *intelligence test*, because the term *intelligence* is so often misunderstood and misinterpreted, counselors are encouraged to describe these tests, particularly those designed for school use, in terms of mental maturity, cognitive ability, school ability, or academic ability.

Group Intelligence Tests for School Use

Because these tests are administered across a number of grades throughout entire school systems, they are administered in the hundreds of thousands each year. The market for these tests is therefore a profitable one, and a large number are available for use. Four of the most popular and most psychometrically sound instruments are briefly described here. Results are typically reported in a variety of forms: national and local age and grade percentiles, stanines, and normal curve equivalents.

Cognitive Abilities Test. The Cognitive Abilities Test, Form 5 is the modern version of the Lorge–Thorndike Intelligence Tests (Riverside Publishing Co., 1994). The test contains three different batteries: one for kindergarten and Grade 1, one for Grades 2 and 3, and a multilevel battery for use in Grades 3 through 12. The Cognitive Abilities Test contains three separate sections providing three separate scores: verbal, quantitative, and nonverbal along with a composite score. The nonverbal section uses neither language nor numbers but geometric figures for tasks that require classification, analogies, or figure synthesis. In this portion, the effects of formal schooling, poor reading ability, or non-native-English speaking are minimized. Raw scores on each section can be converted into stanine and percentile scores for both age and grade levels so that the three scores can be compared both with norm groups and within each individual. In addition, the scores can be converted to standard scores that have a mean of 100 and a standard deviation of 16 to produce a deviation IQ score. The Cognitive Abilities Tests were standardized along with the Iowa Tests of Basic Skills for kindergarten through Grade 9 and the Iowa Tests of Educational Development for Grades 9 through 12.

Kuhlmann–Anderson Test. The Kuhlmann–Anderson Test is made up of seven separate levels for kindergarten through 12th grade, with each level containing eight tests (Scholastic Testing Service, 1997). It is the contemporary version (restandardized and renormed in 1997) of one of the earliest and most popular intelligence tests used in the schools. It is less dependent on language than most similar tests and yields verbal, nonverbal, and total scores. Scores are presented as age- and grade-related percentile bands (confidence intervals) as well as deviation IQ (Cognitive Skills Quotient) scores.

Test of Cognitive Skills. The Test of Cognitive Skills (TCS/2) is the contemporary version of the long-used California Test of Mental Maturity–Short Form (CTB/Macmillan/McGraw-Hill, 1993). In its original form, the instrument was designed to be the group-test equivalent of the Stanford–Binet and to yield scores similar to those that would be obtained by individually administering the Stanford–Binet. In addition to verbal and nonverbal ability subtests, it also contains a section designed to assess short-term memory. There are six levels, each designed for two grade levels ranging from Grade 2 through Grade 12. Age and grade stanines, percentiles, and standard score norms are available for each subtest. A Combined Cognitive Skills Index provides a deviation IQ score. It was standardized with the Terra Nova and the California Achievement Tests–5.

Otis–Lennon School Ability Test. The Otis–Lennon School Ability Test, 7th Edition (OLSAT7) has seven levels ranging from kindergarten to Grade 12 (Otis & Lennon, 1996). The test is published in two forms and yields verbal and nonverbal scores based on 36-item subtests and a total IQ score. The test represents a contemporary version of a series of former Otis tests. The OLSAT7 was jointly normed with the Metropolitan Achievement Tests 8 and the Stanford Achievement Tests 9.

Other Group Intelligence Tests

Shipley Institute of Living Scale. The Shipley Institute of Living Scale–Revised (SILS-R) is a 60-item (40 vocabulary, 20 abstract reasoning) intelligence test that takes approximately 20 minutes to administer. IQ and standard scores are obtained based on age-adjusted norms (Zachary, 1986). Correlations in the vicinity of .8 with Wechsler tests are reported in the manual, along with reliabilities of .8 to .9 for internal consistency and .6 to .7 for test–retest. Originally constructed to assess cognitive impairment, this test is now used as a brief screening device for overall intellectual ability.

Wonderlic Personnel Test. The Wonderlic Personnel Test is a brief 12-minute, 50-item test of mental ability for adults (Wonderlic, 1999). Sixteen forms of this paper-and-pencil intelligence test are available, along with extensive norms. It is administered in business and industry to 2.5 million job applicants each year for the selection and placement of employees. It is available in 14 languages and can be administered on a personal computer. Validity data in regard to job success are undoubtedly available locally in many companies but typically are not found in the research literature. The test's validity has been questioned in regard to selection for certain positions when minorities obtaining lower scores on the instrument are screened out of various entry-level positions. This has resulted in the Wonderlic Personnel Test becoming the subject of various court cases in which its use was declared not legitimate when testing procedures resulted in denying fair opportunities to prospective minority employees but acceptable when test results could be shown to be substantially related to the performance on specific jobs.

Multidimensional Aptitude Battery. The Multidimensional Aptitude Battery–II (MAB-II) was developed by Douglas Jackson as a group-administered paper-and-pencil test to yield the same types of results and scores as the WAIS (D. N. Jackson, 1998). This test battery contains five tests on the verbal scale and five tests on the performance scale that involve very similar tasks to the subtests on the WAIS but in a paper-and-pencil format. Scores on the various subtests have a mean of 50 and a standard deviation of 10, and total scores on the verbal, performance, and full-scale scores have a mean of 100 and a standard deviation of 15.

In the design of the Multidimensional Aptitude Battery, Jackson made use of the capabilities of modern computers in developing items and scales through item analysis and factor-analysis techniques. The battery can be taken directly on most computers with software that presents instructions and practice items, times the subtests, scores them, and produces four different types of interpretive reports. The advantage of the battery is its ease of administration and scoring; the highly trained examiner necessary to administer the WAIS or the Stanford–Binet is not required. As a group-administered battery, however, it does not provide the examiner with the observational data obtained in using individual instruments.

INTERPRETING INTELLIGENCE TEST RESULTS

The typical intelligence test administered in the United States assumes a relatively common cultural background found in contemporary society and English as the native language. For tests above the lower elementary levels, reading ability in English is also necessary to obtain valid results on most of the group-administered tests. To provide valid assessment devices useful in other cultures or for use with subcultures or minority cultures in the United States, test developers have made attempts to develop culture-fair tests that function independently of a specific culture, primarily by eliminating, or at least greatly reducing, language and cultural content. These are discussed in Chapter 16.

Robert Sternberg has refocused attention on some of the fundamental questions regarding intelligence (Sternberg, 1985; Sternberg, Wagner, Williams, & Horvath, 1995). He has proposed a triarchic theory of intelligence with each of the three factors made up of several different elements that interact with one another. The componential (cognitive) factor deals with information processing and is made up of crystallized abilities measured by such subtests as vocabulary and reading comprehension and fluid abilities measured by subtests such as abstract analogies and series completions. His experiential (creative) factor embodies the ability to deal with novel activities and situations and the ability to automatize high levels of information processing. His conceptual (practical) factor contains the components of practical intelligence and social intelligence. His triarchic intelligence test (not yet published) consists of 12 subtests, four for each of the three factors. He believes that a single index of IQ does more to obscure than describe a person's abilities, and his measures vary widely from the tasks typically involved in the more traditional attempts to assess intelligence (Sternberg, 1988, 1998).

Howard Gardner has also proposed a theory of multiple intelligences (called the MI theory) with seven different and relatively independent intelligences: logical-mathematical, linguistic, musical, special, bodily-kinesthetic, interpersonal, and intrapersonal (Gardner, 1993). He and his colleagues are attempting to develop instruments to assess these various intelligences, but at present his theory lacks a strong empirical base (Groth-Marnat, 1997). Meanwhile, John Carroll in England has reanalyzed 461 data sets of various cognitive abilities (Carroll, 1993b). He has described a more traditional theory of intelligence of three strata in a hierarchical model, similar to that of Vernon (1961). It contains a single general ability g at the apex, a second stratum of eight broad abilities, and a third with many narrow abilities. Additional studies have continued to show that cognitive ability as measured by the traditional intelligence test is a valid predictor of educational achievement, occupational success, and work performance (Barrett & Depinet, 1991; Schmidt & Hunter, 1998).

In any case, controversy continues regarding the concept of intelligence, the specific abilities that constitute intelligent behavior, and the magnitude of the roles played by heredity and environment. There has been a curious trend in which mean IQ scores have increased about 3 points per decade over the last 50 years. This trend, known as the "Flynn effect" after James Flynn, who noted it early, is not easily explained—this effect has been variably reasoned to be caused by education, nutrition, and media (Neisser, 1998; Whiston, 2000). Using a sophisticated mathematical model, Dickens and Flynn (2001) suggested that industrialization's rising cognitive demands of work and leisure have created a steadily increasing environmental "social multiplier" effect that could account for the higher IQ scores across many nations. At the same time, academic achievement and scholastic aptitude test scores have not shown similar increases and occasionally have shown actual decreases.

Perhaps the most important point to remember in the interpretation of intelligence test results is that the IQ score obtained does not represent a fixed characteristic of the individual. Instead, it should be interpreted as a particular score obtained on a particular test at a particular time. As has been mentioned, this is especially important for younger clients, for whom test–retest reliabilities are lower, indicating that considerable change and development take place over time. In interpreting the result to a client, rather than say that the client has an IQ of 112, the counselor would provide a better interpretation by saying that the client scored in the top quarter of his or her peers on a test that measures an ability useful in learning academic subjects.

SUMMARY

This chapter dealt with the assessment of intelligence using both individual and group assessment instruments.

1. The concept of intelligence is widely studied in psychology, but IQ scores are widely misunderstood by the general public.
2. Binet designed the first intelligence test in France in the early 1900s; it was revised in 1916 at Stanford for use in the United States. The 1986 revision of the Stanford–Binet intelligence tests contains 15 subtests, only parts of which are administered to any individual, depending on the chronological age and answers on certain of the subtests.

3. Four different Wechsler scales represent individually administered intelligence tests designed specifically for different age ranges.
4. Large numbers of group intelligence tests are administered each year in U.S. schools, and seven of these tests were briefly described in this chapter.
5. Fundamental questions regarding the range of abilities that constitute intelligent behavior are still being explored along with instruments to assess these abilities.

6

ACADEMIC APTITUDE AND ACHIEVEMENT

THE ASSESSMENT of various aptitudes has played an important role in the field of psychological testing. An aptitude is generally thought of as an ability to acquire a specific type of skill or knowledge. In the field of aptitude testing, the assessment of scholastic aptitude is particularly important, because academic or scholastic aptitude is significantly related to achievement in various educational programs in high schools, colleges, and professional schools. Because of the importance of higher education as a prerequisite for entering the majority of higher status occupations and professions in today's society, achieving acceptable scores on scholastic aptitude measures is becoming increasingly crucial for those aspiring to such occupations.

Even counselors in elementary schools or mental health agencies who seldom see scholastic aptitude test scores in their work are expected to be knowledgeable about these tests. They will probably at least be consulted by their relatives, friends, and colleagues whose children are beginning to apply to undergraduate or professional colleges and universities.

In this chapter, information about the two major national college testing programs is presented, along with considerations and data useful in the interpretation of test scores. Academic aptitude tests used for admission to several of the different types of professional colleges are briefly described, followed by a few points regarding the administration and interpretation of academic aptitude tests. Examples of academic achievement test batteries commonly used in the schools are briefly described, along with a discussion of the use and misuse of such test batteries. Finally, the relatively new cognitive development theories and assessment instruments are mentioned because of the expectation that they will be of increasing interest to counselors.

TESTS FOR HIGHER EDUCATION

Scholastic aptitude tests are used as sources of information for the selection and admission of students to institutions of higher education at the undergraduate and graduate or professional levels. They are also used for awarding academic scholarships, in determining athletic eligibility, for awarding financial aid, for placing students in courses, as well as for academic and vocational counseling and advising. The two most commonly required college-level aptitude tests are the College Entrance Examination Board's Scholastic Assessment Test (SAT) and that administered by the American College Testing Program (ACT).

The Scholastic Assessment Test (SAT)

The SAT has been given since 1926 and is now taken by over a million college-bound high school students each year. Its design, administration, and reporting are carried out by the Educational Testing Service (ETS) in Princeton, New Jersey. Originally called the Scholastic Aptitude Test, it was revised in 1994 and given the redundant name—the Scholastic Assessment Test–I (SAT-I). It is now known simply as the SAT-I. It is a 3-hour primarily multiple-choice test with two major sections: (a) Verbal (V), containing multiple-choice items dealing with critical reading, sentence completion, and analogies, and (b) Mathematical (M), with both multiple-choice items dealing with regular mathematics and quantitative comparisons and 10 completion items that require student-produced responses (College Board, 2000b, 2000c). It no longer includes a writing sample, which was moved to the optional SAT-II tests. The SAT-I attempts to measure developed abilities or intellectual skills and is not meant to be an achievement test tied to particular high school courses or curricula. Reliabilities of the SAT-I Verbal and Mathematical portions have generally been found to be in the vicinity of .90 for college-bound students, yielding standard errors of measurement of approximately 30 points.

In 1941, the mean on each section for students taking the test was set at 500 with a standard deviation of 100, and scores therefore range on a scale from 200 to 800. Since 1941, the college-bound cohort completing the test each year had changed drastically, and 500 no longer approximated the college-bound mean. In the spring of 1995, scores on the SAT-I were "recentered" with the mean on each of the two portions reset at 500 (College Board, 1994a). By the year 2000, mean scores had edged up slightly to 505 on the SAT Verbal and 514 on the SAT Mathematical.

The Mathematical portion of the SAT-I is more dependent on curriculum-based learning than is the Verbal portion; the further the student progresses in mathematics courses in high school, the better the student will be prepared for the SAT-I Mathematics. Students who have not taken mathematics courses for several years should be encouraged to review some of their basic algebra and geometry before sitting for the SAT-I.

The College Entrance Examination Board also administers the 1-hour SAT-II subject tests in 18 specific subjects (e.g., biology, Spanish) and a writing test, one or more of which are required by some colleges.

Preliminary Scholastic Aptitude Test/National Merit Scholarship Qualifying Test (PSAT/NMSQT)

The PSAT/NMSQT is typically taken in the 11th grade (College Board, 2000a). It is considered by some students to be a practice or trial run for the SAT to be taken the following year. It is also used to help students choose which colleges to consider in their college decision-making plans. It plays an important role as the initial step in qualifying for National Merit Scholarships.

Scores on the PSAT/NMSQT, which range from 20 to 80, are designed to be comparable—with an additional 0 added—to the SAT scores that students would be expected to obtain when they take that test in their senior year. Like the SAT, it yields both Verbal and Math scores (from two 50-minute sections) and includes a 30-minute Writing Skills section. The PSAT/NMSQT was also recentered in the fall of 1994 in order that those juniors could predict the scores they would receive when they took the recentered SAT-I in 1995 (College Board, 1992a). Thus, a student who receives a 50 on the PSAT Verbal and a 55 on the PSAT Math would be expected to receive scores somewhere in the vicinity of 500 on the SAT-I Verbal and 550 on the SAT-I Mathematical (College Entrance Examination Board, 1988). Such a student who had been planning to enter a very highly selective institution at which the majority of those students admitted score above 650 on both portions of the SAT-I might wish to reconsider his or her chances of admission to that institution. An additional score known as the "Selection Index" is computed for scholarship consideration by summing the Verbal, Math, and Writing Skills scores on the PSAT/NMSQT. The approximately 16,000 highest scoring students become National Merit Scholarship semifinalists, with actual selection index cutoff scores varying among the different states to obtain the top 1% of the scholarship qualifiers from each state.

American College Testing Program (ACT)

The other national college testing admissions program is that of the ACT, established in 1959 and based in Iowa City, Iowa. The ACT tests tend to be used more often by colleges in the Midwest and less often by those on the East Coast, although the majority of institutions in the United States will accept either SAT or ACT scores. The current revision, termed the ACT Assessment, consists of four academic tests, an interest inventory, and a questionnaire regarding student backgrounds and plans (American College Testing Program, 1999b). The academic tests take 2 hours and 55 minutes to complete and are designed to assess academic ability in four areas: English, mathematics, reading, and science reasoning. The item content of the ACT is similar to that of the Iowa Tests of Educational Development, on which the ACT was originally based. Scores are obtained on each of the four academic tests and their seven subscales, along with a total composite score. The mean for college-bound students who take the ACT is approximately 21 on each of the four academic tests and the composite score. Standard deviations vary from 4.5 to 6.0; and standard scores range from 1 to 36. The standard error of measurement is approximately 2 for the academic tests and 1 for the composite score.

The 90-item interest inventory provides scores on six interest areas similar to Holland's (1997) hexagon and a method of plotting interests on the accompanying World-of-Work Map. ACT reports to both the high school and the student contain much information useful in academic and career planning. They include student plans, perceived educational needs, interest inventory scores, and rankings of the students' scores at the colleges to which the scores are being sent.

There is a preliminary ACT battery, the PLAN Program for 10th-grade students (American College Testing Program, 1999a). It consists of (a) four academic tests of 20 to 45 minutes each, yielding standard scores of 1 to 32 that are linked to junior/senior year ACT Assessment scores; (b) a brief interest inventory; (c) a student needs assistance profile; (d) a student information section; and (e) an educational/occupational plans section.

Validity of Scholastic Aptitude Tests

The ACT and the SAT are approximately equal in their ability to predict college grades. Thousands of studies have been conducted assessing the ability of these tests to predict grades, with the typical correlation ranging in the vicinity of .30 to .50 for freshmen grade point averages (GPAs). Correlations tend to be higher at institutions with more heterogeneous freshmen classes and lower among homogeneous student bodies, particularly at the very highly selective institutions with restricted ranges of student scores.

Most studies have found that high school grades are the best predictors of college GPAs but that scholastic aptitude tests are able to improve the prediction over high school GPAs or high school ranks alone (College Board, 2000c). That scholastic aptitude test scores would add to the prediction of college success is not surprising. The particular high school GPA that a student obtains depends on a number of factors: the general competitiveness of the high school attended, the grading curve used in that high school, the types of courses taken, as well as other personal factors. Thus, a high school GPA of 3.2 achieved by a particular student who has taken all college preparatory subjects in a school with a low grading curve and where the majority of classmates are college-bound represents a very different level of achievement than that obtained by a student from a less competitive high school who has taken a number of vocational or commercial courses. A national college admissions test represents a common task for all students and therefore can operate as a correction factor for the high school GPA. In addition, for the student with low grades but with substantially higher scholastic aptitude test scores than would be expected from those grades, the scores may suggest hitherto unrecognized academic potential. These scores may represent a "second chance" for such a student.

These tests are generally equally predictive for different racial groups. In those instances in which differences have been found, the group with the lower scores tends to obtain lower than predicted college GPAs rather than higher, as might be expected.

Test scores tend to be greatly overemphasized by many parents and their college-bound students. Only at the most highly selective institutions are very high scores generally required, and even there, much other information goes into admissions decisions. Students with good high school grades can obtain admission to most colleges unless their test scores are extremely low.

When scholastic aptitude test scores are interpreted to students and their parents, the standard error should be taken into account. On the SAT-Verbal and SAT-Mathematical, the standard error is in the vicinity of 30, suggesting that two thirds of the time the student's true score will fall within 30 points in one direction or the other from the obtained score. For the ACT, with a standard error of approximately 2 points, two thirds of the time students' true scores could be expected to fall within 2 points on either side of their obtained ACT standard scores.

Although the number of U.S. colleges and universities that require very high ACT or SAT scores is not large, almost all 4-year institutions claim to maintain some type of a selective admissions policy.

This selectivity varies greatly. Some public institutions will take any student in the top half of his or her high school class or one who obtains a test score at least equivalent to that level. Others take only those in the top quarter, or in the top three quarters, or have other means of selection using formulas with high school rank or high school grades and SAT scores. A few private institutions admit perhaps only one in five applicants from an already very selective applicant pool. There are many other private colleges that, although maintaining that they are selective in their admissions, in fact will admit almost every high school graduate who applies as will most public community colleges. The result is a great variation in the abilities of the average or typical student on various campuses.

It is definitely not true in the United States that a particular GPA earned at one institution is equivalent to that of another or that college degrees are equivalent from wherever they are obtained (Hood, 1968). Although some differences in levels of competition among colleges are recognized to at least a limited extent by the general public, and perhaps to a greater degree by those in higher education, the actual differences are far greater than all but the most sophisticated observers of American higher education imagine. Levels of competition vary so greatly among institutions that a student obtaining an honors GPA of 3.4 at one institution could easily fail out of a much more competitive institution.

These differences can be understood by examining the scholastic aptitude test scores in various institutions. Scholastic aptitude test scores of entering freshmen at particular institutions of several different types are shown in Table 6-1. This table includes ACT-English and College Board SAT-I Verbal scores as rough equivalents. It should be recognized that the equivalence between these two tests shown in this table was based on a large and relatively heterogeneous population but at a single institution. Populations at particular institutions of varying ability levels and with differing proportions of the two sexes may result in concordance tables that differ substantially from this table. The equivalent scores given in this table should be read as only rough equivalents and not as exact mathematical equivalents. The scores given for the different types of institutions represent a specific institution and are provided here as general examples and do not represent the typical or median institution of that type.

TABLE 6-1. Percentiles of Students With Certain Academic Aptitude Test Scores (Verbal) in Different Types of Institutions

ACT English Standard Score	SAT-I Verbal Standard Score	ACT National Norms English 1999–2000	Ivy League University (SAT-I-V)	A Midwest State University (ACT-E)	A Small Liberal Arts College (ACT-E)	A Southern State College (SAT-I-V)
33	730	99	95	—	—	—
32	700	98	80	99	—	—
30	660	97	60	94	98	—
29	640	94	45	90	95	—
27	600	88	23	74	89	99
24	540	76	3	44	71	91
20	460	52	1	14	34	76
18	420	37	—	8	19	44
12	290	8	—	1	2	11
6	270	1	—	—	—	2
1	230	—	—	—	—	

Note. Institutions shown were selected to show the great variation among them and are not meant to be representative of those types. ACT = American College Testing Program; SAT = Scholastic Assessment Test; SAT = I-V = SAT = Verbal; ACT-E = ACT-English.

By comparing scores in Table 6-1, one can see, for example, that the median student at the Ivy League institution falls above the 90th percentile for students at the midwestern state university. At the same time, the median student at the midwestern university falls in the lower 5% for students at the Ivy League institution. Students at the midwestern university actually tend to score well above college-bound students nationally: The median student at the midwestern university falls at about the 75th percentile of the national college-bound population. The median student at the private liberal arts college included in Table 6-1 is practically never found in an Ivy League school and falls in the bottom quarter among students at the midwestern state university. The median student at the southern state college (an accredited institution) is found only in the lower 1%–2% of students at the midwestern state university, and very few students at this private liberal arts college score that low. The highest scoring student at the southern state college does not reach the mean at the midwestern state university, and only a handful of students at the Ivy League university obtain scores as low as the highest student at the southern state college. Thus, between the southern state college and the Ivy League institution, there is virtually no overlap among the scores of their students.

In assisting college-bound students in their decision making about the institutions they might choose, counselors should consider these types of differences. Information regarding the levels of academic competition at particular institutions can be found in certain college guides, such as *Cass and Birnbaum's Guide to American Colleges* (Cass-Liepmann, 2000), *Profiles of American Colleges* (Barrons Educational Series, 2000), and *The College Handbook* (College Entrance Examination Board, 2000). Anyone involved in college counseling should obtain a guide that contains information regarding high school ranks and test scores of students at different institutions. Armed with the knowledge that the standard deviation on an academic aptitude test at a given institution is likely to be in the vicinity of two thirds or three quarters that of the normative standard deviation of the instrument (4 or 5 points on the ACT or 60 to 75 points on the SAT), and with the mean score or the range of the middle 50% given in one of the college guides, a counselor can easily calculate a rough estimate of the point at which the student is likely to fall in regard to academic aptitude at that institution.

Combining this with a knowledge of the student's achievement level in high school, one can estimate the general level of competition that a student will find at a given institution. Combined with other information about the student, his or her chances of obtaining admission at that institution can also be estimated. A student might therefore be encouraged to apply to several different institutions, including one or two in which chances for admission and satisfactory performance are favorable. The following illustrates how counselors can use academic aptitude test information in their discussions of college choices.

CASE EXAMPLE

Jason is just beginning his senior year in high school, and he and his parents are having a conference with his guidance counselor. He has a 2.9 GPA in the academic program in his high school and received scores ranging from 18 to 22 for a composite score of 20 on the ACT battery that he took the previous spring. His parents want to talk about colleges and universities that he should investigate and his chances of being admitted to them. Included in their consideration is an Ivy League institution that their nephew attends.

The counselor reports to them that Jason's score on the ACT is about an average score for college-bound students in the United States. When he takes the SAT a few weeks hence, if he obtains comparable scores, they are likely to be in the 400s. She suggests that unless he were class valedictorian or a star athlete (which he is not), he has little chance of being admitted to a highly competitive institution. She tells them that because the state university admits any high school graduate who is in the top two fifths of his or her graduating class, and because Jason is at the 65th percentile, he would be admitted to the state university. He would, however, rank toward the bottom at that institution, both in terms of high school record and test scores, and could find it difficult to achieve more than barely passing grades.

Because Jason is undecided as to a career or a major, he is planning to enter a general liberal arts program and therefore has a wide range of institutions from which to choose. At some 4-year institutions, he would fall well above the mean and at others well below the mean. At the particular small college he is considering, he would be below the middle but still above the bottom third. His chances of success there would be better than at a number of other institutions that he and his parents have considered.

The level of competition a student is likely to meet if admitted should also be discussed. Although there are many, including parents, who feel that a student should attend the highest status institution to which he or she can be admitted, some evidence suggests that for many students this is not the wisest move. A 1969 study conducted by Werts and Watley indicated that, holding ability constant, those students who attended an institution at which they fell in the bottom portion of the students at that institution were less likely to go on and attend graduate or professional school than those students who had attended an institution at which they were closer to or above the middle of the distribution. This finding is supported by recent research on the "big-fish–little-pond effect," which indicates that gifted children who participate in regular classes report higher academic self-concepts than do those who are placed in gifted programs (Zeidner, 1999). In essence, it may not always be desirable for students to pursue the most competitive programs for which they can gain admission.

When students transfer from college to college, much of the difference in the GPAs obtained at the new institutions can be accounted for by differing levels of competition. Students transferring from community colleges to more competitive 4-year institutions often experience a drop in grades known as "transfer shock." Students transferring from more competitive institutions to less competitive ones will, on the average, see their GPAs increase.

GRADUATE AND PROFESSIONAL SCHOOL ADMISSIONS TESTS

Graduate Record Examination (GRE)

The GREs are administered by the ETS in Princeton, New Jersey. They consist of two separate types. The first is the GRE General Test, which consists of three portions: Verbal (GRE-V), Quantitative (GRE-Q), and Analytical (GRE-A; Educational Testing Service, 2000a). The Verbal portion includes analogies, antonyms, sentence completion, and reading comprehension items. The Quantitative portion requires mathematical reasoning and an interpretation of graphs and diagrams, and it includes items dealing with arithmetic, algebra, and geometry. The Analytical portion includes analytical reasoning questions and logical reasoning questions designed to measure the ability to apply abstract reasoning to a set of given conditions or facts. The second type is the GRE Subject Tests, which are available in 20 different academic areas, such as physics, psychology, and Spanish.

Scores on each of the three portions of the aptitude test are reported in standard scores, with a mean of 500 and a standard deviation of 100. The scores were standardized on a group of college seniors who took the test in 1952, and scores are equated to this reference group in order that scores remain constant over time. More recent means for students taking the test were in the vicinity of 480 on the Verbal and 520 on the Quantitative portions. The GRE Aptitude Tests show high internal consistency reliabilities (.90 or above).

The GRE General Test is now an adaptive test that can be taken only on a computer, the paper-and-pencil version having been eliminated. Administrations are scheduled on an individual basis at a large number of testing sites around the world, eliminating the requirement that the test be taken on national testing dates. Initially, an examinee is presented with questions of average difficulty, after which the computer selects questions based on the difficulty level of the questions answered correctly and incorrectly. Each correct answer leads to a more difficult question, whereas a wrong answer leads to an easier one. Scores on the three portions are based both on the number of questions correctly answered and on the difficulty level of these questions and are available immediately after the test has been completed.

The GRE Subject (Advanced) Tests are still in paper-based format and are administered on three national testing dates. They are required less often by graduate institutions or by graduate departments than is the General Test. They last 2 hours and 50 minutes and have been developed by committees of faculty members in the appropriate academic departments working with the ETS staff. The results are also reported on a standard scale resembling that of the Aptitude Test with a mean of 500; however, the actual mean, range, and standard deviation of scores are different for each of the advanced tests. Certain of the advanced tests provide subscores for specific subject matter areas within the larger test, for example, a subscore on European history and one on American history within the history examination.

The GRE is used in selecting students for admission into graduate school and into specific graduate departments. Norms on the tests vary greatly among institutions and among specific departments. A physics department could require substantially higher scores on the Quantitative section than on the Verbal section, whereas requirements by an English department would be the opposite. An art department might require a portfolio and pay little attention to either. Because of these differences, use of GRE test scores to assist students in selecting institutions and departments in which they are likely to be admitted and are likely to be successful is difficult without knowledge of the norms in specific graduate institutions and departments.

Using the GRE scores to predict success in graduate school is particularly difficult for a number of reasons. There is likely to be the problem of restriction in range within particular departments, because GREs and undergraduate GPAs are the major criteria on which students are selected for graduate programs, thus eliminating low scores. In addition, graduate school GPAs may be highly restricted in range because grades of A and B are often the only grades given. For a typical department, however, GRE scores plus undergraduate GPAs still provide a better prediction of academic success than any other readily available variables (Educational Testing Service, 1990; Jaeger, 1985; Kuncel & Hezlett, 2001).

The Miller Analogies Test (MAT)

The MAT, published by the Psychological Corporation (1991, 1994), is a second test often used for the selection of graduate students. The test consists of 100 complex analogy items drawn from the subject matter across a number of academic fields. Although the test is administered with a 50-minute time limit, it is largely a power test. It includes items of considerable difficulty so that resulting scores are purported to differentiate reliably among people of superior intellect. It is available in a number of parallel forms, with reliabilities in the general magnitude of .90. Familiarity with the kinds of items on this type of test can significantly affect scores, with substantial improvement resulting from studying practice items or from previous experience with an alternate form. As with the GRE, norms among graduate students in different institutions and different departments vary widely, and knowledge of normative data in relevant comparison groups (provided in the MAT manual) is a necessity if predictive information based on the scores is to have any value. The problems of predictive validity of graduate school success discussed for the GRE are also present for the MAT.

Professional School Tests

A number of aptitude tests have been developed by different professions for selection into their professional schools. In many cases these tests are universally required for admission to such schools. Such tests include the Medical College Admission Test (MCAT; Association of American Medical Colleges, 2000), the Dental Admission Test (DAT; Division of Educational Measurements, 1994), the Law School Admission Test (LSAT; Law School Admission Council, 2000), and the Graduate Management Admission Test (GMAT; Educational Testing Service, 1995). These aptitude tests are typically developed and administered by one of the national testing programs such as the ACT or the ETS and cost $90 to $200.

These tests usually include items similar to those found on scholastic aptitude tests, including measures of verbal and numerical ability. In addition, they usually contain subtests with items relevant to the particular profession. The LSAT includes sections that attempt to assess competence in analytical and logical reasoning. The GMAT, which is administered on demand in a computer-adaptive format only at test centers throughout the world, includes a quantitative and an analytical writing section. The DAT has a perceptual ability portion, and the MCAT includes scores in such areas as the physical and biological sciences as well as a writing sample. Scores on each of the tests are reported in very different types of standard scores with different means and standard deviations. For example, the MCAT yields standard scores ranging from 1 to15 with a mean of approximately 8 and a standard deviation of approximately 2.5. The LSAT now reports scores ranging from 120 to 180 with a mean of approximately 150 and a standard deviation of approximately 10. For the DAT, scores range from 1 to 30 with a mean of 15 and a standard deviation of 5. The GMAT, used by most graduate schools of business, reports subtest scores ranging from 0 to 60 with a mean of 30 and total scores similar to those of the GRE with a range of 200 to 800 and a mean of 500. The writing portion receives a rating of from 1 to 6.

ADMINISTERING AND INTERPRETING ACADEMIC APTITUDE TESTS

Test Anxiety

During aptitude and achievement tests administration, it is generally considered a good procedure to attempt, while building rapport, to reduce test anxiety (Zeidner, 1998). Small but significant negative relationships have been found between test anxiety and scores on these types of tests. This relationship, of course, does not necessarily mean that high levels of anxiety cause lower test scores. Often those who have done poorly on these types of tests in the past are likely to experience more anxiety. Some studies suggest that a moderate amount of test anxiety can actually benefit test scores, whereas a high level of anxiety may be detrimental. Individuals differ in the amount of anxiety that can be considered to be optimal for best test performance.

These results have been obtained when tests have been given under experimental conditions of high tension and of relaxed situations. For example, in an early study on this topic, students took the test under normal conditions when the scores were to be reported to the institutions to which they applied, and a second time on an equivalent form under instructions that the test results were to be used only for research purposes and not otherwise reported (French, 1962). The results showed essentially equal performance under both the anxious and relaxed conditions. The only difference was that certain students under the anxiety conditions attempted more of the mathematical items and therefore achieved slightly higher scores on that subtest than they did under the relaxed conditions. Apparently, under the relaxed conditions they gave up a little earlier and therefore achieved slightly lower scores. In general, testing procedures that are well organized, that are smoothly run, and that reassure and encourage should help to reduce the anxiety felt by highly anxious test takers.

Coaching

The effect of coaching or practice on test scores is a controversial one that has received much attention and has been the subject of a number of studies. Obviously, practice or coaching that provides the answers to, for example, an individual IQ test such as the Stanford–Binet or Wechsler Intelligence Scale for Children would invalidate the results as an accurate assessment. However, completion of a high school course in mathematics that results in a higher score on a mathematics achievement test probably accurately reflects the student's knowledge of mathematics outside of the testing situation. The distinction therefore must be made between broad training and specific training or coaching focused on specific test items.

Coaching has been particularly controversial because of the existence of commercial coaching programs designed to raise scores on admissions tests such as the College Entrance Examination Board's SAT, the GRE, or the MCAT. These coaching programs advertise and almost promise substantially better test performance for those who enroll in their programs. Many of the studies reported have substantial weaknesses that usually include the absence of a noncoached but equally highly motivated control group that is comparable with the coached group in all important ways, including performance on initial tests.

The College Entrance Examination Board (CEEB) has been particularly concerned for two reasons. First, if coaching could help students to improve their scores substantially, then the test results for all students would lose some validity. Second, the commercial coaching programs charge substantial fees and can represent a waste of money if coaching yields little improvement. A number of CEEB's studies investigating different types of coaching methods among different types of students indicate that coaching is unlikely to produce substantial gains on the SAT (Aiken, 2000; Powers & Rock, 1998). An ACT study showed that students' scores tend to increase on a second testing, most of which can be accounted for by the general development that has occurred as students take additional high school courses (Lanier, 1994).

A small amount of increase is perhaps due to a practice effect, that is, familiarity with the types of problems and the problem-solving skills required. As a result, most of the testing programs—the College

Board, the ACT, and the various professional school testing programs—now provide considerable information about the tests, including booklets with a number of practice test items. Thus, all applicants have the opportunity to take practice tests and to become familiar with the types of items that appear. In addition to those provided by the testing programs, a number of test familiarization books have been published, with practice examinations in all of these areas. Usually titled "How to Take the . . . Examination," these books can be found in many bookstores. For certain tests such as the SAT, these materials are not limited to printed booklets but also include a variety of audiovisual and computer software materials as well as programs available on the Internet. The ACT sells a CD-ROM personalized test preparation program using real ACT tests (ACTivePrep), and the ETS sells GRE and GMAT CD-ROMs that contain two complete computer-administered practice tests and hundreds of practice test items (POWERPREP).

It should be remembered that although specific coaching provides little improvement in test performance over that achieved by a little familiarization and practice (and this is particularly true on the verbal portions of these tests), additional training in the form of coursework is likely to result in improvement. In addition, a general review of the subject matter covered can substantially increase scores. For example, a student who has not taken any mathematics during the last 2 years in high school can improve scores on the Mathematics portion of the SAT by review of the courses in algebra and geometry that were taken earlier. A college senior who has not taken any mathematics in college since the freshman year can also improve his or her scores on the Quantitative portion of the GRE by a review of the mathematical and algebraic concepts learned in high school and as a college freshman.

Counselors often receive questions from students, parents, and those involved in the selection and interpretation of such scores regarding the efficacy of coaching programs and other review procedures. They need to be cognizant of the effects of different types of training and other activities on test performance.

ACADEMIC ACHIEVEMENT TESTS

Hundreds of thousands of achievement tests are administered each year, primarily in educational institutions ranging from kindergarten through graduate and professional schools. Others are administered for licensing and certification in trades and professions, in medical specialties, or for the selection and promotion of postal workers.

Achievement tests differ from aptitude tests in that they attempt to assess learning that takes place under relatively standardized conditions or as a result of a controlled set of experiences. Aptitude tests are more typically used for prediction purposes and do not assume previous standardized learning experiences. Achievement tests are designed to measure what has already been learned or knowledge or skills that have been attained, whereas academic aptitude tests attempt to measure learning ability, although such ability is usually related to that which has been developed up to the time of testing. Achievement tests are usually evaluated on the basis of content validity, that is, the extent to which the test includes content similar to that which those tested are expected to have experienced. Aptitude tests are usually evaluated in terms of predictive validity, that is, the extent to which success in whatever it is the aptitude test attempts to measure can be predicted from the test results. The distinction between achievement and aptitude tests is not absolute, however. Some aptitude tests are based on some generally standardized prior experience, whereas some achievement tests are designed to measure some generalized educational experiences that are not especially uniform in nature (Anastasi & Urbina, 1997). For example, the ACT test serves as a scholastic aptitude test to predict success in college; however, its items represent subject matter areas taught in all high school curricula.

Achievement tests vary from the brief achievement test administered by a teacher to evaluate the learning that has taken place during a single lesson to the nationally available achievement test programs produced by the major commercial test publishers. These achievement test batteries are generally designed across a number of grade levels from kindergarten through the 12th grade. The test batteries provide profiles of scores in various academic skill areas. They tend to be based on the "three R's" in the early grades and to measure information and knowledge in specific academic areas at the secondary school levels. The tests are generally carefully prepared in regard to content, with items written by teachers and consultants and examined by expert reviewers. The items are then subjected to analyses of item difficulty and item discrimination, with attempts made to eliminate gender and ethnic bias.

School Achievement Tests

The most commonly used national achievement test batteries include (a) the Iowa Tests of Basic Skills/Iowa Tests of Educational Development, (b) the Stanford Achievement Tests, (c) the Metropolitan Achievement Tests, and (d) the TerraNova Tests. Results are usually reported in a full range of derived scores, including scale scores, national and local percentile ranks, normal curve equivalents such as stanines, and grade equivalents. These four test series are briefly described as examples of such batteries.

Iowa Tests of Basic Skills/Iowa Tests of Educational Development. The Iowa Tests of Basic Skills (ITBS) form a battery of achievement tests covering kindergarten through Grade 8 (Hoover, Dunbar, & Frisbie, 2001). They are considered to be some of the oldest and best of their type (Brookhart, 1998). The tests are designed to measure basic educational skills, including vocabulary, reading, language, and mathematics for the early grades, with the addition of social studies, science, and information utilization tests for the upper grades. Both survey and complete batteries are available. They were normed on large and well-documented samples and were jointly standardized with the IQ-type Cognitive Abilities Test.

The Iowa Tests of Educational Development (ITED) are designed for use at the high school level (Forsyth, Ansley, Feldt, & Alnot, 2001). There are seven tests in the battery measuring achievement in the seven areas mentioned above for the ITBS at levels considered appropriate for high school (plus two supplementary tests in spelling and mathematics computation). Results are reported in a variety of derived scores, including standard scores ($M = 15$, $SD = 5$) and predicted ranges for both the ACT composite (within a 5-point range) and SAT-I college entrance tests (within a 100-point range). Results can therefore be used in counseling for making decisions about high school programs and college planning. ITED interpretive materials are considered to be useful for counselors, school personnel, parents, and students (Mehrens, 1998).

The Stanford Achievement Test. The Stanford Achievement Test Series, 9th edition (Stanford 9) is a series of achievement tests from kindergarten through Grade 12, with separate tests for each year that do not repeat item content except for Grades 11 and 12 (Harcourt Brace, 1996). Each test battery contains a number of different subtests, with the Stanford Early School Achievement Tests available for kindergarten and the first grade and the Tests of Academic Skills for Grades 9–12. The typical battery is composed of 10 to 12 subtests yielding total scores in six to eight subject areas. It was standardized in combination with the Otis–Lennon School Ability Test, 7th Edition.

Metropolitan Achievement Tests. The Metropolitan Achievement Tests, 8th edition (MAT8) provide overlapping batteries from kindergarten through Grade 12 (Harcourt Brace, 2000). The battery consists of a varying number of subtests in basic skills areas beginning with reading, mathematics, and language to which science and social studies are added in the early primary grades and research skills and thinking skills are added in the remaining grades, yielding a total of seven achievement areas. Predicted scores for both the PLAN Program and the PSAT in Grades 9 and 10 and ACT and SAT scores for Grades 11 and 12 are available using MAT8 results.

TerraNova Tests. There are two TerraNova achievement test batteries. The TerraNova Comprehensive Tests of Basic Skills represent the latest edition of the Comprehensive Tests of Basic Skills (CTB/Macmillan/McGraw-Hill, 1996). They assess academic achievement K–12 with two forms and a Spanish edition (referred to as SUPERA). Items have been designed to represent diverse cultures, with topics and content to represent national standards. There are 13 levels (K–12), and the battery was standardized along with the Test of Cognitive Skills. The other TerraNova series are the result of the revision and restandardization of what would have been the sixth edition of the California Achievement Tests Fifth Edition (CTB/Macmillan/McGraw-Hill, 2001). Known as the TerraNova Second Edition or the TerraNova CAT, the test series include assessments of reading/language arts, mathematics, science, and social studies for all school grades using both multiple-choice and student-constructed response items. The TerraNova CAT was standardized with the InView cognitive battery.

These test batteries have traditionally been used to assess the academic strengths and weaknesses of individual students for use by teachers, parents, and counselors. Now, however, they are also found in mandatory statewide programs of "high-stakes" testing that assess student achievement to determine if a student is promoted or graduates and to reward or penalize teachers, schools, or school systems. Some states make use of tests specifically developed for particular grades in those states, whereas others adapt one of these batteries for this purpose. California and Tennessee add a few items to the Stanford 9 to fit their specific curriculum standards. New York City customizes the TerraNova for certain grades, whereas Philadelphia makes use of the unmodified Iowa Tests of Basic Skills. All juniors in Illinois and Colorado take an exam that includes the ACT assessment along with several state-designed tests.

These achievement tests are highly reliable, with internal consistency reliabilities for individual tests ranging from .80 to .90 or above for appropriate populations. Composite scores based on the complete batteries produce internal consistency reliabilities well above .90. The procedures that the authors and publishers of each of the sets of tests have established for ensuring content validity are thorough and detailed. The item pools have been administered to large samples, and sophisticated item analyses to detect gender and cultural biases are used. Although the results of these test batteries are often grossly misinterpreted by users, considerable pains have been taken to provide the results in understandable language and formats.

Most students take standardized achievement tests, which are used for a variety of purposes, at regular intervals during their first 12 years of schooling. They are used in a diagnostic way to identify the strengths and weaknesses of specific skills and achievements in individual students. As a result of such diagnoses, students can be selected for specific types of instruction, either remedial or advanced in nature. For this reason, the tests are often used as a part of the regular guidance and counseling program in an institution. Counselors thus become involved in interpreting the results to the students themselves, to their parents, and to teachers and other professionals.

Achievement tests are also used (and often misused) in attempts to evaluate the quality of the curricula and instruction within courses, programs, schools, or school systems. The tests can provide information regarding what has been actually taught in a course or curriculum, especially in regard to educational goals. They can also be used to assess change in performance over time within a school or school district or to compare the achievement of schools in a district or with national norms. Although the public is asking for accountability in education, which usually involves achievement test results, there are many important factors and complex issues, such as the academic backgrounds of the students and the goals of the educational programs, that make such comparisons difficult and frequently invalid. The complexity of such accountability is often not well understood, but counselors who better understand the effects of ability, socioeconomic status, and ethnic backgrounds should strive to prevent the misuse of achievement testing. In high-stakes testing, it is necessary to be especially wary if there is a suspicion that cultural characteristics affect the validity of the scores and to understand the possible limitations of typical test norms for such students (Frisby, 1998; Scheuneman & Oakland, 1998). As a resource, the Department of Education Office of Civil Rights (2000) has issued a document of principles and warnings regarding the high-stakes testing of students with disabilities or limited English proficiency.

College-Level Achievement Tests

Several college-level testing programs have been created as a basis for awarding college credit other than by enrolling in college courses. These programs include the College-Level Examination Program (CLEP; College Board, 1992b), the Advanced Placement Program (AP; College Board, 1994b) administered by the CEEB, and the Proficiency Examination Program (PEP; American College Testing Program, 1985) administered by the ACT.

The CLEP contains (a) general examinations that assess college-level achievement in five basic liberal arts areas usually covered during the first 2 undergraduate years and (b) 30 multiple-choice subject examinations each taking 90 minutes to complete covering a wide range of popular introductory college-level courses.

The AP provides materials and examinations for college-level courses to be offered in secondary schools for which high school students may gain college credit or obtain advanced placement in college courses. The examinations, which are 3 hours in length, contain both multiple-choice and either essay or problem items. The AP provides 29 different examinations in 16 different academic fields.

The PEP tests are designed to measure subject matter proficiency that has been attained primarily outside of the typical classroom. They cover material usually presented in one- or two-semester courses at the undergraduate level. There are 45 different examinations, many from the fields of business and nursing, with others available in a range of arts and sciences and education subjects. The exams, which range from 3 to 7 hours in length, primarily use a multiple-choice format, with some also including essay portions. Most are taken for the purpose of assigning college credit. Some are used for placement at appropriate levels in the curriculum or to waive particular course requirements.

Both ACT and ETS have developed instruments to assess the proficiency in English of individuals who are not native English speakers. ACT has constructed a computer-adaptive multiple-choice test to assess English as a second language, called the ACT ESL Placement Test (American College Testing Program, 1998a). It consists of three modules—Reading, Listening, and Grammar/Usage—each of which yields a score that classifies students into one of four proficiency levels for course placement. It can be administered along with COMPASS, a program for educational planning and placement (American College Testing Program, 1998c).

The ETS's Test of English as a Foreign Language (TOEFL) has been administered in its paper-and-pencil version since the mid-1960s to international students around the world who have applied for admission to North American colleges and universities. It is now administered only on computer and consists of four sections: Listening, Structure, Reading, and a written essay. Three sections are scored on a 0–30 scale, the essay 0–6, and the total score on a 0–300 scale (Educational Testing Service, 1998, 2000b). It is administered at technology and university centers throughout the world. Tutorials and practice exercises are available on a CD-ROM and by downloading from the TOEFL Web site. Students applying to professional and graduate schools from foreign countries are usually required to obtain certain minimum scores on the TOEFL.

Adult Achievement Tests

Several test batteries have been created to assess the general achievement of adults. These test batteries include the Tests of Adult Basic Education and the Adult Basic Learning Examination. The Tests of Adult Basic Education 7/8 are designed to assess the basic skills that adults need to live and work (CTB/Macmillan/McGraw-Hill, 1994). There are five different forms and a Spanish edition representing difficulty levels ranging from less than a first-grade level to college level. A locator test of 25 vocabulary words and 25 mathematical items yields scores that indicate the appropriate level to use. Although scores are based on adult norms, grade equivalents to California Achievement Test grade levels are reported along with estimated scores on the Tests of General Education Development, or GED (pre-2002 battery), which are taken by candidates for high school equivalency diplomas.

The Adult Basic Learning Examination, 2nd Edition (Karlsen & Gardner, 1986), provides assessment of adult learning in vocabulary, reading comprehension, spelling, language, number operations, and problem solving. All tests are untimed and may be self-scored. A Spanish edition is available. This battery is often used in adult education programs.

Individual Achievement Tests

There are several academic achievement tests administered on an individual basis to obtain diagnostic information about such skills as reading, mathematics, and spelling. These tests include the Wide Range Achievement Test, 1993 Edition (WRAT3; Wilkinson, 1993), the Kaufman Test of Educational Achievement–Normative Update (K-TEA/NU; Kaufman & Kaufman, 1997), and the Wechsler Individual Achievement Test–2nd Edition (WIAT-II; D. Wechsler, 2001). All provide norms based on national samples ages 6 through adult. The WRAT3 has two equivalent forms and a large print form. The K-TEA/NU has a brief screening form and provides an error analysis form for identifying remediation needs for writing Individual Educational Programs. The WIAT-II contains nine achievement subtests (e.g., listening comprehension, reading comprehension, mathematics reasoning) and is linked to the Wechsler Adult Intelligence Scale–III, the Wechsler Intelligence Scale for Children–III, and the Wechsler Preschool and Primary Scale of Intelligence–Revised.

STUDY HABITS INVENTORIES

Counselors in high schools and colleges often work with students who are having difficulties with their coursework or are not achieving academically up to their potential. In working with such students, counselors find that a study habits inventory is often useful for several reasons: first, to allow students to understand how adequate their study habits are as compared with those of other students; second, as a teaching tool, as the items on such inventories have useful instructional value; and third, to point out particular weaknesses, which is useful in discussing specific activities for improvement. In addition to their diagnostic purposes, these inventories also act as structured exercises that can help teach good study techniques and point out ineffective attitudes and behaviors. Several of the achievement test batteries used at the high school level, such as the California or Metropolitan achievement batteries, contain subtests that assess study skills.

The Survey of Study Habits and Attitudes (SSHA) is a 100-item inventory with a high school form and a college-level form (W. F. Brown & Holtzman, 1984). It contains four subscales: Delay Avoidance, Work Methods, Teacher Approval, and Educational Acceptance. Both internal consistency and test–retest scale reliabilities are reported in the general range of .85–.90 for student samples. It also includes a counseling key that can be laid over the answer sheet to assist the counselor in focusing on various critical items.

The Study Attitudes and Methods Survey (SAMS) was developed to assess noncognitive factors associated with success in schools (Michael, Michael, & Zimmerman, 1988). The 148-item inventory provides scores for six factor dimensions: Academic Interest, Academic Drive, Study Methods, Study Anxiety, Manipulation, and Alienation Toward Authority. The survey, which takes approximately 30 minutes to complete, includes both high school and college norms.

The Learning and Study Strategies Inventory (LASSI) is the most widely used learning inventory on college campuses (B. Murray,

1998). The 77-item inventory contains 10 seven- or eight-item scales, 5 of them assessing personal factors related to academic achievement (Attitudes, Motivation, Time Management, Anxiety, and Concentration) and 5 cognitive factors (Information Processing, Selecting Main Ideas, Study Aids, Self Testing, and Test Strategies; Weinstein, Palmer, & Schulte, 1987, 1997). The inventory is available in both secondary school and college forms, and alpha reliabilities are reported in the .7 to .8 range (Weinstein, 1987). The LASSI is also available in a computer-administered and scored format.

Knowledge that individuals prefer different types of learning styles and, in fact, often learn more effectively when the instructional technique matches their preferred learning style has led to the development of inventories designed to assess such individual learning styles. There are four such inventories, all titled "Learning Style Inventory" (Canfield & Canfield, 1988; R. Dunn, Dunn, & Price, 1987; Kolb, 1985; Renzulli & Smith, 1978). They are designed to help individuals assess their preferred methods of learning and to identify differences among individual learning styles and corresponding learning environments. This information can then be used to provide more individualized instructional methods. These inventories typically yield scores on three or four dimensions of learning styles or modes, such as need for structure, active experimenting, or abstract conceptualizing. Robert Sternberg proposed a theory of thinking styles that he termed mental self-government with 13 thinking styles. He constructed the Thinking Styles Inventory to assess them (Zhang & Sternberg, 2001). Because there are significant differences in the types of learning styles assessed by these instruments, the particular purpose for which the inventory is to be administered should be evaluated so that the inventory that best meets that purpose can be selected.

COGNITIVE DEVELOPMENTAL THEORIES

In addition to the learning of substantive knowledge that takes place in school, college, work, and daily life, other types of cognitive development, such as rationality, intellectual tolerance, and intellectual integrity, are now beginning to be assessed as well. One of these areas is ethical development as conceptualized by Kohlberg (1969, 1971), building on the structuralist view articulated by Piaget (1965). Kohlberg's theory holds that moral values are first external, then conventional in upholding and maintaining the social order, and at the highest levels maintained through individually held principles. Rest (1974, 1979) developed a paper-and-pencil instrument using Kohlberg's hypothetical moral dilemmas called the Defining Issues Test to assess this type of cognitive development.

Based in part on the work of both Piaget and Kohlberg, Perry (1970) developed a cognitive developmental scheme of positions of intellectual development that take place during adolescent and adult years. Perry's theory is composed of nine different positions representing a continuum of development that can be clustered into four general categories: dualism, multiplicity, relativism, and commitment in relativism. Assessing cognitive development on Perry's scheme has been difficult, although five different measures have been constructed that attempt to place individuals along these positions. Three of these (Baxter-Magolda, 1992; King & Kitchener, 1994; Moore, 1988) require free responses that must be classified using trained raters—thus making for high costs in terms of money and convenience. Two inventories that make use of objective-style responses to assess cognitive development are the Scale of Intellectual Development (Erwin, 1983) and the Parker Cognitive Development Inventory (Parker & Hood, 1997). Although these inventories are in a form that could be used by counselors, more validity studies and probable revisions need to be undertaken before they will be ready for use by counselors with individual clients.

Stages of cognitive development represent important concepts for counselors to explore, as these stages influence many of the decisions that clients make and the processes by which they arrive at these decisions. These concepts can provide an understanding of why one client seeks only one "right" answer to a problem whereas another is willing to explore a number of alternatives.

SUMMARY

1. Almost all counselors can expect to be consulted about scholastic aptitude tests, even if they work in settings where they seldom make use of them.
2. Test results on the College Board, National Merit, and ACT college admissions tests have often been misinterpreted, even by those with some understanding of their standard score distributions.

3. Scholastic aptitude tests contribute to academic selection and placement by identifying unrecognized academic potential and by acting as a correction factor for high school grades resulting from differing levels of competition.

4. There are great differences in the distribution of students in regard to academic aptitude among the different institutions of higher education in the United States. These differences can greatly affect both the chances for admission and the chances for success at specific institutions.

5. Academic aptitude tests required for admission to graduate and professional programs typically have similar verbal and quantitative sections but otherwise vary considerably in subjects that are assessed and in the types of standard scores with which they report results.

6. Although some practice and familiarity with the types of problems and skills required on academic aptitude tests may make slight improvements in scores, extensive coaching has not been shown to produce substantial gains.

7. Academic achievement batteries are administered in virtually all primary and secondary schools to provide useful diagnostic information regarding the strengths and weaknesses of specific skills and achievements of students. The results are increasingly used and misused in high-stakes testing and to evaluate the quality of instruction within classes, schools, and school systems.

8. Cognitive developmental theories can provide useful concepts in working with adolescent and postadolescent clients, but instruments to assess these stages need considerable additional refinement to be useful to most counselors.

Career and Life Planning Assessment

7

MEASURES OF CAREER CHOICE AND DEVELOPMENT

CAREERS PLAY A PREDOMINANT ROLE in the lives of most people. Counselors help clients with the process of making educational and career choices and adapting to the challenges inherent in career development. To help clients with this process, counselors must assess the clients' readiness for these activities as a first step in a comprehensive career counseling program.

Measures that focus on the *process* of career choice and development are discussed in this chapter. These measures, which evaluate a client's readiness to choose and pursue a successful and satisfying career path, encompass both *attitudinal* and *cognitive* factors (Super & Thompson, 1979; Thompson, Lindeman, Super, Jordaan, & Myers, 1981, 1982). Factors that pertain to the *content* of career choice and development, such as work values, career interests, special abilities, and environmental factors, are considered in subsequent chapters.

The measures of career choice and development discussed in this chapter are important in determining appropriate counseling interventions for clients (Sampson, Peterson, Reardon, & Lenz, 2000). Clients with low levels of readiness for career planning profit from interventions designed to improve the process of career planning, such as future orientation, decision making, and role salience. Clients with high levels of readiness benefit more from interventions focused on the content of career planning, such as interests and values (Toman & Savickas, 1997).

ATTITUDES TOWARD CAREER PLANNING

Attitudinal factors involved in career planning include both career beliefs and career concerns. Career beliefs refer to the client's assumptions regarding career choice and development, for example, the belief that there is one "right" career choice for each individual or that people will not be able to change their careers as they progress through life. Career concerns include difficulties in decision making and in resolving developmental tasks, such as choosing a major or career or making satisfactory progress in one's work.

Measures of Career Beliefs

All of the instruments described below have been influenced by theory and research in the field of cognitive psychology, which states that an individual's actions are based on how he or she thinks about an issue or situation. By examining their thinking in regard to career choice and development, clients should be in a better position to understand and modify their behaviors.

Career Beliefs Inventory (CBI). The CBI identifies beliefs that may block career goals (Krumboltz, 1991). It contains 96 items answered on a Likert scale (*strongly agree* to *strongly disagree*) that provide the basis for scores on 25 scales such as Openness, Control, and Taking Risks. The beliefs are not considered to be "good" or "bad" by themselves; however, individuals frequently possess assumptions about themselves and their careers that may interfere with their career plan-

146

ning. Low scores indicate career beliefs that may be problematic depending on the individual's situation.

Krumboltz (1994) suggested that the CBI be used early in counseling to expose one's assumptions related to career planning that might not otherwise be addressed. The counselor can then help the client to test the accuracy of these assumptions in his or her particular situation. Mitchell and Krumboltz (1987) found that focusing on the career beliefs of undecided clients was more effective than teaching decision-making skills in stimulating career exploration and reducing anxiety.

The CBI provides unique information for career counseling not available by means of traditional interest and aptitude measures (Naylor & Krumboltz, 1994). As such, it can provide valuable information for discussion purposes, but it should not be used as a basis for decision making because of its limited psychometric properties. The CBI scales, most of which contain four items or less, yield relatively low internal consistency coefficients and test–retest reliabilities. In regard to validity, Krumboltz (1991) found that the CBI scores correlated with career satisfaction; however, the correlations were relatively low. As noted by Guion (1995), the CBI should be viewed as "more an interview aid than a measurement tool" (p. 160).

The following case is discussed in the CBI manual (Krumboltz, 1991, p. 10).

CASE EXAMPLE

Ted, a college student, disliked his college major (premed) but did not believe that he had any other options. Ted obtained a low score on Scale 12, Approval of Others, which indicated that approval of his career plans from someone else was very important to him. When the counselor asked Ted about the possible meaning of this score, he said that he wanted to please his father, who wanted him to become a physician. The counselor asked him to discuss this matter with his father, which Ted did despite fears that it was a hopeless matter. In so doing, he learned that his father's actual goal was to be supportive, not demanding, at which point Ted felt free to change his major from premed to art. Ted's desire to enter art had been blocked by his belief that his father would "simply die" if he did not fulfill the ambitions he had for him, a belief that was at the root of his difficulties. Use of the CBI helped to expose his thinking on this matter, which was then addressed in counseling by encouraging him to gather further evidence to test the accuracy of his thinking.

Career Thoughts Inventory (CTI). The CTI measures dysfunctional thinking in career problem solving and decision making for adults, college students, and high school students (Sampson, Peterson, Lenz, Reardon, & Saunders, 1996). It includes 48 items designed to measure misperceptions in eight content areas related to career choice and development, such as self-knowledge, occupational knowledge, and communication. It provides a total score and scores on three scales: Decision-Making Confusion, Commitment Anxiety, and External Conflict. It can be easily administered and scored in a relatively short period of time. Local norms are recommended in addition to those provided in the manual.

Counselors are urged to discuss high scores on any of the scales or individual items with clients. Counselors help clients to reframe negative thoughts regarding the career process into positive thoughts that are true for them. For example, clients who mark *agree* or *strongly agree* to the item "no field of study or occupation interests me" could be encouraged by their counselors to examine extracurricular or leisure-time activities to help identify interests. They could also be encouraged to broaden their life experiences as a means of clarifying and developing their interests.

According to Pickering (1998, p. 6), the CTI is "a well designed, theoretically based, reliable and valid measure of dysfunctional career thoughts" that can be used effectively with career planning clients. The test package includes a workbook for client use (Reardon & Wright, 1999).

Career Decision-Making Self-Efficacy Scale (CDMSE). The CDMSE measures the degree to which people believe that they can effectively decide on a career (Betz & Taylor, 1994). It consists of 50 items that represent critical skills in career decision making. Although it can be scored in terms of five scales, factor-analytic studies indicate that it is best interpreted in terms of the total score as a global measure of career decision-making self-efficacy (Luzzo, 1996).

According to self-efficacy theory, individuals who express confidence in their ability to perform a task (independent of their actual abilities) show greater decisiveness, higher levels of accomplishment, and greater persistence in that activity than do individuals who lack such confidence (Bandura, 1986). In agreement with this theory, individuals who score low on the CDMSE (indicating lack of confidence in career decision-making ability) are likely to have trouble in deciding on an occupation. CDMSE total scores have significantly differentiated among college students with declared majors, tentative majors, and no majors in the expected manner (Betz & Luzzo, 1996).

Strategies for increasing self-confidence in career decision making include successful experiences, vicarious learning or modeling, encouragement or support from others, and emotional arousal (Bandura, 1986). Research indicates that a variety of counseling interventions, including exposure to the DISCOVER computer-based career planning program, verbal persuasion, and career exploration workshops, have successfully increased students' scores on the CDMSE (Betz & Luzzo, 1996). The CDMSE can be helpful both in detecting students in possible need of counseling assistance and in assessing their responsiveness to counselor interventions.

The test authors have developed a shortened, 25-item version of the CDMSE that has produced validity coefficients comparable with or higher than those obtained with the full-scale form (Betz, Klein, & Taylor, 1996). The short version may prove to be particularly valuable as an intake form and in program evaluation research.

Measures of Career Concerns for Students

As suggested by career development theory, the career concerns of students differ from those of adults. The inventories of career concerns discussed below focus on the decision-making process of high school and traditional-age college students.

All of the measures discussed in this section contain scales that assess the degree to which clients may be encountering difficulty in choosing a career. Clients who score high in indecision may be in the precontemplation or contemplation stage of change (Prochaska et al., 1992); that is, they may not be prepared or ready to make a career choice. They may lack the self-confidence, the independence, or the foresight to make a decision (Savickas, 1990). Instead of administering interest inventories or ability tests to these individuals to help them make a decision, the counselor should explore further with them factors that underlie their indecision.

In addition to the scales discussed below, several new instruments have been developed to assess the career concerns of students. These instruments include the Career Factors Inventory (CFI) and the Career Decision-Making Difficulty Questionnaire (CDDQ). The CFI measures factors related to career indecision by means of four scales: Need for Career Information, Need for Self-Knowledge, Career Choice Anxiety, and Generalized Indecisiveness (Chartrand, Robbins, & Morrill, 1997). In a similar vein, the CDDQ considers the various problems that students encounter when attempting to make a career decision (Osipow & Gati, 1998). The CDDQ assesses a student's ability to cope with 10 hindrances to career decision making, such as lack of motivation, lack of information, and inconsistent information.

Career Decision Scale (CDS). The CDS was developed by Samuel Osipow and his colleagues to help identify the antecedents of career indecision (Osipow, 1987). It includes two scales: a 2-item Certainty scale and a 16-item Indecision scale. The 16 items on the Indecision scale represent 16 different reasons for career indecision based on Osipow's interview experiences with clients. For each item, clients indicate on a 4-point scale to what extent the item accurately describes their situation.

The target population for the CDS includes high school and college students in the process of deciding on a career. Because of its brevity, the CDS can be quickly administered (about 10 minutes) and scored (2 minutes). The manual provides normative data for high school students, college students, and continuing education students.

For counseling purposes, the items from the CDS can be used to explore possible causes of a client's indecision. Despite relatively low test–retest reliabilities, results from individual items can be helpful in suggesting hypotheses that can be explored in counseling. In general, factor analysis of the CDS indicates that it primarily measures (a) feelings of indecision, (b) internal and external barriers, (c) approach–approach conflict, and (d) dependency (Savickas, 1990; Shimizu, Vondracek, Schulenberg, & Hostetler, 1988).

According to Harmon (1994, p. 261), there is "probably no better measure" of career indecision than the CDS for use in counseling, evaluation, and research. It has been used effectively in a wide variety of cultural settings (Osipow & Winer, 1996). Although it has some shortcomings, principally in clarifying the meaning of its scores, it has been praised for its ease of use, its applicability in counseling and research, and its extensive research support (Harmon, 1994; Levinson, Ohler, Caswell, & Kiewra, 1998; Savickas, 2000).

My Vocational Situation (MVS). The MVS attempts to identify the nature of problems that may be contributing to career indecision (Holland, Daiger, & Power, 1980). Holland et al. attributed difficulties in decision making to three main factors: (a) problems of vocational identity, (b) lack of information about careers, and (c) environmental or personal obstacles. The MVS includes scales to measure client concerns in each of these areas. The MVS provides diagnostic information regarding career planning problems that should be helpful in selecting the most appropriate type of treatment for the client.

The first scale on the MVS, the Vocational Identity scale, contains 18 items related to career choice uncertainty that must be answered *true* or *false*. True responses suggest problems with one's vocational identity. Normative data indicate that high school students mark about seven true answers on the average, whereas college students usually mark about two or three true responses. Individuals with a large number of true responses compared with people of their age group may profit from career workshops, personal counseling, or additional work experiences.

Each of the two remaining scales, Occupational Information (OI) and Barriers (B), consists of one question with four parts. The OI scale provides data concerning the client's need for occupational information (e.g., how to obtain training or employment in an occupation), whereas the B scale points out barriers (e.g., lack of needed abilities or family support) that may be impeding career development. These scales can be used as checklists to suggest specific steps that counselors can take to assist their clients in the career planning process.

Because of its brevity, clients can easily complete the MVS before the first counseling interview, in the same manner as other problem checklists described in Chapter 4. Counselors can quickly identify clients with vocational identity problems by counting the number of true responses to the first 18 items. They can also determine specific needs of clients by simply noting those items with yes responses on the OI or B scales. Items with such responses can be pursued in individual counseling to determine their significance for the client.

Assessment of Career Decision Making (ACDM). The ACDM is based on Vincent Harren's model of career decision making (Harren, 1979). In its current version (Form F), it contains 94 items scored on nine scales (Buck & Daniels, 1985). Three of the scales assess decision-making styles; the remaining six scales evaluate progress in resolving developmental tasks common to young people.

The Decision-Making Styles scales measure the extent to which clients use rational, intuitive, or dependent styles in making career decisions. Rational types emphasize logic in systematically collecting and weighing data to arrive at a decision. Intuitive types place greater importance on feelings in deciding among alternatives; they may collect data to confirm a choice they have already made. Dependent types rely primarily on the opinions of others in arriving at their decisions. Both the rational and intuitive approaches possess merit as a means of obtaining data and resolving problems.

The Decision-Making Tasks (DMT) scales assess three developmental tasks faced by most young people: adjusting to school, choosing a major, and choosing a career. Adjusting to school is measured by one broad scale, School Adjustment, and three subscales—Satisfaction With School, Involvement With Peers, and Interaction With Instructors. The last two DMT scales, Major and Occupation, measure career development on a continuum ranging from the exploration stage of development to the commitment stage.

The ACDM can be used with either high school or college students. If it is used with high school students who do not plan to attend college, the 20 items pertaining to the Major scale should be omitted. The ACDM must be computer scored. Counselors receive an informative computer-based test interpretation; however, they do not have firsthand access to normative tables or scoring procedures.

Coefficients of internal consistency ranged from .49 (Intuitive scale) to .86 (Occupation and Major scales) with a median value of .72 for a sample of 264 high school students. Besides the Intuitive scale, the three School Adjustment subscales also had alpha reliabilities less than .70. These figures indicate that the content of these four scales is rather heterogeneous and may be somewhat difficult to interpret.

Factor-analytic studies support the arrangement of the profile in three groups of scores. Three factors (Decision-Making Style, School

Adjustment, and Career Decision-Making Progress) that closely resemble the three parts of the ACDM consistently emerge from factor-analytic studies.

The ACDM contributes most to the counseling process with its Decision-Making Styles scales (Prediger, 1988). These scales provide the most new information to clients. Sharf (1994) described the ACDM as an "attractive instrument" that can be beneficial in individual and group counseling, especially with college students. The publisher provides instructional materials (the Western Psychological Services Career Planning Program) that can be used together with the ACDM in high school or college career planning classes.

Measures of Career Concerns for Adults

Several measures have been developed to assess career issues of adults in the working world. In addition to the Adult Career Concerns Inventory (ACCI) and the Career Attitudes and Strategies Inventory (CASI), both of which are discussed below, the Career Transitions Inventory can provide helpful information for the counselor and client. The Career Transitions Inventory can be used to assess the psychological resources, including readiness, confidence, perceived support, control, and decision independence, of clients undergoing a career transition (M. J. Heppner, Multon, & Johnston, 1994). Low scores on any of the five factors represent barriers to career change that may need to be addressed in counseling.

Adult Career Concerns Inventory (ACCI). The ACCI measures the career concerns of adults at different stages in their development (Super, Thompson, & Lindeman, 1988). It contains 61 items, which are scored in terms of four developmental stages (Exploration, Establishment, Maintenance, and Disengagement) and 12 substages. Sample items from each of the 12 substages are listed in Table 7-1. Clients rate each item on a five-step scale ranging from *no concern* to *great concern* based on their present situation. Most clients complete the ACCI, which requires an eighth-grade reading ability, within 15 to 30 minutes. Answers can be hand scored or computer scored.

The manual reports preliminary norms for each sex and for different age groups (Super et al., 1988). Besides making normative

TABLE 7-1. Representative Items From the Adult Career Concerns
Inventory

Scale	Item
	Exploration Stage (typically ages 15 to 25)
Crystallization	"Clarifying my ideas about the type of work I would really enjoy."
Specification	"Choosing the best among the occupations I am considering."
Implementation	"Getting started in my chosen occupational field."
	Establishment Stage (typically ages 25 to 45)
Stabilizing	"Settling down in a job I can stay with."
Consolidating	"Consolidating my current position."
Advancing	"Planning how to get ahead in my established field of work."
	Maintenance Stage (typically ages 45 to 60)
Holding	"Maintaining the occupational position I have achieved."
Updating	"Keeping up with new knowledge, equipment, and methods in my field."
Innovating	"Identifying new problems to work on."
	Disengagement Stage (typically ages 60 and over)
Deceleration	"Developing easier ways of doing my work."
Retirement Planning	"Finding activities I would like in retirement."
Retirement Living	"Having a good place to live in retirement."

Note. From *Adult Career Concerns Inventory* by D. E. Super, A. S. Thompson, R. H.
Lindeman, R. A. Myers, & J. P. Jordaan, 1985, Palo Alto, CA: Consulting Psychologists Press. Reproduced with permission of the authors. All rights reserved.

(interindividual) comparisons, Super et al. also stressed the importance of ipsative (intraindividual) comparisons. Ipsative comparisons
enable the counselor and the client to identify the predominant developmental tasks facing the person. Although most people obtain their
highest score (indicating greatest concern) in the stage that is most
common for their age, adults who are in the process of career change
can be expected to recycle through some of the early developmental
stages.

The test scores show a high degree of internal consistency for samples of employed adults. Factor-analytic studies support the construct
validity of the ACCI. Such studies have identified factors similar to
the four developmental stages that provide the framework for the
ACCI (R. M. Smart & Peterson, 1994).

The ACCI helps to clarify the nature of the developmental tasks of greatest concern to the client at the present time. It can also be used as a teaching device to alert clients to future career challenges. As noted by Cairo, Kritis, and Myers (1996, p. 200), "the ACCI remains one of the few measures capable of illuminating our understanding of the career issues facing adults." The National Career Assessment Services, Inc. will soon become the publisher for the ACCI (R. A. Myers, personal communication, May 18, 2001).

Career Attitudes and Strategies Inventory (CASI). Like the ACCI, the CASI was developed to identify and clarify the career problems confronted by adults (Holland & Gottfredson, 1994b). In contrast with the ACCI, the construction of the CASI was influenced primarily by practical rather than theoretical considerations. It includes a broad range of personal and situational factors known to affect a person's career status.

The CASI consists of 130 items that survey nine aspects of career or work adaptation: Job Satisfaction, Work Involvement, Skill Development, Dominant Style, Career Worries, Interpersonal Abuse, Family Commitment, Risk-Taking Style, and Geographical Barriers. The instrument is designed to be self-administering and self-scoring; however, counselors are usually needed to help interpret the results.

The items for each scale are grouped together in the CASI booklet to facilitate scale interpretation. For example, clients who mark *true* or *mostly true* to items such as "family responsibilities limit my career responsibilities," "I short-change my family or partner by working too much," and "I have changed my work schedule to better meet my family responsibilities" will obtain high scores on the Family Commitment scale. As indicated by the item content, high scores on this scale indicate the realities and some of the difficulties of dual-role responsibilities.

Two large samples of adults who completed the CASI obtained moderately high coefficients of internal consistency (mostly in the .80s). Scores on the scales are correlated with other measures of career concerns according to expectations (Holland & Gottfredson, 1994a). M. B. Brown (1998) recommended that the CASI be used primarily as a checklist to generate discussions with clients and to identify potentially problematic areas for further assessment.

CAREER PLANNING COMPETENCIES

Measures of career planning competencies focus on the cognitive aspects of career development, including occupational knowledge, decision-making skills, and employment-seeking skills. Most of the assessment measures of this nature have been developed for career education programs or for use with vocational rehabilitation clients. General-purpose measures of career planning competencies include the Cognitive Vocational Maturity Test and a vocational card sort, both of which assess primarily occupational knowledge.

Cognitive Vocational Maturity Test (CVMT)

The CVMT, which is designed for use with students beginning in the sixth grade, measures knowledge of the characteristics and requirements of a wide range of occupations in six areas, such as work conditions, education required, and duties (Westbrook, Elrod, & Wynne, 1996). Studies with high school students indicate that CVMT scores are significantly correlated with appropriateness of career choice and other measures of career maturity.

Factor analysis of the CVMT showed that it primarily measures just one broad factor: occupational knowledge. With this fact in mind, Westbrook (1995) revised the CVMT and reduced it in length from 120 to 32 items. Research to investigate the reliability and validity of the shortened version is under way.

The CVMT may be supplemented with information from the Self-Knowledge Scale, a 25-item inventory that asks high school students to estimate their knowledge of different aspects of career planning (Westbrook, Sanford, Merwin, Fleenor, & Renzi, 1987). Scores on the Self-Knowledge Scale correlate with other measures of career planning readiness. Both the CVMT and the Self-Knowledge Scale can be used to evaluate a student's readiness for career planning from a cognitive point of view.

Vocational Card Sort

As an alternative means of assessing one's occupational knowledge, counselors may use a vocational card sort. According to a procedure developed by G. W. Peterson (1998), clients sort occupational titles into separate piles on the basis of their similarity to each other. The clients then label and make comparisons among the piles. They are asked to name the attributes of the occupations in the occupational pile that they believe they most resemble.

As they engage in this process, clients verbalize the reasons for their decisions. This process provides helpful insights regarding the maturity of the client's knowledge and understanding of careers. This procedure can serve as a subjective means of evaluating a client's career development and as a stimulus for career exploration.

COMBINED MEASURES OF CAREER PLANNING ATTITUDES AND COMPETENCIES

Inventories that include scales for both career planning attitudes and competencies provide a comprehensive measure of a client's readiness to engage in career planning. High scores on such measures are associated with *career maturity* or *career adaptability.*

Career maturity, which served as the ultimate goal of career development in Super's early work, indicates a client's readiness to accomplish the career developmental tasks appropriate for his or her age. In later work, Super and others shifted the goal of career development from career maturity to career adaptability (Savickas, 1997; Super et al., 1988).

Career adaptability, which emphasizes situational factors as well as developmental tasks, refers to a client's readiness to cope with both the predictable and unpredictable aspects of a career (Savickas, 1997). It broadens the criteria for evaluating career development by acknowledging the client's need to respond to new or novel circumstances. The concept of career adaptability is more appropriate for nontraditional clients, for adults, and for individuals from different cultures (Vondracek & Reitzle, 1998).

In general, counselors should interpret the results from the measures in this section in terms of career adaptability; that is, what do the measures indicate about the client's readiness to cope with the challenges faced in his or her career development? Such an interpretation should take into account cultural context, situational pressures, and personal goals, as well as normal developmental expectations.

Three comprehensive measures of career planning readiness are discussed below. The first two are designed for use with secondary and postsecondary school students in the exploratory stage of career development (Super, 1990). The third instrument is constructed for use with adults who are in the establishment or maintenance stages of career development.

Career Development Inventory (CDI)

Donald Super and his associates designed the CDI "to assess students' readiness to make sound educational and vocational choices" (Thompson et al., 1981, p. 7). The present version of the CDI includes the School Form (Grades 8 through 12) and the College and University Form.

Part I of the CDI, which includes 80 items, provides two scales each for career planning attitudes and career planning competencies. Scores on the two scales that measure attitudes—Career Planning and Career Exploration—are added together to provide a total score for Career Development Attitudes (CDA). Similarly, scores on the two scales that measure competencies—Decision Making (DM) and World-of-Work Information (WW)—are summed to obtain a total score for Career Development Knowledge and Skills (CDK). A Career Orientation Total (COT) score, which serves as a comprehensive measure of career maturity, combines the scores for all four scales.

Part II of the CDI evaluates the client's knowledge of the occupational field to which he or she is most attracted. The Knowledge of Preferred Occupational Group (PO) scale uses the same 40 multiple-choice items for each occupational group. The correct response for each item (e.g., employment opportunities or educational requirements) varies depending on the occupational field. Part II differs from Part I because of its emphasis on occupational knowledge that pertains to a particular occupational field instead of occupations in general. Under ordinary circumstances, this part of the CDI should not be administered to students below the 11th grade.

The answer sheets must be machine scored by the publisher. For each form, results are reported as standard scores with a mean of 100 and a standard deviation of 20. The manuals provide separate percentile tables by sex and year in school for both forms (Thompson et al., 1981, 1982). Although the normative samples are diverse in their makeup, Thompson et al. acknowledged that they do not represent a cross-section of high school or college students in the United States.

No norms are provided for minority students. The CDI authors encourage test users to develop local norms. When the number of students completing the CDI in any one setting exceeds 100, the test publisher will assist the counselor in developing such norms.

The composite scores (CDA, CDK, and COT) show sufficient internal consistency and test–retest reliability (2- to 3-week intervals) when used with high school and college students (Savickas & Hartung, 1996). Scores on the individual scales, particularly PO, WW, and DM, should be interpreted with caution because of relatively low alpha coefficients and test–retest reliabilities found in studies conducted with high school and college students.

In terms of validity, the items for each scale were selected by expert judges to be representative of the different dimensions of Super's model of career development. The scores for most of the scales increase for each age group in the manner suggested by Super's model (Thompson et al., 1981). Savickas and Hartung (1996) noted that the CDI has been used successfully to predict both career choice perseverance and academic success.

As proposed by its authors, the CDI should be helpful in counseling individuals, in planning guidance programs, and in evaluating programs and research. In a review of the career literature, Savickas and Hartung (1996, p. 185) concluded that research based on the CDI "strongly supports the sensitivity and specificity of the inventory as a measure of readiness to make educational choices, vocational choices, or both."

Career Maturity Inventory (CMI)

The CMI is based on John Crites's (1978) model of career development. According to his model, career maturity encompasses a hierarchy of factors. He hypothesized a general factor of career maturity similar to the g factor in intelligence testing, several group factors, and a large number of specific factors. The group factors pertain to both the process of career planning (attitudes and competencies) and the content of career planning (consistency and realism of career choice).

Crites developed the CMI to measure the career planning attitudes and competencies of secondary school students (Grades 6 through 12). In 1995, he revised the CMI to pertain to college students and young adults as well as adolescents (Crites & Savickas, 1996). He made a conscious effort to shorten the CMI by reducing the number of items and by eliminating subscales. He also added self-help material (a collateral Career Developer) to the test package to aid in the interpretation of the instrument and to help foster the client's career development.

The CMI resembles the CDI in its focus on the career planning process variables. It yields a career planning attitude score, a career planning competency score, and an overall career maturity score in a manner similar to the CDI. It differs from the CDI in its brevity (50 items altogether) and its lack of subscales.

Crites selected items for the CMI in terms of theoretical specifications and age and grade differentiations. Validity studies with the original CMI showed that students in higher grades scored higher (albeit modestly) on the scales than did students in lower grades. Scores on the Attitude Total scale correlated significantly with performance and satisfaction in both academic and work settings. According to Healy (1994), the original Attitude Scale was well supported for studying career development, screening for career immaturity, and evaluating career education, whereas the original Competence Tests lacked validity for use in individual counseling. Although the current version of the CMI resembles the original version in many respects, its reliability and validity need to be examined with new studies (Levinson et al., 1998).

Career Mastery Inventory (CMAS)

The Career Mastery Inventory (abbreviated CMAS to differentiate it from the CMI described above) was constructed by Crites (1993) to assess the career development of adults in the same manner that the CMI assessed the career development of adolescents. Part 1 of the CMAS consists of 90 items on a 7-point Likert scale that assess work attitudes and behavior. Part 2 contains 20 multiple-choice items that measure skill in handling problems in one's work situation.

For Part 1, clients receive a Career Development total score plus scores on six career developmental tasks: Organizational Adaptability ("learning the ropes"), Position Performance, Work Habits and Attitudes, Coworker Relationships ("getting along"), Advancement ("getting ahead"), and Career Choice and Plans ("looking ahead").

For Part 2, they receive a Career Adjustment total score together with scores on three adjustment scales: Integrative (reduces anxiety and solves work problems), Adjustive (reduces anxiety only), and Nonadjustive (neither of the above). The test booklet, which has been uniquely designed so that duplicate copies are provided by means of carbon paper, can be both self-scored to provide immediate feedback and machine scored for aggregate data analysis and program evaluation.

The CMAS has been used primarily in business and industrial settings to help design career development programs, to identify common problems among workers within the organizational culture, and to diagnose individual career development task and job adjustment problems. High total scores on the CMAS are correlated with worker satisfaction and job success as measured by performance appraisals and standardized measures (Crites, 1993). Scores on the career development subscales are associated with one's age in the manner predicted by Crites's career development model.

USE OF CAREER DEVELOPMENT MEASURES IN COUNSELING

Several guidelines concerning the use of career development measures in counseling are listed below:

1. Use the various measures of career development to determine readiness for career planning. Estimate the client's stage of development in terms of both attitudes and competencies. Plan counseling activities that can enhance the client's level of development.

2. Use items from the career development measures themselves as a means of teaching clients about the different aspects of career maturity. "Teaching the test" can help clarify the meaning of career development and can suggest topics for homework.

3. Assign career development measures to clients to stimulate their thinking about career issues. The measures can help focus the attention of clients on matters related to career planning.

4. Assess the client's decision-making style. Teach the problem-solving model to clients who wish to improve their decision-making ability. Help clients to evaluate career myths or distorted beliefs about careers that may be interfering with their career development.

5. Distinguish between indecision and indecisiveness. Clients who are indecisive will probably need personal counseling in addition to assistance for career planning. Use individual items from career decision-making scales as a checklist to identify factors contributing to indecision. Explore these factors in counseling with the client.

6. Administer career development measures to classes or groups of students to help determine needs for different types of educational or counseling interventions. For example, information from career development measures could be used in planning activities for career orientation courses or career exploration counseling groups.

7. When working with multicultural clients, keep in mind the need to evaluate and to address the institutional and personal challenges they may face, both in entering an occupation and in progressing in it. Such challenges include limited educational experiences, low self-confidence, less access to mentors, and lack of political skills and savvy (Eby, Johnson, & Russell, 1998).

8. In addition to paper-and-pencil instruments, counselors should use other assessment techniques, including interviews, observations, situational assessments, or work samples, to help evaluate a client's readiness to engage in career planning (Levinson et al., 1998).

9. In planning interventions, take into account the complexity of a client's situation (family, social, economic, or organizational factors) as well as the client's capability to make appropriate career choices (Sampson et al., 2000). External factors can contribute to or detract from a client's readiness to engage in career planning.

10. Ask students or clients to retake career development measures as counseling or education progresses to assess changes in dealing with developmental tasks. Use career development measures as criteria for evaluating the effectiveness of career counseling programs.

SUMMARY

1. Measures of career development process include both attitudinal (career beliefs and concerns) and cognitive (career planning competencies) factors. These measures are most important for determining the client's readiness for various counseling or educational interventions.

2. It is important for counselors to identify assumptions of clients that may be blocking their career progress. Inventories that counselors can use for this purpose include the Career Beliefs Inventory, the Career Thoughts Inventory, and the Career Decision-Making Self-Efficacy Scale.

3. Several instruments have been designed to evaluate the progress of high school and college students in making a career decision. The Career Decision Scale can help identify different types of indecision, whereas the My Vocational Situation inventory indicates factors contributing to indecision.

4. The Assessment of Career Decision Making enables counselors to distinguish among different decision-making styles (rational, intuitive, and dependent). Counselors should help clients assess the nature and the effectiveness of their preferred style.

5. The Adult Career Concerns Inventory and the Career Attitudes and Strategies Inventory focus on the career difficulties of adults. These instruments can serve as a springboard for discussing critical issues in counseling sessions.

6. Relatively few instruments are available to measure the career planning competencies of clients. The Cognitive Vocational Maturity Test or Peterson's vocational card sort can be used to assess a client's occupational knowledge.

7. Several instruments have been designed to assess both career planning attitudes and career planning competencies. The Career Development Inventory and the Career Maturity Inventory provide comprehensive measures of career planning readiness for high school and traditional-age college students. The Career Mastery Inventory provides a comprehensive measure of career adaptability for adults.

8

MEASURES OF WORK AND PERSONAL VALUES

COUNSELORS OFTEN NEED TO HELP CLIENTS evaluate their motivations in regard to work or other aspects of living. Measures of both values and interests can be helpful for this purpose. Values define what a person thinks is *important*; interests refer to what an individual *likes* to do. According to Nevill and Super (1986b, p. 3), "values are the objectives sought in behavior, whereas interests are the activities in which the values are sought." In essence, values pertain to *why* a person works or undertakes an activity, whereas interests refer to *what* the person chooses to do. Values are more highly correlated than interests with work satisfaction (Rounds, 1990). In contrast, interests are more closely related to academic and career choices (Pryor & Taylor, 1986).

Research indicates that the structure of work values is similar across different cultures (Elizur, Borg, Hunt, & Beck, 1991; Sverko,

1995). Measures of values are considered in this chapter; measures of interests are discussed in the next chapter.

VALUES INVENTORIES

Values can be assessed either by a values inventory or by values clarification exercises. Inventories of both work and personal values are considered in this section. Values clarification exercises are discussed in the next section.

Inventories of Work Values

Work values inventories assess values that pertain primarily to work situations. They measure objectives that can be satisfied in the work itself (intrinsic values) or through work as a means to an end (extrinsic values). Intrinsic values include stimulating work, interpersonal satisfaction, and aesthetic concerns. Extrinsic values include economic security, comfortable existence, and independence. Both types of values need to be taken into consideration in career planning.

Three measures of work values—the Minnesota Importance Questionnaire (MIQ), Career Orientation Placement and Evaluation Survey (COPES), and Values Scale (VS)—are discussed below. The MIQ, which is based on the theory of work adjustment developed at the University of Minnesota, provides a measure of needs or values related to worker satisfaction. The COPES (1995 revision) uses eight bipolar scales to measure 16 work values identified in the career literature. Finally, the VS is a broad measure of values that can be used to assess both work and personal values.

A fourth inventory, the Work Values Inventory (WVI), is currently in the process of revision (D. G. Zytowski, National Career Assessment Services, Inc., personal communication, June 15, 2001). The WVI was originally developed by Donald Super (1970) for career development research and counseling. In a survey conducted by Watkins et al. (1994), counseling psychologists reported that they used the WVI more often than any other values inventory for career assessment. In its revised form, the WVI assesses the importance of 12 values or goals (creativity, intellectual stimulation, achievement, independence, prestige, economic returns, security, surroundings, supervisory relations, associates, way of life, and variety) to clients. Each of the 12 scales consists of six items with four response options ranging from 1 (*unimportant*) to 4 (*very important*). The revised version will provide separate male and female norms for middle school students, high school students, and college students and adults.

Minnesota Importance Questionnaire (MIQ). The MIQ asks individuals to evaluate 20 different work needs or values in terms of their importance in an ideal job (Rounds, Henly, Dawis, Lofquist, & Weiss, 1981). The 20 needs derive from studies of job satisfaction conducted by Dawis and Lofquist (1984) as part of their research on the theory of work adjustment. In the theory of work adjustment, worker satisfaction is predicted by correspondence between worker needs and occupational rewards, assuming that the person has sufficient ability to succeed at the job. The 20 needs have been reduced to six broad factors (called values) by means of factor analysis. Table 8-1 provides a list of the 20 needs, the statements that measure the needs, and the six values that summarize the 20 needs.

Two forms of the MIQ exist. One contains 190 pairs of items by which the respondent can compare every need with every other need. The other form is a simplified version, which requires the respondent to rank five different needs arranged in 21 sets. Most people prefer the simplified version because it can usually be completed within 20 minutes. Computer scoring, available through the publisher, is recommended.

The MIQ measures intraindividual variability; that is, its scores show the range of work needs within the individual. The raw scores are converted to z scores with a mean of 0 and a standard deviation of 1. Each profile is checked for consistency by means of the Logically Consistent Triad (LCT) score. LCT scores are used in setting error bands for each scale score to indicate how much the score might change on retesting.

The MIQ has a fifth-grade reading level; however, it should not be used with individuals younger than age 16. Needs are not well defined for most people until that age.

Work needs as measured by the MIQ can be compared with the rewards or reinforcements provided by different occupations by means of Occupational Reinforcer Patterns (ORPs). The ORPs indicate to what extent different types of reinforcements can be obtained

TABLE 8-1. Description of Scales and Item Content of the Minnesota Importance Questionnaire

Value (Need Factor)	Need Scale	Need Statement
Achievement	Ability utilization	I could do something that makes use of my abilities.
	Achievement	The job could give me a feeling of accomplishment.
Comfort	Activity	I could be busy all the time.
	Independence	I could work alone on the job.
	Variety	I could do something different every day.
	Compensation	My pay would compare well with that of other workers.
	Security	The job would provide for steady employment.
	Working conditions	The job would have good working conditions.
Status	Advancement	The job would provide an opportunity for advancement.
	Recognition	I could get recognition for the work I do.
	Authority	I could tell people what to do.
	Social status	I could be "somebody" in the community.
Altruism	Coworkers	My coworkers would be easy to make friends with.
	Social service	I could do things for other people.
	Moral values	I could do the work without feeling that it is morally wrong.
Safety	Company policies and practices	The company would administer its policies fairly.
	Supervision–human relations	My boss would back up the workers (with top management).
	Supervision–technical	My boss would train the workers well.
Autonomy	Creativity	I could try out some of my own ideas.
	Responsibility	I could make decisions on my own.

Note. From *Manual for the Minnesota Importance Questionnaire: A Measure of Vocational Needs and Values*, by J. B. Rounds, Jr., G. A. Henly, R. V. Dawis, L. H. Lofquist, and D. J. Weiss, 1981, pp. 3–4, 7. Copyright 1981 by Vocational Psychology Research, University of Minnesota. Reprinted with permission.

from a particular occupation (Stewart et al., 1986). An ORP is determined by asking a number of supervisors from an occupation to complete the Minnesota Job Description Questionnaire (MJDQ). The MJDQ lists 20 rewards offered by jobs that match the 20 needs assessed by the MIQ. For example, the work environment for vocational rehabilitation counselors provides the following reinforcements (ranked in order) according to supervisors from that occupation (Stewart et al., 1986):

- Have work in which they do things for other people
- Make use of their individual abilities
- Make decisions on their own
- Plan their work with little supervision
- Get a feeling of accomplishment
- Try out their own ideas
- Have something different to do everyday
- Are busy all the time

The ORPs for 185 representative occupations are listed in the *Occupational Reinforcer Patterns Notebook* prepared by Stewart et al. (1986). Similar information based on the same set of values can be obtained on the Internet as part of the new O*NET database (McCloy et al., 1999; National Center for O*NET Development, 2001; U.S. Department of Labor, 2001).

The test authors have organized the ORPs into six clusters based on the predominant factor (value) scores. For example, Cluster A includes occupations that score high on Achievement and Autonomy values and moderately high on Altruism. Sample occupations include architect, dentist, and school teacher.

An individual's MIQ scores are correlated with the ORP for each occupation to determine the degree of similarity between the worker's needs and the rewards offered by different occupations. Correlation coefficients (also referred to as Correspondence or C scores) above .50 indicate similarity of individual and job characteristics. C scores between .10 and .50 show some similarity. C scores less than .10 indicate no similarity. According to the test authors (Rounds et al., 1981), if the correlation is .50 or greater between an individual's MIQ score and an ORP, the individual stands at least 7 chances out of 10 of being satisfied in that occupation.

Counselors need to be more concerned about profile reliability for the MIQ than they do scale reliability because of the emphasis on rank order of scores for clients. For most people, the shape of the MIQ profiles will be very similar on retesting after a few weeks (Rounds et al., 1981).

Research indicates that when individuals work on jobs providing rewards that match their needs as measured by the MIQ, they will be happy. For example, Elizur and Tziner (1977) found that when social workers expressed needs (high social service, responsibility, and variety needs; low compensation, authority, and social status needs) that matched the reinforcements provided by their work, they were more likely to report satisfaction as defined by the Minnesota Satisfaction Questionnaire. Similar results have been reported in other validity studies (Benson, 1988). In general, test critics have favorably reviewed the MIQ (Lachar, 1992; Layton, 1992).

The case example given below illustrates the use in counseling of the MIQ with an employed adult who wished to consider other career options.

CASE EXAMPLE

Kevin, a 29-year-old college graduate in marketing, wished to consider new career possibilities. He had been employed in sales positions since graduating from college 7 years earlier. Kevin sought counseling at a continuing education counseling service at a nearby university. He completed the MIQ during the course of his counseling contacts.

He obtained his highest MIQ scores on the following scales: Ability Utilization = 3.5, Achievement = 2.7, and Responsibility = 2.7. His sales position was not enabling him to express these values as much as he would have liked. He especially felt the need to obtain work in which he could make better use of his abilities and obtain a sense of accomplishment.

His scores on the six value factor scales were highest for Achievement (3.1) and Autonomy (2.4). These values match the reinforcements provided by occupations in Cluster A (Achievement–Autonomy–Altruism) in the MIQ scoring scheme. He expressed an interest in the following types of occupations included in this cluster: social services, health sciences, and recreation. He obtained Correspondence (C) scores of .79 for dentist and .71 for lawyer, both of which he planned to explore in greater detail. The MIQ helped him to identify occupational possibilities that met his work values.

Career Orientation Placement and Evaluation Survey (COPES). The COPES measures work values on eight bipolar scales as indicated below (Knapp, Knapp-Lee, & Knapp, 1995; Knapp-Lee, 1996):

- Investigative versus Accepting
- Practical versus Carefree
- Independence versus Conformity
- Leadership versus Supportive
- Orderliness versus Flexibility
- Recognition versus Privacy
- Aesthetic versus Realistic
- Social versus Reserved

Each bipolar scale consists of 16 pairs of items that represent the opposite ends of the scale. For each item pair, clients must choose which activity or type of work they value more. For example, "work on my own without direction" versus "work under careful supervision" is an item pair scored on the Independence versus Conformity scale.

The COPES has been designed so that it may be used with the COPSystem Interest Inventory and Career Ability Placement Survey (see Chapter 10). Based on a review of the career literature, the scale authors have identified the three most relevant values for each of the 14 occupational clusters used within this system. For example, outdoor careers are matched with Practical, Independence, and Privacy values.

Studies indicate that the eight COPES scales measure values that are relatively homogeneous and independent of each other. Students in different occupational groups obtain COPES scores according to expectations. Longitudinal data indicate that the COPES scores successfully predict future job or college program placement (Knapp-Lee, 1996).

Values Scale (VS). Donald Super and Dorothy Nevill collaborated with vocational psychologists from a number of different countries as part of the Work Importance Study to construct both the VS and the Salience Inventory (Nevill & Super, 1986a, 1986b). The VS builds on

171

the research conducted by Super on the Work Values Inventory (WVI). It contains 21 scales, which represent the 15 work values originally measured by the WVI plus 6 additional values (such as physical activities, personal development, and cultural identity).

Each VS scale contains five items with four response options ranging from 1 (*of little or no importance*) to 4 (*very important*). For each scale (except Working Conditions), at least two of the five items pertain to nonwork situations, whereas two others pertain to work. Most people complete the inventory in 30 to 45 minutes. The VS, which is intended for people age 13 and older, requires an eighth-grade reading level. It can be easily scored by hand within a few minutes.

Studies of the VS with cross-national samples indicate that five factors (or orientations) account for most of the variance in test scores (Sverko, 1995). The five factors together with the scales that best represent them are listed below:

- Utilitarian Orientation (Economics, Advancement, Prestige, Authority, Achievement)
- Orientation Toward Self-Actualization (Ability, Personal Development, Altruism)
- Individualist Orientation (Lifestyle, Autonomy)
- Social Orientation (Social Interaction, Social Relations)
- Adventurous Orientation (Risk)

These five factors can be used to help organize and explain the information obtained from the 21 scales. The Utilitarian and Individualist Orientations primarily assess extrinsic values that can be satisfied by the outcomes of work, whereas the Self-Actualization, Social, and Adventurous Orientations measure intrinsic values that can be satisfied by participation in the work itself.

From a psychometric point of view, questions have been raised regarding the reliabilities of the scale scores, the representativeness of the norms, and the lack of predictive validity studies (Green, 1998; Schoenrade, 1998). Despite its limitations, the VS can be helpful in counseling in focusing on the importance of values in life and career planning (Nevill & Kruse, 1996). At this point, the VS can be best used for intraindividual comparisons, that is, to help clients determine the relative strength of their values when compared with each other.

Within this context, it can be used as an interview aid to serve as "the basis of fruitful discussion between client and counselor" (Schoenrade, 1998, p. 1115).

Inventories of Personal Values

Inventories of personal values can be used to evaluate what goals or objectives an individual considers to be important in a variety of situations beyond work itself. Among inventories of personal values currently in use, the Rokeach Value Survey is the oldest and best known, especially for use in research. However, the Salience Inventory and the Quality of Life Questionnaire are more likely to be used for counseling purposes. Each of these inventories is discussed below.

Rokeach Value Survey (RVS). The RVS is a short inventory that consists of two sets of 18 words or phrases that measure *instrumental* and *terminal* values (Rokeach, 1973). Instrumental values, such as obedience, forgiveness, and imagination, represent "modes of conduct." Terminal values, such as beauty, adventure, and friendship, represent the "end-states of existence." Respondents must rank each of the two sets of 18 items in order of their preferences for the different values.

Although designed for individuals ages 11 and over, the results tend to be unreliable for younger individuals, especially those who lack the ability to handle verbal abstractions. Brookhart (1995) recommended that the use of the RVS be limited to "literate adults who are used to dealing with abstractions" (p. 879). Although the RVS has been used primarily for research purposes, Sanford (1995) noted that it can be "useful for examining an individual's value system and for determining if change has occurred within [it]" (p. 880). Because of limited norms, the results should be interpreted simply by comparing the ranks of the different values for an individual with each other (i.e., in an ipsative fashion), not by comparison with a norm group.

Salience Inventory (SI). The SI measures the importance of different life roles for individuals in the context of Super's "life-space, life-span" model of career development (Nevill & Super, 1986a; Super, 1990). Five life roles, including Studying, Working, Community Service, Home, and Leisure Activities, are each assessed from three different perspectives: Participation, Commitment, and Value Expectations. The five Participation scales measure the extent of a person's actual behavior in each of the five roles. The five Commitment scales assess the client's emotional attachment to each role. Finally, the five Value Expectations scales measure the degree to which a client expects that his or her values will be fulfilled in each of the five roles.

The instrument, which includes 170 items rated on a 4-point scale, requires about 30 to 45 minutes to complete. It can be hand scored easily without the use of templates.

The SI scales have yielded high coefficients of internal consistency for student and adult samples; however, test–retest coefficients for college students have been somewhat low. A client's test scores can be expected to change somewhat over short time periods. Validity studies indicate that the SI differentiates between different occupational and cultural groups in expected directions. Individuals vary in the relative importance they place on the different roles on the basis of such factors as age, gender, and culture.

The SI provides information for counseling purposes that is not readily available from other instruments. It can help clarify the client's readiness to engage in career planning by indicating the relative significance of career in the client's life. It can be used to identify and explore role conflicts within clients or between clients and their environment. For example, discrepancies between Commitment or Value Expectations and Participation scores may suggest important topics for consideration.

When used in combination with the VS (or other measure of work values), the SI can help identify outlets for values not realized in one's career. Because the SI has been developed for use in multicultural settings, it can be particularly valuable in counseling students from different cultural backgrounds (Nevill & Calvert, 1996). The SI will soon have a new publisher (D. D. Nevill, personal communication, August 20, 2001). In the meantime, SI materials can be obtained from the test author (e-mail: nevill@ufl.edu).

Quality of Life Inventory (QOLI). The QOLI is a short, 32-item instrument that can be used to rate the importance of 16 different aspects of life, such as learning, helping, and health (Frisch, 1994). Individuals also rate the degree to which they are satisfied with each of these aspects of their lives. Total Quality of Life scores can be obtained by multiplying the Importance ratings by the Satisfaction ratings for each of the 16 areas, and then adding these figures together.

The QOLI is a relatively new instrument that is still in a state of development; however, it can serve as a valuable vehicle for the discussion of values with clients. It has the advantages of being brief, comprehensive, easy to administer and score, and based on a quality of life model that can be used to interpret scores and suggest possible interventions (R. W. Johnson, 2001).

Use of Values Inventories in Counseling

The following points pertain to the use of all values inventories in counseling:

1. Use a measure of values when a client wishes to clarify work or life goals and objectives. Integrate measures of values with measures of interests in attempting to understand client motivation for work or other activities.

2. Use the scales or factors from a values inventory to provide a meaningful structure by which clients can consider their values. A structure of this sort enables the client to consider the nature of values expressed in various activities.

3. Ask clients to estimate their own profile. Ask them to separate those needs that are most important for them from those that are least important. This approach will teach clients to apply a values structure to their own situation.

4. Try to estimate the client's profile. This type of exercise helps the counselor to become more familiar with both the values inventory and the client. The counselor is forced to organize his or her thinking about the client's values in a systematic fashion.

5. Compare the client's and the counselor's estimates with the actual profile from the values inventory. If they do not match, try to determine the reasons for the discrepancies. Clarify the meaning of both estimated and measured values.

6. To what extent do the values scores agree with the client's experiences? Clients should report satisfaction with previous occupations and activities that provide rewards that agree with their needs and values.

7. Ask clients to interpret individual items in regard to their situation. What do the items mean to them, particularly those items that they may be most concerned about?

8. Look at the relationship between values scores and rewards provided by different occupations or activities. Use the *Occupational Reinforcer Patterns Notebook* or the occupational reinforcer patterns provided in the O*NET database (National Center for O*NET Development, 2001) to obtain a list of occupations that provide rewards appropriate to clients' values.

9. Consider work values within a larger context of life values and life planning (L. S. S. Hansen, 1999). Help clients to consider a range of values that may be expressed within a variety of roles and situations.

10. Use the results from values inventories to stimulate self-exploration. The results should be used in conjunction with other data that take into account interests, abilities, previous experiences, and opportunities.

11. Keep in mind that values can change. As basic needs (such as survival, safety, and belonging) are satisfied, higher order needs (such as esteem and self-actualization) become more important (Maslow, 1987). Counselors may need to help clients to review their values as their situation changes.

VALUES CLARIFICATION EXERCISES

Values clarification exercises are strategies that enable clients to identify and to make comparisons among their values. Compared with values inventories, values clarification exercises require clients to engage in self-assessment at a deeper level that takes into account actual behavior as well as preferences. The exercises ask clients to review their beliefs and behaviors in response to different situations. They encourage clients to assume a more active role in exploring and expressing their values. They possess all of the advantages of qualitative assessment procedures, including more active participation on the part of the client and a more holistic approach (Goldman, 1992).

For example, a typical values clarification exercise invites clients to list 15 to 20 things they love to do. For each activity, they are then asked to consider such matters as how long it has been since they participated in the activity, if it is something that they do with others or alone, how much the activity costs, how important that activity is compared with other activities, how much planning the activity requires, and whether or not this is a new activity for them. The exercise requires clients to analyze their activities in terms of the values expressed. A value is considered to be fully developed when it meets the following six criteria: It has been (a) chosen freely (b) from among alternatives (c) after careful consideration of the consequences, (d) prized and (e) publicly affirmed, and (f) acted on repeatedly (Raths, Harmin, & Simon, 1978).

Values clarification exercises have been used in regard to a wide variety of issues, including substance abuse, career transitions, grieving, and sex education. Singelis (1998) provides a number of value clarification exercises that can be used to increase understanding of and communication with different ethnic and racial groups.

Most career planning workbooks contain several values clarification exercises (e.g., Figler, 1993; C. F. Wells & Carney, 1998). The workbooks help clients to integrate information derived from the values clarification exercises with other information about themselves and with occupational information. Typical exercises include the values auction, values card sort, and guided fantasy. Other values clarification assessments include the use of stories in which work values are embedded (Krumboltz, Blando, Kim, & Reikowski, 1994) and the use of the Repertory Grid to help clients create their own values categories for making comparisons among occupations (Zytowski, 1994a).

The Life Values Inventory, a relatively new inventory by Crace and Brown (1992), combines qualitative and quantitative assessment of an individual's values (D. Brown, 1995). It is particularly helpful for identifying and addressing both intrarole conflicts (when values held by the individual conflict with values espoused in the workplace) and interrole conflicts (when values held by the individual conflict with his or her values expressed in another role). The scales from the inventory provide a structure for analyzing the types of values demonstrated in one's life experiences or career choice. Clients repeat the quantitative section of the inventory after performing the qualitative exercises as a means of reviewing the priority of their values. This same technique can be used with other combinations of values inventories and values clarification exercises.

177

Kinnier (1995) noted that values clarification exercises have come under attack for the superficial and irrelevant manner in which they have been applied at times. He argued that values clarification can be most meaningful when it is applied to specific values conflicts, such as the relative importance that an individual places on family versus career commitment. He described a number of strategies (both rational and intuitive), such as problem solving, cognitive restructuring, life review, incubation ("sleeping on it"), and the "two-chair technique," that can be used for this purpose. He has designed an assessment instrument, the Values Conflict Resolution Assessment (VCRA), that can be used to identify a values conflict, guide its resolution, and evaluate the desirability of the resolution (Kinnier, 1987). VCRA scores correlated positively with self-reports of conflict resolution and self-esteem for a sample of graduate students.

SUMMARY

1. Values refer to a person's objectives or goals in work or other settings. Counselors usually assess client values by means of values inventories or values clarification exercises.
2. The Minnesota Importance Questionnaire provides a measure of work values based on the theory of work adjustment. Counselors can compare client values identified by the Minnesota Importance Questionnaire with work rewards by means of the *Occupational Reinforcer Patterns Notebook* or the O*NET Occupational Reinforcer Patterns database.
3. The Career Orientation Placement and Evaluation Survey assesses work values by means of eight bipolar scales.
4. The Values Scales provides a broad measure of work and personal values based on research conducted in cross-national settings.
5. Both the Salience Inventory and the Quality of Life Inventory can be used to assess personal values. These inventories enable individuals to compare the relative importance of different life roles or aspects of their life and to determine to what degree their values are being met in their activities.
6. Values clarification exercises require clients to identify and to compare their values with their behaviors. As such, they can be particularly valuable in stimulating exploration and development of client values.

9

ASSESSMENT
OF INTERESTS

S INCE AT LEAST 1909, when Frank Parsons published his classic book, *Choosing a Vocation*, counselors have tried to devise ways to assess people's career interests. Interest inventories, which ask clients to report their likes and dislikes for various activities, have proved to be particularly useful for this purpose. Several interest inventories that counselors use frequently are discussed in this chapter, together with guidelines for their selection and interpretation.

TYPES OF INTEREST INVENTORIES

Interest inventories can be classified in a variety of ways, for example, by age level, occupational level, or type of item. In many ways, the most useful distinction pertains to type of scale. Two types of interest scales predominate. The first type measures the strength of one's interests in broad fields of activity, such as art, mechanical activities, or sports. These scales are frequently described as *general* or *basic* interests. They are *homogeneous* in nature because they refer to one type of activity. For this reason they are relatively easy to interpret.

In contrast, the second type of scale assesses the similarity of one's interest patterns with those of people in specific occupations. These scales, usually called *occupational* scales, are *heterogeneous* in terms of item content. The scales include a variety of items that distinguish between the interests of people in an occupation and those of people in general. Because of the mixed item content, scores on these scales are more difficult to interpret.

The first type of scale is usually constructed by a rational process. The scales are designed to include items that logically fit together. Examples include Occupational Theme scales and Basic Interest scales on the Strong Interest Inventory. Internal validation procedures such as factor analysis are usually undertaken to ensure that the item content of the scales is relatively pure. Scales of this type belong to a "closed system" of scales; that is, the system includes all the scales that are necessary to represent all the different types of interests.

Scales of the second type are based on those items that differentiate between the interests of people in an occupation and people in general. Item selection depends on an empirical process (observed differences between groups), not on theoretical or logical considerations. Examples include the Occupational scales on the Strong Interest Inventory and the Career Assessment Inventory. External validation procedures such as discriminant analysis are frequently used to determine the effectiveness of the scales in differentiating among the interests of people employed in different occupations. Empirical scales are usually part of an "open system"; that is, no one set of scales is established to represent the universe of occupational interests. New scales must be constructed as new occupations emerge or as old occupations change.

Both types of scales contribute to the career or life planning process. Because they are easy to interpret, the basic interest scales can be used in a variety of situations in which counseling contact may be limited. The basic interest scales can also be helpful in interpreting the scores on the occupational scales when both types of scores are available. The occupational scales, on the other hand, provide a means of comparing one's interest pattern as a whole with those of people in different occupations. These scales include in a single score the information that is distributed over a number of basic interest scales.

In most cases, counselors should use interest inventories that provide broad measures of interest with high school age or younger students. Not only are such scales easier to interpret, but they also preclude young students from focusing too early on specific occupations before they have had sufficient opportunity to explore different occupations. Inventories that show scores for specific occupations are more appropriate for college students or other adults.

SELECTION OF INTEREST INVENTORIES FOR COUNSELING

Counselors most often use interest inventories to aid clients with academic or career planning. Interest scores can be used to help clients to explore or discover new academic or career possibilities, to decide among various alternatives, or to confirm a previous choice. Interest scores can also be used for considering ways in which a job might be modified to produce greater job satisfaction or for planning leisure-time activities. As indicated by Harmon, Hansen, Borgen, and Hammer (1994), interest scores can also be used as a catalyst for discussions between client and parents or other significant people in the client's life.

The following guidelines should help counselors to decide when to use an interest inventory with a client. First, counselors should keep in mind that interest inventories measure likes and dislikes, not abilities. Most studies show a negligible relationship between inventoried interests and tested abilities. Interest inventories can help identify careers or work situations that clients should find satisfying, but they do not indicate how successful the person would be in those settings.

Second, clients should be positively motivated to participate in the assessment process. Clients are more likely to benefit from taking an interest inventory if they express an interest in the results beforehand. They are also more likely to present an honest picture of their interests or intentions if they clearly understand and accept the purpose of testing. Large changes in interest scores can occur when clients change the manner in which they approach the test. Sometimes clients answer items in terms of what they think other people (especially parents) would like them to say, or they may respond to the items in regard to their abilities or opportunities instead of their interests. Clients may answer the questions hastily or insincerely, especially if they take the inventory as part of a classroom administration. Test scores will be less valid and reliable under such circumstances.

Third, general interest inventories are of limited value for people who must make rather fine distinctions, such as choosing between civil and electrical engineering. Special purpose inventories such as the Purdue Interest Questionnaire for engineering and technical students (LeBold & Shell, 1986) or the Medical Specialty Preference Inventory for medical students (Savickas, Brizzi, Brisbin, & Pethtel, 1988) can provide some assistance in such cases. Under any circumstance, interest inventories must be supplemented with other information about the person and his or her situation, including abilities, values, previous work experiences, and job availability, before a decision is made.

Fourth, interest inventories may be inappropriate for people with emotional problems. Disturbed people make more negative responses and endorse more passive interests than do people who are not disturbed. Personal issues can interfere with decision making. Counselors usually must address the emotional difficulties before career planning can take place.

Fifth, scores on interest inventories can show significant changes for clients who are young or after long time periods. As a rule of thumb, counselors should consider readministering an interest inventory if it has been longer than 6 months since the client last completed one. Interests are most likely to change for people under age 20 who have experienced large changes in their situation (e.g., new work or school experiences).

Finally, counselors may wish to use an interest card sort instead of an interest inventory if they are interested in the underlying reasons for the client's choices (Slaney & MacKinnon-Slaney, 2000). The card sort functions as a structured interview. As originally designed by Leona Tyler, clients sort cards with occupational titles on them into piles of "would choose," "would not choose," and "no opinion."

They then subdivide the three piles into smaller piles based on their reasons for placing the cards into those piles. This technique helps counselors to understand the reasons for a client's choice. The counselor and the client together look for themes in the client's preferences that can guide the career exploration process. Examples of such card sorts include the Missouri Occupational Card Sort, Missouri Occupational Preference Inventory, Nonsexist Vocational Card Sort, Occ-U-Sort, and Slaney's Vocational Card Sort (Slaney & MacKinnon-Slaney, 2000). The Vocational Exploration and Insight Kit, which includes an 84-item card sort together with other career exploration activities, is especially appropriate for highly motivated clients who wish to consider their career choices in some depth (Holland, 1992).

POPULAR INTEREST INVENTORIES

Several of the most popular interest inventories used for career or life planning are discussed in this chapter. These measures include the Strong Interest Inventory, the three Kuder interest inventories, the two versions of the Career Assessment Inventory, and the Jackson Vocational Interest Survey. Interest inventories that also include self-ratings of abilities, such as the Self-Directed Search, Campbell Interest and Skill Survey, and Career Decision-Making System–Revised, are considered in Chapter 10.

Strong Interest Inventory™ (Strong)

The 1994 Strong is the most recent version of a series of interest inventories that began with the publication of the Strong Vocational Interest Blank (SVIB) by E. K. Strong, Jr., in 1927 (Harmon et al., 1994). The Strong replaces the Strong–Campbell Interest Inventory (SCII), a merged version of the male and female forms of the SVIB, created by David Campbell in 1974 and revised with the help of Jo-Ida Hansen in 1981 and 1985.

The Strong is particularly noteworthy because of its wide usage, its extensive research base, and its innovative role in the field of career assessment. Counseling psychologists use the Strong more frequently for vocational assessment than any other instrument (Watkins, Campbell, & Nieberding, 1994). The Strong has been the subject of extensive research studies in regard to occupational norms, long-term test–retest reliability, concurrent and predictive validity, cross-cultural differences, and counseling applications (J. C. Hansen, 2000; Harmon & Borgen, 1995; Harmon et al., 1994; Lattimore & Borgen, 1999; Lubinski, Benbow, & Ryan, 1995). This "landmark" inventory has led the way for other inventories in the use of criterion-related scale development and in the application of Holland's theory to interest measurement (D. P. Campbell & Borgen, 1999; Donnay, 1997).

The present version of the Strong includes 317 items divided into eight sections (occupational titles, school subjects, general activities, leisure activities, types of people, preferences between pairs of activities, personal characteristics, and preferences between types of work). For most of the items (269 of 317 items), clients indicate whether they *like*, are *indifferent* to, or *dislike* the activity represented by that particular item. Most clients complete the Strong in 25 to 35 minutes.

The answers must be scored by means of a computer program by Consulting Psychologists Press or one of its agents. The scores are reported to the client on a six-page profile or as a computerized narrative interpretation. Besides several Administrative indexes, the Strong produces scores on four sets of scales—the General Occupational Theme scales, Basic Interest scales, Occupational scales, and Personal Style scales—each of which is discussed below.

The different parts of the Strong are discussed in regard to a client who completed the Strong as part of the counseling process at a university counseling center. Juanita, an 18-year-old college freshman of Hispanic origin, sought counseling for help in exploring her career options. While in high school, Juanita planned a career in medicine. After beginning her freshman year at a large university where she could choose from a wide variety of courses and majors, she became less certain of this choice. She took the Strong to help identify occupational fields that she might wish to consider in addition to medicine. Cross-cultural research with the Strong indicates that the results are valid for members of different racial and ethnic groups, including Hispanics (Fouad, Harmon, & Hansen, 1994; Lattimore & Borgen, 1999). The most significant results from her Strong profile are shown in Table 9-1.

Administrative Indexes. The Administrative indexes provide information concerning the manner in which a person completed the

TABLE 9-1. Strong Interest Inventory Scores for Juanita, a Counseling Center Client

Scale	Score	Scale	Score
General Occupational Themes		Organizational Mgmt. (E)	32
Artistic (A)	67	Agriculture (R)	31
Investigative (I)	60	Culinary Arts (A)	28
Social (S)	48		
Enterprising (E)	42	Occupational Scales[a]	
Conventional (C)	40	Musician (A)	63
Realistic (R)	38	Nurse, RN (SI)	62
		Technical Writer (AIR)	61
Basic Interest Scales		Translator (A)	58
Music/Dramatics (A)	68	Librarian (A)	58
Writing (A)	65	Commercial Artist (ARI)	57
Art (A)	64	Fine Artist (AR)	54
Applied Arts (A)	63	Audiologist (IS)	53
Medical Science (I)	62	College Professor (IAR)	53
Medical Service (S)	62	Lawyer (A)	52
Science (I)	58	Photographer (ARE)	51
Public Speaking (E)	56	Reporter (A)	51
Social Service (S)	52	Dentist (IRA)	49
Teaching (S)	51	Psychologist (IA)	49
Law/Politics (E)	50	Occupational Therapist (SAR)	48
Mathematics (I)	48	Physician (IAR)	48
Nature (R)	47	Broadcaster (AE)	47
Sales (E)	45	Respiratory Therapist (IRA)	47
Religious Activities (S)	43	Veterinarian (IRA)	46
Merchandising (E)	42	Optometrist (IR)	45
Military Activities (R)	42		
Athletics (R)	40	Personal Style Scales	
Data Management (C)	40	Learning Environment	68
Mechanical Activities (R)	39	Risk Taking/Adventure	57
Office Services (C)	39	Leadership Style	50
Computer Activities (C)	34	Work Style	44

Note. Scales in each category are ranked from highest to lowest score. All scores are standard scores (T scores) with a mean of 50 and a standard deviation of 10. Holland codes for each scale are shown in parentheses. A = Artistic; C = Conventional; E = Enterprising; I = Investigative; R = Realistic; S = Social.

[a]Only the women's Occupational scales for which Juanita obtained a T score of 45 or higher (indicating similarity of interests with those of women employed in these occupations) are listed.

inventory. Specifically, did the person mark an unusually large proportion of *like, indifferent,* or *dislike* responses; omit a large number of items; or select a large number of unusual responses? The profile reports data on each of these matters.

First, the Response Percentage index shows the distribution of the person's responses to each of the different sections of the inventory. Most people divide their responses about equally among the three possible answers for those sections of the Strong that use a *like–indifferent–dislike* or *yes–?–no* response format. Information concerning the pattern of a client's responses is helpful in interpreting the Strong results. For example, people who mark a large proportion of *like* responses will receive relatively high scores on the General Occupational Theme and Basic Interest scales; those who mark a large proportion of *dislike* responses will receive relatively low scores on these scales.

Next, the Total Response index simply shows the number of items that the client answered. Most people complete all or most of the 317 items found on the Strong. The profile becomes suspect if this number falls below 300 (Harmon et al., 1994).

Finally, the Infrequent Responses index indicates the number of unusual or unpopular responses made by the client. This index consists of item responses infrequently selected (less than 7% of the time) by men or women in the standardization sample. The maximum possible scores on this index are 7 and 5 for men and women, respectively (Harmon et al., 1994). Infrequent responses by clients are subtracted from the maximum score. A score on this index is of concern only if it falls below zero. A subzero score on this index suggests that the client may not have properly understood or cooperated with the inventory's instructions.

Juanita's scores on the Administrative indexes (not shown in Table 9-1) are all well within the normal response ranges. Her subtotal Response Percentages for the different parts of the inventory that use a *like–indifferent–dislike* or *yes–?–no* response format were 32% *like* or *yes*, 28% *indifferent* or *?*, and 40% *dislike* or *no*, which is a fairly typical response pattern. Her score on Total Responses was 317, which shows that she answered all of the items. She obtained a score of 5 on the Infrequent Responses index—the highest score possible for her sex. This score indicates that she made no unusual responses to any of the items and supports the validity of her results.

General Occupational Theme (GOT) Scales and Basic Interest Scales.
The Strong contains two sets of general or homogeneous scales: the

GOT scales and the Basic Interest scales. These scales have been developed by a combination of logical and statistical means to ensure that all of the items for each scale represent a single type of interest.

The GOT scales provide a summary or overview of the Strong profile as well as a framework for interpreting the other scales. Each of the six GOT scales contains items selected to fit Holland's (1997) descriptions of the six types of occupational personalities. Holland found that people (as well as environments) could be broadly classified according to the six types of interests or skills shown in the hexagon in Figure 9-1. This figure shows the nature of the relationship among the six categories, which holds true across both sexes and all major ethnic and racial groups (Day & Rounds, 1998; Fouad et al., 1997). The closer the categories are to each other on the figure, the more they have in common with each other. For example, people with Social interests are more likely also to possess Artistic or Enterprising interests (interests represented by adjacent categories) than they are the other types of interests. The two dimensions underlying

FIGURE 9-1. Holland's Classification of Personality Types

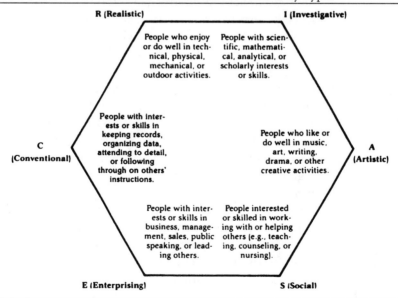

Note. Hexagon showing nature of relationship among different personality types based on Holland's (1997) theory of vocational choice.

this figure can be described as *people versus things* (Enterprising–Social vs. Realistic–Investigative) and *data versus ideas* (Conventional vs. Artistic).

The 25 Basic Interest scales function as subscales for the six GOT scales. They were grouped into the six GOT categories on the basis of correlations between the two sets of scales. Each of the GOT scales subsumes three or more of the Basic Interest scales.

Both the GOT and Basic Interest scales have been standardized by the use of T scores so that the general reference sample of men and women will obtain a mean of 50 and a standard deviation of 10. The T scores are based on combined-sex norms; however, the test authors provide bar graphs beside the scales on the profile sheet to indicate how the scores are distributed for each sex. These bar graphs show that women tend to score higher (about 5 points on average) on the Artistic scales, particularly Culinary Arts, Art, and Music/Dramatics, whereas men tend to score higher (about 6 points on average) on the Realistic scales, particularly Mechanical Activities, Athletics, and Military Activities. Women also score higher (about 4 or 5 points) than do men on the Basic Interest scale for Social Service. Counselors should keep these differences in mind when interpreting scores on these scales, especially for clients who may be considering nontraditional occupations. For example, women who become engineers do not usually score as high on the Realistic GOT scale as do men (Harmon et al., 1994).

High scores on both the GOT and Basic Interest scales are based on *like* responses, whereas low scores are based on *dislike* responses. A large number of likes indicates broad interests; a large number of dislikes indicates fairly focused interests. In either case, the interest scores should be interpreted in relationship to one another. That is, clients should give careful consideration to their highest scores regardless of their absolute level.

The GOT and Basic Interest scales yield results that are highly reliable both in terms of internal consistency and test–retest consistency over extended time periods. Empirical validity studies indicate that both sets of scales effectively discriminate among people employed in different types of occupations (Donnay & Borgen, 1996; Harmon et al., 1994).

The GOT scores can be used to arrive at a Holland code to summarize a person's interest. To determine Juanita's Holland code, we must identify her three highest scores on the GOT scales. As shown in Table 9-1, her highest scores were Artistic (A), Investigative (I), and Social (S), in that order, which remains the same even when sex norms are taken into consideration. Therefore, her Holland code is AIS.

Because the Basic Interest scales are relatively short, scores on these scales can be significantly affected by responses to a few items. The scales range in length from 5 to 21 items. The typical (median) scale possesses 12 items (Harmon et al., 1994). The Military Activities scale, for example, contains only 5 items, 3 of which pertain to marching.

As a counseling technique, it is usually helpful to ask clients to look at their four or five highest and lowest scores on the Basic Interest scales. Do they agree with this description of their interests? Can they think of ways in which they could combine the activities represented by their highest scores in a career or life plan? Juanita received her highest scores on the Music/Dramatics, Writing, Art, Applied Arts, Medical Science, and Medical Service scales. These scores show a pronounced interest in creative activities in addition to medical endeavors.

Occupational Scales. The Strong profile provides scores for 104 Occupational scales for men and 107 Occupational scales for women. The same occupations are represented for both men and women with very few exceptions.

The Occupational scales were developed by selecting items that significantly differentiated between the interests of men or women in the occupation and men or women in general. The typical scale contains 40 to 50 items selected in this manner. Members of occupational criterion groups used to develop the Occupational scales usually possessed the following characteristics:

- Employed in occupation for 3 years or more
- Satisfied with their work
- At least 25 years of age or older

- Belong to a primary professional or business organization associated with membership in that occupation
- Perform typical duties of members of the occupation

Information regarding the specific characteristics of each occupational criterion group can be obtained from the Strong manual (Harmon et al., 1994, pp. 309–376).

Each of the Occupational scales is coded in terms of the predominant interest pattern of people employed in that occupation based on Holland's classification system (see Figure 9-1). For example, the Physician scale is coded IAR (as noted in Table 9-1) for women because women who are physicians more frequently express Investigative, Artistic, and Realistic interests than do other women. The Holland codes are helpful in organizing the Occupational scores and in understanding the nature of the interests underlying the scores.

The Occupational scales have been normed so that men or women in the occupation (depending on which sex was used for constructing the scale) obtain a mean T score of 50 with a standard deviation of 10. Men and women in general obtain mean T scores of approximately 20 to 35 for most scales. Scores above 40 or 45 (referred to as "similar interests" on the Strong profile) indicate that a client endorses many of the same likes and dislikes as those that differentiate men or women in a particular occupation from men or women in general. Scores less than 25 or 30 ("dissimilar interests") indicate a rejection of this interest pattern.

Some clients receive few or no high scores on the Occupational scales. In such cases, scores can still be interpreted in relation to each other. Students with "flat" (undifferentiated) profiles may need additional time and experience to clarify their interests. A 12-year follow-up study indicated that students with flat profiles took longer to get established in their careers; however, at the end of 12 years they were just as satisfied and successful in their careers as those with differentiated profiles (S. A. Sackett & Hansen, 1995). In fact, the male students with flat profiles in this study showed a higher level of satisfaction with their jobs after 12 years than did those with differentiated profiles, possibly because they may have been easier to please.

Separate-sex scales have been established to take into account differences in social conditioning. The Strong printout gives the client's scores for both the male and female Occupational scales but only plots the score on the Strong profile for the same-sex Occupational scales. Scores on the two sets of scales are highly correlated, but men tend to obtain higher scores on cross-sex scales for occupations that have traditionally appealed to men, such as Military Officer, whereas women tend to get higher scores on cross-sex scales for occupations that women have usually preferred, such as Interior Decorator (Harmon et al., 1994). Surprisingly, scores on cross-sex scales seem to be as valid as scores on same-sex scales in predicting future occupational membership (Dolliver & Worthington, 1981).

In contrast with the GOT and Basic Interest scales, high scores on the Occupational scales are based on both *like* and *dislike* responses. People obtain high scores when they share the same likes and dislikes as people in the occupation. In essence, high scores on the Occupational scales point to occupations in which individuals can pursue those activities they enjoy and avoid those they dislike.

Although high scores for most Occupational scales are influenced primarily by *like* responses, some scales, such as Farmer, Plumber, and Radiologic Technologist, include many items with positive weights for *dislike* responses. People in these occupations possess rather narrow or focused interests. If clients mark a large number of *dislike* responses, they will probably obtain elevated scores on these scales. High scores that are based primarily on dislikes can be misleading. It is important to look at the specific likes and dislikes (as revealed by the Basic Interest scales) that underlie an Occupational score.

The Occupational scores are highly reliable, particularly for older people (age 20 and beyond) and over short time periods (less than 1 year). Even over very long time periods (10 to 20 years), the Occupational scales produce similar results for most people based on research conducted with earlier versions of the Strong.

Concurrent validation studies show that the Occupational scales significantly differentiate between people in the occupation and people in general (Harmon et al., 1994). A number of longitudinal research studies (ranging in length from 3 to 18 years) have been conducted to examine the predictive validity of earlier versions of the Strong. These studies found that from one third to two thirds of the people who took the Strong were later employed in occupations related to their high scores (Donnay, 1997).

Scores on the Occupational scales show greater validity when they are supported by scores on the Basic Interest scales that are most relevant. Occupational scores are also more valid when clients report that they have had work or volunteer experiences in those fields.

Research indicates that the Occupational scales predict occupational membership just as accurately for college students who are undecided as they do for those who are decided (Bartling & Hood, 1981). This finding is important inasmuch as the Strong is frequently used with students who are having difficulty in making a career decision.

When Occupational scores agree with expressed interests (career choice stated at the time that the Strong was completed), the predictive accuracy of Occupational scores significantly increases (Bartling & Hood, 1981). When Occupational scores disagree with expressed interests, the latter are more accurate. Expressed interests take into account factors that are not measured by the Strong, such as values, abilities, and opportunities. For example, students may follow family traditions in choosing occupations instead of basing their choices on measured interests. Counselors should recognize the limitations of an instrument such as the Strong. It provides helpful information about one's interests, but it needs to be incorporated with other relevant information.

In general, people report greater job satisfaction when their occupation matches the type of occupation suggested by their Strong scores than when it does not; however, the relationship tends to be modest. Presumably, factors other than interests, such as salary, opportunities for advancement, and relationships with supervisors or coworkers, account for much of one's satisfaction or dissatisfaction.

As indicated in Table 9-1, Juanita obtained high scores (T score of 45 or above) on a relatively large number of the Occupational scales. Her interests resembled those of women in 20 of the 107 Occupational scales for women. Her scores on the Occupational scales for men (not shown in Table 9-1) were similar to those that she received on the Occupational scales for women with several exceptions. She obtained a high score (45 or above) on five scales for men for which she obtained a significantly lower score (10 points or more) on the women's scales. Each of these scales (Art Teacher, Speech Pathologist, English Teacher, Advertising Executive, and Public Relations Director) emphasizes artistic or social interests, areas in which women traditionally express more interests than do men.

Scores on the Occupational scales can be interpreted by referring to both the GOT scales and the Basic Interest scales. All of the Occupational scales for which Juanita obtained a high score (45 or higher) possess Artistic, Investigative, or Social primary codes. Of her 6 highest scores (55 or greater), 5 of the scales (Musician, Technical Writer, Librarian, Translator, and Commercial Artist) can be interpreted in terms of her high scores on the Artistic GOT scale and the Music/Dramatics, Writing, Art, and Applied Arts Basic Interest scales. The sixth scale, Registered Nurse, reflects her high scores on the Investigative GOT scale and the Medical Science and Medical Service Basic Interest scales. The scores on the GOT and Basic Interest scales clarify the nature of the occupational interest patterns represented by the Occupational scales.

Personal Style Scales. The 1994 version of the Strong includes four Personal Style scales that measure personality factors related to educational and career planning. These four scales, each of which is bipolar in nature, are briefly described below.

- Work Style: High scorers prefer to work with people; low scorers prefer to work with ideas, data, or things.
- Learning Environment: High scorers possess academic interests associated with advanced degrees; low scorers possess practical interests associated with technical or trade school attendance.
- Leadership Style: High scorers prefer to direct others; low scorers prefer to lead by example.
- Risk Taking/Adventure: High scorers prefer to take chances; low scorers prefer to play it safe.

Scores on all of these scales correlate highly with scores on the GOT scales (Harmon et al., 1994, p. 164). The Work Style scale is positively correlated with scores on the Social and Enterprising GOT scales and negatively correlated with scores on the Realistic and Investigative scales. The Learning Environment scale possesses much in common with the Investigative and Artistic GOT scales, whereas the Leadership Style scale overlaps to a large extent with the Enterprising, Social, and Artistic scales. The Risk Taking/Adventure scale is highly correlated with scores on the Realistic GOT scale.

Although not as effective as the GOT or Basic Interest scales, the Personal Style scales significantly add to the validity of both of these sets of scales in differentiating among occupational groups (Donnay & Borgen, 1996). The Personal Style scales can be used as a means of introducing personality factors into career planning; however, counselors should be careful not to overinterpret the meaning of these scales.

Counselors can usually best interpret these scales by referring directly to the GOT scales. Juanita's score, for example, was very high on the Learning Environment scale, which can be explained in terms of her high scores on the Artistic and Investigative GOT scales.

Interpretation of Client Profile. Much of Juanita's profile has been discussed in preceding paragraphs. As a means of obtaining some focus, we asked Juanita to select several occupations on the Strong profile that had the most appeal to her. We asked her to look particularly at the scales for which she received scores indicating similarity of interests (including men's Occupational scales as well as women's Occupational scales) but not to exclude any occupations. She chose the following occupations, in addition to physician: technical writer, reporter, and broadcaster. She had obtained scores showing similarity between her interests and those of people employed in each of the occupations listed above. We discussed ways in which she could obtain more information about these career possibilities, which included visiting departmental representatives on campus for each of the academic majors in these fields, interviewing people employed in these fields, reading about the occupations in the current edition of the *Occupational Outlook Handbook* (U.S. Department of Labor, 2000) and related materials, and possibly taking a course in these areas or doing volunteer work in a related field.

She was pleased to obtain information from her Strong profile that suggested several career options other than physician for her to consider. The Strong enabled her to evaluate systematically her interests in regard to different career fields, which was the type of information that she needed at the time.

Skills Confidence Inventory (SCI).   Scores on the Strong may be supplemented with information from the SCI, a new 60-item measure that asks clients to estimate their abilities in the same six Holland categories used to organize scores on the Strong (Betz, Borgen, & Harmon, 1996). Donnay and Borgen (1999) found that the SCI scores enhanced the validity of the Strong in differentiating among members of 21 occupational groups.

The Kuder Interest Inventories

G. Frederic Kuder (1903–2000) developed a number of interest inventories that have had a large impact on counseling. Three of his interest inventories, all widely used, are discussed below. First, the Kuder Vocational Preference Record, which was first published in 1939, served as a popular measure of basic interests until it was replaced by the Kuder General Interest Survey (KGIS) in 1963. Next, the Kuder Occupational Interest Survey (KOIS) was created to provide a measure of occupational interests similar to the Occupational scales on the Strong Interest Inventory. Finally, the Kuder Career Search (KCS), which compares one's interests with those of specific people in various occupations, represented Kuder's most recent efforts to assess vocational interests (Zytowski, 1992). The KGIS, KOIS, and KCS are each discussed below.

All of the Kuder interest inventories present items as forced-choice triads. Clients must select which of three types of activities they prefer most and which they prefer least. For example, one forced-choice triad includes the following items: "Build birdhouses," "Write articles about birds," and "Draw sketches of birds." The use of forced-choice triads controls for response styles such as acquiescence (marking *like* to most items) and deviation (making extreme responses to most items).

The forced-choice item format affects the interpretation of the results. The scores must be interpreted in regard to each other. A high score indicates that the person likes that type of activity more than other activities compared with members of the norm group, but it does not indicate the absolute magnitude of the interest.

The Kuder Task Self-Efficacy Scale (KTSES), a 30-item scale that measures a client's self-confidence in each of the 10 general interest areas found on all of the Kuder interest inventories, may be used in combination with any of the Kuder interest inventories (Lucas, Wanberg, & Zytowski, 1997). The KTSES, which serves the same purpose for the Kuder interest inventories as the Skills Confidence Inventory does for the Strong, enables the counselor and the client to compare self-rated abilities with interests in the same fields.

Kuder General Interest Survey (KGIS), Form E.   The KGIS, which has a sixth-grade reading level, has been designed so that it may be used with students as early as the sixth grade and with adults who have limited reading ability (Kuder, 1988). It provides scores for 10 general scales based on the client's responses to 168 forced-choice triads. These scales are similar to the Holland scales found on many interest inventories as indicated below:

Holland scales	Comparable KGIS scale
Realistic	Outdoor and Mechanical
Investigative	Scientific
Artistic	Artistic, Literary, and Musical
Social	Social Service
Enterprising	Persuasive
Conventional	Clerical and Computational

The verification score (V score) can be used to identify answer sheets that may be answered carelessly, insincerely, or improperly. This scale includes items that are rarely marked by students who are trying to answer honestly and who have paid careful attention to the instructions. Profiles with V scores equal to or above 15 should be reviewed with students for possible problems.

A relatively large number of young people obtain elevated V scores. According to the manual, 25% of middle school boys and 12% of middle school girls obtain V scores of 15 or higher. Such scores may reflect immaturity in regard to development of interests. As a general rule, the KGIS should not be interpreted for such students. These students should be readministered the KGIS at a later point in their educational program.

Answer sheets may be self-scored or scored on the computer. One research study indicated that errors were fairly common on self-scored answer sheets (Lampe, 1985). Counselors should check to make certain that hand-scored answer sheets have been correctly scored. Most people can complete the revised instrument in 45 to 60 minutes. Additional time should be provided if students are asked to score their own answer sheets.

Separate-sex norms are used for middle school (Grades 6 through 8) and high school (Grades 9 through 12) students. Unfortunately, descriptive information regarding the sample, such as ethnicity, social class, and economic class, is not available (Mehrens, 1994). Research indicates that separate norms may be necessary for some minority groups or subcultures. Kuder (1988) encouraged test users to develop local norms if they believe that their student or client population differed from the published norms.

The KGIS scales provide results that are sufficiently reliable for academic or career exploration purposes. The median test–retest reliabilities are close to .80 for middle school boys and girls and for high school boys and girls tested twice over a 2-week period.

Longitudinal research studies indicate that most of the students tested in their teenage years are employed in occupations related to their highest scores in later years (Kuder, 1988). People employed in occupations consistent with their interests also report greater job satisfaction compared with individuals in jobs inconsistent with their interests. These studies support the validity of the Kuder; however, these same studies also show that a surprisingly large number of students also become happily employed in occupations that would not have been predicted by their Kuder scores. The interest scores provide valuable information, but they should be looked upon as just one of a number of factors that need to be considered in academic or career planning.

Kuder Occupational Interest Survey (KOIS), Form DD. The KOIS is similar to the KGIS in its item format but uses fewer items (100 forced-choice triads) and an expanded set of scales based on a different scoring procedure. It includes a shortened version of the 10 general scales (called Vocational Interest Estimates) and a large number of Occupational and College Major scales (Kuder & Zytowski, 1991) that are scored by comparing one's interests with those of different occupational criterion groups. It also includes a modified version of the V score used with the KGIS and several "experimental" scales in the early stage of development.

The KOIS has a sixth-grade reading level but should not be used with students until they are in the 10th grade because of the specificity of the Occupational and College Major scores. Most people complete the KOIS within 30 minutes. A computer must be used to score the answer sheets.

The KOIS resembles the Strong Interest Inventory in its use of Occupational scales; however, the scores on the Occupational scales are determined differently. Instead of selecting items that differentiated between members of an occupation and people in general to form an Occupational scale, Kuder calculated correlation coefficients (called lambda coefficients) directly between an individual's responses to each of the 100 triads and the mean responses of occupational members to each of the 100 triads. High lambda coefficients (.45 or better) indicate that the individual's interests are similar to those of people in the occupational criterion group. KOIS profiles with lambda scores of .50 or better (which indicates a well-differentiated interest pattern) are associated with greater predictive validity and profile stability (Zytowski & England, 1994).

Occupational scales based on lambda correlations offer a number of advantages. Not only are they easier to construct and simpler to interpret than scales based on the use of a general reference group, but they also appear to be more effective in correctly identifying members of different occupational groups. Kuder and Zytowski (1991) reported that lambda scores produced significantly fewer errors of classification than did Strong's system in a study that involved the use of both types of scales.

The current version of the KOIS includes a total of 109 Occupational scales (65 male scales and 44 female scales) and 40 College Major scales (22 male scales and 18 female scales; Kuder & Zytowski, 1991). Men and women are scored on all scales, but scores for the female scales are listed separately from scores for the male scales. Most people will obtain higher scores on scales based on their own sex; however, the rank order of the scores for matching male and females scales will usually be similar.

Profile scores show high levels of reliability for both sexes at both the high school and college level. Median test–retest profile reliabilities over short time periods for the Occupational scales equaled or exceeded .90 for all studies reported in the manual.

Kuder and Zytowksi (1991) studied the validity of the Occupational and College Major scales in differentiating among the interests of 3,000 individuals drawn from 30 "core" occupations and college majors. Two thirds of the 3,000 respondents in their study obtained their highest score on their own Occupational or College Major scale. All but 10% of the total group obtained scores on their own scales that were within .06 points of their highest score (i.e., in their top group of scores). The typical scale showed very little overlap of scores with the other scales. Most overlap occurred with scales that were highly related, such as Clinical Psychologist and Social Caseworker. The scales effectively differentiated among the interests of people engaged in a variety of occupations or college majors.

The scores can also be used to predict future occupation or college major with a fair degree of success. The predictive validities for the two sets of scales compare favorably with those reported for the Occupational scales on the Strong.

Kuder Career Search (KCS) With Person Match. The KCS differs from the KOIS in that it compares one's interests with those of other individuals instead of occupational groups (National Career Assessment Services, Inc., 2000). It contains 60 forced-choice triads, which can usually be completed in 20 to 25 minutes. On the basis of their answers to these items, clients receive scores on 6 occupational cluster scales similar to the 6 Holland scales used on other interest inventories and on 10 activity preference scales. The 10 activity preference scales are the same as those on the KGIS and KOIS, except the Music scale (which did not prove to be as useful as other scales in describing career behavior) has been replaced with a Management scale (Zytowski, 2001).

The client's scores on the 10 activity preference scales are ranked in order and correlated with the rank orders of activity preferences for the 2,500 individuals in the KCS occupational database. Clients receive detailed descriptions of the individual careers and lifestyles of the 25 people (top 1%) who most closely resemble themselves in terms of interests. The descriptions include information about how their career was chosen, specific job duties, likes and dislikes, and future career plans. In essence, this approach provides clients with the equivalent of 25 informational interviews with employed adults similar to themselves who have found satisfying occupations.

Nearly all of the occupations included in the *Occupational Outlook Handbook* (U.S. Department of Labor, 2000) are represented within the KCS occupational database. Occupations with a large number of members are represented by at least several individuals; for example, the database includes descriptive information for more than 10 pilots. All members of the database must be satisfied in their work and must have at least 3 years of work experience.

The KCS has been designed to help clients realize their multipotentiality, as shown by the wide range of occupations typically represented by the 25 individual descriptions. This technique uses "stories instead of scores" to suggest a variety of career paths to a client (Savickas, 1993). The purpose of the KCS is to encourage clients to identify and explore various career possibilities.

The KCS can be completed and scored on the Internet. Separate-sex norms are provided for middle school students and for high school/college students for the activity preference and occupational cluster scales. Because of the emphasis on person match, combined-sex norms have been used to identify individuals with interest patterns most like the client (D. G. Zytowski, personal communication, December 26, 2000).

In terms of reliability, scores on the activity preference scales showed a moderate degree of internal consistency (median $\alpha = .71$) for 146 adults who completed the KCS during an on-line administration. Activity preference profiles were relatively stable (median $r = .81$) for clients who completed a paper-and-pencil form twice over a 3-week period (National Career Assessment Services, Inc., 2000).

In keeping with the purpose of the KCS With Person Match, it needs to be validated in terms of its success in motivating clients to engage in career exploration. Studies of this nature are planned but not yet completed. The client report form includes a number of suggestions to help clients to interpret their test results and investigate career options.

Information concerning the KCS, including a tutorial regarding its use, can be found on its Web site (National Career Assessment Services, Inc., 2000). The tutorial provides several exercises that clients can use to aid them in career planning. For example, clients are taught to search for themes among the 25 individual career descriptions that they receive. A case example describing the use of the KCS With Person Match is included in the tutorial. Clients may use the KCS in conjunction with the lifelong Kuder Electronic Career Portfolio (National Career Assessment Services, Inc., 2001).

Career Assessment Inventory (CAI)

The CAI was first constructed in 1975 by Charles Johansson to measure career interests at the technical and skilled trades level. At that time, it complemented the Strong, which was designed to evaluate interest patterns of men and women considering business or professional occupations. Since that time, both instruments have changed. The Strong now includes a number of scales for occupations that require less than a college education. In 1986, the CAI was expanded so that it now contains a large number of scales for occupations that require a 4-year college degree or advanced training in a professional program (Johansson, 1986).

NCS Pearson, the publisher of the CAI, continues to publish the original (or "blue-collar") version of the CAI as well as the new version. The original version, which has been updated several times, is now known as the CAI–Vocational Version (CAI-VV), whereas the new version is entitled CAI–Enhanced Version (CAI-EV; Johansson, 1984, 1986). CAI-VV is shorter and has a lower reading level than CAI-EV. The former includes 305 items written at a sixth-grade reading level; the latter contains 370 items written at an eighth-grade reading level. CAI-VV should be used with secondary school students or adults who do not plan to obtain a 4-year college degree. The CAI-EV, on the other hand, should be used with individuals in the ninth grade or beyond who wish to consider a broad range of occupations, including those that require a college degree.

Both versions of the CAI consist of three types of items—Activities, School Subjects, and Occupations—each of which uses a five-step response format (L = *like very much*, l = *like somewhat*, I = *indifferent*, d = *dislike somewhat*, and D = *dislike very much*). The most recent version of the inventory provides brief definitions for each of the items that use occupational titles. For example, the term *biologist* is followed by the phrase "Studies plants and animals."

Both versions of the CAI are patterned after the Strong. They both include the same types of scales: Administrative indices, Nonoccupational scales (called Personal Style scales on the Strong), General Theme scales (identical to the General Occupational Theme scales on the Strong), Basic Interest scales, and Occupational scales.

The Nonoccupational scales, which were added to the different forms of the CAI for the first time in 1984, include the Fine Arts–Mechanical scale (an updated version of the Masculinity–Femininity scale that used to appear on the Strong), Extroversion–Introversion scale, Educational Orientation scale (similar to the Learning Environment scale on the Strong), and Variability of Interests scale. These scales provide some insights regarding the personality factors associated with one's career interest patterns; however, they lack the validity of the other scales on the CAI.

Scores on the General Theme scales and Basic Interest scales are highly correlated with parallel scales on the Strong for both the CAI-VV and CAI-EV (Johansson, 1984, 1986). Test–retest studies indicate that scores on these scales are highly consistent over relatively long time periods for college students and adults.

The CAI differs from the Strong by providing combined-sex scales for all of the 111 Occupational scales on the CAI-EV and 32 of the 91 Occupational scales on the CAI-VV. The same scales serve both men and women. Only core items, which differentiate between the interests of both men and women in the occupation and men and women in general, are included on these scales. Items that show significant differences for only one sex have been rejected. For this reason, the scales contain fewer items than do the Occupational scales on the Strong. The reliability coefficients are slightly lower than they would be if longer scales were used; however, use of the combined-sex scales greatly simplifies interpretation of the results.

As with the Strong, the CAI Occupational scales have been coded according to Holland's classification system. The two systems produce similar results in most cases. In a manner similar to the Strong, the Occupational scales have been normed so that people in the occupation will obtain a mean score of 50 with a standard deviation of 10. Scores of 45 and above indicate similarity of interests with those of people employed in the occupation.

Despite the use of fewer items, the CAI Occupational scales for both versions appear to be as reliable and valid as comparable scales on the Strong. The CAI scales clearly distinguish among the interest patterns of people employed in different fields. For the typical scale, workers in the occupational criterion samples averaged about two standard deviations above the mean of those in the general reference samples. The CAI inventories match the success of the Strong is this regard; however, these results have not been cross-validated with independent samples.

The CAI inventories lack the extensive research base that has been established for both the Strong and the Kuder inventories. Test authorities have noted that both versions of the CAI have merit but fall short in some of their technical aspects, such as limited descriptive data for the normative samples, small sizes of some of the occupational criterion samples, and insufficient predictive validity data (Rounds, 1989; Vacc & Hinkle, 1994).

An example of the use of the CAI-EV in counseling is presented below.

CASE EXAMPLE

Tom requested counseling to help him decide on a training program. He had already taken some coursework in his community college but lacked a career direction. The counselor assigned the CAI-EV to Tom to assess his interests in regard to various career possibilities.

Tom obtained high scores (75th percentile or greater) on the Realistic General Theme scale and on each of the following Basic Interest subscales within the Realistic field: Carpentry, Athletics/Sports, Manual/Skilled Training, and Mechanical/Fixing. He also received a high score on the Performing/Entertaining scale from the Artistic field. When his likes and dislikes were compared with people in different occupations, he obtained high Occupational scores (45 or greater) on each of the following scales: Drafter, Painter, Carpenter, Firefighter, Pipefitter/Plumber, Architect, Piano Technician, Card/Gift Shop Manager, and Surveyor.

After studying his results, he expressed an interest in exploring the following occupations: drafter, photogrammetrist or cartographer (suggested by the *Occupational Outlook Handbook* as occupations similar to Drafter and Surveyor), painter, carpenter, and architect. He planned to read about these occupations and to visit with advisers who could provide information to him about training programs in these fields. The CAI thus helped him to focus his career exploration efforts.

Jackson Vocational Interest Survey (JVIS)

The JVIS, which has recently been revised, can serve as an alternative to the interest inventories described above (D. N. Jackson, 1999). The instrument has been designed for counselors to use in educational and career planning with high school students, college students, and other adults. The revised version includes new norms based on a sample of 3,500 individuals.

Respondents must choose between 289 pairs of items that measure interests in different types of job-related activities. The items have been paired to control for response bias. Most people can complete the JVIS in 45 minutes to 1 hour.

Similar to the Strong, the JVIS includes administrative indices, general occupational theme scales, basic interest scales, occupational scores, and a nonoccupational scale (Academic Satisfaction). It differs from the Strong by including measures of academic interests and by its emphasis on occupational clusters instead of specific occupations. Scores are provided for a total of 17 academic major clusters, such as Performing Arts and Environmental Resource Management, and for 32 occupational clusters, such as Agriculturalists and Health Service Workers.

The JVIS differs from most other interest inventories by including items that measure interests in different types of work environments (work style items) as well as different types of work activities (work role items). Of the 34 Basic Interest scales, 8 reflect work style preferences. The work style preference Basic Interest scales, such as Independence and Job Security, are similar to the types of scales often included on values inventories.

The measures of occupational and academic major interests are unique in that these measures are derived from the scores on the Basic Interest scales. Scores for each of the 17 academic major and 32 occupational clusters are reported as correlation coefficients that show the degree of similarity between one's basic interest profile and the basic interests of people in different majors and occupations. In this manner, Jackson has been able to make use of vast amounts of archival data accumulated for the Strong Interest Inventory.

Reliability studies reported in the manual indicate adequate test–retest reliability and internal consistency for the General Occupational Theme and Basic Interest scales for normative samples.

Scores on these scales are highly correlated with similar scales on other interest inventories. Less information is known about the reliability and validity of the academic major and occupational cluster scores; however, one study indicated that the academic major scores were more successful than scores from other interest inventories in correctly identifying college students' academic majors. Jepsen (1994) believed that clients may achieve a "greater breadth and depth in understanding the nature of their interests" (p. 187) with the JVIS than with other interest inventories.

INTERPRETATION OF INTEREST INVENTORIES IN COUNSELING

Suggestions for interpreting interest inventories to clients include the following:

1. Check to make certain that the client has answered a sufficient number of items and to ensure that the client understood and followed the directions. Total response and infrequent response indices should be helpful for this purpose. Check all validity indices, such as the V score on the Kuder interest inventories.

2. Keep the purpose for assigning the inventory in mind. Review this purpose with the client before interpreting the results.

3. Ask clients about their reactions to the inventory before interpreting the results. If possible, allow clients time to inspect their profile and to formulate questions before discussing the results with them.

4. Note the percentage distribution of *like*, *indifferent*, and *dislike* responses for interest inventories with this type of response format. Remember that high scores on general or basic interest scales are based on likes, whereas low scores on these scales are based on dislikes. If a client marks an unusually high or low percentage of either likes or dislikes, be sure to interpret scores relatively; that is, give greatest consideration to the highest scores, regardless of their absolute level.

5. Interpret the general (homogeneous) scales first. Help the client to determine his or her Holland code. Use these scales as a framework for interpreting the occupational scales. Prince (1998) suggested that the interpretation interview be adapted to the client's personality style as suggested by the Holland code. For example, Artistic types may

prefer an interpretation process that is relatively unstructured and that encourages the client to be creative in reflecting on test scores.

6. When available, use separate-sex norms in interpreting scores on the interest scales. The separate-sex norms take into account the differences in the socialization process for men and women, which can affect the validity of the scales.

7. Interpret the occupational scores as measuring similarity of interest patterns compared with those of people in the occupation. Emphasize that the scores reflect interests rather than abilities. The scores can be used to help predict job satisfaction but not job success.

8. Do not overinterpret small differences in scores between scales. If *T* scores fall within 8 to 10 points of each other, do not consider them to be significantly different from each other for most scales.

9. Refer to *dislike* as well as *like* responses in interpreting high scores on Occupational scales. A client can obtain high scores for some Occupational scales simply by sharing the same dislikes that people in the occupation possess.

10. Relate the scores to other information, such as stated interests, work experience, academic background, career plans, and other test data concerning the client. Assist the client in addressing inconsistencies both within the test data and between the test data and other data. Help the client in integrating the assessment data and in generating hypotheses that may be helpful in understanding career conflicts and suggesting directions for further career exploration.

11. Use information from special scales, such as the Personal Style scales on the Strong or the Experimental scales on the KOIS, with caution. The same type of information can often be obtained from the general scales in a more understandable fashion.

12. Bring into consideration occupations that are not on the profile by using Holland's occupational classification system (G. D. Gottfredson & Holland, 1996). Use the O*NET database on the Internet to identify occupations that match the client's interest pattern based on Holland's system (National Center for O*NET Development, 2001; Rounds, Smith, Hubert, Lewis, & Rivkin, 1999).

13. When feasible, use the interest inventory together with other assessment procedures to obtain a more complete picture of the client's situation. For example, the Strong may be used productively with the Skills Confidence Inventory and the Myers–Briggs Type Indi-

cator in career planning (Donnay & Borgen, 1999; Katz, Joyner, & Seaman, 1999) or with the Adult Career Concerns Inventory, Career Development Inventory, Values Scale, and Salience Inventory as part of a career development assessment package (Osborne, Brown, Niles, & Miner, 1997).

14. Ask clients to identify four or five occupations or two or three career-related questions suggested by the interest inventory that they would like to investigate. Suggest sources of occupational and educational information, including the *Occupational Outlook Handbook*, O*NET database (National Center for O*NET Development, 2001), career pamphlets, informational interviews, and volunteer work.

15. Schedule a follow-up interview with clients to help them review their progress and address issues that they may have identified during the career exploration process.

SUMMARY

1. Interest inventories differ in the types of scales they use. General (homogeneous content) scales, which measure interests in different types of activities, provide scores that can be easily interpreted. Occupational (heterogeneous content) scales, which measure the similarity between one's interests and those of people employed in different occupations, yield scores that summarize one's interest patterns.

2. Counselors should carefully consider the circumstances for assigning an interest inventory to a client. These circumstances include the purpose for testing, the client's motivation for taking the inventory, the client's emotional adjustment, and the availability of other interest measures, among other matters. Card sorts should be used to explore underlying reasons for career preferences.

3. The Strong Interest Inventory, which contains both general and occupational scales based on Holland's theory of career choice, represents the most thoroughly developed interest inventory for people considering business or professional occupations.

4. Three different Kuder interest inventories exist for counseling use. The Kuder General Interest Survey, which is most appropriate for younger clients, provides scores on 10 general interest scales. The Kuder Occupational Interest Survey includes a large number of

occupational and college major scales. The new Kuder Career Search, which functions as an informational interview, provides detailed descriptions of the career development of satisfied and successful workers who have interests similar to those of the client.

5. The Career Assessment Inventory–Vocational Version has been designed for use with people considering technical, clerical, or skilled trades occupations. The Career Assessment Inventory– Enhanced Version provides a broader measure of interests than the Vocational Version by also including occupations that require a college degree.

6. The Jackson Vocational Interest Survey provides a comprehensive view of one's preferences for work environments as well as work activities.

7. Counselors should use all of the scales on an interest inventory in combination to understand a client's profile. The Administrative scales, especially response patterns, should be reviewed. The General scales should be used to help interpret the Occupational scales.

10

COMPREHENSIVE ASSESSMENT PROGRAMS FOR CAREER AND LIFE PLANNING

C OMPREHENSIVE ASSESSMENT PROGRAMS MEASURE a combination of one's values, interests, and aptitudes. Most programs include a means for identifying academic, career, or social environments that would be compatible with a person's preferences and abilities. All of these assessment packages use self-reports to measure interests or values; however, they differ in regard to the use of standardization procedures and the manner in which abilities are assessed. Some of the programs adhere to test standardization procedures, whereas others do not. For those programs that are standardized, some use self-ratings to assess abilities, whereas others use objective tests. Each of these different types of comprehensive assessment programs is discussed in this chapter.

NONSTANDARDIZED ASSESSMENT PROGRAMS

Career and life planning programs based on nonstandardized assessments include computer-based programs and career education workbooks. These programs use self-ratings to help clients organize their thinking about themselves and various opportunities. They have been validated primarily in terms of their success in encouraging people to explore various occupations and in enabling individuals to make progress in their career decision making.

Research shows that *informed* self-ratings can predict performance at least as accurately as standardized tests in many situations (American College Testing Program, 1998b; Norris & Cochran, 1977; Shrauger & Osberg, 1981). Self-ratings will be most accurate when clients know specifically what aspects of their behavior are being predicted, when questions are phrased as directly as possible, when the counselor helps the client to recall previous behavior in similar situations, and when clients are motivated to cooperate (Shrauger & Osberg, 1981).

Computer-Based Programs

A number of computer-based career and life planning programs have been developed in recent years. These programs assist clients in self-assessment, environmental assessment (i.e., educational and occupational information), and decision making. The self-assessment modules usually ask clients to evaluate their interests, values, and skills. On the basis of the self-evaluations, the computer generates a list of appropriate occupations.

Two popular programs are SIGI+ (System of Interactive Guidance and Information), a product of the Educational Testing Service, and DISCOVER, a creation of the American College Testing Program (ACT). (Separate versions of DISCOVER have been developed for college students and adults, high school students, and middle school students.) Both programs are comprehensive, interactive, and simple to use, and both are updated each year. Students and counselors react positively to both programs (Kapes, Borman, & Frazier, 1989).

Research indicates that use of computer-based programs leads to increased retention of career information and to greater certainty of occupational choice (Eveland, Conyne, & Blakney, 1998; Pyle, 1984). In a comprehensive review of research on the effectiveness of

DISCOVER, Taber and Luzzo (1999) found that it increased users' vocational identity, level of career development, and self-confidence in career decision making. The programs are most effective when they are used in conjunction with counseling (Eveland et al., 1998; Kapes et al., 1989; Taber & Luzzo, 1999). The effectiveness of computer-based programs does not appear to be influenced by a client's age, gender, or race (Eveland et al., 1998).

In addition to the commercial programs described above, the computer may be used to access free self-assessment instruments on the Internet, such as the Career Key (Jones, 2000) and the Career Questionnaire (College Board, 2001). The National Consortium of State Career Guidance Supervisors (1999) recommends the use of both of these instruments for career planning.

Career and Life Planning Workbooks

Career and life planning workbooks play an important part in comprehensive self-rating programs used by counselors. These workbooks usually include a number of exercises that can be used by clients to assess their interests, values, personality style, and skills. Additional exercises aid clients in exploring the work environment by means of informational interviews and reviews of career literature. The workbooks are well suited to career education classes or career exploration groups. They often use a decision-making or problem-solving model as a framework for presentation of the exercises.

Examples of effective career and life planning workbooks include *What Color Is Your Parachute?* (Bolles, 2001), *Career Development and Planning: A Comprehensive Approach* (textbook, student manual, and instructor's manual; Reardon, Lenz, Sampson, & Peterson, 2000), and *Working Well, Living Well: Discover the Career Within You* (C. F. Wells & Carney, 1998). Exercises provided in the workbooks are informal or qualitative in nature. They are meant to stimulate interest in career exploration by offering a variety of assessment procedures in a systematic fashion.

The *Quick Job-Hunting Map for Beginners*, a short self-assessment workbook, enables clients to identify transferable work skills represented in the different types of activities that they have pursued in their lives (Bolles, 1990). The advanced version of this workbook provides a checklist of over 150 different types of skills that clients use for evaluating their work and life experiences (Bolles, 1991). Similar types of exercises designed to aid clients in self-assessment can be found in workbooks accompanying computer-based career planning programs, such as the *Career Skills Workbook* (Center on Education and Work, 1999).

STANDARDIZED ASSESSMENT PROGRAMS WITH SELF-REPORT MEASURES OF ABILITIES

Although most standardized assessment programs use self-report inventories to evaluate motivational factors such as interests and values, they vary in their approach to measuring abilities. Assessment programs are likely to use self-reports to evaluate abilities when the results are used for counseling. In contrast, assessment programs often use objective tests to assess abilities when the results may be used for selection or placement purposes.

Both procedures for assessing abilities offer certain advantages, which are reflected in the manner in which they are used. On the one hand, self-assessments permit the evaluation of many abilities that are difficult to measure with objective tests, such as interpersonal skills, leadership, organizational skills, and creativity. Prediger and Swaney (1992) found that the effectiveness of multiple aptitude tests in differentiating among students in different career fields could be significantly improved by the addition of self-assessments. On the other hand, objective tests ensure the validity of test results in those situations in which clients' responses may be biased or distorted, such as may occur when tests are used as a basis for selection. Objective tests can also be used in assessing the abilities of clients who may not have an adequate basis for judging their own abilities.

Standardized assessment programs that use self-report measures of abilities are discussed below. These programs include the Self-Directed Search (SDS), Career Decision-Making System–Revised (CDM-R), and Campbell Interest and Skill Survey (CISS). Although both the SDS and CDM-R use raw scores instead of standard scores in interpreting their results, they are standardized in the sense that they use uniform testing and scoring procedures, they use extensive occupational data in interpreting the results and they have been systematically studied in regard to reliability and validity.

Self-Directed Search (SDS)

The SDS (4th edition), which can be self-administered, self-scored, and self-interpreted, is based on Holland's (1997) theory of vocational choice. Holland's theory can be summarized as a "person–environment interaction theory" that assumes that people will be most satisfied and successful if they live and work in an environment that is compatible with their interests and skills (Spokane & Catalano, 2000). Although it is sometimes classified as an interest inventory, the SDS is actually an inventory of both interests and abilities. Holland referred to it as a career counseling simulation.

The SDS consists of sections that ask respondents to indicate their liking for activities (66 items) or occupations (84 items) as well as sections that inquire about competencies (66 items) and abilities (12 self-rating scales). Four versions of this instrument have been created for different populations (Holland, Powell, & Fritzsche, 1994). These versions include the Regular Form (Form R) for high school students, college students, and adults; the Easy Form (Form E) for adults or high school students who possess limited education or reading ability; the Career Planning Form (Form CP) for people who plan to enter a profession or higher level occupation; and the SDS Career Explorer for middle school and junior high school students. The SDS Form R may be completed on the Internet as well as by paper-and-pencil (Psychological Assessment Resources, 1998).

Each part of the SDS includes an equal number of items from each of the six Holland categories (Realistic, Investigative, Artistic, Social, Enterprising, and Conventional) as described in Chapter 9. Based on the test taker's responses, a three-letter Holland code is derived that can then be compared with the Holland code for various occupations or college majors. The *Occupations Finder*, a booklet that accompanies the SDS, lists over 1,300 occupations according to their Holland code and the amount of education required. Holland codes for each of 12,860 different occupations defined in the *Dictionary of Occupational Titles* and its supplements are provided in a separate publication (G. D. Gottfredson & Holland, 1996). Codes for more than 750 postsecondary fields of study are given in *The Educational Opportunities Finder* (D. Rosen, Holmberg, & Holland, 1994). Finally, two-letter codes for over 750 leisure activities have been published for use in life planning outside of careers (Holmberg, Rosen, & Holland, 1990).

Many of the codes that Holland and his colleagues have assigned to different occupations are based primarily on judgments of job analysts. These codes may differ from the codes assigned by authors of interest inventories based on actual test scores. For example, a college or university faculty member is coded as an SEI (Social–Enterprising–Investigative) occupation in the *Occupations Finder*, whereas a college professor is coded as an IAS (Investigative, Artistic, Social) occupation for men and as an IAR (Investigative, Artistic, Realistic) occupation for women on the Strong (Harmon et al., 1994). In most cases, the codes based on the two types of systems agree. When they disagree, codes derived by means of actual data should be given greater weight.

The SDS uses the client's raw scores in determining Holland codes. Holland has been criticized for this approach in that it reinforces sexual stereotypes. With the use of raw scores, men are more likely to obtain high scores on the Realistic, Investigative, and Enterprising scales, and women are more likely to score high on the Social, Artistic, and Conventional scales than they would if scores based on separate-sex norms were used. Holland defended his approach as reflecting the real world, namely, that men and women are in fact attracted to different types of activities (Holland, Fritzsche, & Powell, 1994).

Holland has recommended that the SDS be supplemented with another inventory that he has developed, My Vocational Situation (MVS), which measures aspects of vocational identity not measured by the SDS (see Chapter 7). Clients with a clear vocational identity probably need relatively little assistance from counselors. The SDS may be sufficient for such clients. Clients who score low on the Vocational Identity scale (indicating difficulties in self-perception) are more likely to need individual counseling or other interventions, such as career seminars or volunteer experiences, in addition to the SDS. Similarly, clients who show a need for occupational information or who face external barriers to their career development, such as lack of financial support, parental disapproval of career choice, or lack of ability to complete a training program, probably could profit from individual counseling. The SDS may also be supplemented with the Vocational Exploration Insight Kit for clients who desire a more intensified assessment (Holland, 1992).

A large number of research studies have found that taking, scoring, and interpreting the SDS can be therapeutic in itself even without the aid of a counselor. People who participate in this process report an increased number of career options, increased satisfaction with career choice, and increased self-understanding (Holland, Fritzsche, & Powell, 1994). Results have been equally positive for clients from different cultures.

A case example illustrating the use of the SDS in counseling is presented below:

CASE EXAMPLE

Lisa, a college sophomore, completed both the SDS and the MVS to help her in career exploration after she was dropped from her academic program for poor grades. She had been majoring in biology, with plans to become a dentist, but had lost interest in this career goal some time ago. She planned to reconsider her career plans during the next 3 to 4 months, then reapply to the university the following semester. According to the SDS, her Holland code was ESI (Enterprising–Social–Investigative). In discussing these results, she indicated that she wished to consider the possibility of pursuing a career in business with an emphasis on the environment. The MVS indicated that she lacked occupational information. She planned to take advantage of the time that she would not be in college to explore this type of career direction by talking with people in the field, reading relevant materials, and obtaining volunteer or paid employment in a related field.

Career Decision-Making System–Revised (CDM-R)

The CDM-R, by Harrington and O'Shea (1992), Level 2 (high school students and adults) asks clients to rate themselves in terms of career fields, school subjects, school plans, job values, abilities, and interests. Greatest emphasis is placed on interests, which are assessed by means of 120 items. Each of the six Holland interest categories is represented by 20 items.

Level 1 (Grades 7 through 10) was included as part of the CDM for the first time in the revised edition. It provides a simplified version of Level 2 consisting of 96 interest items. For both forms, clients score their own answer sheets by simply counting the number of responses in each category. Raw scores (instead of standardized scores) are used in the same manner as the SDS. (The authors have published a set of norms for the interest scales in the manual for those who wish to use them.)

The results are used to suggest career clusters to clients that they may wish to investigate. The CDM-R has received favorable reviews from guidance experts as a system for the delivery of comprehensive career planning services (Vansickle, 1994). It is a simple, yet relatively complete, instrument with cross-cultural applicability (Harrington, 1991).

Campbell™ Interest and Skill Survey (CISS®)

David Campbell, who is known for his work in updating and revising early forms of the Strong Interest Inventory (previously titled the Strong–Campbell Interest Inventory), created the CISS after parting company with the publishers of the Strong (D. P. Campbell, 1992, 2000). The CISS is one of several inventories in an integrated battery of psychological surveys called the Campbell Development Surveys (D. P. Campbell, 1993). The CISS is similar to the Strong Interest Inventory in that it includes both general and occupational interest scales; it differs from the Strong by its inclusion of a set of self-report skill scales to match each of the interest scales (D. P. Campbell, Hyne, & Nilsen, 1992).

The CISS provides interest and skill scores for 7 Orientation scales, 29 Basic scales, 60 Occupational scales, and 3 Special scales (Academic Focus, Extroversion, and Variety). The 7 Orientation scales are similar to the 6 Holland scales on the Strong. The Strong Realistic scale has been subdivided into Producing and Adventuring scales to produce the seventh Orientation scale. The Basic scales on the CISS bear much in common with the Basic scales on the Strong.

In contrast with the Strong, the CISS uses unisex Occupational scales instead of separate scales for men and women. These scales were formed by comparing the interests and skills of a combined sample of men and women in the occupation with a general reference sample of men and women. The proportions of men and women in the general reference sample were adjusted for each occupation to match the proportions of men and women in the occupational sample as a means of controlling for gender differences. Based on a study of eight occupations, D. P. Campbell et al. (1992) found that combined-sex scales worked about as well as single-sex scales in representing the interests of people within and without the occupation.

Reliability studies conducted with employed adults indicate that the CISS results are internally consistent (general scales) and stable over a 3-month time period (all scales). In regard to validity, people in the occupation score substantially higher on the interest and skill scales for that occupation than do people in general. On the average, people in the occupational criterion group used in creating an occupational scale scored about two standard deviations higher (18 to 20 points) on the Occupational scale than did people in the General Reference Sample (D. P. Campbell et al., 1992). These results compare favorably with those reported for the Strong Interest Inventory.

Scores on the skill and interest scales for the same activities or occupations are interpreted in terms of the following four categories:

- *Pursue*: high interest, high skill
- *Explore*: high skill, lower interest
- *Develop*: high interest, lower skill
- *Avoid*: low interest, low skill

For example, individuals with a high score on the Accountant skill scale but a relatively low score on the Accountant interest scale are encouraged to explore this occupation with the thought that their interests in it might be enhanced or that they might find a niche in the occupational field that they would enjoy.

The test publishers provide a *Career Planner* booklet that may be used as an aid in interpreting and acting on the CISS results. According to Fuqua and Newman (1994, p. 142), the CISS represents "a well-developed, adequately tested, and user-friendly instrument for the purposes of career exploration."

In addition to the CISS, other instruments in the Campbell Development Surveys include the Campbell Organizational Survey, Campbell Leadership Index, Campbell–Hallam Team Development Survey, and Campbell Community Survey (D. P. Campbell, 1993). These instruments, which possess many characteristics in common to aid interpretation, can help counselors in their work with teams, organizations, and communities in addition to individuals.

An example of the use of the CISS in counseling is presented below:

CASE EXAMPLE

When Tess first came to the Counseling Center as a 31-year-old returning adult student, she had just graduated from college with a degree in Business Administration. At that time she was actively involved in a job search. She wanted to learn more about herself and how her interests and skills related to a variety of occupations and leisure activities. The counselor assigned the CISS to help her in this process.

Her scores on the CISS report summary are shown in Figure 10-1. She produced a valid profile as shown by the Procedural Checks on the bottom of the second page of the report summary. Her response percentages for the interest and skill items were normally distributed, her responses to pairs of similar items were consistent in all but one case, and she omitted no items.

She obtained high scores (T score of 55 or higher) on all seven Orientation skill scales but on only two (Organizing and Analyzing) of the Orientation interest scales. As indicated on the profile, she was encouraged to *pursue* Organizing and Analyzing occupations and to *explore* occupations in the other fields.

The CISS Basic scales showed high interests and self-rated skills in Leadership, Advertising/Marketing, Financial Services, Counseling, and Mathematics, all areas that can be related to her major in Business Administration. She also obtained high interest and skill scores on the Art/Design, Mechanical Crafts, Woodworking, Plants/Gardens, and Animal Care scales, which can be looked on as possible leisure-time pursuits as well as career alternatives.

Tess obtained a large number of high scores on both the Occupational interest and skill scales (see second page of report summary), especially in the Organizing and Analyzing areas. She felt encouraged by the test results. She planned to investigate the following occupations in greater detail, all of which she was advised to *pursue* on the CISS report: Financial Planner, Corporate Trainer, Bank Manager, CEO/President, and Restaurant Manager. All of these occupations were consistent with her major in Business Administration.

In a follow-up interview conducted 4 years later, Tess reported that shortly after completing counseling she obtained a job as a program manager that involved both Organizing and Influencing skills and interests. She disliked the influencing (public speaking) aspect of that job and left it after 6 months. She then obtained a job as a bookkeeper for a public agency, from which she was soon promoted to chief financial officer and assistant director. She thrived in this work, which matched her interests and skills in Financial Services, Mathematics, and Leadership. The CISS helped Tess to identify a career field that proved to be satisfying and fulfilling for her.

FIGURE 10-1. Campbell™ Interest and Skill Survey (CISS®) Report Summary for Tess, a 31-Year-Old Recent College Graduate

TESS — Orientations and Basic Scales

Orientations and Basic Scales	Interest	Skill	Interest/Skill Pattern
Influencing	53	55	Explore
Leadership	60	55	Pursue
Law/Policies	53	49	
Public Speaking	50	39	
Sales	46	59	Explore
Advertising/Marketing	58	63	Pursue
Organizing	65	57	Pursue
Supervision	68	53	Develop
Financial Services	66	66	Pursue
Office Practices	45	46	
Helping	45	63	Explore
Adult Development	51	64	Explore
Counseling	58	61	Pursue
Child Development	44	58	Explore
Religious Activities	37	57	Explore
Medical Practice	36	57	Explore
Creating	44	61	Explore
Art/Design	59	64	Pursue
Performing Arts	44	55	Explore
Writing	46	53	
International Activities	41	44	Avoid
Fashion	52	67	Explore
Culinary Arts	38	62	Explore
aNalyzing	57	59	Pursue
Mathematics	67	61	Pursue
Science	52	53	
Producing	53	60	Explore
Mechanical Crafts	58	56	Pursue
Woodworking	58	60	Pursue
Farming/Forestry	39	50	
Plants/Gardens	59	57	Pursue
Animal Care	58	68	Pursue
Adventuring	48	56	Explore
Athletics/Physical Fitness	52	57	Explore
Military/Law Enforcement	43	52	
Risks/Adventure	51	48	

Scale bands: Very Low (30), Low (35–40), Mid-Range (45–50–55), High (60), Very High (65–70)

FIGURE 10-1. *Continued*

CAMPBELL INTEREST AND SKILL SURVEY INDIVIDUAL PROFILE REPORT

TESS
Female
Age 31

DATE SCORED: 2/06/97
White
College Graduate

Occupational Scales

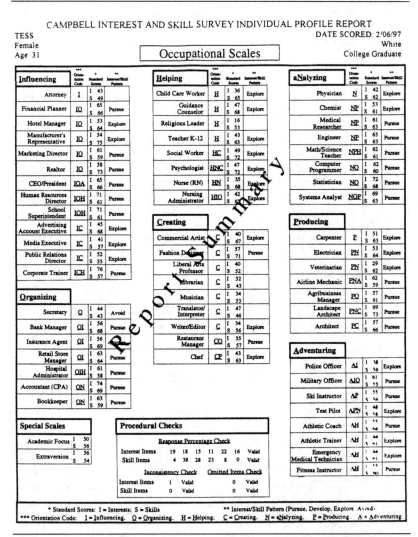

Influencing	Orientation Code	Standard Scores	Interest/Skill Pattern
Attorney	I	I 43 / S 49	
Financial Planner	IO	I 65 / S 66	Pursue
Hotel Manager	IO	I 53 / S 64	Explore
Manufacturer's Representative	IO	I 54 / S 75	Explore
Marketing Director	IO	I 61 / S 59	Pursue
Realtor	IO	I 58 / S 73	Pursue
CEO/President	IOA	I 65 / S 66	Pursue
Human Resources Director	IOH	I 71 / S 61	Pursue
School Superintendent	IOH	I 71 / S 61	Pursue
Advertising Account Executive	IC	I 45 / S 68	Explore
Media Executive	IC	I 41 / S 57	Explore
Public Relations Director	IC	I 52 / S 55	Explore
Corporate Trainer	ICH	I 76 / S 57	Pursue

Organizing	Orientation Code	Standard Scores	Interest/Skill Pattern
Secretary	O	I 44 / S 43	Avoid
Bank Manager	OI	I 56 / S 68	Pursue
Insurance Agent	OI	I 56 / S 69	Pursue
Retail Store Manager	OI	I 63 / S 64	Pursue
Hospital Administrator	OIH	I 61 / S 58	Pursue
Accountant (CPA)	ON	I 74 / S 69	Pursue
Bookkeeper	ON	I 63 / S 59	Pursue

Special Scales		
Academic Focus	I 50 / S 56	
Extraversion	I 56 / S 54	

Helping	Orientation Code	Standard Scores	Interest/Skill Pattern
Child Care Worker	H	I 36 / S 65	Explore
Guidance Counselor	H	I 47 / S 68	Explore
Religious Leader	H	I 16 / S 53	
Teacher K-12	H	I 43 / S 65	Explore
Social Worker	HC	I 49 / S 72	Explore
Psychologist	HNC	I 47 / S 68	Explore
Nurse (RN)	HN	I 35 / S 68	Explore
Nursing Administrator	HIO	I 42 / S 61	Explore

Creating	Orientation Code	Standard Scores	Interest/Skill Pattern
Commercial Artist	C	I 40 / S 67	Explore
Fashion Designer	C	I 57 / S 71	Pursue
Liberal Arts Professor	C	I 40 / S 52	
Librarian	C	I 52 / S 43	
Musician	C	I 34 / S 53	
Translator/Interpreter	C	I 47 / S 46	
Writer/Editor	C	I 34 / S 68	Explore
Restaurant Manager	CO	I 55 / S 57	Pursue
Chef	CP	I 43 / S 63	Explore

aNalyzing	Orientation Code	Standard Scores	Interest/Skill Pattern
Physician	N	I 42 / S 62	Explore
Chemist	NP	I 53 / S 61	Explore
Medical Researcher	NP	I 16 / S 63	Pursue
Engineer	NP	I 61 / S 63	Pursue
Math/Science Teacher	NPH	I 62 / S 61	Pursue
Computer Programmer	NO	I 62 / S 60	Pursue
Statistician	NO	I 72 / S 68	Pursue
Systems Analyst	NOP	I 69 / S 63	Pursue

Producing	Orientation Code	Standard Scores	Interest/Skill Pattern
Carpenter	P	I 51 / S 63	Explore
Electrician	PN	I 53 / S 64	Explore
Veterinarian	PN	I 29 / S 62	Explore
Airline Mechanic	PNA	I 62 / S 59	Pursue
Agribusiness Manager	PO	I 57 / S 61	Pursue
Landscape Architect	PNC	I 69 / S 73	Pursue
Architect	PC	I 57 / S 66	Pursue

Adventuring	Orientation Code	Standard Scores	Interest/Skill Pattern
Police Officer	AI	I 18 / S 56	Explore
Military Officer	AIO	I 61 / S 55	Pursue
Ski Instructor	AP	I 55 / S 56	Pursue
Test Pilot	APN	I 44 / S 48	Explore
Athletic Coach	AH	I 55 / S 54	Pursue
Athletic Trainer	AH	I 44 / S 61	Explore
Emergency Medical Technician	AH	I 44 / S 61	Explore
Fitness Instructor	AH	I 55 / S 61	Pursue

Procedural Checks							
Response Percentage Check							
Interest Items	19	18	15	11	22	16	Valid
Skill Items	4	38	28	23	8	0	Valid

Inconsistency Check		Omitted Items Check	
Interest Items	1 Valid	0	Valid
Skill Items	0 Valid	0	Valid

* Standard Scores: I = Interests; S = Skills   ** Interest/Skill Pattern (Pursue, Develop, Explore, Avoid)
*** Orientation Code: I = Influencing, O = Organizing, H = Helping, C = Creating, N = aNalyzing, P = Producing, A = Adventuring

Note. "CISS" is a registered trademark and the Campbell logo and "Campbell" are trademarks of David P. Campbell, PhD. Copyright 1989, 1992 David P. Campbell, PhD. All rights reserved. Published and distributed exclusively by NCS Pearson, Inc., P. O. Box 1416, Minneapolis, MN 55440. Reproduced with permission by NCS Pearson, Inc.

STANDARDIZED ASSESSMENT PROGRAMS WITH OBJECTIVE TESTS OF ABILITIES

Each of the assessment batteries discussed in this section includes objective tests of abilities in addition to standardized inventories of interests, values, or experiences. In contrast with self-report ability measures, objective tests assess the client's abilities on the basis of actual performance in a test situation. Six frequently used programs— ACT Career Planning Survey, DAT Career Planning Program, WorkKeys, Armed Services Vocational Aptitude Battery, O*NET Career Exploration Tools, and Career Occupational Preference System—are discussed in this section. These measures have been validated most often in terms of educational or occupational membership and performance.

ACT Career Planning Survey (CPS)

The CPS is a comprehensive career guidance program designed to aid students in Grades 8–10 in educational and career planning (American College Testing Program, 1998b). It includes two self-report inventories and a pair of objective tests of ability as indicated below.

- **Inventory of Work-Relevant Abilities (IWRA).** This inventory asks students to rate their skills in 15 areas. Many of the abilities, such as Sales, Helping Others, and Leadership, cannot be measured by objective tests. The results are reported in six categories that correspond to the six Holland types.
- **Unisex Edition of the ACT Interest Inventory (UNIACT).** The UNIACT assesses a student's interests in the same six fields as the IWRA. It consists of 90 items that yield equivalent responses for men and women. All items that produced significant sex differences have been eliminated so that combined-sex norms could be used.
- **Reading and Numerical Skills Ability Tests.** These two tests measure basic concepts and skills essential in reading and mathematics. The tests are intended to identify students in need of remedial or refresher training in either of these areas. High

school teachers and representatives from different cultural groups have reviewed the test items for content and fairness. These two tests (which together require 30 minutes of testing time) may be excluded from the assessment battery if desired.

ACT provides a *Career Planning Guide* to help students apply their survey results in career exploration. The *Guide* includes a Work-Relevant Experiences Checklist and a Job Characteristics Checklist as additional assessment tools. Students use these instruments to review their work experiences and to consider what characteristics (e.g., recognition, physical activity, or variety) they prefer in their work.

Clients can compare their self-rated abilities and interests with those typically expressed by people in different career areas by means of the World-of-Work Map (shown in Figure 10-2). The map shows the relationships among 26 career areas grouped into 12 interest and ability fields. The arrangement of these fields on the map closely resembles that of the Holland hexagon (see Figure 9-1 in Chapter 9). As indicated on the map, the career areas differ from each other in regard to two basic dimensions: *data versus ideas* and *people versus things*. For example, career areas in Region 2 (Management, Marketing & Sales, Employment-Related Services) represent occupations that are people and data oriented.

The CPS Report shows the regions on the World-of-Work Map in which a student obtains his or her highest interest and ability scores by means of a color code (abilities = gray; interests = red; both abilities and interests = red–gray mixture). By inspecting this report, students can easily make comparisons among their abilities, their interests, and relevant career areas.

Self-estimates of interests and abilities are reported as stanine scores (standardized scores ranging from 1 to 9) in the counselor report. Interest self-estimates are simply listed in rank order, and ability self-estimates are reported as bands (instead of single points) on the student profile. Academic Ability test scores are reported in terms of five broad categories (upper 10%, upper 25%, middle 50%, lower 25%, and lower 10%) based on the student's performance in comparison with a national norm group. All these reporting methods have been designed to prevent the overinterpretation of small differences in scores.

FIGURE 10-2. ACT World-of-Work Map (3rd edition—Counselor Version)

Note. The World-of-Work Map arranges 26 career areas (groups of similar jobs) into 12 regions. Together, the career areas cover all U.S. jobs. Most jobs in a career area are located near the point shown. However, some may be in adjacent map regions. A career area's location is based on its primary work tasks. The four primary work tasks are working with DATA (facts, numbers, files, accounts, business procedures), IDEAS (insights, theories, new ways of saying or doing something, e.g., with words, equations, or music), PEOPLE (people you help, serve, inform, care for, and sell things to), and THINGS (machines, tools, living things, and materials such as food, wood, or metal). Copyright 2000 by ACT, Inc. All rights reserved. Reprinted with permission.

Validity studies indicate that both the interest and self-estimated ability measures predict occupational choice for large samples of students with greater-than-chance accuracy. The prediction accuracy is significantly increased when the results of the two measures are in agreement (American College Testing Program, 1998b).

The CPS is well designed for use with individuals or groups of students. It is comprehensive, thoroughly researched, relatively brief, clearly reported, and well integrated with career exploration activities.

Differential Aptitude Tests (DAT) Career Planning Program

The DAT can be used together with the Career Interest Inventory (CII) to generate educational and career planning reports for counselors and students. The DAT, originally published in 1947, was most recently revised in 1990 as the fifth edition, Forms C and D (Psychological Corporation, 1992). The CII measures work and school interests.

Both the DAT and CII include two levels of assessment: Level 1 for Grades 7 through 9 and Level 2 for Grades 10 through 12. Both levels of the DAT and Level 2 of the CII may also be used with adults. When the DAT and the CII are administered together, the results can be integrated by means of a computerized educational and career planning report.

The DAT contains eight subtests: Verbal Reasoning, Numerical Reasoning, Abstract Reasoning, Perceptual Speed and Accuracy, Mechanical Reasoning, Space Relations, Spelling, and Language Usage. The eight tests require 2½ to 3 hours to complete. Although all the tests are timed, they function primarily as power tests except for the Perceptual Speed and Accuracy test. The tests can be hand scored or computer scored.

The CII provides scores for 15 occupational groups for both Levels 1 and 2. In addition, Level 1 reports scores for 16 school subjects and 16 school activities, whereas Level 2 yields scores for 20 postsecondary subject areas.

The DAT has been normed jointly with the CII. Members of the norm groups represent students from different parts of the country, different socioeconomic classes, and different ethnic groups. The norm tables have been subdivided in terms of sex and grade. In contrast with previous editions of the DAT, extensive adult norms are also provided.

The DAT subtests show high internal consistency and acceptable alternate-form reliabilities across samples. Test scores are reported as percentile bands (test score ± 1 standard error of measurement) that take test error into consideration.

The DAT has been validated primarily in terms of educational criteria. Typically, DAT scores have been correlated with course grades from a variety of subjects. In most cases, combined scores on Verbal Reasoning plus Numerical Reasoning (VR + NR) produce the highest correlations with course performance. Except for Perceptual Speed and Accuracy, test scores are highly intercorrelated, so that differential prediction (the goal of the DAT) is questionable. Nonetheless, Wang (1995) noted that "the DAT is still the best battery of its kind" (p. 170).

As part of the scoring service available from the publisher, the Counselor's Report for the combined DAT and CII indicates whether or not a student's occupational plans match his or her aptitude test scores, career interest scores, educational plans, school subjects, and school activities. This report alerts counselors to students who have made inappropriate plans and who may be at risk of failing or dropping out of school.

Schools can use the DAT Partial Battery, which includes the CII together with the Verbal Reasoning and Numerical Reasoning subtests, to save approximately 1 hour of testing time. As noted above, the VR + NR composite score accounts for most of the variance in predicting academic criteria.

Another abbreviated version of the DAT, known as the DAT for Personnel and Career Assessment (PCA), has been developed for use in organizational settings (G. K. Bennett, Seashore, & Wesman, 1989). This version, which has been derived from an earlier edition (Form V) of the DAT, contains 40% fewer items. The technical manual presents extensive data showing the relationship between the test scores and job performance. Willson (1995, p. 307) noted that the DAT for PCA "exhibits excellent criterion-related validity for use as a general screening test for employment with young adults."

Armed Services Vocational Aptitude Battery (ASVAB) Career Exploration Program

The current versions of ASVAB (Forms 18a, 18b, 19a, and 19b), which are administered and interpreted without charge by representatives of the Armed Services, provide scores on 10 individual scales and three composite indices (U.S. Department of Defense, 1992). Test results are used by the military for recruitment, for assessing qualifications of students for different military occupations, and for research. School counselors use the results to help high school students (Grades 10 through 12) and community college students in educational and vocational planning. Testing time, including instructions, is approximately 3 hours. More than 1.5 million students complete the tests each year.

The 10 individual scales include Word Knowledge (WK), Paragraph Comprehension (PC), Arithmetic Reasoning (AR), Mathematics Knowledge (MK), General Science (GS), Auto & Shop Information (AS), Mechanical Comprehension (MC), Electronics Information (EI), Numerical Operations (NO), and Coding Speed (CS). The three composite scores are Verbal Ability (WK + PC), Math Ability (AR + MK), and Academic Ability (Verbal Ability + Math Ability). In addition, a military careers score is also derived that is based on a combination of the Academic Ability score + MC + EI for use in suggesting military careers to students. Only the composite scores are used for counseling and selection purposes.

Besides the ASVAB test scores, the ASVAB Career Exploration Program consists of an interest inventory and a measure of personal preferences. The interest inventory, known as the Interest-Finder, assesses a student's career interests in terms of the six Holland categories used on many interest inventories (U.S. Department of Defense, 1997). The measure of personal preferences focuses on a student's work values (e.g., independence, variety, security) and educational plans. These measures, which are scored by the student, are included in *Exploring Careers: The ASVAB Workbook*.

The student's ASVAB code (based on his or her Academic Ability composite score), Holland code (derived from the Interest-Finder), work values, and educational plans are entered by the student in a booklet titled *OCCU-FIND* to identify occupations that match one's characteristics. Schools that use the ASVAB Career Exploration Program may also use ACES, a new computer software program that automates the person-to-career matching process found in the workbook.

The ASVAB Technical Manual reports high alternate-form reliability coefficients (.92 to .96) for the composite scores for applicants for military enlistment (U.S. Department of Defense, 1994). Studies conducted with earlier versions of the ASVAB found that the composite scores were significantly correlated (.30 to .60) with training and job performance in both civilian and military settings. The ASVAB technical composite scores used to predict training or job performance in military careers have proved to be valid predictors for both males and females and both Blacks and Whites (L. Wise et al., 1992).

In general, the ASVAB, together with its accompanying materials, has shown great improvement since its inception in 1968, especially in selecting candidates for military careers (Elmore & Bradley, 1994). It is most limited in its measurement of specific abilities because of its heavy loading on g (general intelligence). Research indicates that informed self-estimates across a broad range of abilities (e.g., meeting people, leadership/management, and creative/artistic) can greatly enhance the effectiveness of the ASVAB in differentiating among students in various career fields (Prediger & Swaney, 1992).

Prediger and Swaney (1992) suggested that the ASVAB be used as part of a two-step approach in career counseling. First, students should select a career field based on similarity of their characteristics (abilities, interests, and values) with those of people in the career field. In addition to those abilities tested on the ASVAB, students should consider informed self-estimates of abilities not measured by the ASVAB tests, such as those included in the DISCOVER computer-based career planning program. (DISCOVER has been designed so that it can be used in combination with ASVAB.) Second, within the chosen career field, the student should search for an appropriate job level attainable through further education, training, or experience. The ASVAB composite scores are most relevant for the second step in this counseling approach.

WorkKeys

The WorkKeys system was developed by ACT beginning in 1991 (American College Testing Program, 1999d). The program is built around a common scale that measures both the skills of an individual and the skills required for successful job performance. WorkKeys can be used by educators and counselors to help students understand their preparedness for specific jobs and careers and by employers to establish selection and training programs.

WorkKeys measures foundational skills ("skills needed to learn other skills") in eight areas related to work: Applied Mathematics, Applied Technology, Listening, Locating Information, Observation, Reading for Information, Teamwork, and Writing. Additional skill assessments (Computer Skills and Work Habits) are in the process of being developed.

In addition to the skill assessments, the test materials ask clients about their school and work histories, job preferences, and needs in regard to job seeking. UNIACT (the ACT Interest Inventory) may be administered to a group of students at the same time, but the administration uses separate answer documents and provides separate reports. WorkKeys may be used with high school students or adults.

The eight skill tests were defined and developed by panels of employers, educators, and ACT staff. All of the test items are based on work situations. Each of the eight tests is divided into a number of skill levels ranging from Level 1 to Level 7. Depending on the nature of the test, items are presented in paper-and-pencil, video, or audio modes with multiple-choice or constructed-response formats. The eight tests vary in testing time from 45 minutes to 60 minutes. Individuals, educational institutions, and employers select the tests most relevant for their particular situation.

WorkKeys enables students to assess their qualifications for different jobs by using the same set of skills to describe both individuals and jobs. Job analysts work with subject matter experts (usually workers in the job under study) to judge the appropriate skill levels for different jobs. The American College Testing Program (2001) has prepared a table of occupational profiles, which shows the average ratings of relevant skills for nearly 1,200 occupations.

WorkKeys differs from traditional ability tests in that it is criterion-referenced, not norm-referenced. A test taker must correctly answer 80% of the items representing any skill level to be qualified at that level. An individual's skill levels are compared with the skill-level requirements for a particular job or occupation to determine if he or she is prepared to enter that job or occupation. For example, an individual needs to score at Level 6 for Applied Mathematics and at Level 5 for Applied Technology, Locating Information, and Reading for Information to qualify for most jobs as an electronics technician (American College Testing Program, 2001). The specific job requirements vary depending on the employer. For those cases in which a person does not meet the necessary qualifications, the test report includes suggestions for improving one's skills.

WorkKeys has been validated primarily in terms of its content (American Collge Testing Program, 1999d). Outside consultants reviewed the test items for both content accuracy and fairness to minority groups. Statistical analysis was used to identify and eliminate any items that functioned differently for various groups of people, such as males versus females or African Americans versus Whites. Subject matter experts confirmed that the eight skill areas adequately represented the type and the range of skills required in the majority of jobs. Because of the range of skills included in WorkKeys, it appears to have greater potential for the differential prediction of job success than most multiple aptitude test batteries.

An example of the use of this instrument with a group of examinees can be found in *WorkKeys: Score Interpretation Guide– Education* (American College Testing Program, 1999e).

O*NET Career Exploration Tools™

The U.S. Department of Labor (2001) recently developed new comprehensive career assessment tools linked with O*NET™, the Occupational Information Network. The O*NET Career Exploration Tools, which replace the General Aptitude Test Battery (GATB) and the United States Employment Service Interest Inventory (USES-II), include the following three assessment instruments: Ability Profiler, Interest Profiler, and Work Importance Profiler. These instruments may be taken separately or in combination. The results from these tests and client biographical information can be compared directly with occupational profiles by means of the O*NET system.

O*NET is a database of occupational descriptions and worker attributes that has been designed to replace the *Dictionary of Occupational Titles* (DOT; Mariani, 1999; N. G. Peterson, Mumford, Borman, Jeanneret, & Fleishman, 1999). By combining occupations and eliminating obsolete and obscure occupations, the number of occupations included in O*NET has been reduced from the 12,741 occupations defined in the DOT to 974. Compared with the DOT, the O*NET system places greater emphasis on transferable skills than on job duties.

Each occupation is described in terms of six content areas: (a) worker characteristics (abilities, interests, and work styles), (b) worker requirements (education, knowledge, and skills), (c) experience requirements (training, work experience, and licensing), (d) occupational-specific information (job duties and tasks), (e) occupational requirements (work activities and work context), and (f) occupational characteristics (labor market information). The first three content areas describe individual attributes. Worker characteristics refer to worker traits that are relatively stable over time. In contrast, worker requirements and experience requirements refer to worker qualities that are likely to change with the passage of time.

The three O*NET Career Exploration Tools measure worker characteristics—abilities, interests, and work values—that can be expected to be fairly consistent over time (Mariani, 1999). The U.S. Department of Labor (2001) recommends using the three instruments together as part of a "whole person" approach to counseling. These instruments are described below.

The Ability Profiler. This instrument, which replaces the GATB, includes nine scales that are similar to the nine scales that appeared on the GATB. The nine scales comprise three cognitive factors (Verbal Ability, Arithmetic Reasoning, and Computation), three perceptual factors (Spatial Ability, Form Perception, and Clerical Perception), and three psychomotor factors (Motor Coordination, Manual Dexterity, and Finger Dexterity). The GATB General Learning Ability scale has been dropped, and the GATB Numerical Aptitude scale has been divided into Arithmetic Reasoning and Computation scales.

The Ability Profiler differs from the GATB in that it provides new items, revised instructions and scoring procedures, new portions, fewer subtests, and more flexible administration. Additionally, time limits were modified to ensure that examinees had sufficient time to complete subtests where "speed" of answering questions was not important to test performance.

The Ability Profiler includes both paper-and-pencil (first seven scales) and apparatus (last two scales) tests. If preferred, the paper-and-pencil tests can be administered without the apparatus tests. Total testing time for the paper-and-pencil part of the testing process is 1.5 to 2 hours. When apparatus tests are included, total testing time is 2 to 3 hours. The Ability Profiler has been designed specifically for use in counseling and should be used for selection or placement.

The examinee's scores on the Ability Profiler are compared with the ability profiles for the different O*NET occupations. Ability profiles for the different O*NET occupations have been estimated by means of GATB validity data and occupational data from the DOT. The O*NET system includes five job zones that represent five different levels of experience, education, and training. Within each job zone (which the examinee selects), the computer uses a statistical procedure to determine which occupations have ability patterns that most closely match those of the examinee (J. P. Stroupe, personal communication, February 14, 2001).

The Interest Profiler. This inventory measures occupational interests in the same six categories used by most interest inventories: Realistic, Investigative, Artistic, Social, Enterprising, and Convention (see Holland, 1997). Both paper-and-pencil and computerized versions are available. It is designed to be self-administered and self-interpreted. It requires about 30 minutes to complete.

The Work Importance Profiler. The third O*NET assessment tool measures six types of work values: Achievement, Independence, Recognition, Relationships, Support, and Working Conditions. These are the same set of values (with different names) identified in the Work Adjustment Theory and measured by the Minnesota Importance Questionnaire (MIQ; Dawis & Lofquist, 1984). The six work values are subdivided into 21 needs in the same manner as the measures on the MIQ.

Similar to the Interest Profiler, the Work Importance Profiler may be completed in paper-and-pencil form (titled Work Importance Locator) or computer form in about 30 minutes. It is also self-administered and self-interpreted.

At the present time, results for all instruments can be directly linked to over 900 occupations included in the O*NET database (National Center for O*NET Development, 2001). The same variables are used to describe both worker characteristics and job requirements.

For example, according to the O*NET database, the work of an occupational therapist best fits with Social and Realistic interests and Achievement and Relationship work values. The database indicates that the following abilities are most important for occupational therapists: Oral Expression, Oral Comprehension, Written Expression, and Deductive Reasoning. Occupational therapist is listed as an occupation that falls in Job Zone 4 ("considerable preparation needed"). Clients can compare this information with their scores on the O*NET Career Exploration Tools to help determine to what degree this occupation matches their interests, values, and abilities.

In should be noted that many of the abilities included in the O*NET system do not directly match those measured by the Ability Profiler. Abilities not measured by the Ability Profiler must be assessed by other procedures, including self-estimates.

All three of the O*NET instruments are based on extensive research by the U.S. Department of Labor and leading vocational psychologists. The instruments were developed and tested with populations that varied in terms of race, age, gender, ethnic background, geographic location, and educational and economic background. They have been extensively pilot tested in many different education, employment, and training settings. The tools' psychometric properties (e.g., validity, reliability, and fairness analyses) are reported in detailed development reports, which will be published along with user's guides on the O*NET Center Web site as they become available (National Center for O*NET Development, 2001; J. P. Stroupe, personal communication, February 19, 2001).

Career Occupational Preference System (COPSystem)

The COPSystem includes measures of interests, values, and abilities as follows (Knapp-Lee, 2000): (a) The Career Occupational Preference System (COPS) Interest Inventory assesses interests in 14 occupational clusters at different educational levels, (b) the Career Orientation Placement and Evaluation Survey (COPES) measures eight bipolar personal values related to the work one does (see Chapter 8), and (c) the Career Ability Placement Survey (CAPS) measures eight abilities that are important for different types of work. The complete battery can be administered in less than 2 hours. Answer sheets may be self-scored or machine scored.

Several versions of the COPS Interest Inventory have been developed to take into account different grade levels and reading abilities of clients. The COPS Interest Inventory itself may be used with seventh-grade students through adults. The COPS-II (Intermediate Inventory), a highly visual, simplified version of the COPS Interest Inventory based on knowledge of school subjects and activities familiar to younger students, may be used with elementary school children or with adults who have a limited reading ability (fourth-grade level). The COPS-R (Form R) differs from the COPS Interest Inventory in that it contains sex-balanced items, combined-sex norms, and simplified language (sixth-grade reading level). The COPS-R more closely parallels the COPS Interest Inventory than does the COPS-II. The COPS-P (Professional level) provides an advanced version for colleges students and adults who may be considering professional occupations. Finally, the COPS-PIC (Picture Inventory) use pictures only to assess the interests of nonreaders or those with reading difficulties.

The CAPS consists of brief, 5-minute tests in each of the following areas: Mechanical Reasoning, Spatial Relations, Verbal Reasoning, Numerical Ability, Language Usage, Word Knowledge, Perceptual Speed and Accuracy, and Manual Speed and Dexterity. Validation studies indicate that scores on these tests correlate highly with scores for similar tests from other batteries, such as the Differential Aptitude Tests (Knapp, Knapp, & Knapp-Lee, 1992).

Both the COPS Interest Inventory and the COPES were revised in 1995 (EdITS, 1995). The authors developed new norms for all three parts of the COPSystem (COPS Interest Inventory, COPES, and CAPS) in 1996–1997 based on national samples of intermediate, high school, and college students (Knapp-Lee, 2000). Research with earlier versions of the COPSystem indicates that it can be used effectively to predict educational and occupational status.

The COPSystem contributes significantly to the counseling process by stimulating clients to explore career fields from different viewpoints. Test experts have endorsed the COPSystem for its "versatility and usefulness" based on its continued development and refinement (Wickwire & Faldet, 1994, p. 161). Eby et al. (1998, p. 293) noted that "the COPSystem may be particularly useful as a career exploration tool for diverse individuals" who have had less opportunities to engage in career planning.

USE OF COMPREHENSIVE ASSESSMENT PROGRAMS IN COUNSELING

Several recommendations for the use of comprehensive assessment programs discussed in this chapter are listed below:

1. Use self-rating career and life planning programs such as DISCOVER or SIGI+ to promote self-examination and career exploration, especially for people who are unwilling or unable to see a counselor.

2. Use standardized career and life planning programs to identify educational or career fields that match a client's interests, values, and abilities.

3. Use self-report measures of abilities to enlarge the number of abilities under consideration. Use objective tests of abilities with clients who may lack an adequate basis for assessing their own abilities or who may be motivated to distort self-assessments.

4. Disregard small differences between test scores on multiple aptitude tests. When feasible, report test results as a band or range of scores (usually spanning two standard errors of measurement) instead of reporting them as a precise point on a scale.

5. Use combined verbal and numerical ability measures to predict school or job success. Not only is this measure more valid than the other test scores in most cases, but it also yields results with smaller differences between males and females.

6. Develop local norms for interpreting results, especially if the results are used to estimate performance in local courses.

7. Help students with low ability scores consider how they may improve their scores through appropriate coursework or related experiences.

8. Interpret aptitude scores as measures of *developed* abilities. Exposure to the subject matter represented within the test is necessary for the student to perform well on the test.

9. Use nonlanguage tests, such as the Abstract Reasoning and Spatial Relations tests from the DAT, for students with limited English language skills to determine general ability to learn new material or to perform tasks for which knowledge of English is not required.

10. Consult supplementary materials provided by publishers of comprehensive career planning programs. For example, *Using the DAT With Adults* provides suggestions for using the DAT with adults

in various settings. Use student workbooks to encourage active participation on the part of clients.

SUMMARY

1. Comprehensive self-assessments based on computer programs or career and life planning workbooks can be used to stimulate career exploration and to improve capacity for career planning.

2. Standardized assessment programs for career and life planning provide measures of an individual's values, interests, and abilities that can be compared with the requirements of different educational and occupational environments.

3. Standardized assessment programs with self-report measures of abilities permit broad coverage of different types of abilities. Programs with objective tests of abilities help ensure validity of results, especially in situations in which the results may be used for selection or placement.

4. The Self-Directed Search represents a comprehensive self-report inventory based on Holland's model of career behavior.

5. The Campbell Interest and Skill Survey uses self-rated abilities as well as self-rated interests to assess one's similarity to people in 60 different occupations.

6. The ACT Career Planning Survey and the DAT Career Planning Program can be used in educational settings to help students choose an academic field or training course based on their interests and abilities.

7. The Armed Services Vocational Aptitude Battery can be used in military and occupational settings to identify workers most likely to succeed in those settings.

8. Different combinations of WorkKeys skill assessments can be used to predict success in different types of work.

9. The O*NET (Occupational Information Network) database provides a means of directly comparing individual characteristics (as measured by the Ability, Interest, and Work Importance Profilers) with requirements for over 900 occupations.

10. The COPSystem provides an up-to-date set of interest, values, and ability measures that can be used to distinguish among individuals in different majors or careers.

SECTION

IV

Personality Assessment

11

PERSONALITY INVENTORIES

T HE TERM *personality* is often used to cover a very broad concept. When applied to psychological assessment instruments, however, it is used more narrowly to describe those instruments designed to assess personal, emotional, and social traits and behaviors, as distinguished from instruments that measure aptitudes, achievements, and interests. The instruments discussed in this chapter are generally referred to as self-report personality inventories in which respondents check or rate items that they believe are most descriptive of themselves.

This chapter first discusses the different approaches used to construct these inventories, followed by a description of 11 inventories often used by counselors. Personality inventories primarily designed to assess psychopathology are presented in Chapter 15.

INVENTORY DEVELOPMENT

There are four different methods by which personality tests have been constructed (Anastasi & Urbina, 1997). One that uses a deductive approach is the *logical content method*. In this method, the inventory author uses a rational approach to choosing items. Statements related to the characteristic being assessed are logically deduced to be related to the content of the characteristic being assessed. The Occupational Theme scales of the Strong Interest Inventory and the new content scales of the Minnesota Multiphasic Personality Inventory (MMPI-2; discussed in Chapter 15) use this method. The principal limitation of this approach is that it assumes the validity of each item—that individuals are capable of evaluating their own characteristics and that their answers can be taken at face value. If a client checks an item related to "not getting along with parents," this approach assumes that the client is having parental difficulties.

The second approach is the *theoretical method*, in which items are developed to measure constructs represented by a particular theory of personality. After the items have been grouped into scales, a construct validity approach is taken to determine whether the inventory results are consistent with the theory. Two examples of this approach are Jackson's Personality Research Form (PRF), based on H. A. Murray's (1938) theory of needs, and the Myers–Briggs Type Indicator (MBTI), based on Jung's (1960) theory of personality types.

Two methods make use of empirical (data-based) strategies to develop personality inventories. The *criterion group method* begins with a sample with known characteristics, such as a group of individuals diagnosed with schizophrenia. An item pool is then administered to individuals in the known sample and to a control group (usually a "normal" population). The items that distinguish the known sample from the control group are then placed in a scale in a manner similar to the method used to construct the Occupational scales on the Strong Interest Inventory. Typically, these items are then used on another similar sample to determine whether the scale continues to distinguish between the two groups. This method can also be used with groups that present contrasts on a particular trait. For example, members of fraternities and sororities are asked to judge the five most and the five least sociable individuals in their group, and then items that distinguish between these two groups are used in the development of a sociability scale. The MMPI-2 clinical scales and the majority of the scales on the California Psychological Inventory (CPI) are based on the criterion group method of inventory construction.

The *factor-analytic method* is the second method using an empirical strategy in test development. In this method, a statistical procedure is used to examine the intercorrelations among all of the items on the inventory. This technique, which can effectively be completed only on a computer, groups items into factors until a substantial proportion of the variability among the items has been accounted for by the dimensions that have resulted. An example of this approach is Cattell's Sixteen Personality Factor Questionnaire (16 PF), which resulted from a factor analysis of 171 terms that describe human traits and that were, in turn, developed from a list of thousands of adjectives that in one way or another describe humans. Items that appear on particular dimensions resulting from a factor analysis are combined to form homogeneous scales.

Researchers using factor-analytic techniques across a number of personality inventories have synthesized personality traits into five major dimensions nicknamed the "Big Five." These five factors are

1. Neuroticism—insecure versus self-confident
2. Extraversion—outgoing versus shy
3. Openness—imaginative versus concrete
4. Agreeableness—empathic versus hostile
5. Conscientiousness—well-organized versus impulsive

The NEO Personality Inventory–Revised has been developed specifically to assess these Big Five factors (Costa & McCrae, 1992; Costa & Widiger, 1994; Goldberg, 1993; McCrae & Costa, 1986). The four dimensions of the MBTI are related to each of the last four of these factors but not to neuroticism. The MMPI, on the other hand, contains numerous items related to neuroticism and fewer relating to the remaining four factors. These same personality dimensions are also found across diverse cultures as similar factor structures have appeared in Portuguese, German, Chinese, and Japanese samples (McCrae & Costa, 1997). Although there has been considerable agreement regarding the existences of these general dimensions, several authorities, including two of the most famous, disagree. Eysenck says there are only three, and Cattell is convinced there are far more (Goldberg, 1993). There is also disagreement regarding some of the labels that have been given to these dimensions as well as for some of the specific personality characteristics and behaviors deemed associated with certain of these dimensions (Whiston, 2000).

Because most personality inventories are self-report instruments, they can typically be distorted in a negative direction if individuals are motivated to present a poor image or in a positive direction if, for example, they were applying for a desired job. Several inventories contain validity or social desirability scales to detect such distortion. For counselors, this is less often an important problem because the purpose for taking the inventories is self-understanding and counselor understanding. Nevertheless, it is often helpful to point out such purposes and instruct clients to answer openly and honestly to obtain the most valid results.

SELF-REPORT PERSONALITY INVENTORIES

The Myers–Briggs Type Indicator (MBTI)

Work on the MBTI was begun in the 1920s by Katherine Briggs when she developed a system of psychological types by conceptualizing her observations and readings (Myers, McCaulley, Quenk, & Hammer, 1998). Upon finding much similarity between her conclusions and those of Carl Jung, who was working at the same time, she began using his theory. Together with her daughter, Isabel Myers, she developed an inventory now known as the Myers–Briggs Type Indicator. The inventory, in its several forms, was slow in gaining acceptance but is now reported to be the most widely used personality inventory in the world, with 2 million administered each year.

The MBTI is based on Jung's concepts of perception and judgment that are used by different types of people. Each of the several forms of the MBTI (in both self-scored and computer-scored formats) is scored on eight scales (four pairs) yielding four bipolar dimensions. More sophisticated item response theory methods were used for the item development and scoring weights in the latest version, the 93-item Form M. Jung's theory proposes that apparently random variations in human behavior can be systematically accounted for by the manner in which individuals prefer to use their capacities for perception and judgment. The MBTI is a self-reporting instrument designed to identify these preferences.

The first of the four dimensions involves the preference for extraversion versus introversion (E-I). Extraverts prefer to direct their energy to the outer world of people and things, whereas introverts tend to focus energy on the inner world of ideas.

The second dimension measures personal preference for mode of perceiving and is labeled the sensing–intuition (S-N) dimension. Sensing individuals prefer to rely on one or more of the five senses as their primary mode of perceiving. Intuitive people, in contrast, rely primarily on indirect perception by the way of the mind, incorporating ideas or associations that are related to perceptions coming from the outside.

The third MBTI dimension is designed to measure an individual's preference for judging data obtained through sensing or intuition by means of either thinking or feeling (T-F). A thinking orientation signifies a preference for drawing conclusions using an objective, impersonal, logical approach. A feeling-oriented individual is much more likely to base decisions on personal or social rationales that take into account the subjective feelings of others.

The fourth dimension measures a person's preference for either a judging or perceiving (J-P) orientation for dealing with the external world. Although individuals must use both perception and judgment in their daily lives, most find one of these orientations to be more comfortable than the other and use it more often, in the same way that a right-handed person favors the use of the right hand. People with a judgment orientation are anxious to use either the thinking or feeling mode to arrive at a decision or conclusion as quickly as possible, whereas those with a perceptive orientation are more comfortable continuing to collect information through either a sensing or intuitive process and delaying judgment as long as possible. This fourth dimension was not defined by Jung but represents an additional concept of Briggs and Myers.

Although the four dimensions of the MBTI are theoretically independent, significant correlations in the vicinity of .30 have been found between the S-N and J-P scales. This finding tends to support Jung's theory, which included only the first three dimensions. Other than the relationship between these two sets of scales, the remaining scales are statistically independent of each other.

A person's MBTI personality type is summarized in four letters, which indicate the direction of the person's preference on each of the four dimensions. All possible combinations of the four paired scales result in 16 different personality types. Thus, an ENTJ is an extravert with a preference for intuition and thinking who generally has a judging attitude in his or her orientation toward the outer world. An ISFP type indicates an introvert with a preference toward sensing and feeling who has a perceptive orientation toward the outer world. The manual provides a summary of the processes, characteristics, and traits of each of the 16 types.

In computing personality type, scores resulting from forced-choice items are obtained for each of the opposite preferences and then subtracted to obtain the particular type. A large difference between the two scores indicates a clear preference and yields a higher score on that type, whereas a smaller difference yields a low score, indicating a preference on that type that is considered less strong and less clear. Even though the difference is small (the scoring formula eliminates ties), one or the other letter is included in the four-letter code type. These preferences are presumed to interact in complex, nonlinear ways to produce the 16 types. A major criticism of the MBTI is that the variables assessed are assumed to result in dichotomies, although there is little psychological evidence of such dichotomies or bimodal distributions. Instead, the variables can best be represented as continuous bipolar distributions that fall along the normal curve (Pittenger, 1993). An additional dimension of MBTI theory involves dominant and auxiliary functions that are controversial and lack substantial research.

Although an individual's type is supposed to remain relatively constant over a lifetime, norms on several MBTI dimensions change substantially between adolescence and adulthood as well as during the adult years (Cummings, 1995). Internal consistency studies of the MBTI Form M have generally yielded correlation coefficients exceeding .90. In terms of the four letter types, test–retest reliability data tend to be somewhat discouraging in that an individual's four-letter MBTI type has only about a 50–50 chance of being identical on retesting. On the average, 75% of the people completing the instrument will retain three of the four dichotomous type preferences on retesting.

One of the reasons the MBTI is attractive to many individuals is that there are no good or bad scores nor good or bad combinations of types. Because both polarities can be viewed as strengths, this non-judgmental quality facilitates interpreting results to clients. A score indicates a preference to use certain functions or behavioral preferences, although most individuals have the capacity to make use of the opposite preference as well. Each preference includes some strengths, joys, and positive characteristics, and each has its problems and blind spots. In the interpretive materials in the manual, as well as in a number of other publications, the strengths, weaknesses, abilities, needs, values, interests, and other characteristics are provided for scores on each of the scales as well as for the 16 types. Resources include *Gifts Differing* (Myers & Myers, 1995), *People Types and Tiger Stripes* (Lawrence, 1992), *Introduction to Type* (Myers, Kirby, & Myers, 1998), *MBTI Applications: A Decade of Research on the Myers–Briggs Type Indicator* (Hammer, 1996), *I'm Not Crazy, I'm Just Not You* (Pearman & Albritton, 1997), *Applications of the MBTI in Higher Education* (Provost & Anchors, 1987), and *Tools for Team Excellence* (Huszczo, 1996).

The MBTI is used in a number of counseling situations. It is often used to explore relationships between couples and among family members (Chapter 13). It is used to develop teamwork and an understanding of relationships in work situations and in vocational counseling by examining the effects of each of the four preferences in work situations. For example, introverts like a work situation that provides quiet or concentration and may have problems communicating, whereas extraverts like variety in action and are usually able to communicate freely. People with strong thinking preferences are interested in fairness and logic and may not be sensitive to other people's feelings. Feeling types tend to be very aware of other people's feelings and find it difficult to tell people unpleasant things. Thus, preferences and strengths on the MBTI can be discussed in terms of occupational functions and work environments, although solid validity data for such use still need to be obtained.

In addition, the manual lists the types of people found in various occupations from a vast data pool of people in different occupations who have had the MBTI administered to them. People with certain MBTI types are found in substantially higher proportions in cetain occupations. All types may enter all types of occupations, but certain types choose particular occupations far more often than others. For example, although all types are represented among psychologists, 85% of psychologists are intuitive types and only 15% are sensing types, but, like the general population, they are evenly split on the introvert–extravert dimension. The MBTI is seldom used by itself in career counseling but is often used along with interest inventories and other psychological test results to add an additional dimension in vocational counseling (Tieger & Barron-Tieger, 2001).

Individuals who are intuitive, feeling, and perceptive seem to be more likely to seek counseling than individuals with other MBTI types (Mendelsohn & Kirk, 1962; Vilas, 1988). A few counselors administer the MBTI before counseling has begun so that they can use the results, along with the knowledge of their own type, in structuring the counseling process for a particular client.

Because of the wide variety of settings in which counselors use the MBTI, no specific list of guidelines for its use or interpretation is included here. Because of its popularity and seemingly simplistic interpretation of results, however, it is often administered and interpreted by those who are overly enthusiastic about its use or who have little background in psychological assessment. Counselors who make use of this personality inventory should be aware not only of its strengths and usefulness in various settings but also of its various weaknesses, including ipsative scoring and lack of criterion-related validity studies in certain settings.

The MBTI should not be used to label or narrowly categorize people. Although most people have a preferred personality style that they can learn to use to their advantage, they can also learn to express the less dominant aspects of their personality when appropriate. Counselors can teach clients to become more flexible in the manner in which they respond to different situations.

An alternative to the MBTI is the Keirsey Temperament Sorter II (KTS-II; Keirsey & Choiniere, 1998). It contains 70 questions similar to MBTI items and classifies individuals into four temperaments similar to MBTI personality types (Quinn, Lewis, & Fischer, 1992; Tucker & Gillespie, 1993). These temperaments, each of which consists of four MBTI letter codes, are titled Guardians, Artisans, Idealists, and Rationalists. The KTS-II yields an individual's four-letter MBTI type in addition to the Keirsey temperaments. The KTS-II may be taken without cost on the Internet (Keirsey, 2000).

The California Psychological Inventory (CPI)

The CPI (3rd edition) was developed for use with relatively well-adjusted individuals (Gough & Bradley, 1996). Although the MMPI was used as a basis for development of this inventory (over one third of the CPI items), the CPI is designed to measure everyday traits that its author, Harrison Gough, calls *folk concepts*, such as sociability, tolerance, and responsibility—terms that people use every day to classify and predict each other's behavior. The 1995 version of the CPI, containing 434 items and 30 scales, was normed on standardization samples of 3,000 men and 3,000 women. The 1995 form was restandardized in such a way that the scales on the earlier and 1995 forms can be considered interchangeable.

The CPI items deal with typical behavior patterns and attitudes with less objectionable content than that of the MMPI. The scales are designed to assess personality characteristics and to aid in the understanding of the interpersonal behavior of normal individuals. Thus, the CPI is sometimes termed "the sane person's MMPI."

The CPI contains 20 folk scales that are organized into four separate clusters or classes (see Figure 11-1):

1. Class I is designed to assess interpersonal adequacy of poise, self-assurance, and ascendancy and contains seven scales titled Dominance, Capacity for Status, Sociability, Social Presence, Self-Acceptance, Independence, and Empathy.

2. Class II contains measures of socialization, responsibility, and character with seven scales titled Responsibility, Socialization, Self-Control, Good Impression, Communality, Well-Being, and Tolerance.

3. Class III contains scales measuring intellectual and academic themes useful in educational counseling. The three scales in this cluster are titled Achievement via Conformance, Achievement via Independence, and Intellectual Efficiency.

4. Class IV contains a mixed group of three scales that do not fit well together or are not highly related to scales in the other three clusters. They include Psychological-Mindedness, Flexibility, and Femininity–Masculinity.

Of the 20 CPI scales, 13 were developed by the criterion group method, 4 by internal consistency analysis (Social Presence, Self-Acceptance, Self-Control, and Flexibility), and 3 by a combination of

FIGURE 11-1. California Psychological Inventory Report

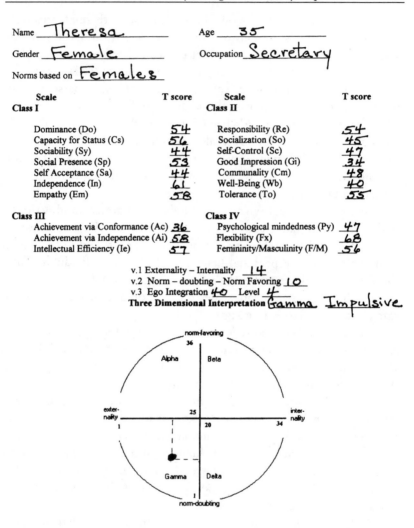

Name __Theresa__   Age __35__

Gender __Female__   Occupation __Secretary__

Norms based on __Females__

Scale	T score	Scale	T score
Class I		**Class II**	
Dominance (Do)	54	Responsibility (Re)	54
Capacity for Status (Cs)	56	Socialization (So)	45
Sociability (Sy)	44	Self-Control (Sc)	47
Social Presence (Sp)	53	Good Impression (Gi)	34
Self Acceptance (Sa)	44	Communality (Cm)	48
Independence (In)	61	Well-Being (Wb)	40
Empathy (Em)	58	Tolerance (To)	55

Class III
Achievement via Conformance (Ac) 36
Achievement via Independence (Ai) 58
Intellectual Efficiency (Ie) 57

Class IV
Psychological mindedness (Py) 47
Flexibility (Fx) 68
Femininity/Masculinity (F/M) 56

v.1 Externality – Internality __14__
v.2 Norm – doubting – Norm Favoring __10__
v.3 Ego Integration __40__ Level __4__
Three Dimensional Interpretation Gamma Impulsive

these two methods (Good Impression, Communality, and Well-Being; Gough & Bradley, 1996).

Three of the scales are validity scales developed to detect faking or other test-taking attitudes. "Faking bad" is detected by *T* scores of 35 or less on the Well-Being, Communality, or Good Impression scales.

Low scores on the Well-Being scale reflect endorsement of items representing various physical and psychological complaints. Scores on the Communality scale are based on a frequency count of popular responses, with low scores ($T = 29$ or less for men, 24 or less for women) suggesting that the inventory has been taken in a random or idiosyncratic fashion (Groth-Marnat, 1997). When a "fake bad" profile is obtained, the counselor should ask why the individual feels a need to create an impression of serious problems. The person might in fact have very serious problems or might be malingering for some reason, or the low score might represent a cry for help. The Good Impression scale is based on responses by normal individuals asked to "fake good" to identify persons who are overly concerned about making a good impression. "Faking good" is suggested by a Good Impression T score of 65 or more with this score as the highest on the profile. Generally, most other scales will also show scores in the positive direction, which makes it difficult to differentiate between an individual with an excellent level of adjustment and one who is faking good. Here an individual's history can usually help the counselor to differentiate between faking good and superior adjustment. There are an additional 13 special purposes or research scales (e.g., Amicability, Creative Temperament, and Management Potential) derived for different practical and experimental purposes (McAllister, 1996).

Standard scores (T scores) are reported with a mean of 50 and a standard deviation of 10 (see Figure 11-1; Gough, 1999, 2000; Groth-Marnat, 1997). High scores (T scores of 60 or above) tend to indicate psychological health and lower scores (40 or below) psychological inadequacy or distress (except for the Femininity–Masculinity scale). Different profiles are used to plot scores for men and women. Norms in the current version are based on 3,000 men and 3,000 women representing heterogeneous samples from high school and college students, teachers, business executives, prison executives, psychiatric patients, and prison inmates.

Reliability coefficients for some scales show substantial reliability, whereas for others coefficients are more moderate. Median alpha coefficients for the 20 folk concept scales were .72 for men and .73 for women. The large numbers of validity studies conducted with the CPI, usually exploring either predictive or concurrent validity, have yielded validity indices that have varied widely among the scales.

On the basis of factor-analytic work, Gough developed three "vector" scales to measure broad aspects of personality structure. Because a number of the 20 scales on the CPI show considerable overlap, the three dimensions (vectors) can be used to facilitate understanding and interpretation of the 20-scale profile. The three vectors are described generally as (a) internality versus externality, (b) norm favoring versus norm questioning, and (c) self-realization versus self-actualization. These factors have been placed in an interpretive three-dimensional model (see Figure 11-1). The first two vectors measure personality type, whereas the third vector measures levels of personality adjustment.

- Vector 1: High scorers tend to be viewed as reticent, modest, shy, reserved, moderate, and reluctant to initiate or take decisive social action. Low scorers are talkative, outgoing, confident, and poised.
- Vector 2: High scorers are viewed as well organized, conscientious, conventional, dependable, and controlled. Low scorers are seen as rebellious, restless, self-indulgent, and pleasure-seeking.
- Vector 3: High scorers are described as optimistic, mature, insightful, free of neurotic trends and conflicts, and as having a wide range of interests. Low scorers are seen as dissatisfied, unsure of themselves, uncomfortable with uncertainty and complexity, and as having constricted interests.

The intersection of Vectors 1 and 2 form four quadrants or lifestyles. Personality characteristics can be inferred from membership in one of these four quadrants: Alphas are ambitious, productive, and socially competent; Betas are responsible, reserved, and conforming; Gammas are restless, rebellious, and pleasure-seeking; and Deltas are withdrawn, reflective, and detached. These four lifestyles are related both to college going and college majors (Gough, 2000). Among almost 3,500 high school graduates in 16 cities, the college-going rate for Alphas was 61%, who were most likely to major in engineering or business; for Gammas 40%, who were most likely to major in the social sciences; for Betas 39%, who were most likely to major in teaching or nursing; and for Deltas only 27%, who were most likely to seek out the humanities or music.

In addition to the 20 folk scales, there are 13 special purpose or research scales: Management Potential, Work Orientation, Creative Temperament, Baucom's unipolar masculinity scale, Baucom's unipolar femininity scale, Leventhal's anxiety scale, Dicken's scale for social desirability, Dicken's scale for acquiescence, Leadership, Amicability, Law Enforcement Orientation, Tough-Mindedness, and Narcissism (Gough, 1999, 2000).

The CPI has been shown to be useful in predicting success in a number of educational and vocational areas. Achievers in both high school and college have been shown to obtain relatively high scores on the Achievement via Conformance, Achievement via Independence, Responsibility, and Socialization scales. Studies making use of CPI scale scores have been shown to predict school and college performance beyond that using IQ scores or Scholastic Assessment Test scores alone. Other scores (Achievement via Conformance, Capacity for Status, Sociability, Good Impression, and Intellectual Efficiency) have been shown to be related to achievement in different types of professional training programs (Groth-Marnat, 1997). The Dominance scale has proved to be effective in differentiating leaders from nonleaders. The CPI has not been shown to be effective for clinical assessment, as it was not designed for that purpose. An individual's general level of adjustment or maladjustment is indicated by the overall level of the profile, but the scales do not yield much information related to a specific diagnosis. Juvenile delinquents and criminals tend to have low scores on the Responsibility and Socialization scales. Solitary delinquents tend to obtain lower scores on the Intellectual Efficiency and Flexibility scales, whereas social delinquents tend to obtain higher scores on the Sociability, Social Presence, and Self-Acceptance scales.

When interpreting the CPI results, one should inspect the three validity scales first. If the CPI results are valid, the three vector scales should then be reviewed to provide a broad overview of the results. After that, the profile for the 20 individual scales should be analyzed.

In analyzing the CPI profile, the counselor should begin by paying attention to the overall height of the profile. Higher scores represent psychologically healthy responses, and these should be compared not only with the standard scores on the profile but also, where possible, with an appropriate norm group. The mean on most of the scales, for example, is higher for college students than for high school students.

Next, the counselor should pay attention to the highest scores (*T* score of 60 or above) and the lowest scores (40 or below) on the profile. The next step in examining the profile is to attend to the height of the scores within each of the four classes. The class in which the scores tend to run the highest and those in which they tend to run the lowest are examined and interpreted. Continuing to examine the profile, the counselor should interpret and discuss the highest scales within each class and the lowest scales within each class. Finally, the counselor should pay attention to the remaining scales on the profile to be described and interpreted. With this method, the most important aspects of the profile are discussed first and receive the most emphasis and are less likely to become lost by the client in the detailed interpretation that follows. Finally, all of the data, including scale interactions where appropriate, are integrated with other client information in the overall interpretation (P. Meyer & Davis, 1992).

The manner in which the elevation of the scales can be interpreted is seen in Table 11-1 for the Dominance scale of the CPI (Craig, 1999; Gough, 2000; Groth-Marnat, 1997; McAllister, 1996). Similar information for all the CPI scales can be found in these sources.

TABLE 11-1. Sample Interpretive Descriptions for the CPI Dominance Scale

---

Very High (T = above 65): Highly assertive, frequently seeks power and leadership positions in a direct manner, is confident, ambitious, and dominant, may be overbearing.

High (T = 60–65): Reasonably dominant and assertive, likely to take charge of situations, confident, optimistic, task oriented.

Moderately High (T = 55–60): generally self-confident, can assume leadership roles when called upon.

Average (T = 45–55): Neither strongly dominant nor inhibited, not characterized by strongly assertive or unusually nonassertive behavior.

Moderately Low (T = 40–55): Likely to be hesitant to take the initiative, generally uncomfortable in leadership positions, may have difficulty making direct requests.

Low (T = 35–40): Likely to appear dependent, generally prefers a nonassertive participant role, may resist change and be seen as lacking in self-confidence.

Very Low (T = below 35): Likely to be socially withdrawn, appears shy and insecure, tends to avoid tension and pressure situations, usually seen as submissive and inhibited.

Because of the care with which the CPI was originally constructed and has since been revised, along with the many hundreds of studies using this instrument, the CPI has become one of the best and most popular personality inventories available. Because the majority of the scales were empirically constructed and scale scores can be compared with different norm groups, the counselor can make use of the instrument in assessing and comparing the strength of various personality characteristics of clients, and clients can use the interpretation to assess their own strengths and weaknesses in comparison with normative samples. Computer-based profile interpretation is also available. A limitation of the CPI is that few studies have examined the meaning of elevations on more than one scale, in contrast to the considerable research that has been conducted on two and three high-point codes of the MMPI. An example of an interpretation of a CPI profile is provided below:

CASE EXAMPLE

The CPI profile of scores for Theresa, a 35-year-old divorced secretary, is shown in Figure 11-1. She sought counseling because of a general dissatisfaction with her current situation. She is not happy with her job; she has had three serious relationships with men since her divorce, none of which have developed into marriage; and she is often in conflict with her 15-year-old daughter. After graduation from high school, she attended college sporadically for 2 years, earning less than 40 credits and a grade point average of 1.6. She attributes her poor record to a lack of goals and interest in liberal arts subjects and to "too much partying."

The validity scales from Theresa's CPI profile show a tendency to present herself in a negative fashion (Good Impression = 35). Her personality type, Gamma, suggests self-confidence and social competence together with restlessness, pleasure-seeking, and nonconforming beliefs and behaviors. At Level 4 (out of 7 levels) on Vector 3 (Realization), she shows average integration and realization of potential. As a Gamma at this level, she may feel somewhat alienated from society. At a higher level, she might be seen as creative or progressive; at a lower level, she might be viewed as antisocial.

In general, the scores on Theresa's profile fall near the midpoint, which corresponds with her Level 4 score on Vector 3. Her two high scores (*T* score of 60 or above) indicate that she is "self-sufficient, resourceful, detached" (Independence) and that she "likes change and variety," that she is "easily bored by routine life and everyday experience," and that she "may be impatient, and even erratic" (Flexibility; Gough, 1987, pp. 6–7).

253

Her three low scores (T score of 40 or below) indicate that she "insists on being herself, even if this causes friction or problems" (Good Impression), that she is "concerned about health and personal problems; worried about the future" (Well-Being), and that she "has difficulty in doing best work in situations with strict rules and expectations" (Achievement via Conformance; Gough, 1987, pp. 6–7). Theresa used the information from the CPI together with other information to gain a better understanding of herself and her situation.

The Sixteen Personality Factor Questionnaire (16 PF)

The 16 PF (5th edition) is a personality inventory developed through the factor-analytic technique by Raymond B. Cattell and others (Cattell, Cattell, & Cattell, 1993; Karson, Karson, & O'Dell, 1997; Russell & Karol, 1993). Based on the theory that if a human trait exists, a word in the language would have been developed to describe it, Cattell began from a list of all adjectives that could be applied to humans from an unabridged dictionary and produced a list of 4,500 trait names. These were combined to reduce the list to 171 terms that seemed to cover all of the human characteristics on the longer list. He then asked college students to rate their acquaintances on these terms and, through factor analysis, arrived at 16 different primary factors that were developed into the 16 scales. Additional scores are now also obtained on five global factors—extraversion, anxiety, tough-mindedness, independence, and self-control (note resemblance to the "Big Five")—as well as for a number of additional derived scales.

The adult edition now contains 185 items. High and low scores on each of the scales represent opposite characteristics. Thus, the scales are labeled by such terms as Practical versus Imaginative, Trusting versus Suspicious, Concrete versus Abstract, Shy versus Socially Bold, and Relaxed versus Tense. Separate-sex and combined-sex norms are available for adults, college students, and high school juniors and seniors. Scores are given in terms of "stens"—standard scores with a mean of 5.5 and a standard deviation of 2.0. Scores below 4 (10%) are considered low, and scores above 7 (10%) are considered high. Because the scales are bipolar, both high and low scores can be interpreted as representing a particular characteristic (Schuerger, 2000). Several sets of equivalent forms of the inventory have been developed. In addition, the adult level has been extended downward to develop a form for high school students ages 12 to 18 (the High School Personality Questionnaire) and another one for use with children ages 8 to 12 (the Children's Personality Questionnaire).

Three different validity scales have been developed, one to detect random responding, one to detect faking-good responses (called the Motivational Distortion scale), and a third to predict attempts to give a bad impression (called the Faking Bad scale). Additional adaptations and computer-generated interpretations of the 16 PF have been published and promoted for use in marriage counseling, career counseling, job proficiency, and the assessment of managers.

The following steps constitute a suggested strategy for interpreting the 16 PF. After considering client information and the context of the assessment, the counselor should first inspect the three validity scales to determine if the results are trustworthy. Second, the counselor should interpret global scores and their patterns and evaluate overall adjustment level (Craig, 1999). Third, the counselor should interpret very high or very low primary factor scores, and fourth, the counselor should interpret patterns (interrelationships) of primary factor scores. The counselor should pay attention to any inconsistencies among the primary scores within the global factors that may affect the interpretation of the global scores (Karson et al., 1997; Schuerger, 2000). Another approach in using the 16 PF is to compare the client's overall profile with that of typical profiles of certain groups. This approach is aided by the use of computer programs available for such interpretation.

The 16 PF is based on a large amount of research both in the construction of the instrument and in the examination of its reliability and validity (Schuerger, 1992). Test–retest reliability coefficients over short periods tend to range from .60 to .85. The reliability coefficients are somewhat low because the scales are made up of relatively few items (10 to 13 items per scale). A wide variety of validity data are available, including the prediction of academic grades and mean profiles for many groups such as delinquents, neurotics, and workers in a variety of different occupations.

The NEO Personality Inventory–Revised (NEO PI-R)

The NEO PI-R was developed to assess the Big Five personality factors previously mentioned (Costa & McCrae, 1992). It consists of five 48-item scales answered on a 5-point agree–disagree continuum.

Scores are obtained on each of the five domains of Neuroticism (high scores: poor adjustment and emotional distress), Extraversion (high scores: sociable, energetic; low scores: reserved, even-paced), Openness (high scores: imaginative, curious; low scores: practical, traditional), Agreeableness (high scores: sympathetic, dependent; low scores: egocentric, antagonistic), and Conscientiousness (high scores: organized, self-controlled; low scores: easy going, disorganized), as well as on 30 facet subscales. Each of the five global dimensions is composed of six subscales of eight items each designed to measure facets of the global dimension. The Neuroticism domain includes facet subscales such as anxiety, hostility, and depression, whereas the Conscientiousness domain includes facets such as competence, order, and self-discipline. Except for the Neuroticism scale, higher scores are indicative of positive characteristics, but on two of the scales (Agreeableness and Conscientiousness) very high scores can indicate a lack of balance in the individual's personality structure.

Reliability coefficients ranging from .8 to .9 are reported for the global dimensions with the facet scales ranging from .6 to .8. Separate profile sheets are provided with differing norms for males, females, and college students. The inventory is easy to administer and hand score, although computer administration, scoring, and interpretation are available. Concurrent validity studies (primarily with other personality measures) have yielded moderate to strong correlations in expected directions.

The NEO PI was originally developed on populations available from two large studies of aging adults, indicating that the inventory can be used throughout the full range of adult ages. Because it was developed primarily with adults, different norms must be used with adolescents and college-age adults, as they tend to achieve particularly high scores on certain of the inventory's five dimensions. In addition to the individual form (Form S), an additional form (Form R) is available with the same items but designed to be completed on an individual by another rater—someone who knows the individual well, such as a spouse or peer. The scores representing an individual's self-perception and another's perception can then be compared. Correlations that range from .5 to .7, which are typically obtained between individual and spouse or peer ratings, can be interpreted as evidence of the validity of the instrument. A form for use in employment and career counseling settings where the Neuroticism factor is not relevant is the NEO-4. It can provide feedback in nonthreatening terms appropriate for both group and individual sessions. Again, two forms are provided: self-reports (Form S) and ratings by another individual (Form R). A shortened version, the NEO Five Factor Inventory, which yields scores only on the five domains, is also available. A rapidly increasing number of research studies using the NEO PI-R have been conducted, and it has emerged as one of the better inventories available for the assessment of normal adult personality.

Eysenck Personality Questionnaire–Revised (EPQ-R)

The EPQ-R offers a brief, broad, and well-researched measure of personality characteristics (Eysenck & Eysenck, 1993). It yields scores for three personality scales, an addiction scale, and a validity scale. The three personality scales—Extraversion, Neuroticism, and Psychoticism—measure independent factors that account for most of the variance among different personality measures. The scales were designed to be used primarily with a nonpathological population; however, extreme scores on the Neuroticism or Psychoticism scales usually indicate psychopathology. The Lie scale measures the extent to which a client may have distorted his or her answers to give a good impression. The 96 items on the EPQ-R describe behaviors that fall primarily within the normal range, not psychiatric symptoms.

For normal clients, the Neuroticism scale can be relabeled as a measure of "emotionality" and the Psychoticism scale as a measure of "tough-mindedness." The Lie scale, although primarily a measure of dissimulation, also may reflect social naivete. A scoring algorithm has been developed to provide an addiction scale.

The EPQ-R has been validated primarily in terms of factor analysis and related procedures. The statistical analyses show that the scales do represent independent dimensions of personality that are important in describing variations in human behavior. The scales significantly discriminate among different groups (e.g., mental patients, criminals, business leaders) in the expected manner. The scales exhibit satisfactory test–retest reliabilities for short time periods and moderately high alpha reliabilities.

Separate age and sex norms are needed. Men score higher on the Psychoticism scale; women score higher on the Neuroticism and Lie scales. Men score higher than women on the Extraversion scale when they are young (less than age 50) but lower than women as they get older. Both sexes obtain lower scores on the Psychoticism and Neuroticism scales as they get older. Scores on the Lie scale are positively correlated with age. A separate form of the EPQ-R, the EPQ Junior, should be used for younger age groups.

The Personality Research Form (PRF)

The PRF is one of two personality inventories authored by Douglas Jackson that represent a method of test construction using the availability of high-speed computers (D. N. Jackson, 1997b). It is based on H. A. Murray's (1938) personality theory and yields scores on 20 personality traits, such as Affiliation (friendly and accepting of others), Endurance (patient and persevering), Nurturance (sympathetic and comforting), and Play (easygoing and participates in many "fun" activities). In addition to the 20 personality scales, there are two validity indices: a Social Desirability scale and an Infrequency scale. High scores on the Social Desirability scale indicate that the clients may be distorting their answers by primarily saying socially desirable things about themselves. Low scores suggest faking bad or malingering by saying undesirable things about themselves. High scores on the Infrequency scale, which is based on items with highly unlikely responses, suggest careless or random responses. The manual contains norms for sixth grade through college.

Jackson Personality Inventory–Revised (JPI-R)

The JPI-R was also developed by D. N. Jackson (1997a) to assess normal personality characteristics but is designed to provide a more practical orientation than the PRF. It consists of 300 true–false items yielding 15 scales organized into five higher order clusters measuring traits such as anxiety, tolerance, energy level, responsibility, risk taking, and social astuteness. The norms are based on samples of college students and white- and blue-collar workers. Each of the 15 scales yields a standard score with a mean of 50 and a standard deviation of 10. The instrument is designed to be easily and quickly scored (10 minutes). High scores represent the traits mentioned by the scales. For example, a high scorer on the Cooperativeness scale is described as susceptible to group influence and pressure and tends to modify behavior consistent with standards set by others.

High scorers are described as compliant, agreeing, and cooperative. Low scorers are described as individualistic, self-reliant, and contradicting. Low scorers tend not to go along with the crowd and are independent in thought and action.

Alpha reliabilities, which are somewhat low, range from .65 to .90 with a median of approximately .80. Validity studies, primarily correlations with appropriate scales on other personality inventories, indicate reasonable concurrent validity.

Both of the Jackson instruments represent contemporary methods of constructing psychometrically sound personality instruments, but they are not well known and have not yet received much use in counseling and other applied settings. Jackson has accomplished the construction of psychometrically sound inventories but has been slower to produce the validity data and the interpretive materials that make them useful in applied settings.

Millon Index of Personality Styles (MIPS)

The MIPS is a newly developed inventory designed to assess personality styles for adults within the normal range (Millon, 1995). It is intended for various counseling situations involving relationships, career placement, or clients experiencing problems in daily living. It contains 24 scales that measure opposite styles on 12 personality dimensions, plus an overall adjustment index. The scales are grouped into four categories: (a) motivating aims, which assess a person's style of adapting to the environment, such as modifying/accommodating, individuating/nurturing; (b) cognitive styles, which assess a person's preferences for information processing, such as sensing/intuiting, thinking/feeling; (c) interpersonal behaviors, which assess the ways people relate to others, such as outgoing/retiring, controlling/yielding; and (d) response sets, such as negative or positive impressions. The inventory is useful for counseling and helping professionals, including those in family and career settings. As a newly developed instrument, it does not possess an extensive research base (Choca, 1998). Millon has also authored the Millon Adolescent Personality Inventory, which can be used to assess the personality of adolescents who have at least a sixth-grade reading level (Millon & Davis, 1993).

Hogan Development Survey (HDS)

The Hogan Development Survey (HDS) is one of several instruments from Hogan Assessment Systems developed for use in particular contexts (Hogan, 1997). Although designed for normal clients, this 168-item instrument measures 11 dysfunctional dispositions that disrupt relations with others and hamper occupational, career, or marital success. It can be used for selection for high-stress jobs, for working clients with interpersonal or situational adjustment problems, or in career development programs.

Coopersmith Self-Esteem Inventories (SEI)

Stanley Coopersmith, who devoted a large part of his career to the study of factors related to self-esteem, defined self-esteem as "the evaluation a person makes and customarily maintains with regard to him- or herself" (Coopersmith, 1993, p. 5). He reasoned that people who have confidence in their abilities will be more persistent and more successful in their activities than will those who perceive themselves negatively. He looked on self-esteem as a global construct that affects a person's evaluation of his or her abilities in many areas. Because of its importance to the individual, in terms both of school or work performance and of personal satisfaction, he believed that counselors and teachers in particular should be aware of deficits in children's self-esteem and that they should be aware of methods for helping to improve self-esteem.

He developed three forms of the Coopersmith Inventory (so named to avoid influencing responses) to measure self-esteem. The longest and most thoroughly developed form is the School Form. This form, which contains 58 items and six scales, was designed for students ages 8 to 15. An abbreviated version of this form, the School Short Form, was constructed from the first 25 items in the School Form for use when time is limited. (The School Form requires about 10 to 15 minutes for most students, whereas the School Short Form can usually be answered in about 5 minutes.) The Adult Form, which also contains 25 items, was adapted from the School Short Form. All items, such as "I'm a lot of fun to be with," are answered *like me* or *unlike me*.

The School Form provides six scores: a total self-esteem score; four scores derived from subscales that measure self-esteem in regard to peers, parents, school, and personal interests; and a score based on a

Lie scale that checks for defensiveness. The School Short From and the Adult Form yield only one score: the total self-esteem score. Measures of internal consistency show high reliabilities for both the subscores and the total scores. Studies based on the School Form show significant relationships between self-esteem and school performance (C. Peterson & Austin, 1985; Sewell, 1985).

As a check on the individual's self-report on the SEI, Coopersmith and Gilberts (1982) developed the Behavioral Academic Self-Esteem (BASE) rating scale for teachers to use in evaluating a student's performance in 16 situations. The scale contains items similar to "this child likes to work on new tasks" and "this child readily states his/her opinion." Teachers rate students on a 5-point scale based on the frequency with which they perform the behavior indicated. The BASE provides outside information to check the accuracy of one's self-perception. Counselors can profit from both types of information in helping clients to enhance their self-esteem.

Tennessee Self-Concept Scale (2nd Edition)

This revision of a famous measure of self-concept is a 90-item instrument that yields a total of 14 scales for counseling purposes. The scales assess self-concept in terms of identity, feelings, and behavior (Fitts, 1996). Items are answered on a 5-point scale ranging from *completely false* to *completely true*. Nine different measures of self-concept have been derived for areas such as identity, physical self, moral/ethical self, self-satisfaction, and social self. In addition, there are two summary scores and four validity scales. The second edition was standardized on a nationwide sample of 3,000 individuals ages 7 to 90. There is a child form for ages 7 to 14 and an adult form for ages 13 and older. The first 20 items on either version can be administered as a short form when only a quick summary is needed. A similar instrument designed especially for younger children is the Piers–Harris Children's Self-Concept Scale, an 80-item instrument designed for children in Grades 3 through 12 and written at a third-grade level (Piers & Harris, 1996).

Computer Administration and Interpretation

Computers are playing an increasing role in the administration, scoring, and interpretation of personality instruments. Almost all publishers offer mail-in computer-scoring services that provide results with colorful and easy-to-interpret profiles. For additional fees, computer-generated narrative reports can be obtained for specific purposes such as selection for sales or police positions, staff or leadership development, or career counseling. Counseling agencies can often purchase software for their own computers that can provide immediate scoring and interpretation as well as actual administration of the inventory itself on computer screens. These features have substantial costs associated with them, so that in addition to determining the most appropriate inventory to use, counselors must decide which type of scoring and interpretation report to purchase on the basis of usefulness, value, and cost.

SUMMARY

1. To interpret results of a personality inventory competently, the counselor must understand both the personality characteristics being assessed and the approach used to develop the various inventory scales.
2. The Myers–Briggs Type Indicator has gained great popularity and is used in many settings in addition to its use by counselors and clinicians.
3. The California Psychological Inventory, the Sixteen Personality Factor Questionnaire, and the Eysenck Personality Questionnaire–Revised are carefully developed inventories with much research backing that assess everyday personality traits.
4. The NEO Personality Inventory–Revised provides measures of the "Big Five" personality factors that account for most of the variance among personality measures.
5. The Personality Research Form and the Jackson Personality Inventory–Revised are two relatively new personality inventories that have capitalized on the capabilities of modern computers in their construction. The Millon Index of Personality Styles and the Hogan Development Survey are other new inventories that have potential usefulness for counselors.
6. Two inventories useful in assessing self-concept are the Coopersmith Self-Esteem Inventory and the Tennessee Self-Concept Scale (2nd Edition).

12

PROJECTIVE TECHNIQUES AND OTHER PERSONALITY MEASURES

T ECHNIQUES USED TO ASSESS personality include the interview, behavioral observations, and personality inventories, as discussed in the previous chapter. In this chapter, four of the most commonly used projective personality measures are discussed briefly. Projective techniques are less often used by counselors than other personality assessment procedures for both practical and psychometric reasons.

Influences on personality include both environmental and developmental factors. Several instruments are described that have been constructed to assess different environments in which individuals find themselves. The chapter concludes with a summary of the assessment of adolescent and postadolescent psychosocial development.

PROJECTIVE TECHNIQUES

In using projective techniques as a method of assessment, counselors present unstructured tasks to the examinee, whose responses to these tasks are expected to reflect needs, experiences, inner states, and thought processes. This concept is known as the *projective hypothesis*—that responses to ambiguous stimuli reflect a person's basic personality. People often reveal more about themselves in their interpretation of a situation than they do about the situation itself, especially if the situation is ambiguous. A variety of ambiguous stimuli have been used for assessment purposes, such as inkblots, pictures, and incomplete sentences. Examinees usually respond in the form of stories, descriptions, completed sentences, or associations. Interpretations have generally drawn on psychoanalytic theory.

Because there is an infinite variety of possible responses to ambiguous stimuli, no particular conclusion can be drawn from any single response. Responses may be classified, however, and from a number of responses general impressions and inferences regarding a person's personality may be derived. The administration and scoring of most projective instruments require considerable training and experience on the part of the examiner. The scoring process may be quite complex or subjective. In addition, even highly experienced examiners frequently disagree on the interpretations and inferences drawn from projective data.

Rorschach Ink Blot Test

The most widely used projective test has been the Rorschach Ink Blot Test (Goldfried, Stricker, & Weiner, 1971; Ulett, 1994), developed in 1921 by Hermann Rorschach, a Swiss psychiatrist. Placing ink on a piece of paper and folding the paper to form ink blots, he asked people to say what images the ink blots suggested to them and used the responses to assess personality.

A series of 10 ink blots have become the standardized stimuli, some of them in gray and several with combinations of colors. Several different methods of administration have been developed along with various systems to score the responses. Responses are classified and scored according to set criteria, such as the location of the response on the ink blot, the feature that determined the response, and the content of the response.

264

Exner's (1993, 2001) procedure has emerged as the most popular scoring scheme and has been shown to have considerable interscorer reliability. Each response given to each ink blot is scored for (a) location—which part or whole of blot; (b) determinant—which feature or color; (c) content—clouds, geography, anatomy; and (d) popularity—common or original. Numbers and ratios of responses in different categories are related to the interpretation given to the test protocol. The Exner system has been shown to have considerable validity in identifying certain personality characteristics.

Although the Rorschach is difficult to evaluate because of its complexity, a meta-analysis of validity studies conducted with the Rorschach indicated that it showed more success than the Minnesota Multiphasic Personality Inventory (MMPI) in predicting objective criterion variables. The MMPI proved to be more effective in predicting psychiatric diagnoses and self-report criteria (Hiller, Rosenthal, Bornstein, Barry, & Brunell-Neuleib, 1999). An extensive amount of training is required to adequately understand and interpret the Rorschach, and the instrument continues to elicit variable reliabilities and validities and mixed reviews. Nevertheless, the Rorschach continues its popularity in many clinical settings (Groth-Marnat, 1997).

Thematic Apperception Test (TAT)

The TAT was developed by Christina Morgan and Henry Murray based on Murray's theory of needs (*apperception* means to perceive in terms of past perceptions; H. A. Murray, 1943). It consists of 30 black-and-white picture cards, most containing one or more human figures, and 1 completely blank card. Twenty of the 30 cards are presented in a test administration, the selection of the 20 depending on the age and sex of the examinee. The examinee is asked to make up a story about each picture and to include what is currently happening in the picture, what led up to that situation, how the people in the story feel, and how the story ends. If examinees fail to include any of these elements, they are asked to fill in the information after the initial story has been completed. They are expected to identify with the hero in their story and project their needs, attitudes, and feelings on this character (Groth-Marnat, 1997).

When the entire test is administered, it is usually broken down into two sessions on 2 different days with 10 cards administered at each session. The cards that illustrate more threatening material are usually included in the second session. Many of those who use the TAT do not use all 20 cards but select 8 to 12 of them and administer them (in the sequences noted by numbers on the back) in a single session. The TAT is usually not scored in any objective fashion, but the frequency of various themes, the intensity and duration of the stories, and the outcomes are taken into account. It is assumed that the hero in the story is the person with whom the examinee identifies. The assumption in interpreting the results is that examinees reveal their conflicts, experiences, needs, and strivings in their storytelling responses. A number of more objective scoring systems have been developed for the TAT to assess such concepts as achievement, ego development, or gender identity, but most are complex and do not provide the overall qualitative view of the individual usually sought by those using this instrument. There is a modified 10-card version for African Americans.

The TAT is widely used and has many supporters, but it has been attacked primarily on psychometric grounds. Subjective interpretations of TAT results often result in different or opposite conclusions even by experienced users.

Instead of administering the entire TAT, counselors often select a few cards for use in an early interview. The cards can be used as a method of initially gaining rapport and as a method of encouraging the client to open up and talk during the counseling session. At the same time, the storytelling responses can yield considerable insight into the needs and personality of the client.

House–Tree–Person (HTP)

The House–Tree–Person Projective Drawing Technique evolved from the earlier "draw-a-person" method of attempting to assess a child's level of cognitive maturity. It is one of the more widely used projective techniques because it often yields considerable clinical information and is easy to use (Buck, 1992). The individual simply draws a house, a tree, and a person, usually on three separate sheets of paper. Then the individual is asked to describe, define, and interpret each of the drawings. Characteristics of the drawings are scored, and interpretive concepts are applied to the characteristics and the responses. Interpretive guidelines are available, but they lack independent validation and any extensive research base (Groth-Marnat, 1997).

Rotter Incomplete Sentences Blank

In the sentence completion technique, a person is asked to complete a number of sentence fragments that are related to possible conflicts or emotions. The most popular sentence completion test is the Rotter Incomplete Sentences Blank, Second Edition (Rotter, Lah, & Rafferty, 1992), which consists of 40 sentence fragments. It has been updated with new norms and more reliability information. Most of the sentence fragments are written in the first person, such as "my mother . . ." or "what bothers me most is . . . ." There are three forms: one for high school, one for college, and one for adults. It is expected that attitudes, traits, and emotions will be expressed in the responses. Responses are compared with sample answers in the manual and scored on a continuum of 6 to 0, from unhealthy or maladjusted through neutral to healthy or positive responses (higher scores suggest greater maladjustment). Thus, a single overall adjustment score is produced that makes this particular form useful as a gross screening instrument.

Because sentence fragments are easy to construct, counselors often develop their own incomplete sentence instruments to deal with various types of conflicts and problems presented by clients. Thus, one counselor-constructed incomplete sentence instrument will deal with problems and conflicts revolving around educational/vocational decision making, another might deal with family conflicts, another with interpersonal conflicts, and yet another with school difficulties.

Early Recollections

Alfred Adler's use of early recollections has been described as the first truly projective test (Aiken, 1999). Emphasizing the importance of early experiences in the formation of personality, the technique involves asking the client to "tell me your earliest memory." It is sometimes used by counselors as a brief projective device. The memories, which should be specific rather than general, are analyzed for cognitive and behavioral patterns. The themes, outlooks, and attitudes revealed by the recollected behavior are examined and interpreted rather than the behavior itself. Standardized questions and a scoring system have been developed to assess these early memories.

PERSON–ENVIRONMENT INTERACTION

Almost all of the developments of applied psychology on which the field of counseling is based have concentrated on the individual and the individual's specific traits, states, aptitudes, and attitudes. Except for the fields of academic and career planning, relatively little attention has been paid to the environments in which individuals function, although some theorists such as Williamson (1939) have emphasized environmental manipulation as a counseling tool. Certain behavioral settings have a very strong and often coercive influence on individuals, and it is necessary to pay particular attention to the perceived situations and environments that influence human behavior. The emphasis thus far has been an attempt to assess the environment and thereby help people to understand and organize their behavior in the social environments in which they find themselves, in order to behave more effectively. Several theories have been developed that emphasize the importance of the environment to the way that individuals think and behave. They emphasize the value that can often result from changes in the environment, as opposed to the more typical counseling approach of assisting the individual to adapt to the situation.

Person–environment interaction theories are usually based on the work of Kurt Lewin (1935) and his famous formula $B = f(P \times E)$, in which behavior (B) is a function (f) of the interaction of the person (P) and the environment (E). These theories give particular attention to the environment portion of this formula, emphasizing the important role that environments play in shaping behavior. Another theorist (Barker, 1968) maintained that individuals tend to behave in similar ways in similar environments (e.g., in church versus at a football game) even though, as individuals, they differ from each other in many important ways. He pointed out that human environments often have a coercive effect on behavior. Environmental or situational variables are seen as the primary influences on behavior, with individuals behaving in a variety of ways depending on the social environments in which they find themselves.

According to Holland's theory (introduced in Chapter 9), human behavior is a function of the interaction between personality and environment, and the choice of a vocation is in part an expression of personality. The ways people think about occupations and vocational stereotypes influence vocational preferences. People with particular personality types create the environments within these occupations, and thus the process is a circular one. People in each of Holland's six personality and environmental types create an atmosphere that reflects that type, and people search out and choose environments in which their interests, attitudes, and personalities fit. Their behavior is thus determined by an interaction between their personality and their environment. Individuals choose environments because of their personalities and remain in these environments because of the reinforcements and satisfactions they obtain in these environments.

Holland developed the Position Classification Inventory (G. D. Gottfredson & Holland, 1991), an 84-item inventory that enables an employee or a supervisor to assess and classify work environments in terms of their demands, rewards, and opportunities. Occupational positions are thus assessed on Holland's six-category classification system and can be used to examine person–job fit and for understanding satisfaction and dissatisfaction with a position or occupation.

Several researchers have developed instruments to use in the assessment of different environments. Rudolph Moos (1974; Moos & Moos, 1994b, 1994c) studied social climates in such widely varying institutions as hospitals, military companies, nursing homes, school classrooms, and university student living units. He developed a series of Social Climate Scales to assess the psychosocial dimensions of environment in these settings. His scales provide information about how those in a particular psychosocial environment perceive that environment. The inventories can be used to compare perceptions of different environments over time or to evaluate how individuals or groups of people differ in their perceptions of an environment.

One of Moos's findings was that the social environments in a variety of settings can be described by common sets of dimensions. These dimensions generally fall under three categories. The relationship dimension refers to the extent to which individuals are involved in the setting, the extent to which they generally support and help each other, and the extent to which they feel able to express themselves. The personal growth dimension includes the extent to which personal growth and self-enhancement occur within the basic functions of the setting. The third dimension is that of system maintenance or change and includes the extent to which the environment is structured and expectations are clear, the extent to which control is maintained in the setting, and how changes can occur.

Individuals are usually more satisfied and successful in those environments where positive social climates exist. Under these circumstances, workers report greater satisfaction with their jobs, psychiatric patients become less depressed, and students show more interest and become more engaged in their course materials (Moos, 1976).

Pace (1987) developed the College Student Experiences Questionnaire to assess the quality of students' college experiences. Now in its fourth edition, the questionnaire assesses 10 dimensions of college environments in addition to 13 dimensions of college activities and 25 estimates of outcomes of undergraduate education (Pace & Kuh, 1998). The College Environment scales are composed of 10 one-item rating scales, of which 7 reflect the purposes of the environment: scholarship, aesthetic awareness, critical analysis, understanding diversity, vocational emphasis, information skills, and personal relevance emphasis. The other 3 dimensions focus on the supportiveness of interpersonal relationships at the college among students, with faculty, and with the administration.

PSYCHOSOCIAL DEVELOPMENT

Several theories have been advanced regarding the developmental changes that occur as an individual moves through various life stages. Instruments designed to assess the effect of these influences and to substantiate the relevant theories have been constructed, but at this point they are not yet ready for use in individual counseling. Nevertheless, these concepts are important for counselors to take into consideration in their work with individuals and groups, and several examples of theories related to these concepts are presented.

These theories have generally built on the work of Erik Erikson (1968), who believed that an individual develops through a sequence of stages that define the life cycle. Each phase or stage is created by the convergence of a particular growth phase and certain developmental tasks. These tasks include learning certain attitudes, forming particular facets of the self, and learning specific skills that must be mastered if one is to successfully manage that particular life phase. In these theories, the development follows a chronological sequence: At certain times of life, a particular facet of the personality emerges as a central concern that must be addressed. The particular timing and methods by which the concerns are addressed are influenced by the individual's society and culture. Psychosocial theorists examine these particular concerns or personal preoccupations that occur at various points in the life cycle. The adolescent is likely to be preoccupied with the concerns of "Who am I?" or "What am I to believe?" The young mother wonders, "What type of parent shall I try to be?" and the older worker, "What type of identity will I have when I retire from my professional position?"

Analogous to the moral and cognitive theories in Chapter 6 advanced by Kohlberg and Perry, Arthur Chickering (Chickering & Reisser, 1993) developed a theory of college student development that is an elaboration of Erikson's stages of identity and intimacy. Chickering focused on the particular developmental concerns of students that are relevant to the social situation in which they find themselves during their years at the university. He attempted to construct a framework of the developmental changes occurring in young adulthood in a more detailed way than did the psychosocial theorists such as Erikson. This framework has been presented in a form that draws on and gives coherence to the wealth of empirical data on college student change reported by a variety of researchers who have studied college students.

Chickering postulated seven vectors or dimensions of development, rather than the developmental tasks or developmental stages used by other theorists. The seven vectors along which development occurs in young adulthood are as follows: Achieving Competency, Managing Emotions, Developing Autonomy, Establishing Identity, Freeing of Interpersonal Relationships, Developing Purpose, and Developing Integrity.

Two sets of inventories have been developed to assess status on these developmental vectors. They include the Student Developmental Task and Lifestyle Assessment (Winston, Miller, & Cooper, 1999) and the Iowa Student Development Inventories (Hood, 1997). These inventories are designed to assess status on these vectors and the changes on them that occur during the college years. Recommendations regarding activities students might undertake to help them develop on those vectors on which they feel they would like to grow might be made from an individual's scores on these instruments. At this point, however, they do not represent instruments on which reliance can be placed in regard to differential diagnoses or selection.

SUMMARY

1. For both practical and psychometric reasons, projective instruments such as the Rorschach Ink Blot Test and the Thematic Apperception Test are seldom used by counselors.

2. Condensed or adapted versions of projective tests such as the Thematic Apperception Test and Rotter Incomplete Sentences Blank are sometimes used by counselors as rapport-building techniques that may also yield insight into the client's personality.

3. Person–environment theories and inventories emphasize situational variables that often have been overlooked by counselors who have traditionally placed more emphasis on the assessment and treatment of individuals. Environmental assessment inventories include the Position Classification Inventory and the Social Climate Scales.

4. Psychosocial developmental theories offer useful concepts (e.g., life stages and developmental vectors) for assessing individuals with particular concerns that occur at various points in the life cycle.

CHAPTER

13

ASSESSMENT OF INTERPERSONAL RELATIONSHIPS

OUNSELORS WHO DEAL WITH educational and vocational issues often make extensive use of interest and aptitude tests, and those who deal with personal adjustment problems often make use of personality tests. Although a number of instruments have been designed specifically for marriage and relationship counseling, relatively few of these instruments are used as a part of the counseling process. When tests are used in relationship counseling, they are often those commonly used in other types of counseling, such as the Minnesota Multiphasic Personality Inventory (MMPI), the California Psychological Inventory (CPI), or the Myers–Briggs Type Indicator (MBTI). The relationship inventories most likely to be used in counseling are briefly discussed in this chapter. Most of the other instruments lack substantial amounts of normative and validity data. Many of these instruments, which can be considered experimental at this point, are primarily used in research studies in this field.

INVENTORIES FOR MARRIAGE, COUPLES, AND FAMILY COUNSELING

Myers–Briggs Type Indicator (MBTI)

The MBTI (see Chapter 11) is the standardized assessment instrument most often used by marital and family therapists in counseling with couples and families (Boughner, Hayes, Bubenzer, & West, 1994). Here its use is to help couples understand their differences in the four dimensions measured by the MBTI and therefore to help them use these differences constructively rather than destructively. Data accumulated by the Center for Applications of Psychological Type indicate that people are only slightly more likely to marry individuals of similar than of opposite types (Myers, McCaulley, Quenk, & Hammer, 1998). The proportion of couples alike in three or all four dimensions is only slightly higher than would be expected from a random assortment of types. The MBTI thus can be used to assist couples in understanding their differences and similarities.

When couples differ on the thinking–feeling dimension, feeling spouses may find their partner cold, unemotional, and insensitive, whereas the thinking spouse can become irritated with the seeming lack of logic of feeling types. Counselors can help thinking types to improve relationships by openly showing appreciation and by refraining from comments that sound like personal criticism. They can encourage feeling types to state wishes clearly, so the thinking partner does not have to guess their wishes. One spouse may be an extrovert who needs considerable external stimulation, whereas the other may be an introvert who needs sufficient time alone. This becomes a problem when the introverted partner expends a good deal of energy in extroverted work all day and has little energy left for sociability in the evening. The extroverted partner, on the other hand, may work in a more solitary setting and look forward to an evening of social stimulation and activity. Problems arising from judging–perceiving differences can be found when planning, order, and organization are important to the judging partner whereas freedom and spontaneity are important to the perceptive partner, who also has a great deal more tolerance for ambiguity.

In using the MBTI with couples, counselors sometimes ask couples to guess the types of their partners after describing the types briefly. It is also possible to have each partner answer the MBTI twice, once for themselves and once as they believe their partner will respond. In either case, the accuracy of type descriptions of partners can be discussed, and these differences can be useful to them as they see how they affect their relationship.

The MBTI can also be useful in family counseling in discussing difficulties in communication and differences in child-rearing styles and in attitudes toward other family members. For example, a counselor can help an orderly, practical, sensing–judging parent to see that it is easier for him or her to raise a sensing–judging child, who desires structure and organization, than it is for that parent to raise an independent, intuitive–perceptive child, who rebels against structure and order.

Taylor–Johnson Temperament Analysis (TJTA)

The TJTA is second only to the MBTI in popularity for use in premarital and marital counseling (Boughner et al., 1994). It consists of 180 items equally divided among nine scales measuring traits such as Nervous–Composed, Depressive–Lighthearted, Responsive–Inhibited, Dominant–Submissive, and Self-Disciplined–Impulsive (Taylor & Morrison, 1996). Norms are based on large but not necessarily representative samples, including a separate set of norms based on high school students. An additional edition is available for use with populations whose vocabulary and reading comprehension are below the eighth-grade level.

A unique feature of this instrument is the "crisscross" procedure in which one person records his or her impressions of another person. This use can be valuable in family counseling involving parent–adolescent interaction, in situations involving sibling conflict, or in premarital or marital counseling.

Marital Satisfaction Inventory, Revised (MSI-R)

The MSI-R is a self-report inventory designed to assess marital interaction and the extent of marital distress (Snyder, 1997). Scores are obtained on 11 different scales with titles such as Affective Communication, Problem-Solving Communication, Disagreement About

Finances, Sexual Dissatisfaction, Conflict Over Child-Rearing, and a Global Distress scale, which measures general unhappiness and uncertain commitment in the marriage. A Social Desirability scale (conventionalization) and an Inconsistency scale are included as a check on the response set of the test taker, and an Aggression scale has been added. The scales contain 9 to 19 true–false items per scale. In the revised version, items were changed to be appropriate for both traditional and nontraditional couples, and the inventory was restandardized on a larger and more representative sample of couples.

The MSI-R is intended to be used in couples counseling, with both the husband and wife taking the scale and the results being displayed on a single profile that indicates areas of agreement and disagreement. It is typically administered during the initial contact with the counselor or agency so that results are available for the ensuing counseling sessions. The MSI-R provides useful information for counselors by providing a picture of the couple's overall marital distress, the general quality of their communication, and the differences between their perceptions of aspects of their relationship. Validity studies of the MSI-R scales generally show reasonable correlations with other measures of marital satisfaction. The MSI-R significantly differentiates between various criterion groups experiencing marital dissatisfaction. The manual for the MSI-R reports internal consistency coefficients and test–retest reliability coefficients in the .80 to .95 range.

Derogatis Sexual Functioning Inventory (DSFI)

The DSFI yields 12 scores consisting of 10 scales with titles such as Information, Experience, Psychological Symptoms, Gender Role Definition, and Sexual Satisfaction (Derogatis, 1979). A total score and the client's evaluation of current functioning are also included. The Information subscale consists of 26 true–false items measuring the amount of a client's accurate sexual information. The Experience subscale lists 24 sexual behaviors ranging from kissing on the lips to oral–genital sex. The Sexual Drive subscale measures the frequency of various sexual behaviors, and the Attitude subscale measures the diversity of liberal and conservative attitudes.

The entire inventory can be expected to take 45 minutes to an hour to complete and was designed to assess individual rather than couple sexual functioning. The DSFI primarily measures current functioning, although the Sexual Experience and the Sexual Fantasy subscales ask the client to report lifetime experiences. Because the DSFI is one of the most thoroughly studied instruments in sexual research, several different types of norms are available for the instrument. Certain of the subscales, such as Sexual Information, Sexual Desire, and Gender Roles, have produced relatively low internal consistency coefficients (below .70). Others tend to be more adequate, falling in the .80 to .92 range. The instrument can provide counselors with considerable information regarding sexual functioning. A computer-administered version is also available that yields extensive interpretive information.

Couple's Precounseling Inventory (CPCI)

The CPCI is a revision of the former Stuart Couple's Precounseling Inventory (Stuart & Jacobson, 1987). Norms are based on a small representative sample (60 couples) that includes nonmarried heterosexual and homosexual couples. The purpose of the instrument is for use in planning and evaluating relationship therapy based on a social learning model. From a 16-page form, scores are obtained in 12 different areas of relationships, such as Communication Assessment, Conflict Management, Sexual Interaction, Child Management, Relationship Change Goals, General Happiness With the Relationship, and Goals of Counseling. The manual reports high levels of internal consistency reliabilities (from .85 to .91). In taking the instrument, couples describe current interaction patterns rather than personality characteristics. Items tend to emphasize positive characteristics, and, if taken with some seriousness by the couple, the instrument can be educational and therapeutic. The CPCI is based on social learning theory and is designed to examine relationship characteristics and motivations that can be useful in suggesting avenues of treatment if the relationship is to survive (Touliatos, Perlmutter, & Holdon, 2001).

Family Environment Scale (FES)

The FES (3rd Edition) is one of a number of social climate scales developed by Moos and his associates (Moos & Moos, 1994a). It consists of three forms that assess the client's perception of the family as it is (the Real Form, R), as he or she would prefer it to be (the Ideal Form, I), and as he or she would expect it to react to new situations (the Expecation Form, E). The three 90-item inventories yield standard scores for 10 scales with titles such as Cohesion, Intellectual–Cultural Orientation, Active Recreational Orientation, Moral–Religious Emphasis, Expressiveness, and Control. Any of the three forms can be used alone or in combination with various family members to allow the counselor to explore differences between spouses' perceptions and between parent and child perceptions as a means of identifying family treatment issues. There is also a children's version (CVFES).

The 10 scales are grouped into three underlying domains: the relationship domain, the personal growth domain, and the system maintenance domain. The assumption behind all of the Social Climate Scales is that environments, and in this case families, have unique personalities that can be measured in the same way as individual personalities. Norms are based on a group of 1,432 normal and 788 distressed families. The items on the FES are statements about family environments originally obtained through structured interviews with family members. Validity evidence is based primarily on the difference in mean scores between normal and distressed families.

Family Assessment Measure–III (FAM-III)

The FAM-III consists of three interrelated forms: a 50-item General Scale that examines general family functioning, a 42-item Dyadic Relationship Scale that examines how a family member perceives his or her relationship with another family member, and a 42-item Self-Rating Scale on which each individual rates his or her own functioning within the family (Skinner, Steinhauer, & Santa-Barbara, 1995). It yields scores on seven scales such as Role Performance, Affective Expression, and Communication and two validity scales. It is available in paper-and-pencil and computer formats, in several languages, and in a brief screening version (Brief FAM).

Triangular Love Scale (TLS)

The TLS is a 45-item scale that measures the three components of romantic relationships identified by Sternberg (1987): intimacy, passion, and commitment. According to Sternberg, all three components must be assessed in evaluating the quality of a romantic relationship.

NEO Couples Compatibility Report (NEO-CCR)

A software program for the NEO Personality Inventory–Revised (NEO PI-R; see Chapter 11) has been developed to identify aspects of each partner's personality that may be affecting a couple's compatibility. Each partner takes the NEO PI-R, and his or her NEO facet scores are entered into the computer program. A report is generated that indicates how the partners' personalities fit together and how each partner's personality characteristics are likely to influence the couple's compatibility.

INTERPERSONAL ASSESSMENT INVENTORIES

Contemporary theories of interpersonal functioning assert that an individual's behavior can be understood only in relation to transactions with others and not for the individual in isolation. In the generally accepted model of interpersonal theory, each interaction represents a combination of two basic dimensions of interpersonal behavior: control (dominance vs. submission) and affiliation (friendliness vs. hostility; VanDenberg, Schmidt, & Kiesler, 1992). In any interaction (including client and counselor), individuals continually negotiate these two relationship issues: how friendly or hostile they will be and how much in control they will be in their relationship. This approach uses a circular rather than a linear model; behavior is viewed not solely by situational factors or psychic motivation but instead within a group of two or more people exerting mutual influence. These two dimensions are incorporated into a model called the *interpersonal circle* or *circumplex*. It is organized around the horizontal and vertical axes representing affiliation and control (Tracey & Schneider, 1995).

Among the inventories designed to assess interpersonal interactions are the Checklist of Interpersonal Transactions (CLOIT), a 96-item interpersonal behavior inventory, and the Checklist of Psychotherapy Transactions, a parallel version of the CLOIT for rating clients and counselors, both developed by Kiesler (1987). Other promising measures of interpersonal functioning include the Interpersonal Compass (Fico & Hogan, 2000) and the Impact Message Inventory (Kiesler, Schmidt, & Wagner, 1997).

279

The Interpersonal Adjective Scales (IAS), a self-report instrument that assesses the two primary interpersonal dimensions of dominance and nurturance, builds on experience gained with previously developed interpersonal assessment inventories (Wiggins, 1993). The IAS yields scores on eight interpersonal variables that are ordered along the two primary axes of the interpersonal circumplex. It is designed to provide information about how an individual typically behaves in different interpersonal situations. The instrument consists of 64 adjectives that are descriptive of interpersonal interactions and are responded to in an 8-point Likert format, with respondents rating how accurately each word describes them as individuals. Responses yield octant scores, which are then plotted on the circumplex. The titles of the eight interpersonal octants are shown on the circumplex profile in Figure 13-1. Based on scores shown in this example, this individual would be described as cold-hearted, aloof, introverted, unassured, and submissive.

In interpreting the results of the circumplex profile, counselors should use all of the information provided on the profile and not focus solely on the highest segment score or scores. By paying attention to only one or two octants, the counselor may miss considerable information regarding the client's interpersonal behavior, and the advantage of the circumplex model is lost. Because interpersonal transactions include those between the client and counselor, the counselor's perception of client interactions should be compared with those of the client's self-report represented by the circumplex profile. Counselors can examine the components of a client's interpersonal functioning and identify topics that will be more or less anxiety provoking to a client. Many client difficulties can be viewed as maladaptive transactional patterns. Clients can be helped to understand the predominantly automatic and unaware manner in which they communicate to others through their verbal and nonverbal behavior. Individuals often use a narrow range of interpersonal responses that may not be appropriate to the situation.

The Thomas–Kilman Conflict Mode Instrument is an inventory often used in situations calling for conflict resolution (Thomas & Kilman, 1974). Individuals respond to 30 statement pairs to determine their preferred style or mode of handling conflict: competing, avoiding, compromising, collaborating, or accommodating. According to a

FIGURE 13-1. Interpersonal Adjective Scales Profile of Extreme Depression in a Former Bank Manager

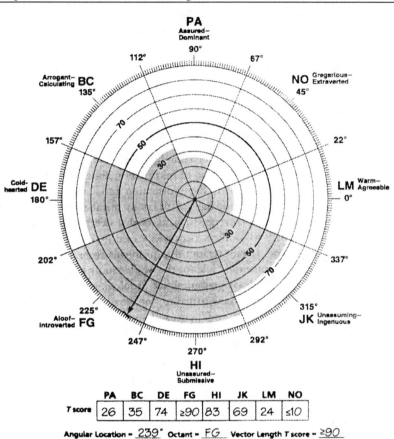

	PA	BC	DE	FG	HI	JK	LM	NO
T score	26	35	74	≥90	83	69	24	≤10

Angular Location = 239° Octant = FG Vector Length T score = ≥90

recent study that compared MBTI types with conflict resolution styles, thinking types preferred collaboration, and introverts preferred conflict avoidance (A. K. Johnson, 1997). Results can lead to a discussion about how conflict affects personal and group relations and present a practical approach to conflict resolution.

GENOGRAMS

A genogram is a map that provides a graphic representation of a family structure and is usually associated with Bowen's family system theory (Marchetti-Mercer & Cleaver, 2000). It involves the collection of information for about three generations of a family and organizes the information into a kind of family tree. It contains the names and ages of all family members along with information about major events such as births, deaths, marriages, divorces, adoptions, and conflicts. As the information is collected in this way, it allows family relationship problems to be seen in the context of the developmental cycle for the whole family in addition to that of the individual who is presenting the problem.

By examining the relational structure, including family composition, sibling constellations, and unusual family configurations, the counselor can hypothesize certain roles or relationships that can then be checked out by eliciting further information. Repetitive patterns of functioning and relationships often occur across generations, and by recognizing these patterns, counselors can help family members to alter them.

In drawing a genogram, some counselors obtain the basic information to structure the genogram and then go back and question each individual about it and their relationships with other family members, both within and across generations. Others obtain this information as each individual is placed on the genogram. Some counselors obtain only a basic genogram illustrating the general family structure; others, through the use of figures, abbreviations, and symbols, develop a genogram that contains a great deal of organized data, including educational and occupational patterns, about the generations of a family system (McGoldrick & Gerson, 1985). A sample basic genogram for the couple Joseph and Paula is shown in Figure 13-2.

The construction of a genogram is a cooperative task between the counselor and the client. Clients readily become interested and involved in the construction of a genogram; they enjoy the process and usually reveal much significant information about various relatives and their relationships with them. While seemingly deceptively simple, genogram construction provides much insight into both the family constellation and the individual's interpersonal relationships within the family system. Even from reticent clients, both the quantity and the emotional depth of the data produced are often superior to that obtained through the typical interview process and are more easily obtained as well. The genogram can easily be adapted for

FIGURE 13-2. Genogram of Joseph and Paula

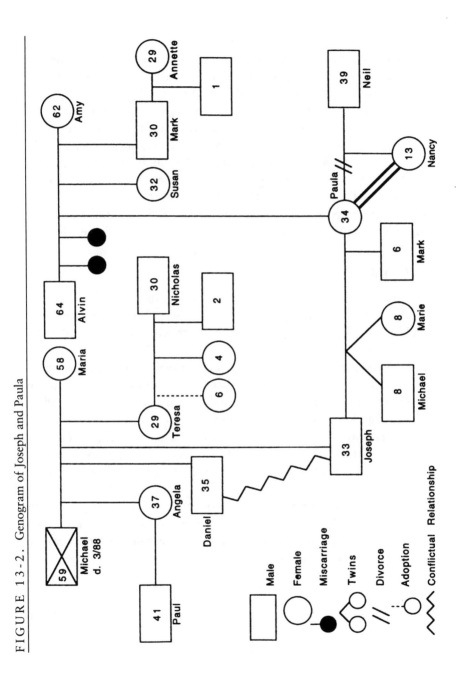

counseling clients from diverse backgrounds on a variety of issues. Particular attention is usually paid to two opposite types of interactions linked to family dysfunction: enmeshed (too emotionally close) or disengaged (too emotionally distant; Penick, 2000).

The construction of genograms in marriage and relationship counseling as well as in other types of counseling has thus been enthusiastically embraced by many counselors and has become an increasingly commonly used assessment technique. Although popular, the technique has not been subjected to more than a few studies of reliability, and there is little validity evidence. Therefore, counselors should consider such interpretations as only hypotheses and use caution in drawing conclusions from genograms without other confirming evidence.

SUMMARY

1. Personality inventories such as the MMPI, the CPI, and especially the MBTI, commonly used in other types of counseling, are most likely to be used by counselors with clients concerned with marriage or relationship issues.
2. There are instruments specifically developed to assess marital satisfaction, sexual functioning, communication issues, and family environments with which counselors can assist clients to understand and deal with relationship problems.
3. Interpersonal assessment instruments usually evaluate an individual's interaction with others in terms of two dimensions: control (dominance vs. submission) and affiliation (friendliness vs. hostility).
4. Through the cooperative construction of a multigeneration graphic family structure—the genogram—insight into family constellations and interpersonal relationships within the family can be revealed to both the counselor and the client.

14

MENTAL HEALTH ASSESSMENT: INTERVIEW PROCEDURES

I
N THE COURSE of helping people solve problems, counselors will work with a number of clients who could be diagnosed as mentally ill. In the first national survey of a representative sample of the population based on a structured psychiatric interview, Kessler et al. (1994) found that nearly 30% of the respondents suffered from a mental or addictive disorder within a 12-month period. The most common disorders occurring during this time period were anxiety disorders (17%), substance abuse disorders (11%), and affective disorders (11%). Approximately one half of the participants in the survey met the psychiatric diagnostic criteria for a mental disorder sometime in their lifetime. These figures are higher than those of previous epidemiological studies based on less comprehensive procedures (Regier et al., 1988; Robins et al., 1984).

Other research also shows that a significant number of the clients at university counseling centers or mental health centers are psychopathologically disturbed (Pledge, Lapan, Heppner, Kivlighan, & Roehlke, 1998). In one study, more than 40% of the students at a university mental health clinic qualified as psychiatric cases (Todd, Deane, & McKenna, 1997). In another study, at least one fourth to one third of the clients at a university counseling service showed signs of a psychiatric disorder (R. W. Johnson, Ellison, & Heikkinen, 1989).

These studies indicate the need for counselors to be familiar with procedures for assessing mental illness. Many of their clients will exhibit symptoms of mental illness, especially depression and anxiety. Many of the people in the population the counselors serve will also show signs of mental illness even though they do not seek treatment. Counselors must be able to recognize the symptoms of mental illness and to provide at least a preliminary assessment of the client's mental state. They must be able to determine when services such as crisis intervention, psychiatric consultation, and long-term treatment may be necessary. Interview procedures to aid counselors in this endeavor are presented in this chapter. The use of standardized inventories for this purpose are discussed in the next chapter.

DIAGNOSTIC AND STATISTICAL MANUAL OF MENTAL DISORDERS, FOURTH EDITION (DSM-IV)

The *DSM-IV* provides a means of classifying psychiatric and psychological disorders for treatment and research purposes (American Psychiatric Association, 1994). The *DSM-IV*, which assumes an atheoretical position, classifies disorders based on descriptive, not etiological, factors. The diagnostic categories used by the *DSM-IV* serve as the official means of classifying mental disorders in most medical and psychological settings in the United States.

The *DSM-IV* uses a multiaxial classification system as indicated below:

- Axis I: Clinical disorders and other conditions that may be a focus of clinical attention
- Axis II: Personality disorders and mental retardation

- Axis III: General medical conditions
- Axis IV: Psychosocial and environmental problems
- Axis V: Global assessment of functioning

The clinical disorders included on Axis I encompass all mental disorders except personality disorders and mental retardation. The Axis I disorders are classified into 15 broad categories, such as mood, anxiety, and adjustment disorders. The broad categories are further subdivided into subcategories, such as major depressive, dysthymic, bipolar I or II, or cyclothymic disorders for the mood disorder category. Developmental disorders such as learning, motor skills, and communication disorders, which used to be classified on Axis II, are now classified on Axis I. In addition to the clinical disorders, non-psychiatric conditions that may be a focus of clinical attention are noted on Axis I. These conditions include the V-codes, which pertain to relational problems, bereavement, identity problems, phase-of-life problems, academic problems, occupational problems, and other issues often addressed in counseling.

Each disorder is defined in terms of specific criteria. For example, the diagnostic criteria for dysthymic disorder (*DSM-IV* code number 300.4), a chronic state of low-grade depression, are summarized below (American Psychiatric Association, 1994, pp. 345–349):

- Depressed mood for most of the day during the majority of the days over a 2-year period (1-year period for children and adolescents)
- Presence of at least 2 of the following 6 symptoms while depressed: poor appetite or overeating, insomnia or hypersomnia, low energy, low self-esteem, poor concentration or difficulty making decisions, and feelings of hopelessness
- Symptoms must cause significant distress or impairment in social, occupational, or other areas of functioning

In addition, the person must never have been without these symptoms for more than 2 months during the 2-year period (1 year for children and adolescents) and must not meet the criteria for a major depressive episode during this time period. It is also important to differentiate this disorder from other disorders such as cyclothymic disorder, chronic psychotic disorders, and substance-related disorders, and from general medical conditions such as hypothyroidism.

Note that the criteria describe the frequency, duration, and severity of the symptomatic behaviors. A person must meet all of these criteria to be classified as an individual suffering from dysthymic disorder.

Axis II differs from Axis I in focusing on personality disorders or mental retardation conditions that may underlie the presenting problem. These conditions, which are often longstanding in nature, may be overlooked if not recorded on a separate axis (American Psychiatric Association, 1994). Personality disorders refer to lifelong maladaptive behavior patterns that are often triggered by specific events in the person's life. *DSM-IV* identifies a total of 10 personality disorders grouped in three clusters as indicated below.

- Cluster A: *Emotional withdrawal and odd behavior* includes paranoid, schizoid, and schizotypal personality disorders
- Cluster B: *Exaggerated, dramatic emotionality* includes antisocial, borderline, histrionic, and narcissistic disorders
- Cluster C: *Anxious, restive submissiveness* includes avoidant, dependent, and obsessive–compulsive disorders

In addition, "personality disorder not otherwise specified" also serves as a diagnostic category for individuals who meet the general definition for personality disorder but who do not fit neatly into any of the 10 categories.

Personality disorders represent extreme forms of personality traits (i.e., enduring and pervasive patterns of behavior) that have become dysfunctional for the person. The trait is expressed in such a rigid or inappropriate manner that it interferes with that person's adjustment.

People with personality disorders usually lack insight regarding the source of their difficulties. Clients usually do not seek counseling because of a personality disorder itself but because of difficulties associated with the disorder. For example, a person with a dependent personality disorder might seek counseling because of loneliness or indecisiveness but not for dependency. The counselor needs to look beyond the symptoms to find the personality disorder.

According to Fong (1995, p. 636), any of the following signs may suggest a client with a personality disorder:

- Counseling comes to a sudden stop in progress after initial success
- The client is unaware of the effect of his or her behavior on others
- The problems are acceptable to the client
- The client is underresponsive or noncompliant with therapeutic regime
- The client enters into intense conflictual relationships with institutional systems

Fong recommended the use of a semistructured interview such as the Personality Disorder Interview–IV (Widiger, Mangine, Corbitt, Ellis, & Thomas, 1995) to ascertain the presence of a personality disorder.

The third axis of *DSM-IV* lists any current physical illness or condition of the individual. In some cases, a physical illness may mask itself as a psychiatric ailment. The counselor needs to be aware of physical disorders that might be influencing a client's mental state.

The first three axes provide the official classification of psychiatric patients for most purposes; however, information provided by the last two axes allows the counselor to gain a more complete picture of the person. The fourth axis identifies psychosocial stressors faced by the client, such as problems with primary support group or occupational problems. The fifth axis rates the client's general level of functioning on a 100-point scale at the time of evaluation. The five axes together offer an integrated view of a client's problems from the standpoint of a biopsychosocial model of human functioning.

The current version of the *DSM* includes a number of changes designed to enhance its use with clients from different cultures. D. W. Smart and Smart (1997) noted the following five improvements: (a) Specific culture, age, and gender features are described for many of the disorders; (b) a glossary of culture-bound syndromes limited to certain societies or cultural areas has been added; (c) an "Outline for Cultural Formulation" is provided in the Appendix as a means of systematically taking into account cultural context; (d) Axis IV has been broadened to include psychosocial and environmental problems such as difficulty with discrimination, inadequate housing, and inadequate health care services; and (e) the V-codes now include "Acculturation Problem" as a nonpsychiatric condition that may be the object of clinical attention.

The *DSM-IV*–Text Revision (*DSM-IV-TR*; American Psychiatric Association, 2000a) provides updated information regarding many of the mental disorders; however, the specific criteria used in making the different psychiatric diagnoses remain unchanged.

As a diagnostic system, the *DSM* has continued to evolve since its first edition in 1952. Widiger and Clark (2000) suggested that future versions of the *DSM* be based on a dimensional model of classification that makes systematic use of laboratory or psychological tests in determining diagnoses. A dimensional model recognizes a "continuum of functioning" in various psychological domains (such as personality or cognitive ability factors) that can be used to differentiate between psychopathology and normality and among different types of mental disorders. Such a model (based on cognitive ability factors) is now used in diagnosing learning disorders and mental retardation but not for any of the other *DSM* disorders. They also argued that the *DSM* should place more emphasis on assessments made over a period of time, in contrast with those made at just one point in time.

The following points should be considered in using the *DSM-IV* in counseling:

1. Use the *DSM-IV* with clients who appear to be suffering from a psychiatric disorder. Use of the *DSM-IV* classification system improves the reliability and validity of the assessment process. Diagnoses of mental disorders made by means of specific criteria such as those listed in the *DSM-IV* are as reliable as diagnoses of general medical disorders (U.S. Public Health Service, 1999).

2. Become familiar with case study materials and interviewing techniques for determining *DSM-IV* classifications (LaBruzza & Mendez-Villarrubia, 1994; Morrison, 1995a, 1995b; Spitzer, Gibbon, Skodol, Williams, & First, 1994). Appropriate use of the *DSM-IV* requires systematic training and experience in its use.

3. Consider using a structured interview, such as the Primary Care Evaluation of Mental Disorders (Spitzer, Williams, et al., 1994), to assist in the screening and diagnostic process. Use the decision-tree approach described in the back of the manual to help make differential diagnoses (American Psychiatric Association, 1994, Appendix A).

4. Take into account both inclusion and exclusion criteria. A person who meets the inclusion criteria for a mental disorder actually may be suffering from a related disorder, a physical illness, or substance abuse, which may not be clear until exclusion criteria are considered. *DSM-IV* places greater emphasis on exclusion criteria than did earlier versions of this manual.

5. Assess for the possibility of more than one disorder occurring at the same time. Dual and triple diagnoses of mental disorders for the same person are relatively common (Kessler et al., 1994).

6. Keep in mind the distinction between symptom-oriented interviewing and insight-oriented interviewing (Othmer & Othmer, 1994). The first yields descriptions of the client's behavior, which is necessary for *DSM-IV* classifications. The second provides possible explanations for the client's behavior. Both types of interviewing need to be pursued in counseling.

7. Be careful to use the *DSM-IV* categories to classify a client's condition, not to label the client. For example, a client should be viewed as a person with schizophrenia, not as a schizophrenic. Labeling can lead to stereotyping and self-fulfilling prophecies.

8. In making *DSM-IV* diagnoses, consider a person's strengths as well as weaknesses. For example, all personality disorders represent the client's attempts to cope with his or her environment. Psychopathology can often be reframed as a logical response to developmental history (Ivey & Ivey, 1998).

9. Use the *DSM-IV* classification system to enhance communication with medical and mental health referral sources (Geroski, Rodgers, & Breen, 1997; Hinkle, 1999). Most agencies require that clients or patients be assigned a *DSM-IV* code for diagnostic and treatment purposes as well as for third-party payments.

10. Consult guidebooks such as *Selecting Effective Treatments* (Seligman, 1998) or *Therapist's Guide to Clinical Intervention* (S. L. Johnson, 1997) for treatment suggestions for the different types of mental disorders listed in *DSM-IV*.

11. In planning treatments, take into account the client's environment and developmental history as well as the *DSM-IV* diagnosis (Axis IV can be helpful for this purpose). Ivey and Ivey (1999) noted that the *DSM-IV* diagnoses primarily focus on the individual without giving sufficient attention to the context in which the problem developed.

12. Be careful not to equate cultural differences with psychological deficits (Rollock & Terrell, 1996). As noted by D. W. Smart and Smart (1997), the *DSM-IV* is biased toward the North American culture in which it was developed. Counselors need to develop a broad awareness of social and cultural issues to be able to apply the *DSM-IV* effectively with multicultural clients.

13. Keep in mind the limitations of the *DSM-IV* classification system. Because of its categorical nature, it does not adequately indicate the severity of a particular condition, nor does it sufficiently differentiate among individuals classified within the same broad categories (Clark, Watson, & Reynolds, 1995). Furthermore, the categories themselves suffer from artificial boundaries and extensive overlapping.

14. Consider the *DSM-IV* diagnosis as a hypothesis that is subject to review as circumstances change or as additional data are collected. Determining a *DSM-IV* diagnosis should be looked on as a process, not a static event (Hinkle, 1999).

SUICIDE RISK ASSESSMENT

Counselors must always be ready to evaluate the risk of suicide among the clients they see. As indicated in Chapter 4, it is a good practice to routinely ask clients about any recent thoughts of suicide. The National College Health Risk Behavior Survey found that 10% of college students had seriously considered attempting suicide during the 12 months preceding the survey (Brener, Hassan, & Barrios, 2000). Approximately 30% of the clients (474 of 1,589) seen at one university counseling service during a 1-year period indicated that they had experienced "thoughts of ending their life" during the week prior to their first counseling session (R. W. Johnson, Heikkinen, & Ellison, 1988). Counselors need to respond to this issue by undertaking a systematic assessment of suicide risk. The counselor should be careful to establish rapport with the client so that the assessment can be as complete and as accurate as possible.

Clients should be asked directly about their suicidal thoughts if there is any hint of suicidal thinking. The counselor can usually approach this with a series of graded questions. For example, the counselor might ask, "How have you been feeling lately?" "How bad does it get?" "Has it ever been so bad that you wished you were dead?" and "Have you had thoughts of suicide?" If the client has had thoughts of suicide, the counselor needs to inquire about the extent of these thoughts.

Some counselors are apprehensive about bringing up the topic of suicide with a client for fear that this will encourage the client to think about suicide as an option. In reality, clients who have had suicidal thoughts need the opportunity to talk about these thoughts. The great majority of clients are receptive to the routine assessment of suicide risk, including past suicide attempts. Only 3% of the clients in one study did not think that it was a good idea to assess past suicide attempts routinely (Hahn & Marks, 1996).

In essence, suicide risk assessment becomes part of the treatment. Talking about suicidal thoughts helps to validate the client's experience. It provides a sense of relief and communicates hope to the client that the problem can be addressed. In contrast, clients who have not had suicidal thoughts will usually reassure the counselor that this is not a concern. In fact, it is sometimes a relief for such clients to see their problems from this perspective: Even though they are struggling with a problem, things are not so bad that they think of suicide.

In making a suicide risk assessment, counselors should be both calm and direct. Calmness indicates that it is acceptable for clients to talk about the things they find to be most troubling. Counselors help clients to look at problems in depth and from different points of view. They should make a point of using the words *suicide* or *kill yourself* while conducting the suicide risk assessment. The enormity of the act should be faced directly. It should not be romanticized.

Significant Factors in Suicide Risk Assessment

The assessment of suicide risk is basic to the formulation of a treatment or intervention plan. The assessment should involve a consideration of the six significant sets of factors discussed below (Cesnik & Nixon, 1977; Stelmachers, 1995).

Self-Reported Risk. After clients have acknowledged suicidal ideation, they will usually tell the counselor of their perception of their risk level when asked. Questions such as "How likely do you think it is that you will act on your thoughts of suicide?" or "How long can you continue to tolerate the situation as it is?" will often generate responses that will be helpful in the assessment process. A self-report of high risk must always be taken seriously.

Suicide Plan. For those clients with thoughts of suicide, the counselor should ask if they have considered a plan. If they have a plan, do they intend to act on it? Information about the plan is critical in helping to assess a client's suicide potential. The counselor should evaluate the plan in terms of (a) its lethality, (b) the availability of the means, and (c) the specificity of the details.

First, some plans are much more lethal, or likely to succeed, than others. Firearms, jumping from great heights, and hanging are highly lethal. More people kill themselves with firearms than by any other method (National Institute of Mental Health, 1999). Holding one's breath until one dies or starving oneself to death is much less likely to succeed.

Second, does the client have access to the means of killing himself or herself? Is a gun available? Has ammunition been purchased? The counselor needs to get clear answers to these specific questions. At times, it may be necessary to interview friends or family members to obtain this information.

Finally, how detailed are the client's plans? The risk of suicide increases as plans become more detailed and specific. For example, has the client made plans to give away possessions? Has the client considered what he or she might write in a note? Where would the suicide take place? When would it take place? Clients who have worked out a detailed suicide plan with a high likelihood of success demand immediate attention. Even more alarming are clients who have started to act on their plans, for example, those who have written a suicide note or given a pet animal to a friend. Provisions for further psychological or psychiatric assessment and treatment must be undertaken at once for these people.

Suicide History. A history of suicide attempts, the medical seriousness of previous attempts, and a family history of suicide are all critical factors in assessing the suicide risk of clients with depression, according to a survey of practicing psychologists (Peruzzi & Bongar, 1999). About 10% of those who have attempted suicide in the past will eventually succeed in killing themselves (Suicide Risk Advisory

Committee, 1996). If a person has attempted or seriously thought about suicide at some earlier time, particularly by lethal means, the risk of suicide for that person is significantly increased.

The counselor should check on the history of suicide in the family and among friends. Have family members or friends committed suicide or made suicide threats or attempts? If so, what was the nature of the relationship between that person and the client? Did that person represent a model for the client? How does the client feel about these situations? When did the suicide or suicide attempt take place? Anniversary dates can sometimes provide the impetus for suicide attempts.

Psychological Symptoms. Clients who are suffering from mental disorders or psychological distress are much more likely to commit suicide than those who are not (Klerman, 1987; National Institute of Mental Health, 1999). All client symptoms should be reviewed. Critical symptoms include acute suicidal ideation, severe hopelessness, attraction to death, and acute overuse of alcohol (Peruzzi & Bongar, 1999).

Suicidal ideation can be predicted by asking clients if they had relatively long periods of time (2 weeks or more) during the past year in which they experienced sleeping problems, felt depressed or lost interest in things they usually enjoyed, felt guilty or worthless, or felt that life was hopeless (Cooper-Patrick, Crum, & Ford, 1994). Clients who respond positively to any of these items should be asked if they have thoughts of suicide. According to experts on the topic, hopelessness stands out as "the most powerful antecedent" of suicide (Stelmachers, 1995, p. 374). Restlessness or agitation associated with any of the above symptoms increases the risk for suicide.

Alcohol or other drug abuse significantly increases the risk of suicide for a client. Approximately 15% to 25% of people with alcoholism eventually commit suicide (Klerman, 1987). Counseling programs designed to prevent suicide must also address the related problem of alcohol or other drug abuse (Brener et al., 2000).

Medications can also be associated with suicide. The side effects of many medications include depression. The counselor should note if the client is taking any medications, including any recent change in medications. Medications are also frequently used as a means of suicide. As a safety precaution, someone else should control anti-depressant medications prescribed for highly suicidal clients.

Symptoms that suggest severe mental illness such as schizophrenia, bipolar disorder, or other psychotic disorders demand prompt attention. Has the client lost contact with reality? Does the client hear voice commands (auditory hallucinations) telling him or her what to do? All psychotic individuals with thoughts of suicide should be hospitalized immediately to provide protection and relief from their psychosis. Many people who kill themselves are people with severe and persistent mental illness.

Sometimes signs of improvement can increase the risk of suicide. Clients may become more actively suicidal as they begin to come out of a deep depression, that is, when they acquire enough energy to act on their suicidal thoughts. In a similar fashion, clients sometimes will give an appearance of improvement when they have resolved their ambivalence by deciding to commit suicide.

Environmental Stress.   Stressful situations are often the precipitating cause of suicidal ideation. What is the nature of the client's environment? Why is the client feeling suicidal at this particular time? What are the precipitating factors? How would the client benefit from suicide? Clients who wish to commit suicide to escape from stressful situations represent a greater risk than clients who see suicide as a means of manipulating the environment.

Has the client encountered significant changes in his or her life, such as divorce, death of a family member, sickness, loss of job, academic failure, or an overwhelming work assignment? Any change, even one that is positive, such as a job promotion or the end of an unhappy relationship, can be perceived as stressful. Change involves loss. Losses that pose the greatest threat include loss of a relationship, loss of a significant role, loss of a dream, or a large financial loss. Sometimes anticipating a loss can be more stressful than the actual loss. Loss can be particularly stressful if the client accepts most of the blame. Client stress can be systematically assessed by means of the Life Experiences Survey (Sarason, Johnson, & Siegel, 1978) or the Life Stressors and Social Resources Inventory–Adult or Youth Form (Moos & Moos, 1994b, 1994c).

Sometimes stress can be associated with an event that happened years earlier if this event has not been addressed. Such events include sexual abuse, physical abuse, the suicide of a parent or sibling, and other traumatic events. Ask clients if there are things from their past that they find very difficult to talk about. If so, help them to begin to look at these issues in a supportive atmosphere. Recognize the need for long-term treatment for many of these issues.

Available Resources. Counselors need to determine what resources are available for the client. Three levels of resources should be considered: (a) internal; (b) family, close friends, neighbors, co-workers, and others who may have contact with the client; and (c) professionals.

First of all, what are the client's internal resources? In trying to assess these resources, the counselor should ask what has helped the client in the past in similar situations. What is keeping the client from committing suicide? Does the client have plans for the future?

To what degree can the client cope with the stress that he or she may be encountering? For example, can the client identify a solvable problem? Can the client distinguish between wanting to die and wanting to be rid of a problem? Can the client see more than one solution to a problem? Some clients experience "tunnel vision" so that they cannot conceive of options other than suicide for dealing with their stress. Does the client benefit from the counselor's attempts to provide assistance? Positive answers to these questions help to reduce the risk of suicide for the client.

Second, find out what type of support system the client has. If nobody seems to be involved with the client at the present time, ask who used to care. Does the client have regular contact with anyone else? Does the client have any confidants? Would the client be willing to share his or her concerns with family members or close friends? In some respects, suicide can be looked on more as a social than as a psychiatric phenomenon. Evaluation of the client's social support system is critical from this point of view. One's social support system can be evaluated by means of the Multidimensional Scale of Perceived Social Support (Zimet, Dahlem, Zimet, & Farley, 1988) or the Life Stressors and Social Resources Inventory–Adult or Youth Form (Moos & Moos, 1994b, 1994c).

Finally, what community resources are available for the client? Possibilities include a 24-hour crisis phone line, emergency treatment center, or mental health specialist with whom the client has good rapport. Would the client make use of these resources in case of a crisis? Will the client sign a contract that he or she would contact the counselor or another mental health professional before attempting to commit suicide?

In addition to the six sets of risk factors discussed above, suicide risk is affected by both personality and demographic characteristics. Individuals with impulsive personality styles are more likely to attempt suicide than other individuals (Joiner, Walker, Rudd, & Jobes, 1999). Women make twice as many suicide attempts as men; however, men are four times as likely to succeed in actually killing themselves (National Institute of Mental Health, 1999). The suicide rate is significantly higher for both adolescents and older adults than it is for the general population (Westefeld et al., 2000). Married people or people with dependent children at home are less likely to attempt suicide (Rogers, Alexander, & Subich, 1994). Personality factors such as impulsivity, perfectionism, and negativity, and demographic factors such as sex, age, and marital status, should be considered together with the other risk factors in making a suicide risk assessment.

Suicide Risk Assessment Aids

As indicated above, a large number of factors are associated with suicidal thinking and behavior. An assessment aid can help ensure that the counselor does not overlook crucial factors in making a risk assessment.

Three aids for assessing suicide risk are described below. These aids are designed for use as part of the interview process. All of these aids emphasize the importance of assessing current suicidal symptoms and suicide history. They can provide a guide both for the assessment interview and for documenting the comprehensiveness of the assessment.

SAD PERSONS Scale. This scale provides a convenient acronym for 10 factors to keep in mind when assessing a client for suicidal risk (Patterson, Dohn, Bird, & Patterson, 1983). These 10 factors (arranged in order of the first letter for each factor to spell SAD PERSONS) include *s*ex, *a*ge, *d*epression, *p*revious attempt, *e*thanol abuse, *r*ational

298

thinking loss, social support loss, organized plan, *no* spouse, and sickness. All of these risk factors have been discussed above.

Clients receive 1 point for each of these factors that pertain to them based on the counselor's judgment. All clients who receive more than 2 points should be considered for psychiatric referral or hospitalization. The counselor needs to weigh all aspects of the situation in making a decision. Some factors may deserve greater consideration than others depending on the particular situation. An organized plan is always cause for serious concern. When working with children, counselors may use the Adapted–SAD PERSONS Scale, which takes into account such factors as negligent parenting and school problems (Juhnke, 1996).

Students who have been taught how to use the SAD PERSONS Scale make judgments similar to those of experienced psychiatrists (Juhnke & Hovestadt, 1995; Patterson et al., 1983). Those who do not know how to use the SAD PERSONS Scale tend to overestimate the suicide risk of the people they evaluate.

Suicide Assessment Checklist (SAC).   Based on a review of the literature, Rogers et al. (1994) developed the SAC. It includes 12 items based on the client's suicide planning, suicide history, psychiatric history, drug use, and demographic characteristics and 9 items based on the counselor's ratings of significant factors (hopelessness, worthlessness, social isolation, depression, impulsivity, hostility, intent to die, environmental stress, and future time perspective).

The items are weighted in terms of their criticalness. The authors of this checklist assigned the highest weights to the following factors: having a definite suicide plan, planning to use a highly lethal method (including firearm, hanging, car exhaust, drugs/poison, and suffocating), making final plans (such as giving away possessions), writing a suicide note, and being a suicide survivor (having a close friend or relative who has committed suicide). In general, higher scores indicate greater risk; however, counselors also need to take into account other pertinent information such as third-party reports and their own clinical judgment in making a final assessment of suicide risk.

Research evidence indicates that the instrument can be used effectively by counselors with a broad range of education and experience. The SAC yielded high interrater and test–retest reliabilities for counselors (both experts and crisis-line volunteers) who judged the suicide risk of audiotape role-play clients. In addition to its value in initial suicide risk assessment and documentation, the SAC provides a standardized means of measuring changes in a client's status over time.

A Decision-Tree Assessment Strategy. This approach uses three risk factors—(a) past suicide attempts, (b) suicide plans and preparation, and (c) suicidal desire and ideation—as a basis for assessing suicidality (Joiner et al., 1999). All clients with these risk factors are assessed further. Clients who have made more than one previous suicide attempt (multiple attempters) or who have made suicide plans and preparation are classified as at least moderate suicide risks if they possess one other significant risk factor, such as depression, alcohol abuse, or impulsivity. Clients who express suicidal ideas and desires (but who have not made multiple attempts or who have not developed plans and preparations) are regarded as at least moderate risks if they possess two other significant risk factors. Clients with none of the three risk factors listed above are considered to be at low risk.

The decision-tree approach helps the counselor to readily identify clients who need further assessment. It provides a systematic means for determining which clients are at greatest risk for attempting suicide.

The authors of this assessment strategy suggest a range of possible interventions for clients judged to be at least moderate risks for committing suicide. These interventions include increase of frequency and duration of counseling sessions or telephone contacts, a detailed emergency plan (presented in writing to the client), 24-hour availability of emergency or crisis services for the client, professional consultation or referral for psychiatric treatment or hospitalization, active involvement of family and supportive others, and frequent reevaluation of suicide risk and treatment goals.

In summary, counselors should use some form of systematic assessment to determine a client's suicide risk. Each of the interview aids described above focuses attention on significant factors that should be included in a suicide risk assessment. By using a systematic approach, the counselor can be sure to assess critical factors relevant to most situations in addition to other factors that may be pertinent in particular situations. Counselors should ask for more detail in those areas in which a problem is detected.

Suicide risk factors should be reviewed during each counseling session for clients who may be suicidal. Such a review can serve both as a risk management strategy and as a basis for ongoing treatment planning.

When the counselor makes a suicide risk assessment, it is often important to consult with another mental health professional. Clients who are at risk for suicide may need to be referred for psychiatric evaluation. Psychiatrists can evaluate the client's need for medication, hospitalization, or long-term treatment. The assessment and treatment of suicidal clients frequently require a team approach.

ASSESSMENT OF ALCOHOL USE

A section on the assessment of alcohol use is included in this chapter because of the prevalence of abusive drinking and alcohol-related problems in American culture. According to a national study of psychiatric disorders, more than 25% of the U.S. population will meet the diagnostic criteria for substance abuse or dependence some time in their lifetime (Kessler et al., 1994). Most of the substance use disorders involve the use of alcohol. Because denial is a central issue in the abuse of alcohol or other drugs, counselors may not learn of the problem if they do not systematically review this matter with clients.

A variety of assessment procedures may be used to evaluate alcohol use. In most cases, the interview will probably be used to determine the nature and the gravity of drinking problems. Self-monitoring methods and physiological indices such as blood alcohol concentration (BAC) levels can be used to supplement the interview. Standardized measures (discussed in the next chapter) may also be used as part of the assessment process. In addition to individual assessment, the counselor will often need to assess the environment in which the drinking takes place.

Diagnostic Criteria for Alcohol Dependence or Abuse

Although this chapter focuses on assessment of alcohol disorders, similar diagnostic criteria are used to determine dependence or abuse for all psychoactive substances. Psychoactive drugs include all drugs that alter one's mood or thought processes by their effect on the central nervous system. *DSM-IV* recognizes 10 classes of psychoactive drugs (alcohol, amphetamines, cannabis, nicotine, cocaine, PCP or phencyclidine, inhalants, hallucinogens, opioids, and sedatives) that can lead to dependence. The drugs show some differences in respect to tolerance and withdrawal symptoms as indicated in the *DSM-IV*.

The specific criteria used to determine alcohol (or other substance) *dependence* are summarized below (American Psychiatric Association, 1994):

- Tolerance to the effects of the substance, so that markedly increased amounts of the substance are needed over time to attain intoxication or desired effect, or markedly diminished effect occurs with continued use of same amount of the substance
- Withdrawal symptoms that significantly interfere with everyday functioning when the substance is no longer available
- Compulsive use of the substance as indicated by consuming the substance in larger amounts or over a longer time period than intended
- Unsuccessful efforts to cut down on use of the substance
- Expenditure of a great deal of time in obtaining the substance, using it, or recovering from its effects
- Reduction or cessation of important social, occupational, or recreational activities because of substance use
- Continued use of the substance despite the physical or psychological problems that it is known to produce

Of the seven criteria listed, three or more must be manifested over a 12-month period for a person to be diagnosed as alcohol dependent. The diagnostic classification includes the specifier "with physiological dependence" if the person shows evidence of either tolerance or withdrawal (American Psychiatric Association, 1994, p. 181). Alcohol withdrawal symptoms include "the shakes," transient hallucinations or illusions, anxiety, depressed mood, headache, insomnia, rapid heart rate, or sweating.

Alcohol *abuse* refers to problematic drinking that does not fulfill the criteria listed above for alcohol dependence. People who suffer from this condition continue to drink within a 12-month period despite significant problems. These problems include failure to fulfill major role obligations at work or home, repeated use in dangerous situations (e.g., driving while intoxicated), recurrent legal problems, or recurrent social and interpersonal problems.

Counselors will often see clients because of the problems produced by drinking, such as deterioration in work performance, conflicts with others, depression, or poor health. The counselor will need to be careful to assess for drinking (or other substance) abuse that may have caused the problem. In general, counselors should assess clients' ability to control their use of alcohol and the degree to which alcohol usage causes problems in their lives.

Interview Schedules

A number of interview schedules have been developed to aid in the assessment of alcohol use. The schedules vary in length from a few questions designed to be used for screening purposes to extensive forms that may require as much as 3 hours to complete (Evans, 1998).

The CAGE questionnaire (named for the key words in each of four questions) can be readily used to screen clients for problems related to alcohol use (Ewing, 1984; Kitchens, 1994). The interviewer asks clients if they have (a) felt the need to *cut down* their drinking, (b) become *annoyed* when others ask them about their drinking, (c) felt *guilty* about their drinking, or (d) needed to take an *eyeopener* to start the day. If clients acknowledge any of these feelings or behaviors, they are likely to have experienced problems with alcohol, and additional inquiry should be undertaken.

Heck (1991) found that the effectiveness of the CAGE questionnaire in identifying problem drinkers could be significantly improved by asking clients about their social drinking habits, driving habits, and the age at which they began to drink. Problem drinkers rarely or never choose nonalcoholic beverages at social events, frequently drive while under the influence of alcohol, and started drinking on a regular basis while they were still in high school.

In a recent study, Cherpitel (2000) found that a shortened version of the Rapid Alcohol Problems Screen (RAPS) was more effective than the CAGE and other standard screening instruments in detecting alcohol dependence across gender and ethnic groups. The RAPS4 contains four items, each of which has shown high sensitivity and specificity in identifying individuals with alcohol dependence. These four items relate to guilt about drinking (Remorse), blackouts (Amnesia), failing to do what was normally expected (Perform), and need for an eyeopener or morning drink (Starter). Individuals who respond positively to any one of these items should be referred for a more thorough assessment of alcohol problems.

Several structured interviews have been developed to assess a client's current and past alcohol or other drug use in considerable detail. These measures include the Addiction Severity Index, Comprehensive Drinking Profile, and Time-Line Follow-Back.

The Addiction Severity Index (ASI) assesses the impact of the client's use of alcohol or other drugs on the client's medical status, employment or school status, legal status, family and social relationships, and psychiatric status (McLellan et al., 1992). According to Budman (2000), this instrument has become the standard measure of substance abuse in many agencies, with more than 1 million administrations a year in the United States. Research indicates that it yields internally consistent and valid information regarding a client's functioning even when administered in less-than-ideal circumstances, such as inner-city alcohol and drug abuse clinics (Leonhard, Mulvey, Gastfriend, & Schwartz, 2000). The ASI may also be administered in a multimedia version (called the ASI-MV) by virtual interviewers. The ASI-MV provides computer-generated ratings of addiction severity that match (or surpass) those of trained interviewers in terms of reliability and validity (Budman, 2000).

The Comprehensive Drinking Profile (CDP) is a structured intake interview procedure requiring 1 to 2 hours for completion (Marlatt & Miller, 1984). It provides detailed information regarding the history and current status of an individual's drinking problems and related matters. It assesses both consumption and problematic behaviors. A short form of the CDP, the Brief Drinker Profile, is also available, as well as the Follow-Up Drinker Profile (a measure of client progress) and the Collateral Interview Form (an instrument for obtaining information from other people who are close to the client).

The Time-Line Follow-Back (TLFB) enables the client and the counselor to reconstruct the client's drinking or other drug-using behavior for the past year (Sobell et al., 1980). It analyzes the patterns (e.g., daily, weekly, sporadically) and the intensity (light, heavy) of such behavior. Connections between drinking or other drug-use episodes and significant events ("anchor points") in the person's life are studied. Research indicates that the TLFB is highly reliable and relatively accurate (Fals-Stewart, O'Farrell, Feitas, McFarlin, & Rutigliano, 2000). TLFB reports obtained from clients agree reasonably well with those that are obtained from clients' spouses or partners or from urine assays. This procedure yields information that is enlightening to clients as well as to counselors (Vuchinich, Tucker, & Harllee, 1988).

Self-Monitoring Methods

Self-monitoring can enhance assessments made by means of interview procedures in a number of ways. Because self-monitoring is based on planned observations, data obtained in this manner should be more accurate and more complete than data based on recall. Self-monitoring has the added advantage of helping clients to see more clearly the relationship between certain events and their drinking behavior. Finally, self-monitoring provides a means of plotting the client's progress in controlling drinking behavior.

Self-monitoring charts typically include the amount of alcohol consumed in a given period of time, the situation in which the alcohol was consumed, and the presence of other people (Vuchinich et al., 1988). The thoughts or feelings of the person at the time may also be recorded. Temptations to drink, as well as actual drinking behavior, may be tracked.

Situational Factors

Besides assessing individual factors, counselors should help clients look at environmental factors that may encourage abusive drinking. Miller and Munoz (1982, p. 75) provided a checklist of 10 such situations:

- Drinking after work, especially after hard days
- Drinking after a stressful or emotional experience
- Drinking beer from barrels, kegs, or pitchers
- Drinking directly from the bottle (except beer)
- Drinking during automatic or boring activities
- Drinking during or with rewarding activities
- Drinking with heavy drinkers

- Drinking when thirsty or hungry
- Drinking with those who pressure you to drink faster or more
- Drinking "the usual" in the usual place

In a survey conducted by Ziemelis (1988), approximately 60% of college students reported that they often found themselves in situations in which they were encouraged to drink more than they wished.

Use of Alcohol Assessment Procedures in Counseling

Guidelines concerning the assessment of problems related to alcohol or other substance use are listed below:

1. Be alert to possible substance abuse problems of individuals with other *DSM-IV* diagnoses. Dual diagnoses involving substance abuse with other mental disorders are relatively common (Kessler et al., 1994).

2. Be sure to ask about the use of alcohol or other drugs as part of the intake procedure. Evans (1998) pointed out that it is important to diagnose and treat substance use disorder early in counseling when the client is under duress and less well defended.

3. Be aware of crucial signs ("red flags") that indicate possible substance abuse. In the case of adolescents, these red flags include such matters as physical or sexual abuse, parental substance abuse, peer involvement in substance abuse or serious delinquency, sudden downturns in school performance or attendance, marked change in physical health, HIV high-risk activities, and severe depression (Winters, 1999).

4. Inquire about problems related to drinking. Abusive drinking may be most evident in the problems it produces. Ask if other people have been concerned about the client's drinking behavior. Use the CAGE or RAPS4 questions as part of the screening process.

5. Keep the *DSM-IV* criteria in mind in assessing for alcohol dependence or abuse. Determine frequency, duration, and severity of pertinent symptoms. Remember that these same criteria can be used in assessing other types of psychoactive substance dependence or abuse.

6. If alcohol or other drug problems are detected, use a more thorough assessment procedure to gain a better understanding of the problem, or refer the client to specialists for this purpose. Interview

schedules such as the CDP or TLFB or the Alcohol Use Inventory (briefly discussed in the next chapter) could be used for a more extended assessment.

7. Engage the client in self-assessment. Self-monitoring of drinking behavior can be helpful both in defining the problem and in gauging the success of treatment efforts.

8. Help clients to become aware of those situations that may trigger drinking behavior for them. Also help them to identify problems associated with drinking. Checklists can be helpful for this purpose. For example, the Alcohol and Other Drugs Self-Test includes 50 items that can be used to stimulate greater self-awareness (Wisconsin Clearinghouse, 1996).

9. Teach the use of blood alcohol concentration (BAC) tables to clients with drinking problems so that they can assess the influence of alcohol consumption on their judgment and reaction time (Kishline, 1994). Help them to use these tables to set alcohol consumption limits.

10. When clients do not accept the fact that they have a problem of control of their drinking behavior (an essential feature of dependency), ask them to try to limit their drinking to a certain amount (e.g., no more than three drinks) on any one occasion for a period of 3 months. This has sometimes been referred to as the "acid test" of one's ability to control drinking behavior.

11. If denial appears to be a problem, obtain permission from the client to speak with family members or friends as a means of gaining information about his or her drinking behaviors. Interview these people with the client present in the room.

12. Use information from all available sources, including work, school, and community records or personnel. Assessment will be more accurate if it is based on multiple sources of information.

13. Seek supervision to avoid frustration and to improve skills for gathering information from clients who may be in a state of denial (Evans, 1998).

14. Refer clients with persistent drinking problems to specialists for assessment and treatment. Assessment should include a physical exam by qualified medical personnel. Inpatient or intensive outpatient treatment in a multidisciplinary setting may be necessary.

SUMMARY

1. Mental illnesses, particularly anxiety and mood disorders, occur frequently in the United States. Counselors need to be able to detect psychopathology among clients within their caseload.
2. The *DSM-IV* offers a clear and comprehensive means of diagnosing possible mental disorders among clients.
3. All counselors should be able to undertake suicide risk assessments and substance abuse assessments within the counseling session.
4. If counselors are concerned about a client's suicide risk, they should ask about suicide intentions, specific suicide plans, previous suicide attempts, psychological symptoms, environmental stress, and available resources.
5. Alcohol assessment should focus on the client's ability to control his or her drinking and the problems in the client's life associated with drinking. The *DSM-IV* criteria can be used to diagnose alcohol dependence or abuse.

15

MENTAL HEALTH ASSESSMENT: STANDARDIZED INVENTORIES

S TANDARDIZED MEASURES of mental health are presented in this chapter. General-purpose measures contain a variety of scales that assess different aspects of psychopathology, whereas specific-purpose measures focus on a particular type of mental health problem, such as depression, anxiety, alcohol abuse, or eating disorders. The use of both types of measures in counseling is discussed below.

GENERAL-PURPOSE MEASURES

The Minnesota Multiphasic Personality Inventory (MMPI) has been used more than any other personality inventory to assess psychopathology for both adults and adolescents (Archer, Maruish, Imhof, & Piotrowski, 1991; Watkins, Campbell, Nieberding, & Hallmark, 1995). In the past several years, the MMPI has been updated and restandardized as two distinct versions: one for adults (MMPI-2) and one for adolescents (MMPI-A). The characteristics and use of both of these instruments are discussed below. In addition, three other broad measures of psychopathology that can serve as alternatives to the MMPI-2 are also reviewed.

Minnesota Multiphasic Personality Inventory–2 (MMPI-2)

The MMPI-2 replaces the MMPI, which was first published in 1943 (Graham, 2000). This instrument, which requires a sixth-grade reading level, may be used with clients beginning at age 18. The MMPI-A, the adolescent version of the MMPI, should be used with boys and girls ages 14 to 18.

The original MMPI, as developed by Starke Hathaway and J. Charnley McKinley, contained a total of 4 validity scales and 10 clinical scales that formed the standard MMPI profile (see Table 15-1). The validity scales enable the counselor to assess the client's attitude toward the testing process. Most of the clinical scales consist of items that significantly differentiated between people in a particular psychiatric diagnostic category (e.g., depression) and people in the general reference group (often referred to as "the Minnesota normals"). For example, the Depression scale (Scale 2) contained 60 items that people with depression endorsed significantly more (or less) often than did the Minnesota normals (Butcher, Dahlstrom, Graham, Tellegen, & Kaemmer, 1989).

Subsequent research has indicated that the MMPI scales cannot be used to classify individuals into psychiatric categories with a high degree of accuracy. Instead, the scales are most useful in providing descriptions of personality and as a source of inference regarding a person's behavior. Because of the large amount of research that has been conducted with the MMPI, the scales convey a wealth of information about an individual's personality that transcends the original purpose of the scales. For this reason, the original names for the MMPI scales have been replaced by the scale numbers for most purposes (e.g., Scale 7 instead of Pt or Psychasthenia).

The MMPI-2 authors have corrected problems with the original normative sample and brought the instrument up to date (Butcher et al., 1989). The total number of items (567) remains about the same.

TABLE 15-1. Description of Standard Scales on Minnesota
Multiphasic Personality Inventory–2

Scale	Original Name and Abbreviation	Behaviors Associated With Elevated Scores
Validity scales		
?	Cannot say (?)	Indecisiveness, rebelliousness, defensiveness
L	Lie (L)	Faking good, naivete, scrupulosity
F	Frequency (F)	Faking bad, unusual behavior, confusion while taking test, self-critical
K	Correction (K)	Faking good, defensiveness, self-reliance
Clinical scales		
1	Hypochondriasis (Hs)	Bodily complaints, fatigue, weakness
2	Depression (D)	Dejection, dissatisfaction, tendency to give up
3	Hysteria (Hy)	Denial of problems, desire for social acceptance, psychosomatic symptoms
4	Psychopathic deviate (Pd)	Impulsivity, acting out, not bound by rules
5	Masculinity–femininity (Mf)	Men: Cultural-aesthetic interests, passivity, academic achievement Women: Outdoor-mechanical interests, dominating, competitive
6	Paranoia (Pa)	Sensitive, suspicious, preoccupied with rights and privileges
7	Psychasthenia (Pt)	Anxious, obsessive, compulsive
8	Schizophrenia (Sc)	Unusual thoughts or behavior, detached, introspective
9	Hypomania (Ma)	High energy level, restless, distractible
O	Social introversion–extroversion (Si)	Introverted, reserved, reticent

Ineffective, offensive, and repeated items have been eliminated. Sexist or dated items have been reworded. New items tap areas not well represented in the original MMPI item pool, including family relationships, eating disorders, and drug abuse.

In contrast to the original standardization procedures, members of the new normative sample (1,462 women and 1,138 men) were selected so that they would be representative of the adult U.S. population in terms of age, marital status, ethnicity, and geography. The percentage of college graduates in the new normative sample is much higher than that found in the original sample or reported by the U.S. Census Bureau. According to Butcher, Ben-Porath, et al. (2000), the change in the educational level of the normative sample has a minimal impact on the interpretation of the MMPI-2 scores.

With the new norms, the cutoff score used to detect psychological problems has dropped from 70 on the MMPI to 65 on the MMPI-2. Research indicates that a T score of 65 provides optimal separation between clinical groups and the standardization sample (Butcher et al., 1989). The scores on the MMPI-2 have also been adjusted so that the distribution of the profile scores will be the same for the eight clinical scales (Scales 1, 2, 3, 4, 6, 7, 8, and 9) used to assess psychopathology. For example, a T score of 65 equals the 92nd percentile (based on the restandardization sample) for each of these scales.

A number of new validity scales have been developed for the MMPI-2. In addition to number of item omissions (? score), the original MMPI validity scales measured "fake good" (L and K scales) and "fake bad" (F scale) response tendencies. The new validity scales include TRIN (True Response Inconsistency, which measures acquiescence or negativity), VRIN (Variable Response Inconsistency, which measures random responding), and Back F (a "fake bad" measure for the back, or new, part of the inventory). Counselors should check the validity scores first to make certain that the client has been honest and cooperative in responding to the inventory before they attempt to interpret the other scores.

The MMPI-2 scales should be interpreted in conjunction with the other scales on the profile, not in isolation. A number of MMPI-2 reference books provide personality descriptions and possible psychiatric diagnoses associated with different profile configurations (e.g., Butcher, 1997, 1999; Butcher, Williams, & Fowler, 2000; Duckworth & Anderson, 1995; A. F. Friedman, Lewak, Nichols, & Webb, 2001; Graham, 2000; Greene, 1999). Counselors should be acquainted with the vast literature pertaining to the MMPI-2 if they work with clients who are mentally disturbed; however, they cannot expect to become proficient in its use without specialized training and extensive clinical experience.

Counselors should note critical items that the client has checked as well as scale scores. For example, if the client marked *true* to Item 506, "I have recently considered killing myself," or Item 524, "No one knows it but I have tried to kill myself," the counselor should review these items with the client. Clients might not bring these topics up on their own. They may assume that the counselor already knows this information from their responses to these items on the MMPI-2.

Several critical item lists have been developed. For example, the Koss–Butcher critical item set contains 78 items related to six crisis areas. These items typically differentiate normal from psychiatric samples. Most computer-based MMPI-2 scoring programs will flag critical items checked by the clients. This information can also be obtained by means of hand scoring. The critical item lists provide a simple and straightforward means for counselors to discuss MMPI-2 results with clients and to identify topics that may need additional inquiry.

A number of additional scales have been created for the MMPI-2 that can be used to help interpret the clinical scales. Most of the clinical scales have been divided into subscales that can help clarify the meaning of scores on the scales (Graham, 2000). The Depression scale, for example, has been divided into the following subscales: Subjective Depression, Psychomotor Retardation, Physical Malfunctioning, Mental Dullness, and Brooding.

Besides the subscales, 15 content scales devised by Butcher, Graham, Williams, and Ben-Porath (1990) can also be used to clarify the meaning of the MMPI-2 clinical scales. In contrast with the clinical scales, which were developed by empirical means, the content scales were constructed by logical analysis of the item content on the MMPI-2. The scales were refined by statistical procedures to ensure homogeneity of item content. Scales developed in this fashion are easier to interpret than empirical scales. The content scales also assess aspects of personality not measured by the standard scales, including Type A behavior, work interference, family problems, and negative treatment indicators. The content scales significantly add to the validity of the clinical scales in predicting symptomatic and personality characteristics of clients (Barthlow, Graham, Ben-Porath, & McNulty, 1999).

In addition to the scales discussed thus far, many other scales have been constructed from the MMPI item pool for various purposes. Popular supplementary scales include A (Anxiety), R (Repression), and Es (Ego Strength). A and R represent the two main factors derived from factor analyses of the clinical scales. As such, they offer a quick summary, or overview, of the MMPI-2 results. Scale A provides a measure of anxiety or general maladjustment; Scale R shows the client's tendency to repress or deny psychological difficulties. The Es scale is based on items that distinguished between clients with psychological problems who responded to therapy and those who did not. In contrast with most of the scores on the MMPI-2, high scores on the Es scale should be interpreted favorably.

Research on the MMPI-2 indicates that it can be used effectively with clients from minority groups if moderator variables such as socioeconomic status, education, and acculturation are taken into account (Anderson, 1995; Greene, 1999; Tsai & Pike, 2000). These variables have a greater influence than ethnic status on MMPI-2 scores. Timbrook and Graham (1994) found that the MMPI-2 predicted criterion variables (based on partner ratings) as accurately for African Americans as it did for White men and women. Similarly, McNulty, Graham, Ben-Porath, and Stein (1997) found no evidence of test bias in a study of African American and White mental health center clients. A review of 25 MMPI and MMPI-2 comparative studies found no substantive differences in test scores among European Americans, African Americans, and Latino Americans (Nagayama Hall, Bansal, & Lopez, 1999).

Although the MMPI-2 has many advantages, it is not without faults. In a comprehensive critique of the MMPI-2, Helmes and Reddon (1993) noted the following shortcomings: (a) lack of a consistent measurement model, (b) heterogeneous item content within clinical scales, (c) suspect diagnostic criteria, (d) overlapping of item content among scales, (e) lack of cross-validation of scoring keys, (f) inadequate measures of response styles, and (g) suspect norms. They urged clinicians to consider alternative measures such as the Millon Clinical Multiaxial Inventory, Personality Assessment Inventory, and Basic Personality Inventory, because these measures are "more likely to incorporate modern developments and have fewer serious conceptual problems" (Helmes & Reddon, 1993, p. 467).

The use of the MMPI-2 in a counseling situation is illustrated in the following case example.

CASE EXAMPLE

Janet, a 19-year-old college sophomore, requested counseling because of low self-esteem, relationship difficulties, family conflict, and eating concerns. She marked 5 (*very much*) to the following items on the Inventory of Common Problems:

- Feeling irritable, tense, or nervous
- Feeling fearful
- Feeling lonely or isolated
- Eating, appetite, or weight problems

She also completed the Beck Depression Inventory as part of the initial contact session, for which she received a raw score of 32, indicating "severe depression." The counselor asked Janet to complete the MMPI-2 during her next visit to the counseling center to assess more thoroughly the nature and the level of her psychological problems. She obtained the profile shown in Figure 15-1.

The scores on the three validity scales (L, F, and K) indicate self-criticism and a possible plea for help. Her low L and K scores indicate that she is

FIGURE 15-1. MMPI-2 Profile for Counseling Center Client

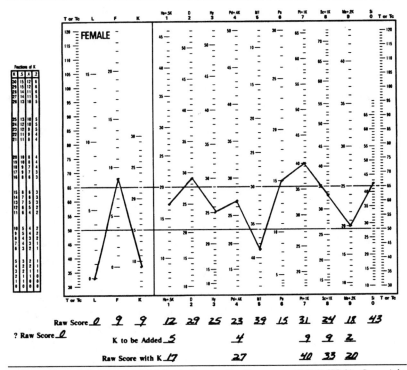

Note. From Minnesota Multiphasic Personality Inventory–2 (MMPI-2). Copyright 1942, 1943 (renewed 1970), 1989 by the Regents of the University of Minnesota. This profile form 1989. Reprinted with permission.

describing herself in a negative fashion. The elevated F score suggests self-criticism together with moderately severe psychopathology. Among the clinical scales, she obtained elevated scores on Scales 2, 6, 7, and 0. Her highest two scores are on Scales 7 and 2. According to Graham (2000, p. 96), individuals with this code type (27 or 72) "tend to be anxious, nervous, tense, high-strung, and jumpy. They worry excessively, and they are vulnerable to real and imagined threat. They tend to anticipate problems before they occur and to overreact to minor stress. Somatic symptoms are common." Because of their acute discomfort, they are likely to respond well to psychotherapy. They are most likely to receive a psychiatric diagnosis of anxiety disorder, depressive disorder, or obsessive–compulsive disorder.

Janet's elevated scores on Scales 6 and 0 indicate possible difficulties in interpersonal relationships. According to the MMPI-2 manual, scores between 66 and 75 on Scale 6 can possibly be interpreted as follows: angry and resentful, displaces blame and criticisms, hostile and suspicious, rigid and stubborn, and misinterprets social situations (Butcher et al., 1989, p. 39). Similarly, scores between 66 and 75 on Scale 0 suggest behavior that is introverted, shy, lacking self-confidence, moody, submissive, and rigid (Butcher et al., 1989, p. 43).

The counselor provided counseling to Janet to help her deal with her immediate situation. At the same time, she made arrangements to refer Janet to a psychiatrist for a more complete assessment of some of the psychological problems suggested by the MMPI-2 and other assessment procedures.

Minnesota Multiphasic Personality Inventory–Adolescent (MMPI-A)

Prior to the construction of the MMPI-A in 1992, adolescents were frequently administered the adult version of the MMPI despite the difficulties in adapting this version for adolescents (Archer et al., 1991; Butcher et al., 1992). The adolescent version of the MMPI is similar to the new adult version in that it retains the same basic scales as the old MMPI and also includes a new set of content scales.

The MMPI-A differs from the MMPI-2 in regard to its norms, its item content, and the nature of some of its scales. The MMPI-A provides separate-sex norms for adolescents ages 14 through 18 years. (The test authors recommend that the MMPI-2 be used with 18-year-olds who have moved away from their parental home.) The MMPI-A contains 89 fewer items than the MMPI-2 to help encourage client cooperation. Most of the omitted items are items that were not scored on any of the clinical scales, items found on Scales 5 and 0 (both exceptionally long scales on the MMPI-2), or items on the Fears content scale (which has been dropped from the MMPI-A). The MMPI-A includes a number of items from the original MMPI that have been rewritten to pertain to adolescents, as well as a number of new items that deal specifically with adolescent circumstances (such as school, peers, teachers, and parents).

Whereas 11 of the 15 content scales on the MMPI-A are similar to those found on the MMPI-2, 4 of the scales—School Problems, Low Aspirations, Alienation, and Conduct Disorder—have been designed specifically to address issues common to adolescents. The F validity scale, which often produced high scores for adolescents on the MMPI, has been redesigned for the MMPI-A by including only those items answered infrequently (20% of the time or less) by adolescents. The MMPI-A also includes a new supplementary scale, the Immaturity scale, not found on the MMPI-2.

Research reported in the manual indicates that the basic and content scales demonstrate adequate test–retest reliability and internal consistency when used with adolescents. The content scales have proved to be valid in predicting external criteria, such as record reviews and ratings by parents and treatment staff (Williams, Butcher, Ben-Porath, & Graham, 1992). Much of the validity for the MMPI-A can be inferred from validity established for the MMPI because of the comparability of the instruments. As with the MMPI-2, T scores of 65 or greater suggest possible psychopathology. Scores between 60 and 65 should be viewed as indicating possible psychological problems.

Millon Clinical Multiaxial Inventory–III (MCMI-III)

The MCMI-III provides an alternative to the MMPI-2 for diagnosing psychopathology (Millon, Millon, & Davis, 1994). It is considerably shorter than the MMPI-2, containing 175 items compared with 567 items on the MMPI-2. Most people can complete the MCMI-III in 20 to 30 minutes. It is also more closely tied to the *DSM-IV* than is the MMPI-2, so that psychiatric classifications can be made more easily. The MCMI-III is also more closely related to psychological theory than is the MMPI (Millon, 1990).

The MCMI-III provides two broad sets of scores that correspond with Axis I (clinical syndromes) and Axis II (personality disorders) on the *DSM-IV*. The scales are scored in terms of base rates so that the percentage of people classified by means of the MCMI-III as suffering from a particular psychological problem corresponds with the actual percentages found in society. Because of the scoring procedure, it is important that the MCMI-III be used only with people who fit the normative population, that is, people suspected to be suffering from a mental disorder. The MCMI-III will overpathologize for people who do not fit this population. Clients should be screened by other criteria such as an interview, the Beck Depression Inventory–II, or the Inventory of Common Problems before they are assigned the MCMI-III.

The MCMI-III has been validated in terms of its effectiveness in differentiating individuals with particular psychiatric diagnoses from other psychiatric patients. This is a more rigorous criterion than differentiating these same types of individuals from a "normal" population, such as that originally used with the MMPI. The technique used with the MCMI-III has proved to be more accurate in identifying the psychiatric diagnoses of patients in subsequent studies than has the technique used with the MMPI.

Although hand scoring is possible, MCMI-III answer sheets can be much more efficiently scored by means of computer-based scoring programs available from the publisher. The scoring programs provide comprehensive narrative interpretations of the scores, together with suggested psychiatric diagnoses and treatment possibilities.

Counselors should consider the use of the MCMI-III with adult clients whom they believe may be suffering from psychiatric disorders. For adolescents, counselors should use the Millon Adolescent Clinical Inventory, the "junior version" of the MCMI-III (Millon & Davis, 1993). Considerable training and experience are required for the use of either instrument. As noted by Millon et al. (1994), the instruments provide a series of "tentative judgments" rather than a set of clinical statements. The counselor can use information gained from these instruments in the referral of clients for psychiatric assessment and treatment (Choca & VanDenburg, 1997).

Personality Assessment Inventory (PAI)

The PAI was designed to provide information on "relevant clinical variables" for individuals 18 years of age and older (Morey, 1991). Content areas for the PAI were selected on the basis of current diagnostic schemes and treatment planning. The PAI consists of 344 items (selected from an original item pool of 2,200 items) that are scored on 22 scales. Final items for the PAI were selected on the basis of expert ratings, statistical analysis, and related criteria in a 10-stage process.

The 22 full scales on the PAI include 4 validity scales (Inconsistency, Infrequency, Negative Impression, and Positive Impression), 11 clinical scales, 5 treatment scales, and 2 interpersonal scales. The 11 clinical scales, which resemble many of the MMPI clinical scales, can be subdivided into three broad categories of disorders: (a) neurotic spectrum scales—Somatic Complaints, Anxiety, Anxiety-Related Disorders, and Depression; (b) psychotic spectrum scales—Mania, Paranoia, and Schizophrenia; and (c) behavior disorder scales—Borderline Features, Antisocial Features, Alcohol Problems, and Drug Problems. The 5 treatment scales, which focus on issues important in treatment not necessarily apparent from the clinical scales, include Aggression, Suicidal Ideation, Stress, Nonsupport, and Treatment Rejection. Finally, the 2 interpersonal scales measure two critical dimensions in interpersonal relations: domination versus submission (Dominance scale) and friendliness versus hostility (Warmth scale). Information is also provided on the client's answers to 27 critical items, which were selected because of their potential seriousness and low endorsement rates.

Because of the heterogeneous nature of the clinical scales, 9 have been divided into subscales. For example, the Anxiety scale includes Cognitive, Affective, and Physiological subscales, and the Anxiety-Related Disorders scale includes Obsessive–Compulsive, Phobias, and Traumatic Stress subscales. The treatment scale for aggression has also been divided into three subscales: Aggressive Attitude, Verbal Aggression, and Physical Aggression.

The PAI, which has a fourth-grade reading level, requires about 50 minutes to complete. The item response format provides four alternatives: *false–not at all true, slightly true, mainly true,* or *very true.* All of the scales can be easily hand scored without the use of a template in 10 minutes or less. In contrast with the MMPI-2, none of the full scales contain overlapping items.

The PAI has been normed on a sample of 1,000 community-dwelling adults selected to match the characteristics of the U.S. population in terms of sex, race, and age. In addition to adult norms, comprehensive norms have also been established for college students and clinical populations.

The full scales exhibit adequate test–retest reliabilities over short time periods and relatively high internal consistency coefficients for samples of college students and community-dwelling adults. The PAI shows substantial convergent and discriminant validity based on its correlations with scales from other psychological measures.

The PAI is an appealing instrument because of its ease of scoring and interpretation. It has been carefully constructed and appears to be psychometrically sound. In a short period of time, it has become one of the most frequently used personality tests in practice and clinical training (Piotrowski, 2000).

The author of the PAI has recently developed a brief, 22-item version of the PAI, the Personality Assessment Screener, that can be used as a screening device to distinguish between those clients free from psychopathology and those in need of follow-up evaluation with the full PAI (Morey, 1998).

Basic Personality Inventory (BPI)

The BPI is intended for use with both adolescents and adults in clinical and normal populations (D. N. Jackson, 1989). It consists of 240 true–false items scored on 11 clinical scales and 1 critical-item scale (20 items per scale). The categories for the clinical scales were derived from factor analysis of other personality inventories including the MMPI. As a result, the clinical scales on the BPI hold much in common with the clinical scales on the MMPI.

The 11 clinical scales measure neurotic tendencies (Hypochondriasis, Depression, Anxiety, Social Introversion, and Self-Depreciation), psychotic tendencies (Persecutory Ideas, Thinking Disorder), and antisocial tendencies (Denial, Interpersonal Problems, Alienation, and Impulse Expression). Items for each scale were selected to maximize item–scale correlations and minimize interscale correlations.

The BPI, which requires approximately 35 minutes to complete, can be hand scored in less than 10 minutes. The manual provides separate-sex norms for both adults and adolescents. The manual reports respectable reliability and validity data. Validation procedures primarily involved correlating the scores on the BPI scales with clinical ratings and other measures of psychopathology.

In comparison with the MMPI-2, the BPI has been praised for its brevity, ease of administration and scoring, and "purity" (homogeneity) of its clinical scales (Urbina, 1995; Yelland, 1995). However, it lacks the diagnostic utility and extensive normative data, especially for ethnic populations, of the MMPI-2.

SPECIFIC-PURPOSE MEASURES

A number of standardized inventories have been developed to assess mental health problems in specific areas of interest to counselors. These areas include emotional states such as depression, anxiety, and anger, as well as behavioral problems such as alcohol abuse, eating disorders, and attention deficit disorders. Measures of emotional states serve as "emotional vital signs" that can be used to assess the individual's psychological well-being in the same sense that physical vital signs such as heart rate and blood pressure are used to evaluate one's physical health (Spielberger, Sydeman, Ritterband, Reheiser, & Unger, 1995). Measures of specific behavioral or psychological disorders can be used to determine to what extent an individual may be suffering from a particular problem.

Most of the specific-purpose instruments (sometimes referred to as focus measures, rapid assessment instruments, or "narrow-band" scales) discussed in this section are relatively brief and easy to administer and score. For this reason, they can be readily readministered to monitor a client's progress in dealing with a specific issue.

Depression

One of the most common psychiatric disorders suffered by people in the United States is depression. In the National Comorbidity Study conducted by Kessler et al. (1994), more than 17% of the sample reported lifetime incidences of a major depressive episode, and more than 10% reported such an episode within the past year.

A large number of self-rating scales have been devised to assess depression. Ponterotto, Pace, and Kavan (1989) identified 73 different self-report measures for depression used by mental health professionals for research or counseling purposes. Among these instruments, the Beck Depression Inventory was used 10 times as often as the next most popular measure.

Beck Depression Inventory–II (BDI-II). The BDI-II replaces the BDI, which was first published in 1961 (Beck, Steer, & Brown, 1996). The current version reflects *DSM-IV* criteria for depression more closely than did earlier versions. The instructions have been changed to pertain to a 2-week period instead of a 1-week period, four items have been replaced with new items, and two items have been reworded. Item responses have been simplified so that the BDI-II can be used with clients as young as 13 years of age.

The BDI-II includes 21 items that describe symptoms of depression of an affective, cognitive, behavioral, or physiological nature. Each item uses a 4-point scale of severity ranging from 0 to 3. Clients mark the level of severity for each symptom that best describes how they have been feeling over "the past 2 weeks, including today." The BDI-II instructions and sample items are shown in Figure 15-2.

Most clients complete the BDI-II within 5 to 10 minutes. Scoring, which involves tallying answers for 21 items, takes just a minute. For

FIGURE 15-2. Instructions and Sample Items From the Beck Depression Inventory–II

BECK DEPRESSION INVENTORY–II

Instructions: This questionnaire consists of 21 groups of statements. Please read each group of statements carefully, and then pick out the *one statement* in each group that best describes the way you have been feeling during the *past two weeks, including today*. Circle the number beside the statement you have picked. If several statements in the group seem to apply equally well, circle the highest number for that group. Be sure that you do not choose more than one statement for any group.

Sadness
0   I do not feel sad
1   I feel sad much of the time
2   I am sad all the time
3   I am so sad or unhappy that I can't stand it.

Suicidal Thoughts or Wishes
0   I don't have any thoughts of killing myself
1   I have thoughts of killing myself, but I would not carry them out
2   I would like to kill myself
3   I would kill myself if I had the chance.

this reason, it can easily be administered, scored, and interpreted as part of a regularly scheduled counseling interview.

Ponterotto et al. (1989) rated the original BDI higher in terms of its overall effectiveness than any other self-report measure of depression. They gave it the highest possible rating for utility, that is, ease of use by counselor and client. They also rated it highly (4 on a 5-point scale) for both reliability and validity.

Scores on the BDI-II are internally consistent for college students and psychiatric outpatients but are subject to change over time (Beck et al., 1996). The BDI-II was designed to be highly sensitive to changes in mood over short time periods. If people experience significant changes in their lives, or if they are responding positively to a counseling program, their BDI-II scores should reflect these events. Validity studies indicate that the BDI-II total score effectively differentiates between depressed and nondepressed individuals (Beck et al., 1996).

The BDI-II manual recommends that scores be interpreted as follows:

0–13 = minimal depression
14–19 = mild depression
20–28 = moderate depression
29–63 = severe depression

The cutoff scores shown above should be looked upon as general guidelines. The counselor will need to obtain more information to judge the severity of a client's depression. The duration of the symptoms and the possible cause of the symptoms (e.g., loss of a loved one) need to be considered. If the symptoms are of short duration (less than 2 weeks) or if they can be attributed to a grief reaction, they are less likely to indicate psychopathology.

As a general rule, if the score exceeds 28, especially for two administrations of the BDI-II separated by 2 weeks, the counselor should consider referring the client for psychiatric evaluation. The item content of the BDI-II can be easily reviewed with clients to obtain more information about a symptom. It usually helps to ask clients which items they are most concerned about. Counselors should pay particular attention to symptoms of hopelessness (Item 2) and suicidal thinking (Item 9). The counselor should be sure to evaluate the risk of suicide for such clients.

Hammen (1980) noted that BDI scores for college students often dropped upon retesting, even without treatment. Depression for these students may be caused by situational factors, such as impending exams or relationship conflicts, which could change rather quickly. Such factors must be taken into account. For this reason, it is a good idea to readminister the BDI-II periodically during the course of counseling to help monitor changes that may occur. Information obtained from readministrations of the BDI-II can often be helpful in trying to decide if the client should be referred for additional assessment or treatment or if the client has made sufficient progress so that regular sessions are no longer needed.

In general, clients can be considered to be full responders to treatment if their scores on the BDI drop by 50% or more from their baseline score. Clients whose scores decrease by 25% to 50% show partial improvement, whereas clients whose scores drop by less than 25% should be thought of as nonresponders (Ambrosini, Bianchi, Metz, & Rabinovich, 1994).

Children's Depression Inventory (CDI). The CDI is a self-report measure of depression for children and adolescents ages 8 to 17 years (Kovacs, 1992). This instrument, which is a downward extension of the BDI, consists of 27 self-report items written at a third-grade reading level. For each item, the child or adolescent chooses the one statement from among three listed that most closely describes his or her thoughts, feelings, or behaviors for the past 2 weeks. The CDI yields a total score together with five factor scores: Negative Mood, Interpersonal Problems, Ineffectiveness, Anhedonia (inability to find enjoyment in any activities), and Negative Self-Esteem. The manual provides separate-sex norms for children (ages 7 through 12) and adolescents (ages 13 through 17). Kovacs has also created a 10-item version of the CDI for group administration when time is limited.

The CDI is one of the most thoroughly researched of all instruments designed to measure depression in children. Although it was developed primarily for research purposes, it has been used increasingly for clinical purposes because of the lack of effective instruments in the field. Kovacs recommends that a T score of 65 be used to indicate possible depression in screening situations. If a client obtains a T score of 65 or greater on two administrations, he or she should then be evaluated by means of a diagnostic interview.

Although some studies support the validity of the CDI in differentiating between adolescent inpatients diagnosed with major depression and those diagnosed with other psychiatric disorders, studies reported in the manual indicate mixed results (Craighead, Curry, & Ilardi, 1995; Kovacs, 1992). At this point, the CDI can best be used as an adjunct to other diagnostic tools, including the clinical interview.

Geriatric Depression Scale (GDS). The GDS is a short, self-administered inventory that effectively differentiates between depressed and nondepressed elderly clients (Yesavage et al., 1983). It consists of 30 yes–no items that focus on affective and cognitive symptoms of depression. Items that assess somatic symptoms have been largely excluded because these items do not detect depression as well in the elderly as they do in younger populations. Holroyd and Clayton (2000, p. 6) concluded that the GDS is "the best validated instrument" for measuring depression in geriatric clients who are not cognitively impaired.

Hamilton Depression Inventory (HDI). The HDI is a relatively new paper-and-pencil version of the Hamilton Depression Rating Scale, a well-established measure of depression for adults based on a clinical interview. In contrast to the BDI-II, the HDI measures the frequency as well as the intensity of symptoms. Some of its 23 questions contain subquestions so that a total of 38 items are included. In addition to the total score, the HDI also provides a relatively pure measure of melancholia, that is, endogenous depression. Scores on the HDI have proved to be highly effective in differentiating individuals diagnosed with clinical depression from nondepressed individuals (W. M. Reynolds & Kobak, 1995).

The Harvard Department of Psychiatry/National Depression Screening Day Scale (HANDS). The HANDS is a new 10-item scale developed by staff at the Harvard Department of Psychiatry for National Depression Screening Day and other uses (Baer et al., 2000). It assesses the degree to which a person has experienced the major symptoms of depression during the past 2 weeks. The scale authors found that the instrument performed as well as the BDI-II in differentiating between depressed and nondepressed individuals. The

National Mental Health Association (1999) maintains a Web site on which individuals may take the HANDS without charge, have their answer sheet scored and interpreted on a confidential basis, and receive pertinent information concerning community and professional resources.

Anxiety and Fear

Approximately one fourth of the population in the United States can be expected to suffer from an anxiety disorder sometime during their lifetime (Kessler et al., 1994). Anxiety disorders, which tend to be chronic, include social phobias, panic disorder, agoraphobia, simple phobia, generalized anxiety disorder, and related ailments. Approximately 17% of the population are likely to have experienced an anxiety disorder during any given year.

Popular measures of the symptoms of anxiety and fear are discussed below. *Anxiety* can be defined as "a pervasive feeling of dread, apprehension, and impending disaster" (Goldenson, 1984, p. 53). The cause of the anxiety is usually unknown or unclear. In contrast, *fear* is an intense emotional response to a known danger, such as snakes or crowded places.

State–Trait Anxiety Inventory (STAI). The STAI, the most popular and well researched of all anxiety measures, was first published by Charles Spielberger and his associates in 1970; the current version (Form Y) was published in 1983 (Spielberger, Gorsuch, Lushene, Vagg, & Jacobs, 1983). The STAI consists of two scales: a State–Anxiety scale (S-Anxiety) that measures transitory anxiety and a Trait–Anxiety scale (T-Anxiety) that measures persistent anxiety. Both scales contain 20 items marked on a 4-point scale.

Instructions for the S-Anxiety scale ask clients to indicate how they feel "at this moment"; they indicate to what degree (*not at all, somewhat, moderately so,* or *very much so*) they may be experiencing different feelings, such as tension or calmness. Instructions for the T-Anxiety scale ask clients to rate how they "generally feel"; they indicate how often (*almost never, sometimes, often,* or *almost always*) they experience different feelings, such as restlessness or self-satisfaction. Responses to the S-Anxiety scale show the *intensity* of one's anxious response at the time of measurement; responses to the T-Anxiety scale show the *frequency* of such responses.

The STAI is untimed but can usually be completed within 10 minutes. The instrument can be easily hand scored; however, the scorer must take into account that approximately one half of the items measure the absence of anxiety whereas the other half measure the presence of anxiety. For those items that measure the absence of anxiety, the scoring must be reversed.

Reliability studies indicate that scores on the S-Anxiety scale are internally consistent but can change substantially over time depending on the individual's circumstances. For example, scores on this scale can be expected to rise markedly when a person is confronted with a threatening situation, such as an exam or surgery. Individuals who score high on the S-Anxiety scale are usually experiencing a number of symptoms associated with activation of the autonomic nervous system, such as rapid heart rate, perspiration, shortness of breath, shakiness, and hot or cold flashes.

Scores on the T-Anxiety scale are both internally consistent and relatively stable over time for most populations. Individuals who score high on the T-Anxiety scale will usually show a larger increase in their S-Anxiety scores in a threatening circumstance, especially in situations that involve social evaluations, than will individuals who score low on this scale. In addition to measuring anxiety proneness, the T-Anxiety scale also taps a range of other psychological problems. According to Chaplin (1985), the T-Anxiety scale can probably best be viewed as a measure of general dissatisfaction with one's life.

A children's version of the STAI, The State–Trait Anxiety Inventory for Children (STAIC), has also been established for counselor use. The STAIC provides extensive norms for fourth, fifth, and sixth graders. Because the reading level for the STAIC is relatively high (above sixth-grade level), the STAIC should be used only with elementary school students who possess above-average reading ability (Walker & Kaufman, 1984).

Beck Anxiety Inventory (BAI). The BAI was designed to measure symptoms of anxiety that are relatively independent of depression (Beck & Steer, 1993). The BAI parallels the BDI-II in its manner of construction and interpretation. Similar to the BDI-II, the BAI contains 21 items, each of which is answered on a 4-point scale. Each item measures a separate symptom of anxiety. Raw scores on the BAI are interpreted in terms of four categories (minimal, mild, moderate, or severe anxiety). As with the BDI-II, the BAI can easily be administered as part of the counseling interview to monitor a client's progress over time. The BAI results can be analyzed in terms of four clusters of scores—neurophysiological, subjective, panic, and autonomic—that can be helpful in differentiating among different types of anxiety disorders.

Other Measures of Anxiety or Fear.   Other standardized inventories of anxiety or fear that are of interest to counselors include the Test Anxiety Scale (Sarason, 1980), Mathematics Anxiety Rating Scale–Revised (Plake & Parker, 1982), Maudsley Obsessional–Compulsive Inventory (Hodgson & Rachman, 1977), Posttraumatic Stress Disorder Symptom Scale (Foa, Riggs, Dancu, & Rothbaum, 1993), and Fear Questionnaire (Marks & Mathews, 1978). These instruments assess specific types of anxieties or fears often encountered by clients. The Fear Questionnaire measures the extent to which a client may be suffering from a particular type of phobia (i.e., agoraphobia, blood-injury phobia, or social phobia).

Anger

Anger is a universal emotion that underlies hostile attitudes and aggressive behaviors. Assessment of anger can aid in crisis intervention and increase understanding of factors related to one's anger.

An individual's anger can be assessed by means of the State–Trait Anger Expression Inventory–2 (STAXI-2; Spielberger, 1999). This instrument is designed to measure the experience, expression, and control of anger in individuals who are 16 years of age or older. It consists of 57 items that can be completed in 5 to 10 minutes and scored in about 5 minutes. Norms are available for both adolescents and adults.

The STAXI-2 is analogous to the STAI in that it provides measures of anger both as a state (actual anger at any point in time) and as a trait (potential anger). The Trait–Anger (T-Anger) scale consists of two subscales: Angry Temperament and Angry Reaction. The State–Anger (S-Anger) scale has been subdivided into three subscales: Feeling Angry, Feel Like Expressing Anger Verbally, and Feel Like Expressing Anger Physically. In addition to the Trait– and State–Anger scales, the STAXI-2 contains several measures of anger expression and anger control. An Anger Expression Index provides an overall measure of total anger expression. Factor-analytic research supports the creation of the separate scales (Forgays, Forgays, & Spielberger, 1997).

Although initially developed for research purposes, the STAXI-2 can also be helpful in counseling situations by providing a format for considering the different dimensions of anger. The STAXI-2 provides a broad assessment of one's anger that can be useful in counseling clients with issues related to anger, hostility, and aggression.

Alcohol Abuse

As indicated in Chapter 14, alcohol abuse is relatively common in the United States. No single personality type represents all individuals with alcoholism. Graham and Strenger (1988) identified six different personality types for individuals with alcoholism, but none were unique to these individuals. The authors emphasized the individual differences among the alcoholic patients they studied.

The instruments described below have been designed to identify and evaluate individuals with alcohol problems.

Michigan Alcoholism Screening Test (MAST). The MAST, which has received wide usage over the years, is a brief instrument that can be answered by the client in less than 15 minutes (Evans, 1998; Selzer, 1971). The items describe symptoms of excessive drinking, various problems (e.g., social, family, work, legal, and health) that one may have encountered as a result of drinking, concerns expressed by others about one's drinking, and efforts that one may have made to control drinking or to obtain treatment for excessive drinking. The instrument and the scoring weights for each item are shown in Figure 15-3. Scores of 5 or more indicate alcoholism, scores of 4 suggest the possibility of alcoholism, and scores of 3 or less indicate the absence of alcoholism.

Research indicates that the MAST can effectively identify individuals with alcohol-related diagnoses (Teitelbaum & Mullen, 2000). MAST results should be confirmed by means of other assessment procedures.

FIGURE 15-3. Items and Scoring Weights (Shown in Parentheses) for the Michigan Alcoholism Screening Test

MICHIGAN ALCOHOLISM SCREENING TEST (MAST)

Instructions: Please answer each question "Yes" or "No" as it pertains to you.

(2) *1. Do you feel you are a normal drinker?

(2) 2. Have you ever awakened the morning after some drinking the night before and found that you could not remember a part of the evening before?

(1) 3. Does your spouse (or do your parents) ever worry or complain about you drinking?

(2) *4. Can you stop drinking without a struggle after one or two drinks?

(1) 5. Do you ever feel bad about your drinking?

(2) *6. Do friends or relatives think you are a normal drinker?

(0) 7. Do you ever try to limit your drinking to certain times of the day or to certain places?

(2) *8. Are you always able to stop drinking when you want to?

(5) 9. Have you ever attended a meeting of Alcoholics Anonymous (AA)?

(1) 10. Have you gotten into fights when drinking?

(2) 11. Has drinking ever created problems with you and your spouse?

(2) 12. Has your spouse (or other family member) ever gone to anyone for help about your drinking?

(2) 13. Have you ever lost friends or girlfriends/boyfriends because of drinking?

(2) 14. Have you ever gotten into trouble at work because of drinking?

(2) 15. Have you ever lost a job because of drinking?

(2) 16. Have you ever neglected your obligations, your family, or your work for two or more days in a row because you were drinking?

(1) 17. Do you ever drink before noon?

(2) 18. Have you ever been told you have liver trouble? Cirrhosis?

(5) 19. Have you ever had delirium tremens (DTs), severe shaking, heard voices, or seen things that weren't there after heavy drinking?

(5) 20. Have you ever gone to anyone for help about your drinking?

(5) 21. Have you ever been in a hospital because of drinking?

(2) 22. Have you ever been a patient in a psychiatric hospital or on a psychiatric ward of a general hospital where drinking was part of the problem?

(2) 23. Have you ever been seen at a psychiatric or mental health clinic, or gone to a doctor, social worker, or clergyperson for help with an emotional problem in which drinking had played a part?

(2) 24. Have you ever been arrested, even for a few hours, because of drunk behavior?

(2) 25. Have you ever been arrested for drunk driving after drinking?

*Negative responses to these items indicate alcoholism; for all other items, positive responses indicate alcoholism.

Note. From "The Michigan Alcoholism Screening Test: The Quest for a New Diagnostic Instrument" by M. L. Selzer, 1971, *American Journal of Psychiatry*, 127, p. 1655. Copyright 1971 by the American Psychiatric Association. Reprinted with permission.

The MAST, or abbreviated versions of it (Evans, 1998), can be used with all clients in an agency to detect possible alcohol problems that otherwise might be missed. According to one study, 22% of new clients at a university counseling center scored high enough on the MAST to suggest possible alcoholism (Hay, 1988).

A case example showing the use of the MAST in counseling is presented below.

CASE EXAMPLE

Sally, a client at a community counseling service, received a score of 16 on the MAST. She answered Items 1, 2, 5, 6, 8, 10, 11, 12, and 23 in the scored direction. Friends had brought Sally to the counseling agency because of problems related to her drinking. Her score of 16 far surpasses the cutoff score of 5 used on the MAST to signal alcoholism.

The MAST contributed to counseling by emphasizing the importance of Sally's drinking problem. Information obtained from the MAST was confirmed by other information related to Sally's drinking habits. Her alcohol consumption (13 drinks per week) surpassed more than 82% of American adults who drink (Miller & Munoz, 1982). Counseling with Sally revealed that she came from a troubled family, and she frequently fought with her mother while she lived at home. Sally suffered from low self-esteem and a perfectionistic nature. She was demanding and dependent in her relationships. Testing with the California Psychological Inventory revealed that she was highly critical of herself (low Good Impression score; $T = 34$), undercontrolled (low Self-Control score; $T = 39$), and lacking confidence (low Capacity for Status score; $T = 39$). Her personality type was Gamma (externally oriented and norm-questioning) at the midpoint (Level 4 of 7 levels) of self-realization.

The counselor worked with her on family issues and relationship matters. Sally became more self-sufficient during the course of counseling and more confident in her relationships with others. She began to deal with some of the personal issues represented by her drinking problem. By addressing unresolved problems and by the use of self-monitoring techniques, Sally was able to reduce the amount of her drinking during the course of counseling.

Additional measures of alcohol or other drug problems that counselors may wish to use for screening purposes include the Personal Experience Screening Questionnaire (Winters, 1991), Alcohol Use Disorders Identification Test (Saunders, Aasland, Amundsen, & Grant, 1993), Substance Abuse Subtle Screening Inventory–3

(Lazowski, Miller, Boye, & Miller, 1998), and Adolescent Drinking Index (Harrell & Wirtz, 1989).

Alcohol Use Inventory (AUI). The AUI is a comprehensive self-report inventory that assesses patterns of behavior, attitudes, and symptoms pertaining to the use of alcohol for individuals 16 years and older (Horn, Wanberg, & Foster, 1986). Most people complete the AUI, which requires a sixth-grade reading level, within 35 to 60 minutes. It contains 24 scales based on 228 items organized at three levels: 17 primary scales, 6 second-order scales, and 1 general alcohol use scale. The scales evaluate alcohol usage in terms of benefits, styles, consequences, and concerns. It is most appropriate for individuals who enter a treatment program as a result of alcohol dependence or abuse. It can be used to establish a treatment plan for a person with alcohol-related issues.

Other comprehensive measures of substance abuse include the Personal Experience Inventory for adolescents ages 12 to 18 years (Winters & Henley, 1989) and the Personal Experience Inventory for Adults (Winters, 1996). Both inventories include a problem severity section and a psychosocial section. The Inventory of Drinking Situations can be used to identify personal or social situations in which a person may drink excessively based on that person's previous experiences in those situations (Annis, Graham, & Davis, 1987).

Eating Disorders

The major eating disorders include anorexia nervosa (self-induced starvation), bulimia nervosa (binge–purge syndrome), and eating disorders not otherwise specified (American Psychiatric Association, 1994). The *DSM-IV* does not list obesity as an eating disorder because it is not usually associated with a specific psychological or behavioral syndrome.

Women are 6 to 10 times as likely as men to suffer from an eating disorder. The lifetime prevalence of anorexia nervosa among women ranges from 0.5% to 3.7% depending on the breadth of definition. The lifetime prevalence of bulimia nervosa among women ranges from 1.1% to 4.2% (American Psychiatric Association, 2000b). A number of women also suffer from eating disorders not otherwise specified. In addition, studies indicate that many women express some of the symptoms of eating disorders, such as binge eating and purging, without meeting the diagnostic criteria for an eating disorder (Mulholland & Mintz, 2001).

According to the *DSM-IV*, the essential features of anorexia nervosa include refusal to maintain normal body weight (e.g., the person weighs less than 85% of expected body weight), intense fear of gaining weight, a disturbed body image, and loss of menstrual cycle for females. Anorexia nervosa, which means nervous loss of appetite, is a misnomer; the person resists eating, but actual loss of appetite is rare. Bulimia nervosa, in contrast, is characterized by binge eating (rapid consumption of food in a short period of time), a feeling of lack of control of one's eating behavior while binge eating, drastic attempts to prevent weight gain (e.g., self-induced vomiting, use of laxatives or diuretics, strict dieting or fasting, or vigorous exercise), and persistent overconcern with body shape and weight (American Psychiatric Association, 1994). Some individuals share the symptoms of both disorders.

Individuals suspected of meeting the *DSM-IV* criteria for an eating disorder should be referred to an eating disorders clinic or health service with a multidisciplinary team that includes a physician, nurse, dietitian, and mental health professional. The person may require a complete medical examination, nutritional assessment, and psychological assessment. Treatment also entails cooperation among the different disciplines to help clients address medical complications, alter eating habits, and alleviate psychological problems by such means as improving social skills and self-image.

Individuals with eating disorders typically wait several years from the onset of the disorder before entering treatment. Early assessment of a person's eating problems can reduce the length of this time period. Counselors can use standardized tests to assess the severity of one's eating problems and to help structure a discussion on this topic in counseling. To ensure full and honest reporting, the counselor must establish a trusting relationship with the client before undertaking the assessment.

The Eating Attitudes Test and the Eating Disorders Inventory–2, both discussed below, are two widely used standardized measures available for evaluating eating problems (Rosen, Silberg, & Gross, 1988). In addition to these measures, the Questionnaire for Eating Disorder Diagnoses is a new instrument based on *DSM-IV* criteria that shows promise for use in counseling (Mintz, O'Halloran, Mulholland, & Schneider, 1997).

Eating Attitudes Test (EAT).   The EAT is a 40-item screening inventory that measures the symptoms and behaviors associated with anorexia nervosa and other eating problems (Garner & Garfinkel, 1979). Total scores on the EAT have clearly differentiated between individuals with and without eating disorders in research investigations (Mintz & O'Halloran, 2000). The scores are sensitive to treatment so that recovered anorectics obtain scores similar to normals.

The EAT can be scored in terms of three subscales—Dieting, Bulimia, and Oral Control—to help determine the nature of the eating problems. Rosen et al. (1988) found that scores on each of the three subscales correlated significantly with scores on the Restraint Scale (a measure of restrained eating) and self-reported diet behavior (skipping meals, fasting, using diet pills, vomiting, and taking laxatives).

The following case illustrates the use of the EAT with a client in an intake interview.

CASE EXAMPLE

Joan's intake counselor asked her to take the EAT as a means of reviewing her eating habits and assessing the need for a referral to an eating disorders clinic. Joan had come to the community mental health service for assistance with relationship issues, family conflicts, and eating problems. She ate large quantities of bakery goods and sweets about once a week, then used laxatives to purge the extra food.

Joan obtained a score of 36 on the EAT, which placed her almost two standard deviations above the mean (98th percentile) of adult women. Scores above 30 suggest serious eating concerns. She marked *always* or *very often* to items such as "am terrified about being overweight," "am preoccupied with a desire to be thinner," and "feel that food controls my life." Her EAT score and other intake data indicated that she could probably benefit from a referral to an eating disorders clinic with a multidisciplinary staff for a more thorough assessment of her eating and nutritional habits as well as her physiological and psychological well-being. After discussing the matter with her, the counselor made arrangements for such a referral.

Eating Disorders Inventory–2 (EDI-2). The EDI-2 consists of 91 items that assess the psychological and behavioral characteristics that underlie anorexia nervosa and bulimia (Garner, 1991). It differs from the EAT by the inclusion of personality items as well as behavioral and symptomatic items. The EDI-2 retains the eight scales originally found on the EDI, five of which measure psychological traits— Ineffectiveness, Perfectionism, Interpersonal Distrust, Interoceptive Awareness, and Maturity Fears—and three of which measure behavioral or attitudinal factors—Drive for Thinness, Bulimia, and Body Dissatisfaction. In addition, it includes three new scales—Asceticism ("oral self-restraint"), Impulse Regulation, and Social Insecurity— that assess constructs important in the diagnosis and treatment of eating disorders.

Clients also complete a four-page checklist concerning symptoms they may be experiencing in regard to eating disorders. Information obtained from the checklist on matters related to dieting, exercise, binge eating, purging, laxatives, diet pills, diuretics, and menstrual history can be helpful in forming a *DSM-IV* diagnosis.

The EDI-2 manual provides normative tables for patients with anorexia nervosa (restricting type), anorexia nervosa (bulimic type), and bulimia nervosa as well as for the total eating disorder sample. Separate norms are also provided for college women, college men, high school girls, and high school boys. The normative study for high school students found that girls scored particularly high on two of the three scales that directly pertain to eating disorder symptoms (Drive for Thinness and Body Dissatisfaction; Rosen et al., 1988). Although separate-sex norms are necessary, separate norms based on age, socioeconomic class differences, and race do not seem to be warranted.

The EDI-2 scales produce reliable (internally consistent) results for people with eating disorders. The results are somewhat less reliable for nonpatient samples, presumably because of the restricted range of scores for these samples. Validity studies show that scores on the EDI-2 scales differentiate patients with eating disorders from various control groups (general psychiatric patients, recovered patients, and nonpatients) in a variety of cultures (Niv, Kaplan, Mitrani, & Shiang, 1998; Podar, Hannus, & Allik, 1999; Schoemaker, Verbraak, Breteler, & vanderStaak, 1997).

Attention-Deficit/Hyperactivity Disorder (ADHD)

In recent years, ADHD has become a popular, but somewhat controversial, diagnosis for children and adolescents with behavioral problems (Panksepp, 1998; Zwi, Ramchandani, & Joughin, 2000). Professionals have been accused of both overdiagnosing and underdiagnosing ADHD in the populations they serve (Higgins, 1997). According to the Practice Guidelines of the American Academy of Pediatrics (2000), ADHD is the most common neurobehavioral disorder of childhood, with prevalence rates varying from 4% to 12% for school-age samples. Between 30% and 70% of children diagnosed with ADHD continue to meet the criteria for ADHD as adolescents and adults (Heiligenstein, Guenther, Levy, Savino, & Fulwiler, 1999; B. Jackson & Farrugia, 1997).

The *DSM-IV* provides diagnostic criteria for three subtypes of ADHD: predominantly inattentive, predominantly hyperactive, and combined (American Psychiatric Association, 1994). An individual must exhibit (a) six of nine symptoms for inattention (such as makes careless mistakes, easily distracted, disorganized, and forgetful) to meet the criteria for ADHD Predominantly Inattentive Type or (b) six of nine symptoms for hyperactivity–impulsivity (such as fidgets, runs about, talks excessively, and interrupts others) to satisfy the criteria for ADHD Predominantly Hyperactive Type. Individuals who exhibit six or more of the nine symptoms in both categories fulfill the criteria for ADHD Combined Type.

Symptoms must be pervasive, maladaptive, and inconsistent with normal developmental expectations. They must have occurred for at least 6 months, must occur in more than one setting (such as school and home), and must interfere with one's functioning. Some of the symptoms must have been present before age 7. Symptoms must not be attributable to some other disorder, such as a learning disability, anxiety, or depression.

Because of potential problems with misdiagnosis, a multimodal approach should be used in assessing a client for possible ADHD (M. B. Brown, 2000). Such an approach should include reports from parents and teachers (or other school professionals) as well as the client. Historical information and observational data may be obtained by interviews, questionnaires, and rating scales. Evidence should be obtained regarding the core symptoms of ADHD, age of onset, duration of symptoms, extent of functional impairment, and associated conditions (American Academy of Pediatrics, 2000).

"Broad-band" behavior rating scales, such as the Behavior Assessment System for Children (C. R. Reynolds & Kamphaus, 1992) and the Child Behavior Checklist (Achenbach, 1991), can be used as screening devices to identify possible ADHD problems among a number of other behavioral problems. Broad-band instruments can be helpful in identifying children in need of further evaluation; however, they should not be relied on as a basis for diagnosing ADHD (American Academy of Pediatrics, 2000).

"Narrow-band" scales, such as the Conners' Rating Scales (Revised)–ADHD Index and *DSM-IV* Symptoms Scales (Conners, 1997), ADHD Rating Scale (DuPaul, 1991), and Child Attention Profile (Barkley, 1991), focus specifically on ADHD symptoms. These instruments are relatively short, able to discriminate between children with and without ADHD, and sensitive to treatment effects (M. B. Brown, 2000). Studies indicate that ADHD-specific checklists are much more accurate than broad-band scales in distinguishing between children with and without ADHD (American Academy of Pediatrics, 2000). The Adult Attention Deficit Disorders Evaluation Scale (McCarney & Anderson, 1996), Conners' Adult ADHD Rating Scales (Conners, Erhardt, & Sparrow, 1998), and Brown Adult ADHD Rating Scales (T. E. Brown, 1996) are narrow-band instruments that may be used to assess symptoms among adults.

SUMMARY

1. The MMPI-2 provides a more comprehensive assessment of a client's mental health than any other personality inventory. The MMPI-A provides comparable information for adolescents.

2. The MCMI-III represents a viable alternative to the MMPI-2 for assessment of client psychopathology. It is shorter and more closely related to theory and to the *DSM-IV* categories than is the MMPI-2.

3. Two promising new measures of psychopathology are the Personality Assessment Inventory and the Basic Personality Inventory. Both of these instruments can be self-scored, contain scales that are relatively easy to interpret, and circumvent some of the difficulties inherent in the MMPI-2.

4. The Beck Depression Inventory–II serves as a quick, yet relatively thorough, measure of a client's state of depression. It is particularly helpful for monitoring changes in depression over time.

5. The State–Trait Anxiety Inventory yields valid and reliable scores for anxiety that can be distinguished as either transitory (state anxiety) or enduring (trait anxiety). In a similar fashion, the State–Trait Anger Expression Inventory measures one's actual and potential anger and provides information on how anger is likely to be expressed.

6. Problems related to alcohol use can be detected by the Michigan Alcoholism Screening Test. Individuals with problems can be further evaluated by means of the Alcohol Use Inventory.

7. The Eating Attitudes Test can be used to screen clients for possible eating disorders. The Eating Disorders Inventory–2 provides information regarding the psychological traits and symptom clusters of clients with eating disorders.

8. A multimodal approach based on the use of interviews, questionnaires, and rating scales with clients, parents, and teachers should be used in the assessment of attention-deficit/hyperactivity disorder.

Professional Practices and Considerations

16

ASSESSMENT OF MINORITY AND SPECIAL POPULATIONS

ONTROVERSY HAS SURROUNDED psychological tests almost from their beginnings. The development of the Army Alpha for testing World War I recruits caused much debate (Haney, 1981), particularly when differences between socioeconomic and ethnic groups became known. Since then, controversy has continued, especially regarding the fairness of aptitude tests used for selection procedures for people of different ethnic or racial groups (Gross, 1962; Neisser et al., 1996; Sandoval, 1998). Assessment of individuals with disabilities is a complex problem often requiring modifications of standardized instruments and caution in interpreting the results. This chapter examines the issues of psychological and aptitude assessments for different racial/ethnic groups, people with mental and physical disabilities, and older populations.

CULTURAL BIAS IN TESTING

There are three commonly considered ways in which tests may be biased against a person or groups of persons. First, they may contain items that favor one group over another (lack of content equivalence). For example, an item on a verbal analogies test that includes the word *toboggan* might tend to favor people from northern states over those from southern states. Similarly, a test may be biased because it includes language or values that are typical to White middle-class people but not to Blacks, Hispanics, or other distinct cultural groups (Lonner & Sundberg, 1987). Many sociocultural factors—ethnicity, socioeconomic class, region, and situation—contribute to mismatches between the language of test takers and that of test makers (lack of conceptual equivalence). Most test authors now include carefully chosen normative samples to include members of diverse groups, and counselors should consult the test manuals for specific information about translations and different gender and minority norm groups (Fouad & Chan, 1999; Geisinger, 1998).

The second source of bias comes from test-related factors such as the motivation, anxiety, or test sophistication of those taking the test—sources of bias that are external to the test itself. Extreme forms of test anxiety, self-esteem, and achievement motivation have been found to be related to test performance, but there has been little evidence that there are substantial differences in these areas among races, sexes, or social classes. However, clients from minority groups who are not motivated to perform well on a test or who are not sophisticated in regard to the nature of the test items cannot be expected to perform as well on tests as those from the dominant culture in which these factors have been emphasized.

A third possible source of bias comes from the use of test results in selection for employment or college admissions—if the model used for selection and prediction produces results that vary greatly among different groups. When the use of a test or other selection procedure results in a substantially higher rejection rate for minority candidates than for nonminority candidates, the use of the test must be justified by proving it is valid for the job in question (Anastasi, 1988). In general, a test used in selection can be defined as fair if it does not lead to differential prediction for any minority group (Geisinger, 1998).

Recognizing that increasing diversity in counselee backgrounds presents special challenges in testing, a committee of the Association for Assessment in Counseling developed a set of multicultural counseling standards containing 34 standards grouped according to the assessment-related task (Prediger, 1994a). Of the 34 standards, the majority addressed the selection of assessment instruments appropriate to multicultural populations because if the instrument is inappropriate, counseling based on interpretations will also probably be inappropriate (Prediger, 1994a). Both the American Psychological Association (1993) and the American Counseling Association (1995) have stated in their ethical codes that professionals should consider socioeconomic, ethnic, and cultural backgrounds, beliefs, and values when administering and interpreting psychological tests.

In discussing the problem of test bias or group differences, one must distinguish between test results and innate aptitude. The statement that men as a group achieve higher levels of competence in mathematics than women is a statement regarding past achievement on a given test. This does not imply that men possess a greater aptitude for mathematics than women—a statement that suggests innateness or biological or genetic determinism. Almost no one these days believes that intellectual functioning, no matter how it is measured— by tests or academic achievement—is exclusively a function of either one's heredity or one's environment; it is a complex function of both.

An understanding of the client's worldview is important, because the initial step in the counseling process is to understand the client and his or her issues and problems. Worldview includes the individual's perceptions of human nature (good or evil) and the individual's focus on the past, present, or future; it also includes the emphasis given to individual or group goals and locus of responsibility (internal or external) including causes of behavior. Based on the knowledge of the client's worldview and the client's cultural group, counselors are better able to determine the approaches, techniques, and goals needed for a specific client (Lonner & Ibrahim, 1996; D. W. Sue, 1978). If counselor and client worldviews clash, the client may find the services not understandable or unacceptable (Dana, 1998).

It is important in the assessment and treatment of multicultural clients for the counselor to display both the sensitivity to be aware of the cultural variables that affect assessment and the competence to translate this awareness into effective assessment (Arbona, 1998). To competently assess and counsel members of multicultural groups, counselors must consider the level of the client's acculturation and determine the potential impact of this variable (Dana, 1993). *Acculturation* is defined as the degree of integration of new cultural patterns into one's original cultural patterns. To assess the level of a client's acculturation, the counselor should take into account the age of the client, the number of generations in the new culture (e.g., first, second, third), the language generally preferred, and the extent of activities and relationships within and beyond the client's own cultural group (Paniagua, 1998).

In using standardized tests in counseling with a person from another culture, a general rule is that the less the counselor knows of the client's culture, the more errors the counselor is likely to make. It is important for the counselor to be knowledgeable about the culture of the person being assessed and to develop skills for dealing with culture-related behavior patterns. Conversely, it is important not to "overculturalize." Culture is important in understanding an individual, but it is not the only variable influencing human behavior. Attempting to remove all cultural differences from a test is likely to compromise its validity as a measure of the behavior it was designed to assess. There are many factors that all people experience that lead them to seek counseling, and these are all important in assessing a person (Lonner & Sundberg, 1987).

Culture has an influence on psychopathological expression, and differences on personality tests across cultures should be taken into account. Psychological tests are measures of behavior, and to the extent that culture affects behavior, its influence is going to be detected by tests. Resulting psychological and educational diagnoses made as a result of such testing data should be made with caution (Sue, 1990).

APTITUDE AND COGNITIVE ASSESSMENT

A basic assumption of standardized testing is that it is perfectly appropriate for the test taker to be willing to provide obvious information and to give a performance for a total stranger—the examiner. These basic social assumptions may be in conflict with the interactional rules for individuals in some cultures. For example, it might be hypothesized that Black working-class children or Native American working-class children are less oriented to public performance for unfamiliar adults than are White middle-class children. It might even be argued that child-rearing practices of many White middle-class parents, which encourage public verbal performance for strangers, program their children for eventual success on standardized tests.

The combination of constriction imposed in most American schools and the competition encouraged there can conflict directly with aspects of African American and Native American cultures. Such conflict may lead to alienation of these students from both the experiences and products of education, of which assessment instruments are a part (Neisser et al., 1996).

African Americans

Counselors must remember that there are large within-group differences among the 37 million African Americans in regard to social class, rural/urban, and racial/bicultural identities. For example, the middle-class African Americans who make up 25% of their minority group tend to be similar to their Anglo American middle-class counterparts in regard to personal resources and expectations (Dana, 1998).

Although tests could be biased against any minority, the most serious controversy exists over the fact that, as a group, African Americans score approximately one standard deviation below White Americans on most standardized tests of cognitive ability (Lichtenberger & Kaufman, 1998). Even more aggravating is the fact that the magnitude of this difference persists from preschool children through college applicants. There is, however, some evidence that this differential is decreasing among children and adolescents (Neisser et al., 1996). Of course, there is a great deal of overlap between the two distributions, with almost 20% of Blacks scoring above the mean for Whites and 20% of Whites scoring below the mean for Blacks. Because counselors usually deal with individuals rather than total populations, group differences are of less importance. The counselor is concerned only with the particular ability of a particular individual, whether Black or White. The counselor is not concerned with overall mean differences among populations but with the question of whether a particular aptitude test score has equal validity, that is, whether it predicts equally well for Black as for White Americans.

Because African Americans as a group have experienced great racial discrimination in the past and this discrimination has had an impact on their socioeconomic status, their opportunities, and their home environments, it is not surprising that this would have an effect on test results. Much of the controversy centers on the cause of the differences. Some attribute the differences to the disadvantages that African Americans suffer in their economic status and their educational and occupational opportunities. Others attribute much of the difference to genetic factors, although little direct evidence supports this position (Neisser et al., 1996).

A frequently offered argument is that intelligence tests and other measures of cognitive aptitude are constructed by and for White middle-class individuals and therefore are biased against lower socioeconomic individuals and others who are not members of the majority culture. Some of this cultural bias could be found in the items on which suburban children might have more familiarity than inner-city or rural children. Children brought up using a Black dialect or nonstandard American English might be less able to comprehend the language used on such instruments. Test developers have now become extremely sensitive to this issue and have established panels of experts that include representatives from many cultural groups. Most of this content bias has therefore been eliminated from many of the current forms of these tests, although such changes have been shown to have little if any effect on the scores obtained by minority individuals (Friedenberg, 1995; Walsh & Betz, 2000).

If the validity of cognitive aptitude tests is different for majority and minority groups, and if counselors encourage or discourage clients about pursuing different levels of education or types of jobs on the basis of these test results, then this type of bias could affect counseling outcomes. Numerous studies have been conducted predicting various criteria for both education and job performance for Black and White groups. In general, results have shown that ability tests are equally valid for both minority and majority groups. These studies have used IQ tests to predict school achievement, scholastic aptitude tests to predict college grades, and job-related aptitude tests to predict job success. Both correlations and regression lines tend to be similar for both groups, and in the cases in which minor differences have occurred, there has been a tendency for the test to slightly overpredict the achievement of Black students—contrary to what might be expected if the tests were significantly racially biased (Messick, 1980; Neisser et al., 1996).

Hispanics

There are now 35 million Hispanic Americans, and this number is expected to grow to 47 million (15% of the U.S. population) within the next two decades. Counselors need to recognize the diversity within this minority group both in regard to acculturation to the U.S. society and in regard to cultural background. The largest group is of Mexican origin, most of whom have settled in the southwestern states. Puerto Ricans are concentrated in the eastern states, Cubans in Miami, and Central and South Americans in Florida and Texas. Although heterogeneous in many ways, their worldview is shaped by several common influences: the Catholic religion (85%), some presence of folk beliefs, and a Hispanic group cultural identity (Dana, 1998).

Although Spanish-speaking individuals often share the poor economic conditions of other minorities, their difficulties do not lie solely in their poverty. The Spanish-speaking student meets difficulties in communication and understanding from whatever social background. A Hispanic student who scores low on a standardized test in English may actually have obtained a remarkably good score if the student has been learning English for only a short period. A Hispanic client or one from another cultural background may receive a very low score on the Information subtest of the Wechsler Adult Intelligence Scale (WAIS) not because of a lack of intelligence but because the client lacks information about the total population of the United States, the number of senators, and other general knowledge expected from the average American. Similar problems would arise from the vocabulary section and scores on the Picture Completion and Picture Arrangement subtests, because they include materials that are not part of the client's culture (Paniagua, 1998). The counselor must consider individual differences and circumstances in interpreting the test results of clients for whom English is not their native language.

For Hispanic individuals, a Spanish edition of an assessment instrument may be appropriate, and Spanish language editions have been developed for most of the widely used tests, including the Strong Interest Inventory, the Myers–Briggs Type Indicator, the Wechsler intelligence scales, the Self-Directed Search, the Sixteen Personality Factor Questionnaire (16 PF), and Cattell's Culture-Fair Intelligence Test.

Native Americans

In counseling Native American individuals, caution must be used in interpreting the results of various assessment procedures. There is a wide range of differences with regard to culture among various Native American tribes, and because of such large differences few generalizations are possible. For example, Sioux children are likely to be more integrated into the American society than Navajo children, who more often live on a reservation and speak primarily Navajo (Lichtenberger & Kaufman, 1998). Therefore, assessment of Native American clients should begin with an attempt to understand the client's cultural identity. In norming samples of tests, very small numbers of Native Americans are likely to have been included in the sample, and even those are likely to represent only a few of the many different cultures from which Native Americans come.

As a group, Native Americans have lost much of their original self-sufficient heritage and now represent major challenges for counselors and the entire mental health community because they have the highest rates of poverty, unemployment, alcohol abuse, and suicide (Dana, 1998). In testing situations, Native Americans may underestimate the seriousness of tests, lack test-taking skills, or lack motivation to perform on tests. For some, tribal beliefs may discourage the type of competitive behavior often present in test-taking situations. They may also have learned English as a second language and learned their first language as a nonwritten language—factors that can easily affect English reading skills (Brescia & Fortune, 1989). In addition, because they often come from isolated, rural, or impoverished settings, they may lack the type of knowledge and experience expected on certain test instruments. There is a 20-item Native American Acculturation Scale that yields an estimate of an individual's extent of acculturation to American society (Garrett & Pichette, 2000).

Asian Americans

Test results and the interpretations of these results vary greatly for different Asian American clients. They come from widely diverse cultural backgrounds and range all the way from fourth- and fifth-generation Asian Americans to the more recent Filipino and Vietnamese immigrants.

The later generations of Japanese and Chinese Americans come from backgrounds in which the mean income level equals or surpasses that of Whites, and they hold many attitudes and values similar to the majority culture. There are aspects of their cultures, however, that influence them to place increased emphasis on the results of achievement and aptitude tests and less on other types of performance. In addition, education, especially higher education, is much valued and supported, with particular value placed on attending prestigious institutions of higher education. Thus, there is considerable pressure to attain high enough scores on academic aptitude tests to gain entrance to prestigious colleges and universities.

Test results for recent Southeast Asian immigrants have much less validity because these individuals are affected by all of the language problems, vast cultural differences, and economic difficulties common to newly arrived immigrants.

Ethnicity, Social, and Educational Variables

In attempting to understand and competently interpret cognitive assessment results of clients from various backgrounds, the counselor must remember that social class is correlated with race and ethnicity and that many cultural differences disappear when socioeconomic status is controlled (Arbona, 1998). Academic aptitude and achievement test scores are far more related to school academic variables (e.g., grades achieved, types of courses taken, particular school attended) than to race or ethnicity. In a study conducted by the American College Testing Program (ACT) of students in four racial/ethnic groups (African American, Hispanic/Native American, Asian American, and Caucasian), over 50% of the variance in ACT scores could be explained by high school academic variables, with an additional 15% explained by student background characteristics and noncognitive, education-related factors. Race/ethnicity or gender explained only 1% to 2% of additional variance in ACT scores over and above the other variables considered in this study (Noble, Davenport, Schiel, & Pommerich, 1999).

Culture-Fair Tests

The typical intelligence test administered in the United States assumes a relatively common cultural background found in contemporary society along with English as a native language. For tests above the lower elementary levels, literacy in reading English is also necessary to obtain valid results on most of the group-administered tests. To provide valid assessment devices useful in other cultures or for use with subcultures or minority cultures in the United States, attempts have been made to develop culture-fair tests that function independently of a specific culture, primarily by eliminating, or at least greatly reducing, language and cultural content (Samuda, 1998b).

Cattell's Culture-Fair Intelligence Test. This test is a paper-and-pencil test that has no verbal content and is designed to reduce the effects of educational background and cultural influences (Cattell, 1973). The test consists of four parts in multiple-choice formats: (a) series—a figure must be chosen to complete the series; (b) classification—the object is to choose the figure that is different from the series; (c) matrices—the pattern of change occurring in the figures must be completed; and (d) conditions—the alternative with similar conditions to the example figure must be chosen. The test is available in two parallel forms and for three different age or ability levels: (a) children ages 4 through 8 years and adults with mental retardation, (b) children ages 8 through 14 years and average adults, and (c) college students and adults with above-average intelligence. Within particular age levels, the raw scores can be converted to normalized deviation IQ scores that have a mean of 100 and a standard deviation of 16.

Raven's Progressive Matrices. Raven's Progressive Matrices is a widely used culture-fair test that requires the examinee to solve problems involving abstract figures and designs by indicating which of various multiple-choice alternatives complete a given matrix (Raven, Court, & Raven, 1993). Progressive changes occur in the vertical dimension, horizontal dimension, or both dimensions in a series of matrices. For each item, the examinee must determine the principle by which the matrices are progressively changing and select the correct alternative from six answers that are provided. It is available in two forms: a black-and-white version for Grade 8 through adulthood and the Coloured Progressive Matrices for children ages 5 to 11 years and for adults with mental retardation. Developed in England, Raven's Progressive Matrices has been used in a large number of cross-cultural studies in many countries. These studies suggest that although this test is one of the best available, it might better be described as culturally reduced rather than culture-fair or culture-free. Norms are based on samples of English children and adults, and one drawback for its use in the Unites States is its lack of normative U.S. data.

Naglieri Nonverbal Ability Test (NNAT). The NNAT provides a measure of nonverbal reasoning and problem-solving ability based on the use of progressive matrices with shapes and designs that are not unique to any cultural group (Naglieri, 1996). This test can be administered at seven different levels for students in kindergarten through Grade 12. Administration time requires about 30 minutes. The test can be used with children with hearing, motor, or color vision impairments. The NNAT has been standardized for group administration. A new version of this test, the NNAT–Individual Administration form, has been created for individual administration for those students who need special attention (Naglieri, 2000). Research indicates that the NNAT produces comparable results for children from different cultural backgrounds and that it can be used to provide a fair assessment of White and minority children (Naglieri & Ronning, 2000).

Other Culture-Free Attempts

The Beta IQ III, which was first developed as the Beta IQ test for nonreaders in the army in World War I, is language-free and useful for nonreaders and those with limited English proficiency (Kellogg & Morton, 1999). The Test of Nonverbal Intelligence, which requires only pointing or gesturing responses, uses instructions and illustrative examples that can be pantomimed (L. Brown, Sherbenou, & Johnsen, 1997).

Raven's Progressive Matrices and other attempts to develop culture-fair tests not only represent attempts to increase the fairness of intelligence tests but also provide interesting ways of studying this type of ability. Most studies in the United States have found that children in lower socioeconomic groups score substantially lower than middle-class groups on these tests as well as on the more common culturally loaded intelligence tests. In addition, culture-fair tests typically do less well in predicting academic achievement or job performance than do the standard culturally loaded tests. This is not surprising, because academic achievement and job performance often include much culturally important content.

Cultural Differences

Some authorities state that test results based on norms of White middle-class students or adults cannot usually be appropriately applied to ethnic minorities and are therefore of limited usefulness for counselors with minority clients (Dana, 1993). Counselors should understand that the actual results of cognitive tests often contain less bias than that held by test critics. In addition, studies show that the removal of biased items does not affect overall test scores and that many cognitive tests continue to provide mostly accurate predictions for most minority clients (Groth-Marnat, 1997). Developers of those cognitively loaded tests used in making high-stakes employment or admissions decisions have undertaken a number of strategies to attempt to reduce racial and ethnic subgroup differences (P. R. Sackett, Schmitt, Ellingson, & Kabin, 2001). These strategies have included identifying and removing culturally biased items, experimenting with alternative modes of presenting test items, relaxing time limits, and conducting test orientation and coaching programs, but they have not resulted in substantially reducing subgroup differences.

The melting-pot philosophy of cultural assimilation of all minorities into the Anglo American culture has been generally rejected in favor of a multiethnic culture. Counselors who hold positive attitudes toward cultural differences are better able to accommodate the cultural predispositions of students from other ethnic backgrounds. The positive attitudes of counselors are more valuable than specific techniques or special materials. As students are accepted by counselors, they accept themselves and their abilities, as well as their limitations. In schools in which the counselor has considerable influence in determining guidance and testing procedures for these students, he or she can influence the adoption of appropriate programs and policies to prevent the misuse of test results.

CAREER ASSESSMENT

A major question with regard to the use of vocational interest inventories is whether minority students are sufficiently familiar with the vocabulary, the examples, the occupational terms, and the problems that are used in these tests. Because many minority students differ from middle-class White students in their experiences, orientations, and values, their view of available occupations may be restricted even though the minority students' aspirations may equal or exceed those of the middle-class White student. Students from disadvantaged backgrounds are likely to be less aware of the great variety of occupations and the skills required for certain occupations. They may also view potential occupations in ways that are quite different from that which is implied in occupational literature. Minority students tend to enter narrower ranges of fields of study (Arbona, 1990; Bowman, 1995; Leong & Gim-Chung, 1995; Muhs, Popp, & Patterson, 1979).

Within minority communities, there is often a lack of continuity of values between school and family as well as a lack of diversity in the occupations that exist as models for children from these backgrounds. Family cultures vary considerably among different ethnic groups, which influence career roles and expectations. The genogram (Chapter 13) and its accompanying discussion can be a useful tool to help counselors understand the career values and motivations of minority clients (Penick, 2000). On various interest inventories, minority students may achieve relatively low scores, because such students indicate liking fewer occupational titles or interests than students in the norm group.

Studies have shown that despite these differences, interest measures have similar validities among various minority groups in the United States. Interest inventories can therefore be used with minority clients with the same amount of confidence as with Whites, with the possible exception of those coming from particularly disadvantaged backgrounds. Studies have also shown that interest measures predict college majors similarly for students from various minority backgrounds. Differences have been found on interest measures among different minorities, but these differences have equal predictive value (Fouad, Harmon, & Hansen, 1994; Lamb, 1974; Lattimore & Borgen, 1999). For example, Blacks who tend to score higher on social interests are more likely to enter social occupations, whereas Asian American students who obtain higher scores on biological and physical science interests and lower scores on social and sales interests are more likely to pursue scientific occupations. Counselors should also be aware that some of the female–male differences found among Whites are similar but more extreme for Hispanic women.

There is a tendency among Asian Americans to choose vocations in business, science, mathematics, or engineering fields to the exclusion of humanities, social sciences, or law. When interpreting the results of interest inventories in educational and vocational counseling, the counselor should keep in mind this tendency by the minority client to consider a narrow range of possible career goals. Expanding the range of occupations being considered may well be one of the goals of such counseling.

For minority students, the development of appropriate attitudes and behaviors can be enhanced by using representative minority models and pointing out their accomplishments in various fields. In this way, counselors can assist minority students in understanding and appreciating the contributions that have been made and continue to be made by members of their own group.

Counselors must evaluate the testing and appraisal instruments to determine whether they meet criteria for nondiscrimination. Are data provided that assist in making sound occupational choices? What is the racial and socioeconomic makeup of the population on which the test is based?

Several interest inventories have been translated into a number of other languages. A question that needs to be asked in administering such a version of the inventory is whether the person taking the test is from a culture that has similar expectations and social customs as that for the culture in which the test was devised. Unfamiliarity with the nature and purpose of tests could be a problem, as could different ways of responding. Clients from a culture in which the emphasis is on agreeing with nearly everything (because it is considered impolite to disagree) may obtain test results that lack validity.

PERSONALITY ASSESSMENT

Although racial bias has less often been a major issue in personality measurement, there is some evidence that various minority groups obtain scores on personality inventories that differ from those typically obtained in a White majority population. For example, Asian clients are more likely to express psychological problems in terms of somatic complaints. Therefore, an elevation on the Hypochondriasis scale (Scale 1) on the Minnesota Multiphasic Personality Inventory (MMPI) with Asian clients should be interpreted in light of this cultural phenomenon (Gray-Little & Kaplan, 1998; Paniagua, 1998). A Pacific Islander's deviant scores on the MMPI could easily be accounted for by cultural and language differences from the original sample on which it was normed. Diagnoses of schizophrenia are more commonly found with Black clients than with White clients, whereas depression is reported more frequently for White clients than for Black clients (Paniagua, 1998). Differences on personality tests among minority groups and those from other cultures are to be expected, and counselors should take these into consideration in their interpretations of personality test results. Studies of various personality inventories, however, usually indicate that the scales predict the same types of behavioral and personality characteristics for both minority and majority group members, and therefore, when used with caution, these scales can be appropriately used in counseling and psychiatric situations (Duckworth & Anderson, 1995; Novy, Nelson, Goodwin, & Rowzee, 1993).

Greene (1987), in reviewing a large number of studies examining differences between Black and White Americans on the MMPI, reported no consistent pattern to such differences on any of the standard validity and clinical scales. Although Blacks frequently score higher on the F scale and Scales 8 and 9 of the MMPI than White Americans, differences usually disappeared if the groups were matched on education and severity of psychopathology. Black Americans may also score higher on Scales 8 and 9 because of higher levels of nonconformity, alienation, or impulsivity or because of different types of values and perceptions (Groth-Marnat, 1997). Timbrook and Graham (1994) also reported only small differences on MMPI-2 scales between Black and White Americans when matched by age, education, and income. Although there were some statistically significant differences—for example, Black men scoring higher on Scale 8 and Black women scoring higher on Scales 4, 5, and 9—these differences were less than 5 *T*-score points and therefore of little clinical significance. They reported a slight underprediction of psychopathology for Black men, which is in the opposite direction of that suggested in the literature.

Few consistent differences have been found in comparing Hispanics and White Americans on the MMPI scales. A number of other variables such as socioeconomic status, education, and intelligence seem to be more important determinants of MMPI performance than ethnic status. Alcohol abuse combined with depression is more often found among Hispanic male clients as compared with White male clients. Hispanic women's expected traditional roles are often in conflict with the greater female role flexibility in American society. Failure to meet these gender-specific roles as wives and mothers can lead to guilt, anger, and depression that may be revealed on personality instruments (Prieto, McNeill, Walls, & Gomez, 2001).

In a meta-analysis of 25 studies that compared the MMPI scores of African Americans, Hispanics, and European Americans, only slightly higher or lower scores were found among these groups, none of which suggested substantive statistical or clinical differences (Nagayama Hall, Bansal, & Lopez, 1999). The only nontrivial difference was for Hispanic men scoring lower on the Masculinity–Femininity scale. This is not a pathological scale and perhaps suggests a stronger masculine identity in this group.

There is some evidence that Native Americans tend to score higher on the clinical scales on the MMPI compared with Whites (Greene, 1987). A Native American client with a particular score on a personality inventory might be told, "This score suggests that you are quite reserved and timid, lack interest in many activities, and that you are a shy person. My understanding is that among many American Indian tribes, these behaviors are culturally accepted so we probably need to talk more about these behaviors to ensure that they are not a part of the [problem] you reported earlier to me" (Paniagua, 1998, p. 124).

Asian Americans tend to underuse counseling and mental health services and less often share experiences and emotions with those outside the family. They are more likely to express concerns in an indirect manner, such as physical symptoms. There have been few studies of the scores on personality inventories of Asian students as compared with White students.

Projective techniques, personality assessment instruments that have generally not shown high validity, undoubtedly have even less value as assessment tools for minority clients. This is probably true for

lower socioeconomic groups in general, as interpretations of protocols of people from different cultures or lower socioeconomic classes
tend to result in diagnoses of more severe illness (Garb, 1998; Jenkins
& Ramsey, 1991).

Inaccuracies in the assessment and diagnosis of mental disorders
can have three consequences: overdiagnosis, underdiagnosis, and
misdiagnosis. Bias in testing can be an important factor in such inaccuracies. Attempts have been made to eliminate or control bias in the
assessment and diagnosis of multicultural groups by the translation
of tests into the language of the group being tested or through
the development of culturally appropriate norms. For example, for
the 5th edition of the 16 PF, all items were reviewed for gender, racial,
and cultural bias by African American and Hispanic bias consultants,
with norms based on age, gender, and racial 1990 census data (Conn
& Rieke, 1997). Despite these attempts, the general sense among
researchers and counselors is that biases in cross-cultural testing still
exist (Dana, 2000). Thus, although it is important for counselors to
use tests and inventories in the assessment of multicultural groups,
they need to determine how to best use these instruments with clients
from different cultural backgrounds (Paniagua, 1998).

ASSESSMENT OF CLIENTS WITH DISABILITIES

According to recent estimates, nearly one fifth of the U.S. population
ages 15 years and over suffer from a physical disability (Whiston,
2000). Assessment of clients with physical disabilities in rehabilitation
settings may involve three different approaches to vocational evaluation. One approach is that of psychological testing, a second involves
the use of work activities or work samples, and the third is evaluation
of actual on-the-job activities (Berven, 1980).

For some clients with disabilities, psychological testing that provides relatively objective and reliable measures of individual abilities
and interests can yield sufficient data to assist in decisions regarding
vocational choice, training, and job placement while avoiding the
great additional amount of time and expense involved in the other
types of evaluation. For others, employability can better be explored
through work samples and on-the-job evaluations. The employer
becomes directly involved with the problems of the client, client characteristics can be ascertained (particularly in relation to the ultimate

objective of more independent living), and a functional appraisal of job-related characteristics can be provided. Disadvantages include dependence on the goodwill of potential employers, as well as insurance, wage laws, and regulations that make cooperation by employers difficult. Considerable evaluative information about clients must be obtained in advance if job tryouts are to be successful.

Personality measures, interest inventories, general intelligence tests, measures of specific aptitudes, and tests of achievement or current skills have potential for use with various types of special populations. In using such instruments, however, counselors must view results with caution; for example, items related to general health and physical symptoms on a personality test may be answered in a "deviant" direction by people who are physically ill or disabled and therefore yield scores that are difficult to interpret or are easily misinterpreted.

Section 504 of the 1973 Rehabilitation Act requires that testing be adapted for disabled students so that it measures what it is designed to measure while allowing for the students' disability. For students with disabilities, academic standards should be maintained while appropriate accommodations in test administration are made. Considerable information regarding the assessment and testing of people with physical disabilities can be found in the professional literature (Frank & Elliott, 2000; Sandoval, Frisby, Geisinger, Scheuneman, & Grenier, 1998; Technical Education Research Centers, 1977). Included in these publications are lists of assessment instruments appropriate for particular types of disabilities, with recommendations for modifications where necessary.

The Americans With Disabilities Act of 1990 includes a section that speaks directly to the testing (primarily employment testing) of individuals with disabilities. Any tests administered to a job applicant or employee who has a disability must accurately reflect the skills or aptitudes the test purports to measure rather than reflecting the individual's particular disability. As employers must make reasonable accommodations for otherwise qualified employees to perform a particular job, so must reasonable accommodations be provided in the testing process to ensure that the test accurately measures the abilities of the candidate rather than reflecting the disability (unless the disability relates directly to the skill the test measures). Reasonable accommodations can include administering tests in accessible locations or modifying the testing materials (timed vs. untimed, written vs. braille, or oral vs. sign language; LoVerde, McMahon, & Morris, 1992).

The 1997 revision of the Individuals With Disabilities Education Act requires states and districts to devise appropriate testing procedures for students with disabilities by 2003 (Azar, 1999). Recent statistics indicate that up to 15% of school children (11% because of disabilities and 4% because of limited English proficiency) will need special testing accommodations. Test experts are challenged to find ways that allow the students with disabilities to show their skills without giving them an unfair advantage. Research conducted thus far indicates that the accommodations often must be tailor-made for the student.

The national testing programs such as ACT and the College Board provide special test forms and special testing arrangements for examinees with disabilities who are unable to take the test under standard testing conditions. These options include audiocassettes, braille, large-type editions, use of a reader, use of an amanuensis to mark responses, or extended time for testing. In general, predictions of college grades obtained from the special testing situations are less accurate, and more emphasis should be placed on other data (Laing & Farmer, 1984). When college admission tests are administered with accommodations, the resulting scores are "flagged" to indicate nonstandard conditions. This policy is consistent with standardized testing procedures (American Educational Research Association, American Psychological Association, & National Council on Measurement in Education, 1999) but is seen as a violation of privacy by many with disabilities.

People who are functionally blind must be assessed through senses other than sight, such as by auditory (readers) or tactile (braille) means (Bradley-Johnson & Ekstrom, 1998). Fewer than 25% of those classified as legally blind (corrected visual acuity of less than 20/200, which determines eligibility for government benefits) have no usable vision. Those not functionally blind are described as *low vision* or *partially sighted* and can often use large-type print or magnifiers. Individuals born without sight who have no visual memories may have difficulty with some concepts such as color, canyon, skyscraper, or elephant. They may also find it difficult to develop competent social skills as they cannot see others' social behaviors and nonverbal communications.

Several individually administered test and major testing programs such as the Scholastic Assessment Test (SAT), the achievement tests, and the statewide testing programs provide a number of accommodations. These include braille, large-type print, magnifiers, dictating arrangements, or prerecorded audiotapes. Extra time is provided as all, including reading large type, are slower; reading braille, for example, takes $2\frac{1}{2}$ times as long. A study of the SAT results of visually impaired students using different accommodations (all with extra time) yielded results comparable with those of sighted students. The only exception was that those using braille found certain graphics or novel-content mathematics items to be more difficult (R. E. Bennett, Rock, Kaplan, & Jirele, 1988).

The verbal scales on the Wechsler Intelligence Scale for Children (WISC) and the WAIS and certain parts of the Stanford–Binet are widely used with blind and partially sighted individuals. Some of the comprehension items need rephrasing to be appropriate, and attention should be paid to the possibility that lower scores on certain subtests may result from experiential deprivation. The performance scales have less validity if visual impairment is more than minimal. Interest inventories such as the Strong or Kuder are frequently used with visually impaired people by reading items aloud or by tape recording.

The deaf or hard of hearing also represent a heterogeneous population ranging from mild, to severe, to profound. Some have been deaf since birth (congenital), others later due to disease or trauma (adventitious; Brauer, Braden, Pollard, & Hardy-Braz, 1998). Therefore, any assessment should begin with a discussion of communication preference—spoken, written, or signed. Deaf children are nearly always delayed in their speech and language skills, and this deficit continues into adulthood (Braden & Hannah, 1998). They develop a smaller vocabulary, which affects reading, spelling, and writing scores. Verbal IQ tests are therefore never used, but normal scores can be expected on performance tests. The performance scales on the Wechsler tests are the most commonly used. Other nonverbal IQ tests such as the Raven Progressive Matrices or the Matrix Analogies Test can be administered when appropriate.

Norms for the hearing impaired are available for the WISC and the Metropolitan and Stanford Achievement Tests. Mean ACT assessment scores of students with auditory disabilities fall below the means obtained by students with visual, motor, or learning disabilities (Laing & Farmer, 1984). Certain tests and inventories may be administered to the population with American Sign Language (ASL), and responses can also be communicated through an ASL interpreter. The WAIS-III and the MMPI-2 are available in ASL translations.

The Peabody Picture Vocabulary Test and the Raven Progressive Matrices are two intelligence tests that require only a pointing response and are useful for the assessment of individuals with cerebral palsy or other physical handicaps. Verbal scales of the Wechsler tests can also be used for severely motor-impaired clients. Some of the performance subtests are not easily adapted because they require both adequate vision and some arm and hand use.

Adaptive devices for computers can provide clients with disabilities with options other than paper-and-pencil responses or the traditional computer keyboard. As a result, individuals with disabilities can complete a test with minimal staff assistance. Examples include voice input, simplified keyboards, joysticks, pneumatic controls, head pointers, and braille keyboards. Without the computer, individuals with disabilities have typically completed tests with the assistance of another person who read or responded to test items for the test taker. The problem with an intermediary is that that person may influence the test taker's response or the test taker may modify his or her responses because of the presence of another individual. The practice also has the potential of reinforcing dependence of people with disabilities on others (Sampson, 1990).

Because cognitive disabilities cause problems adjusting to the demands of the environment, the diagnosis of mental retardation is usually made not only on the basis of individual intelligence tests but also on the basis of an assessment of adaptive behavior. Intelligence and adaptive behavior are obviously closely related, but adaptive behavior is more synonymous with such terms as *social maturity*, *personal competence*, and *social competence*, that is, how effectively individuals cope with and adjust to the natural and social demands of their environment. Can they function and maintain themselves independently, and can they meet the culturally imposed demands of personal and social responsibility? Measures of adaptive behavior generally consist of behavioral rating scales administered in an interview or by observation (Cohen, Swerdlik, & Smith, 1992).

The Vineland Adaptive Behavior Scales (Sparrow, Balla, & Cicchetti, 1985) are available in an interview, an expanded interview, and a classroom edition. These scales were developed from the original measures designed to assess social competence by Edgar Doll of the Vineland Training School in Vineland, New Jersey. The interview, which follows a semistructured format, is conducted with the client's parents or caregivers. The classroom edition, which is designed to be completed by either the general school teacher or the special education teacher, deals primarily with adaptive behavior in the classroom. The interview is conducted without the client being present. The interview edition contains 297 items and takes 20–60 minutes to complete, the expanded interview edition contains 577 items and takes 60–90 minutes to complete, and the classroom edition with 244 items takes 20–30 minutes. The items tap four domains: daily living skills (self-care, dressing, washing), communication (receptive and expressive language), socialization (interpersonal interactions and play), and motor skills (gross and fine coordination). The expanded form also includes the maladaptive behavior domain assessing undesirable behaviors that interfere with adaptive behavior.

The standardization sample for the current version of the Vineland scales included 3,000 individuals, 100 in each of 30 age groups stratified to represent the U.S. Census population. Test–retest reliabilities are reported from .80 to over .90, and interrater reliability from .60 to .75 (Sattler, 1989). As might be expected, the expanded form was the most reliable of the three forms and the short classroom form the least reliable. The scales are designed to assess adaptive behavior from birth to 18 years old and among low-functioning adults. The instrument is used not only with individuals with mental retardation but also with those who are emotionally disturbed or who are physically, hearing, or visually impaired to develop individually educative treatment programs or vocational rehabilitation programs. Supplementary norms are available for each of these groups.

A cornerstone of the 1975 Education of All Handicapped Children Act (also called P.L. 94-142) has been the requirement that an Individualized Education Program (IEP) be written for each eligible student. Renamed the Individuals With Disabilities Education Act, or IDEA, the amendments passed in 1997 (IDEA-97) placed additional emphasis on the assessment of students' needs and the evaluation of their progress toward observable goals. The team that develops the IEP now must include not only (a) the student's special education teacher, (b) the student's general education teacher, (c) the student's parents, and (d) a local education agency representative but also (e) a professional educator such as a counselor or school psychologist who has the knowledge and expertise to interpret the assessment and evaluation results (Yell, Drasgow, & Ford, 2000).

An IEP must include (a) a statement of the student's present level of performance and the student's needs, (b) the special educational services that are to be provided to meet these needs, and (c) a valid measure of annual goals and short-term objectives (Shinn & Shinn, 2000). Several test publishers (e.g., Harcourt, American Guidance Service) now provide materials to assist in the writing and assessment of IEPs that accompany their educational achievement tests.

The 1997 IDEA Amendments also include requirements regarding the question of the participation of students with disabilities in statewide and districtwide assessments. Such participation becomes especially controversial when high-stakes testing programs are involved.

ASSESSMENT OF OLDER ADULTS

The number of older people living in the world has grown dramatically. In the United States, one person in seven is over 65, and by the year 2025 this figure will be one in five. The need to assess both mental health and cognitive functioning has led to the development of instruments specifically designed for the assessment of older clients.

The Clinical Assessment Scales for the Elderly (CASE) provide information for diagnosing *DSM-IV*, Axis I disorders (C. R. Reynolds & Bigler, 2000). There are 10 clinical scales, for example, Anxiety, Depression, Psychoticism, and Substance Abuse, along with 3 validity scales. Two forms are provided; one can be completed by the client and a second by a knowledgeable caregiver such as a spouse, son or daughter, or health care worker. Norms are based on 2,000 adults ages 55–90 matched to census data. A brief version (CASE–Short Form) is also available.

Several standardized methods have been devised to assess cognitive functioning and cognitive deficits among older people that involve tasks such as drawing a clock, making change, or answering certain questions. The most popular of these is the Mini-Mental State Examination (MMSE; Folstein, Folstein, & McHugh, 1975; Folstein, Folstein, McHugh, & Fanjiang, 2001). The MMSE represents a brief standardized method to assess mental status and consists of 11 questions on which the maximum score for each ranges from 1 to 5 for a total maximum score of 30. Sample questions (and maximum score) include: "What is the [year] [season] [date] [month]?" (5) and "Begin with 100 and count backward by subtracting 7. Stop at 65." (4). The individual is asked to perform the three-step command: "Take the paper in your right hand, fold it in half and put it on the floor." (3). Normal-functioning adults usually obtain scores of 28 or higher, whereas scores less than 24 suggest some cognitive impairment (New England Medical Center, 2000). The full MMSE can be found on the Internet at http://heartcarefoundation.org/health_tests.

Alzheimer's disease is the most common disorder causing cognitive decline in old age and is progressive and irreversible. Therefore, if the MMSE reveals cognitive impairment, the next step is to determine if it is due to Alzheimer's disease or if it is a more treatable impairment such as depression, vascular dementia, or substance abuse dementia (American Association for Geriatric Psychiatry, Alzheimer's Association, & American Geriatrics Society, 1997). The further diagnostic screening includes both medical and psychological tests often involving the administration of certain portions of the WAIS.

SUMMARY

1. The increasing diversity of cultural backgrounds in the U.S. population will present challenges both now and in the future, so that counselors who make use of psychological assessment instruments will need to become more culturally competent as the population becomes more diverse.

2. Counselors need to be aware of problems associated with the cross-cultural use of psychological tests, which include the difficulty in establishing equivalence across cultures, the difficulty of not possessing appropriate norms, differences in response sets

across different cultures, the nature of the test items, and the differing attitudes toward psychological testing across cultures.

3. Cultural factors influence not only aptitude test results but also scores on interest and personality inventories.

4. When used appropriately, psychological assessment instruments such as the WAIS, the Strong Interest Inventory, and the MMPI have produced results that are equally valid for individuals from different racial and ethnic backgrounds.

5. With different types of accommodations, psychological test data can provide useful information in counseling individuals with disabilities, but results obtained under atypical testing conditions must be viewed with caution.

17

COMMUNICATION OF TEST RESULTS

COUNSELORS ARE CONSTANTLY REQUIRED to communicate assessment results both to clients and to others—parents, agencies, and other professionals. The evaluation, selection, administration, and interpretation of assessment instruments receive much emphasis in texts, course curricula, and the counseling literature. In contrast, the communication of assessment results, which is one of the most important aspects of the assessment process, typically receives scant attention. In fact, of course, it is the understanding by the client or other individual who will be making decisions on the basis of the results that will, in the end, determine the actual application, if any, to which the assessment results will be put.

This chapter contains four sets of guidelines for such communications. The first set lists some general guidelines regarding the communication of assessment procedures and the results. The second set pertains to the actual interpretation of tests in the interview with the client. The third discusses reporting results to children, parents, and others. In the final section, suggestions regarding the format and content of a typical written report on an assessment procedure are provided.

Most of the research studies on the interpretation of test results have been related to career counseling and have been conducted with either high school or college students as participants. These studies have usually shown that clients who receive test interpretations experience greater gains than those in control conditions who do not. Thus, counselors may have confidence that the interpretation of test results to clients generally has a positive effect. There is little research evidence that outcomes are differentially affected by one type of interpretation over another, although clients generally prefer individual integrative interpretations over self-interpretations or group interpretations (Goodyear, 1990).

The counselor's theoretical orientation usually determines how the test scores are interpreted to the client. Counselors whose orientation is client-centered are likely to present clients with key scores or percentiles and encourage the clients to join in the process of interpretation. They pay particular attention to how clients feel about the test results and the interpretations. More directive counselors typically review the purpose of testing, present the scores, clarify what they mean, and discuss their implications. Both types should consider assisting clients to make their own interpretations. The advantage of helping clients to interpret and react to test results is that it assists the counselor in obtaining more insight about the client. Also, clients may become accepting of the results more readily by participating in the discussion and may be more likely to use the information when making decisions. It should also assist their memory of the results since studies of the accuracy of recall of test data have not been encouraging (Zytowski, 1997). Client participation in the interpretations, of course, usually takes more time on the part of both the counselor and the client, and this must be weighed when determining the type of approach to be used.

It is necessary to have a thorough understanding of tests, particularly of their theoretical foundations, if a counselor is to function as a professional interpreting the test rather than as a technician using a simple cookbook approach. Two of the most important steps in interpreting tests are, first, to understand the method used to develop the test and, second, to learn about the evidence of its reliability and validity (J. C. Hansen, 1999). Tests are used to diagnose and predict; interpretations must lead to the desired understanding and results. It must be remembered that a huge number of factors are involved in producing a particular test score. These factors include clients' inherited abilities; their educational, cultural, family, and other experiences; their experiences with other tests, particularly psychological tests; their motivation; their test anxiety; the physical and psychological conditions under which they took the test; and the lack of consistency in the test itself.

Psychological and educational diagnoses of culturally diverse clients made as a result of testing data should be made with extreme caution. Culture has a strong influence on psychopathological expression, which can yield significant bias related to the assessment of psychopathology across cultures. There have been studies indicating that ethnically and racially diverse individuals have received more negative psychological diagnoses, although recent meta-analysis studies have shown no substantive differences for ethnic minorities on such instruments as the Minnesota Multiphasic Personality Inventory (Nagayama Hall, Bansal, & Lopez, 1999). In any case, counselors should be knowledgeable of culture-specific behaviors that may influence the traditional diagnostic process.

In writing reports of psychological and educational assessments, counselors should be aware of the implications of test scores. All of the factors that have contributed to the scores should be considered when reporting predictions and recommendations. Counselors know very well that Miller Analogies Test or Graduate Record Examination scores account for only a small fraction of the variance in predicting which students, for example, will become skillful counselors. Therefore, test results should always include a statement about the validity of the entire testing situation. Counselors should also include in their report social, ethnic, racial, and cultural variables that may affect intelligence, achievement, or personality test scores (Hinkle, 1994). Counselors should interpret cross-cultural test scores with caution and, when necessary, include a disclaimer for limitations in the report.

It is in the interpretation of the test that the various types of validity become extremely important. In every kind of test interpretation, there is the assumption of a definite relationship between the person's score or result on a test and what it is being related to in the interpretation. It is therefore important to understand the construction and development of the test as well as its validity as determined by the relationship of the test score to that aspect or construct that the test has been designed to measure. Often this relationship is expressed in statistical terms, such as correlation coefficients, descriptive and comparative statistics, or expectancy tables. These statistics can often be presented to clients through profiles and other graphic means.

Claiborn (Claiborn & Hanson, 1999) has argued that test interpretations offer clients alternative ways of considering their experience and constitute messages of varying discrepancy to clients about their behaviors and their relationships to the world. Such discrepancies are important variables in the counseling process to which counselors should pay particular attention.

GENERAL GUIDELINES FOR COMMUNICATING TEST RESULTS

1. Professional codes of ethics and standards stipulate information that test authors and publishers should include in their manuals to facilitate test interpretation. Therefore, the first step in interpreting a test is to know and understand the test manual. In this way, the validity of a test can be related to the purpose for which the test was used. The manual is also likely to contain information regarding the limits to which the test can be used and suggestions for interpreting the results.

2. In interpreting test results, the counselor must review the purposes for which the client took the test and the strengths and limitations of the test.

3. In interpreting results, the counselor must explain the procedure by which the test is scored, along with an explanation of percentile ranks or standard scores if they are to be included in the interpretation.

4. Where possible, the counselor should present results in terms of probabilities (which are now better understood by clients because

of weather reports) rather than certainties or specific predictions. Keep in mind standard errors of measurement and the intervals they represent.

5. Unlike other testing situations, in counseling the tests are used to assist the client in his or her decision making. It is the understanding of the results by the client, not the counselor, that is ultimately important as it is the client who will use, misuse, or ignore them. The emphasis should be on increasing client understanding and, where appropriate, encouraging clients to make their own interpretations.

6. The test results should be presented as they relate to other available information about the client.

7. The counselor should ensure that the interpretation of the test information is understood by the client and that he or she is encouraged to express reactions to the information.

8. Any relevant information or background characteristics, such as sex or disabilities, should be examined, along with any apparent discrepancies or inconsistencies that appear.

9. Both strengths and weaknesses revealed by the test results should be discussed objectively.

Some of the more difficult tests to interpret are those in which a pattern or profile of scores is provided and one on which the client's pattern is a flat profile with no particularly high or low scores. In educational and vocational counseling, flat profiles on interest inventories are often encountered by the counselor because it is the client's indecision that both brings the client into counseling and yields a flat profile. In other circumstances, the individual's response set when taking the test may be a factor. The client makes little differentiation among the responses—all are high, neutral, or low. Validity indices and response patterns should therefore be examined before results are interpreted. With some inventories on which some scale scores are either slightly higher or slightly lower, there may be patterns that can be pointed out and discussed. Other relevant information such as past experiences, values, lifestyle goals, and previous work activities can be investigated.

On aptitude and achievement tests, flat profiles indicate a general level of performance in all areas that may be average, above average, or below average. Again, results from other types of tests and relevant past experiences may be taken into consideration in assisting with decision making.

GUIDELINES FOR THE TEST INTERPRETATION INTERVIEW

1. Show confidence in the client's ability to understand and make use of the test information. Emphasize the importance of adding the test data to other information that clients have about themselves. Emphasize the importance of clients themselves using the test information to help to assist them in making the decisions they are facing.

2. Ask clients to tell how they feel about the particular tests they took before beginning the interpretation process. This may yield information about their attitudes toward the particular tests and provide information about the usefulness or validity of some of the test results. An understanding of how clients perceive the test is often useful in the interpretation process. Stress to clients that they can ask questions; that you, as a counselor, are particularly interested in their reactions to the interpretation; and that you want to know their thoughts about the results.

3. Do not begin discussing the results of any test without reminding clients which test is being discussed. Refresh their memory about it, for example, "Remember the test where you checked whether the two sets of names and numbers were exactly the same or were different? That was a test designed to measure clerical aptitude or ability. . . ."

4. Try to make sure that clients are involved in the interpretation process. Do not merely state the results. Ask clients about their reactions before disclosing the results of a particular measure. After refreshing the clients' memories about an instrument, ask, "What were your reactions to that test? How do you think you did on it?"

5. Be prepared with a brief, clear description of what the instrument measures, including what the results mean and what the results do not mean. Be sure to clarify the differences between interests and aptitudes or abilities and personality characteristics. For example, "These are some of the activities you indicated you liked and these are some that you said you did not like. Your interests seem to be more

like those of people in social service fields and unlike those of most people in mechanical and technical occupations."

6. Emphasize the usefulness of the tests for the client's decision making rather than for information it provides to the counselor: "With this set of scores, you can see how you compare with other college-bound students regarding your ability to learn academic subject matter," rather than "These results confirm my belief that you have the ability to do well in most colleges."

7. Discuss the test results in the context of other information, particularly relating the test results to past, present, and future behavior. Past information and current test results should be related to current decisions and to future longer range plans rather than treating each of these subjects separately.

8. Present the purpose of a test in useful and understandable terms, trying to stay away from psychological jargon. Adjust the pace of the instructions and interpretations to clients' ability and understanding. Have clients summarize often to make sure the results are being understood. If necessary, additional information or alternative methods of interpretation can be used.

9. Where possible, use a graphic representation of the results in addition to a verbal explanation. Remember to turn test profiles so that clients can read them directly. If anyone is going to have to read the profile upside-down, it should be counselors, who are familiar with profile sheets, rather than clients. It is probably better to position chairs so that you and your clients can go over the results together from similar angles. Complicated profile sheets should be grouped and summarized; this way a number of scores can be more easily assimilated by the client. It should not be assumed that most clients have the ability to do this on their own. The results should be explained simply, without the use of elaborate statistics. Verbal interpretations that can be given for particular T scores or percentile ranks, assuming they are based on appropriate norms, were presented in Table 3-1. The normal curve with 100 figures drawn on it was illustrated in Figure 3-1; when covered with plastic for continuous use, this figure is particularly helpful for interpreting scores to students and adults.

For interpretation of test results to children (and occasionally to parents as well), a simple line drawing of five identical children of the appropriate gender and ethnicity can be a very practical device. They can be verbally labeled from right to left (as viewed by the child) as superior, above average, average, below average, and low. The child is then asked to point to which of those children he or she is like on various characteristics. Begin with some neutral or positive characteristics to ensure the child understands—how tall, how fast a runner, how cute (most children have been told they are cute), and then move to test results. First, ask the children to point to the appropriate figure where they predict they fall in regard to reading, for example, and then you can point to what the test results indicate.

10. Avoid overidentifying with the test results. Discuss a client's rejection of low test scores. The primary concern is what the results mean to the client, not what they mean to the counselor. Low performance scores should be expressed honestly but with perspective. They should not be ignored or attributed to inadequate measures or chance.

11. Listen attentively to what the client says and be alert for unexpressed or nonverbal emotional reactions especially when the test results are not what are expected or desired. Accept the client's right not to agree with them.

12. Make alternative plans sound respectable without imposing the biases of the typical middle-class counselor. Encourage clients to make their own plans rather than simply agreeing with the counselor's suggestions.

13. Be certain that you and your client relate the test information to other data available on the client. For example, scholastic aptitude scores should be related to school grades. It should be remembered that the usual purpose of a scholastic aptitude test is to predict academic course grades. When such grades are available, emphasis should be placed on actual grades rather than on test results that merely predict those grades.

14. Whenever possible, use the types of norms that are most relevant to clients. When such norms are not directly appropriate, information about this should be presented to clients, and the interpretation of the results should make certain that this is clear.

15. Use only tests that you, the counselor, have personally taken, scored, and interpreted for yourself. Know the reasons a particular test was administered, what was expected from its interpretation, and the validity of the test for the purpose for which it was used.

16. Be aware that psychological tests should not be used to provide information that can be easily gathered in other ways. Only in an exceptional circumstance would a student with high academic achievement or scholastic aptitude test scores need to be administered an IQ test. Tests should not be overused.

17. Toward the end of the interview, have clients summarize the results of the entire interview rather than attempting to do this for them. Allow enough time to discuss this summarization and to discuss discrepancies or misunderstandings. Attempt to end on a positive note even though some portions of the interview have not yielded information that the client has been happy to receive. If clients have received discouraging information about educational, vocational, or other types of plans, try to broaden the scope of alternatives that might be considered. Emphasis should be placed not only on narrowing the focus of future plans but also on broadening them.

18. Remember that in counseling there is almost always an implicit future orientation. Even though the immediate goal may be to help clients to make a particular decision, clients also gain the opportunity to understand themselves better. Ultimately, the self-knowledge acquired in counseling and testing will enable individuals to pursue more effective and satisfying lives and to make wiser and more realistic plans.

GUIDELINES FOR THE CASE CONFERENCE

Counselors often meet together with other professionals and people interested in the client's welfare to discuss assessment results and their implications for treatment. Guidelines for conducting these conferences are listed below.

1. Make certain that all present are introduced. You may be familiar with everyone and their roles but others may not—the social worker, the parents, the school psychologist, the grandparent.

2. Structure the session by briefly outlining how you will proceed and the contributions each will be making and encourage feedback, discussion, and questions.

3. Recognize and accept the fact that as the possessor of assessment information you may be perceived by parents as "the enemy" or perhaps the messenger with the bad news. Point out that the main concern of all present is the welfare of the child. All are trying to help the child and thus have a common goal.

4. Begin by covering the history that leads up to the meeting and the context in which it is taking place. Summarize previous meetings or interviews.

5. Draw useful nontest information from those present. The teacher sees the child in relation to many other children, and parents know much about the child's leisure-time interests and nonschool activities.

6. If the child is present, pay particular attention to him or her. It is easy for the adults present to become involved in their conversations and ignore the child.

7. In presenting information to parents, many professionals recommend the "bad news sandwich" approach: first some positive information, then any negative, and ending on a positive note. When the conference is due to a diagnosis of a child's disorder or disability, it is especially important to also focus on some of the child's abilities, not just the disabilities.

8. When finishing, summarize the assessment information and any conclusions that have been reached in the meeting. Encourage and allow time for final questions and discussion.

9. Recognize that the receipt of a diagnosis of a serious disorder can cause strong feelings of loss, guilt, or frustration and that additional sessions may be useful because you, as a counselor, can help those who are affected work through these issues.

GUIDELINES FOR REPORT WRITING

Counselors often need to summarize assessment results in a written report. In writing a report, the counselor must have some understanding of what is necessary to include and a conceptualization of the client or person about whom the report is being written. The focus of the report and the way it is to be used are the first considerations in determining its content, including the reasons for referral testing and whether the report will be primarily oriented toward an objective summary of test results or an overall description of the individual being examined. Often there is a large amount of information available, and the report writer must decide what information should be included and what should be excluded (Drummond, 1996).

The writer should first decide the principal idea that should be communicated and what other types of information play an auxiliary role. One of the ways of emphasizing material is by the order in which it is presented, with the most important information first. Another way is through the adjectives and adverbs used in describing the person and his or her behavior. It can also be done through illustrations, by using a vivid example to point out critical information. Another mode is through repetition. Obviously, repetition needs to be handled skillfully to avoid repeating the same material more often than necessary. Repeating information in the summary or conclusion is another way of adding emphasis. The psychological test results themselves can often be used as a framework to describe the client— for example the "Big Five" factors from the NEO Personality Inventory, the interpersonal circumplex from the Interpersonal Adjective Scales, or the Holland hexagon.

Problems that should be avoided include (a) poor organization, in which the results are not integrated as a whole; (b) use of psychological jargon that will not be understood; (c) use of terms that do not have clearly understood definitions; or (d) lack of integration between the test results and information based on other data such as observations or client history.

What Gets Included in a Case Report

The following is an outline of a typical case report.

1. *Brief description of client.* Including some of the demographic information, a counselor might begin a report by saying "This is a 32-year-old man of medium build, with wrinkled and soiled clothes, who was extremely verbal and articulate in the interview." This beginning gives a bit of an impression and should include some identifying information, such as age, race, occupation, or year in school.

2. *Reason for counseling or referral.* The next piece of information is the reason that the person is seeking counseling, the problem he or she presents, or the reason the person was referred for testing. A brief description of a client along with a brief description of the nature of the problem and the reason for undertaking the evaluation give a general focus for the report.

3. *Relevant background information.* Next to be included might be some additional descriptive data and some of the information available from the referral source. The background information should be relevant to the purpose of the testing, should be related to the overall purpose of the report, and should be as succinct as possible. It is likely to include the client's educational background, occupation, family background, health status, and current life situation. It should also include other aspects of personal history that are related to the reason for testing and that help to place the problem or reason for testing in its proper context.

4. *Evaluation procedures.* Evaluation procedures should be briefly described, giving the rationale for testing, the names of the tests used, and why the particular tests were selected.

5. *Behavioral observations.* Specific behaviors that were observed during the interviews and during the tests can be included in the next section. The way the client approached the test, any problems that arose, and any other factors that might bring into question the validity of any of the tests used should be mentioned. Only relevant observations should be included. This section is likely to be very brief if the behaviors were normal and much more lengthy if behaviors were unusual.

6. *Test results and their interpretation.* Next is a report of the test results, an overall interpretation, and diagnostic impressions. The description of the test results does not necessarily need to include the actual test scores, but they should be included if the report is for other professionals who are knowledgeable about testing. The most important part of this section is the interpretation of the results. Here all of the test data are integrated, along with the behavioral observations and relevant background information. A discussion of the client's strengths and weaknesses is included. A statement regarding the client's future prospects in relation to the reason for the testing often needs to be included. This statement would include both favorable and unfavorable predictions.

7. *Recommendations.* The primary reason for testing and the subsequent case report is usually to make recommendations. Particularly if the case is a referral, recommendations can include further testing or activities that the client or others should undertake in relation to the problem. Recommendations should relate to the problem and

to the general purpose of the testing and report. They should be as practical and specific as possible.

8. *Brief concluding summary.* A summary paragraph should succinctly restate the most important findings and conclusions (Maloney & Ward, 1976).

Writing Style

Writing a report is often much easier if an overall case conceptualization is developed first. Reports often include the general theoretical framework that is followed by the counselor. When psychoanalytic theory was the primary theory followed by counselors, a great deal of emphasis was placed on early childhood experiences. Those who follow Rogerian theory probably pay particular attention to the person's self-concept. The Gestalt theorist looks specifically at current relationships, and the behavioral counselor will be interested in things that reinforce particular behaviors. Counselors may not feel they have a particular theory of behavior, but in the case report their general theory of personality often emerges because it influences what they perceive from the interviews and test results and therefore what they report.

In reporting test results, it is a good idea to stay away from testing jargon. It is also important in writing a report to avoid the extremes of focusing either too much or too little on the test results themselves. It is possible to report extensive test results without relating them to the individual and the individual's situation and future plans, and thus not offer much in the way of conclusions or practical suggestions. It is also possible to depart too much from the test results and downplay them, particularly if the test information does not come out as expected or if it is not likely to be seen in positive terms by the client.

Counselors should also remember that it is better to get to a report immediately after counseling and testing rather than letting a considerable period of time go by. Counselors enjoy working with people much more than writing reports, so it is easy to put these aside. Timeliness becomes particularly important when a number of clients are seen each day. It is important to at least write down the information that will be needed to write a report, even if it is not possible to write the final report immediately. In writing a report, the counselor should come out and say what needs to be said, making clear statements and clear recommendations. Conversely, where results must be considered inconclusive, this also needs to be said.

SUMMARY

The influence of the counselor's theoretical orientation and the importance of case conceptualization are related both to the interpretation of the test results and to the content of a test report. Nine general guidelines for communicating test results were presented in this chapter, along with 18 counselor behaviors useful in the test interpretation interview and 9 guidelines for a case conference. A sample outline provided 8 topics typically included in a written case report.

18

ETHICAL AND SOCIAL ISSUES IN TESTING

T HERE ARE A NUMBER of situations when psychological tests are used in counseling and placement in which ethical principles are called into question. In this chapter, important ethical issues related to tests are discussed, along with the accompanying ethical principles that need to be considered. The second portion of the chapter includes several social issues related to testing that have not been included in previous chapters.

PROFESSIONAL ETHICAL STANDARDS

Because of the number of cases that have arisen in the past regarding the ethical use of psychological tests, each of the professional organizations whose members make use of tests have developed, among their codes of ethics, principles that deal specifically with psychological testing. The American Counseling Association's (ACA, 1995) *Code of Ethics and Standards of Practice* and the American Psychological Association's (APA, 1993) *Ethical Principles of Psychologists and Code of Conduct* each contain a section related to educational and psychological testing. ACA's relevant standards are reemphasized in the Measurement and Evaluation section of the *Ethical Standards for the National Board of Certified Counselors* (NBCC, 1997a; see NBCC, 1997b, for the on-line version of the code). In addition, The Responsibilities of Test Users (The RUST Statement Revised; American Association for Counseling and Development & Association for Measurement and Evaluation in Counseling and Development, 1989) and the Joint Committee *Standards for Educational and Psychological Testing* (American Educational Research Association, American Psychological Association, & National Council on Measurement in Education, 1999), both of which were discussed in Chapter 2, contain statements of test user responsibilities and ethical standards. The Joint Committee on Testing Practices (1998) has produced a statement on the rights and responsibilities in the testing process and outlines the responsibility of those professionals involved in the testing process and the steps they should take to ensure that test takers receive these rights (see Chapter 2). Excerpts from the ACA Code, the RUST Statement, and the Joint Committee Standards most relevant for test use in the counseling process are presented in Appendices A, B, and C, respectively. In their review of the codes of ethics of 13 mental health professions, Vacc, Juhnke, and Nilsen (2001) concluded that the ACA Code addressed more of the standards than those of the other professional groups.

ETHICAL STANDARDS FOR TEST QUALITY

A portion of the Joint Committee *Standards for Educational and Psychological Testing* deals with the technical quality of tests and test materials and standards to be followed by test developers and test publishers before distributing the test. Test publishers and authors make money from the royalties on tests that are sold, and there is an obvious temptation to exaggerate the usefulness or the validity of such tests. The committee that developed the standards placed considerable emphasis on the importance of "truth in advertising" in test publishing. Test manuals should provide evidence of reliability and validity, including information regarding the methods of estimating reliability and the populations on which reliability was measured, and types of validity studies, including validity relevant to the intended use of the test.

Certain of the standards are designed to prevent the premature sale of tests for general use and to specify when the test is to be released for research purposes only. The standards emphasize that the test manual should not be designed to sell the test but should include adequate information about the administration, scoring, norms, and other technical data to permit the potential user to evaluate the test itself and its potential use, as well as to properly interpret its results.

Counselor Competence in Testing

An important ethical issue lies with competence of the counselor to use the various available assessment instruments. The issue is whether those who use various tests have sufficient knowledge and understanding to select tests intelligently and to interpret their results (ACA Code E.2). Because different tests demand different levels of competence for their use, users must recognize the limits of their competence and make use only of instruments for which they have adequate preparation and training. The administration and interpretation of individual intelligence tests such as the Stanford–Binet or the Wechsler tests, certain personality tests such as the Minnesota Multiphasic Personality Inventory (MMPI), or projective personality tests such as the Rorschach or the Thematic Apperception Test require advanced training and practice to obtain the necessary background and skill for their appropriate use.

In an attempt to deal with this problem, a number of publishers will sell tests only to those who are qualified and require a statement of qualifications from purchasers of psychological tests. In cooperation with the Test User Qualifications Working Group (see Chapter 2), publishers have produced forms that must be completed by those purchasing the tests regarding their educational background and experience. Tests are graded by levels in regard to the amount of background and experience required and are sold only to those who meet the standards required for particular tests. These levels of qualifications are usually included in the test publishers' sales catalogs. In most cases, Level A tests may be purchased by schools and other organizations with no special qualifications required. Counselors must provide relevant information regarding their qualifications before purchasing test supplies. Typically, a master's degree and a course in psychological assessment are the minimum qualifications required to purchase many of the Level B tests commonly used by counselors. Level C tests usually require verification of a doctoral-level degree in psychology or education, or licensure or certification recognized as requiring advanced training in a relevant area of assessment. Graduate students who need to purchase particular tests for training or research purposes must have the order signed by the graduate instructor, who takes on responsibility for seeing that the tests are properly used.

High standards for publishers and purchasers of tests, however, do not guarantee that tests will be properly used. The major responsibility is that of the professional who makes use of them (ACA Code E.6; Standards 9.1–9.6). Is the test appropriate for the person who is being tested? How are the results going to be used? Are the test scores reliable enough? Does the test possess enough validity to be used for the purpose for which it is planned? Counselors who are well trained select tests that are appropriate both for the person to whom they are administered and for the specific purpose for which the person is being tested. They are also sensitive to the many conditions that affect test performance. They are knowledgeable enough about individual differences and human behavior not to make unwarranted interpretations of test results.

CLIENT WELFARE ISSUES

Occasionally, an ethical issue arises regarding the welfare of the client in the testing process. Is the welfare of the client being taken into consideration in the choice and use of tests (Standards 6.4–6.7)? Except in such cases as court referrals or custody determinations, this is seldom an issue in counseling because tests are usually used to help the client and not for other purposes.

Another client welfare issue deals with the questions of privacy and confidentiality (ACA Code E.4; RUST Statement, VIII). In counseling situations, clients are typically willing to reveal aspects about themselves to obtain help with their problems; thus, the invasion-of-privacy issue, often a concern in psychological testing elsewhere, is seldom a concern in counseling. Clients obviously would not wish this information to be disclosed to others. Test data, along with other records of the counseling relationship, must be considered professional information for use in counseling and must not be revealed to others without the expressed consent of the client. Certain types of test results, such as those assessing intelligence or aptitude and those that ask for or reveal emotional or personality or attitudinal traits, often may deal with sensitive aspects of personal lives or limitations that an individual would prefer to conceal and certainly not have disclosed to others.

Problems of confidentiality often arise when the counselor is employed by an institution or organization, which results in conflicting loyalties. In these circumstances, counselors should tell clients in advance how the test results will be used and make clear the limits of confidentiality. In general, ethical principles state that the test results are confidential unless the client gives his or her consent for the test results to be provided to someone else. The limits of confidentiality and the circumstances under which it can be broken (such as clear and present danger or court subpoena) must be communicated to and understood by the client. These issues are included in the various associations' codes of ethics (e.g., ACA Code E.4) and in the American Psychological Association's (1996) "Statement on the Disclosure of Test Data."

In addition, the Family Education Rights and Privacy Act of 1974 requires that educational institutions release test result information to parents of minor students and to students who are 18 years of age or older. In reporting results to others who have a reason and need to make use of the results, counselors must ensure that the results of the assessment and their interpretations are not misused by others. Is the person receiving the information qualified to understand and interpret the results? It is incumbent on the counselor to interpret the results in a way that they can be intelligently understood by those receiving them, including teachers and parents (RUST Statement, VII, VIII). In addition, the counselor has an obligation to point out the limitations of the results and any other important information about reliability or validity, as well as a description of the norms used and their appropriateness.

Clients, of course, have the right to know the results of tests, with interpretations of the results communicated to them in a language they can clearly understand. The results must be interpreted to clients in such a way that clients understand what the tests mean and also what they do not mean. It is important that clients not reach unwarranted conclusions from the interpretation that they receive (RUST Statement, VII).

The manner in which test results are communicated to others (when appropriate) should be carefully considered. Results should usually be presented descriptively rather than numerically. The use of labels that can be misinterpreted or damaging should be avoided. Labeling someone as schizophrenic or intellectually retarded can stigmatize a person even when such terms can be justified. They not only suggest a lack of any chance to grow or change but may also become self-fulfilling prophecies. Instead, interpretations should be presented in terms of possible ranges of achievement or formulations of interventions to assist the individual in behaving more effectively.

To help ensure confidentiality, counselors should keep test results in a place where they are accessible only to authorized individuals. They should be maintained in school or agency files only so long as they serve a useful purpose. With the advent of computerized record keeping, the difficulty of keeping test results secure and inaccessible to all but authorized users has increased. Effective measures for protecting the security of individual records must be maintained.

Tests must be administered in a standardized fashion if the results are to be adequately interpreted. One problem in the area of test administration involves test security (ACA Code E.10). It is obvious that test results will not be valid if people can obtain the tests in advance. For tests such as the College Board tests or the Medical College Admission Test, elaborate procedures are established to ensure that there is adequate security for these tests on which important decisions will be based. In addition, tests need to be accurately scored and accurately profiled if the results are to have valid meaning.

Another ethical issue, probably a minor one for counselors, is in regard to what might be called impersonal service in using tests. It is possible for a counselor or a psychologist to use tests in which test booklets are sent to clients, returned, scored, and interpreted through the mail. A fee is charged, but the counselor does not meet the client face to face. Considerable money in fees could be generated by this service. Without knowing why the person is requesting the tests, the purposes for which test results are to be used, or the interpretation that clients could give to the results, such a practice would constitute a misuse of testing. Therefore, this practice, along with other types of impersonal psychological services, is considered unethical.

The opportunity for such practices has increased with the use of computer interpretations. As noted in Chapter 4, test publishers have increasingly relied on computers to prepare often elaborate narrative reports of test results. Computer interpretations of such inventories as the Strong Interest Inventory or the MMPI can produce interpretations that run 10–20 pages in length. Such interpretations provide a distillation of the information that has been accumulated in the professional literature and of the pooled experience of a number of experts. Narrative computer printouts are obviously no better than the wisdom and clinical experience on which they are based; however, they protect the client from possible bias or inexperience of an individual counselor while expediting what can be a time-consuming and tedious chore of report writing. The client may either take the test itself on a computer or have the test scored and interpreted by a computer. These computer interpretations are, of course, based on norms, which are not necessarily appropriate for a particular individual. They should be used only in conjunction with the counselor's professional judgment. The narrative needs to be evaluated by the counselor who knows other facts about the client, the rationale for testing, and the reasons for such evaluation. The misuse of such computer-generated test interpretations has become an issue of increased concern to the counseling and psychological professions.

A final issue deals with the ethical use of psychological tests in research. When tests are given for research purposes, the first principle is that of informed consent: Having had the procedures explained to them, individuals must have the opportunity to choose whether or not to participate. Minors should also be informed, to the extent of their comprehension, and parental consent is often necessary as well. A particular problem arises in testing research when knowledge regarding the specific objectives of a test has a substantial effect on the attitude of the person taking it, therefore yielding invalid research results. In research studies, there are also the ethical issues of privacy and confidentiality.

In general, counselors have had fewer ethical problems in the use of tests than have various other professionals, because counselors typically use tests in their activities on behalf of the client—to assist the client in regard to decision making or to provide additional information for treatment and self-understanding. They do not usually use tests for "high-stakes" purposes such as selection, promotion, or placement.

CONTROVERSIAL ISSUES IN TESTING

During the past several decades, testing has been a controversial subject that has become involved with a number of social issues. Persistent controversies occur when tests are used in making high-stakes decisions. Here concerns are expressed that the tests are unfair to minorities and women, that they are too much a measure of social class or income, or that they assume special knowledge not available to many groups. Other concerns include the effect of coaching for the test, teachers teaching to the test, and tests being improperly used to judge schools and teachers (Fremer, 1992). In particular, testing has been attacked for its discrimination against minority groups (see Chapter 16). Tests are designed to measure differences among individuals, but when they reveal differences among ethnic or gender groups, they are considered to be biased.

These issues have led to much disenchantment with psychological tests, particularly intelligence and academic aptitude tests. Much of the controversy has resulted when test scores have shown group differences. There is less controversy when the discussion is restricted to individual differences, and it is individual differences with which counselors are typically concerned.

Gender Bias in Aptitude Testing

Intelligence tests have not been shown to produce significant differences between men and women. Mean scores for both sexes are essentially the same. On specific aptitudes, however, women tend to score higher than men on tests of verbal ability, whereas men tend to obtain higher scores on numerical and spatial aptitudes (Eagly, 1995; Maccoby & Jacklin, 1974; Neisser et al., 1996). Women tend to achieve higher grades in elementary school, high school, and college (Han & Hoover, 1994), although the difference in college tends to diminish when controlled for types of majors and types of courses (Hood, 1968).

The question regarding lower scores on mathematical ability is a controversial one at the present time; some argue that the difference is an inherent sex-related difference, whereas others argue that it is due to stereotypical attitudes on the part of parents and teachers, which result in the two sexes being differentially encouraged to learn mathematics. Recent evidence yields at least partial support for the latter explanation as the gap has decreased among adolescents over the past 40 years and has virtually disappeared in unselected populations (Eagly, 1995; Hoover & Han, 1995). Substantial gender differences are now found only in selected populations such as among college-bound youths on the SAT or on the National Merit test. Again, this mean difference is of less consequence to counselors as they work with individual students of either sex who may obtain scores anywhere throughout the entire range.

A recent development dealing with the gender bias of tests is related to the awarding of scholarships to the top 1% or 2% of scorers on the basis of a scholastic aptitude test. In the case of awarding certain scholarships, this practice has resulted in a higher proportion of men receiving scholarships than women. A major cause of this problem is the difference in the variance on test scores between the sexes in a number of academic areas including mathematics (Eagly, 1995; Han & Hoover, 1994). On such measures, including quantitative reasoning, men vary over a greater range than do women (Benbow, 1988). Thus, as the top 1% contains more men than women, so does the bottom 1%. There is pressure to develop tests to qualify for scholarships that eliminate this type of bias, but if the variance hypothesis holds, this will be a difficult task. In the case of the National Merit Testing Program, different cutoff scores are already used for different states, so that the top 1% of the students in each state qualify. If this practice were extended to the sexes, then qualifying scores could be established to ensure that the top 1% of both men and women would qualify.

Gender Bias in Personality and Interest Measurement

Although most of the controversy regarding bias in tests has centered around aptitude or intelligence tests, certain of the tests used in counseling, such as interest and personality measures, have not been entirely free of bias. Most personality measures are scored on norms developed for each sex, and thus the bias that would result if men and women tended to score differently on a personality characteristic is eliminated. Counselors using particular tests, such as the MMPI, should be aware that behavior patterns attributed to certain profile types often differ for men and women.

During the decades of the 1960s and 1970s, charges of gender bias were leveled against vocational interest inventories and their use in the vocational and educational counseling of women. Several of the interest inventories used only male pronouns and male-oriented occupational names and listed primarily stereotypical occupations for each sex. Earlier versions of both the male and female forms of the Strong Interest Inventory were particularly criticized for this bias. The bias that existed has been examined by several national committees, with resulting recommendations to eliminate both the sexually stereotypical language that exists among the inventories and the tendency of test results to channel students on the basis of sex and limit their consideration of certain careers.

There are several methods by which publishers have attempted to eliminate, or at least reduce, gender bias on interest inventories. One is by using separate-sex norms. In the case of the Strong Interest Inventory and the Kuder Occupational Interest Survey, the occupational scales are based on separate criterion groups for each sex. All clients receive scores on both the male and female scores. Thus, individuals can compare their interests with those of both sexes in a wide variety of occupations. On basic interest scales, profiles now show scores for both male and female norm groups; thus, gender bias is eliminated by use of the inclusion of norms for both sexes. In the case of the earlier forms of these instruments, many more occupations were shown for men than for women, which had the tendency to limit the number of careers considered by women. In recent years, test authors have attempted to develop the same number and type of scales for both men and women. The only exceptions are occupations in which it is very difficult to find a norm group of one sex, such as male home economics teachers or female pilots. Virtually all inventories have eliminated sexist language, for example, replacing *policeman* with *police officer* and *mailman* with *postal worker*.

Another method by which publishers of interest inventories have attempted to make them free of gender bias has been to include only interest items that are equally attractive to both sexes. For example, on an interest inventory containing items related to the six Holland themes, many more men than women respond to a realistic item such as "repairing an automobile" and many more women to a social item such as "taking care of very small children." Through the elimination of items that are stereotypically masculine or feminine, such differences can be largely avoided. For example, realistic items such as "refinishing furniture" or "operating a lawn mower" or a social item such as "teaching in high school" tend to receive approximately equal responses by both men and women (Rayman, 1976). An interest inventory such as the unisex edition of the ACT Interest Inventory, or UNIACT, published by the American College Testing Program (1995), is a sex-balanced inventory that increases the probability that men will obtain higher scores on the social scale and women on the realistic scale, and thus that each sex would be more likely to give consideration to occupations in a full range of fields.

Holland has resisted constructing sex-balanced scales on his Self-Directed Search, believing that the use of sex-balanced scales destroys much of the predictive validity of the instrument (L. S. Gottfredson, 1982; Holland & Gottfredson, 1976). An inventory that predicts that equal numbers of men and women will become automobile mechanics or become elementary school teachers is going to have reduced predictive validity given the male and female socialization and occupational patterns found in today's society. When such inventories are used primarily for vocational exploration, however, an instrument that channels individuals into stereotypical male and female fields can be criticized for containing this gender bias.

By including scores on all occupational scales for both sexes, by showing norms for both sexes on interest scales, by eliminating stereotypical language, and, for some instruments, by developing sex-balanced items, gender bias in interest testing has been greatly reduced. It must be remembered, however, that gender-based restrictions in interest preferences and career choices will continue as long as societal influences limit the experiences that men and women are exposed to or are able to explore (Walsh & Betz, 2000).

COUNSELING PROCESS ISSUES

It is probably to be expected that tests used for selection into desirable programs and occupations will be criticized, particularly by those not selected. The use of tests in counseling situations, however, has been much less controversial. Counselors and human development professionals typically use tests for problem-solving purposes to assist the client. In other settings, test results do not necessarily get shared directly with clients; in counseling, test results are almost always discussed with clients because the goal of counseling is usually to assist clients in making choices and in developing self-awareness. The client is seen as the primary user of test results, with the counselor acting more as a facilitator. Although counselors use the clinical interview and behavioral observation, tests provide an opportunity to obtain standardized information concerning individual differences that can be useful both to plan counseling interventions and to promote clients' understanding of themselves. Counselors help clients explore and identify their abilities, personality characteristics, patterns of interests, and values for the purpose of making choices and changes that can improve their sense of well-being or their lifestyles.

Personality inventories reveal information that can be useful in the counseling process, and interest and aptitude test results can assist in educational and vocational planning. Diagnostic tests in academic areas such as reading or arithmetic skills can help to identify those who need special instruction in particular areas and to plan future educational programs. Because of criticisms leveled against psychological tests when used in selection procedures (and perhaps in part because of some counselors' own experiences with scholastic aptitude tests used for selection purposes), counselors occasionally develop a bias against psychological tests. They refuse to use them even in individual counseling programs, where they can often be valuable.

Much of the criticism of psychological testing and assessment and attacks on their use in educational institutions and employment situations has resulted mainly in constructive effects. Increased awareness of the utility and limitations of testing has resulted in the need for more carefully trained users of test results as the personal and social consequences of testing have become increasingly apparent. Consistent with these needs, the primary objective of this book has been to improve the knowledge and understanding of counselors who administer and interpret the results of these assessment procedures.

Counselors should not blame the tests themselves when tests have been used inappropriately. Obviously, tests are often misused and occasionally misused by counselors and other human development professionals, but that does not mean the tests are at fault. When pliers are used on a bolt when an adjustable wrench is called for, it is not the pair of pliers or its manufacturer that is criticized.

One of the earlier criticisms of psychological tests was that they were dominating the counseling process. With the development of many new counseling theories and techniques, there are few, if any, strict practitioners of what used to be known as trait-and-factor counseling, for whom psychological tests totally dominated their counseling practices.

When using tests in counseling, the counselor must attempt to understand the frame of reference of the client. If the counselor is knowledgeable about tests, the counselor can then better help the client understand the information that tests can provide. In interpreting test results, the counselor must help clients to understand their implications and their limitations and help clients integrate the test information into their self-perceptions and decision-making strategies.

It has been suggested (and even mandated by legislative action) that tests should not be used because certain disadvantaged groups make poor showings on them. In these situations, the test results are often indicative of symptoms of a societal ailment, analogous to a fever thermometer that indicates an illness. When the tests reveal that the disadvantaged have not had the opportunity to learn certain concepts, there should be an attempt to provide these opportunities, not to dispose of the instruments that reveal such symptoms.

Another criticism of using tests in counseling is the point that validity coefficients are based on groups of individuals, and it is not possible to discern the validity of any test score for any one individual. It is in the counseling process that the counselor attempts to help clients determine the validity of that test score for that individual. To use tests properly in counseling, the counselor must know as much about the client and the client's environment as possible. Counselors must also be well informed about tests and have a basic familiarity with them. Although they may not need to have a great deal of understanding regarding the technical aspects of test development and standardization, they do need to have a clear understanding of the general purposes of the particular tests they use, the uses to which they can be put, and the role these tests can play in the counseling process.

In the information age, test results will continue to provide important data needed for many decisions. In addition to individual personal and career decisions, there will be increased reliance on tests to determine minimum skills and competencies for educational institutions, licensing and certification, and personnel selection.

The increasing automation of psychological assessment will make the administration and scoring of tests, as well as the interpretation of their results, more efficient, more extensive, and more complex. Already many tests commonly administered by counselors are available for administration, scoring, and interpretation with a microcomputer (e.g., California Psychological Inventory, Differential Aptitude Tests, Millon Index of Personality Styles, MMPI, Myers–Briggs Type Indicator, 16 Personality Factors Questionnaire, Strong, and Wechsler tests). Standardized interview data can also easily be obtained through interaction with a computer.

FINAL STATEMENT

Psychological tests are used by personnel staff to select employees, by school psychologists to track pupils, by clinical psychologists to diagnose patients, by college admissions staff to admit students, and by forensic psychologists to determine sanity. In the counseling setting, however, psychological tests are used to help clients to understand themselves. With the prevalence of negative attitudes toward psychological tests, counselors may be reluctant to make adequate use of them in assisting clients, but they should remember that the use of tests in counseling differs from other test use. Counselors use tests primarily to assist individuals in developing their potential to the fullest and to their own satisfaction. Test results are designed to be used by the clients themselves, and only in the ways in which they decide to make or not to make use of them. In counseling, tests are not used by others to make decisions for or against a client.

The concept of individual differences is a basic tenet of counseling. Assessment procedures enable counselors to measure and compare the different characteristics of clients and their environments. Tests and assessment data can provide important behavior samples useful in the counseling process to assist counselors to understand their clients better and clients to understand themselves.

The purpose of this volume has been to help current and future counselors, as well as others in the helping professions, to become better consumers and interpreters of psychological and educational tests and assessment procedures. We have attempted to cover some of the philosophical and ethical principles related to the use of tests, basic knowledge about certain tests, when tests should be used, and how to interpret and report tests and other assessment results.

By using tests ethically, appropriately, and intelligently, counselors can assist their clients to understand their problems, make use of their potential, function more effectively, make more effective decisions, and live more satisfying lives.

Appendices

VI

Appendices

A

Excerpts From American Counseling Association *Code of Ethics and Standards of Practice* (1995)

CODE OF ETHICS, SECTION E: EVALUATION, ASSESSMENT, AND INTERPRETATION

E1. General

a. *Appraisal Techniques.* The primary purpose of educational and psychological assessment is to provide measures that are objective and interpretable in either comparative or absolute terms. Counselors recognize the need to interpret the statements in this section as applying to the whole range of appraisal techniques, including test and nontest data.

b. *Client Welfare.* Counselors promote the welfare and best interests of the client in the development, publication, and utilization of educational and psychological assessment techniques. They do not misuse assessment results and interpretations and take reasonable steps to prevent others from misusing the information these techniques provide. They respect the client's right to know the results, the interpretations made, and the bases for their conclusions and recommendations.

E.2. Competence to Use and Interpret Tests

a. *Limits of Competence.* Counselors recognize the limits of their competence and perform only those testing and assessment services for which they have been trained. They are familiar with reliability, validity, related standardization, error of measurement, and proper application of any technique utilized. Counselors using computer-based test interpretations are trained in the construct being measured and the specific instrument being used prior to using this type of computer application. Counselors take reasonable measures to ensure the proper use of psychological assessment techniques by persons under their supervision.

b. *Appropriate Use.* Counselors are responsible for the appropriate application, scoring, interpretation, and use of assessment instruments, whether they score and interpret such tests themselves or use computerized or other services.

c. *Decisions Based on Results.* Counselors responsible for decisions involving individuals or policies that are based on assessment results have a thorough understanding of educational and psychological measurement, including validation criteria, test research, and guidelines for test development and use.

d. *Accurate Information.* Counselors provide accurate information and avoid false claims or misconceptions when making statements about assessment instruments or techniques. Special efforts are made to avoid unwarranted connotations of such terms as IQ and grade equivalent scores (See C.5.c).

E.3 Informed Consent

a. *Explanation to Clients.* Prior to assessment, counselors explain the nature and purposes of assessment and the specific use of results in language the client (or other legally authorized person on behalf of the client) can understand, unless an explicit exception to this right has been agreed upon in advance. Regardless of whether scoring and interpretation are completed by counselors, by assistants, or by computer or other outside services, counselors take reasonable steps to ensure that appropriate explanations are given to the client.

b. *Recipients of Results.* The examinee's welfare, explicit understanding, and prior agreement determine the recipients of test results. Counselors include accurate and appropriate interpretations with any release of individual or group test results (See B.7.a and C.5.c).

E.4. Release of Information to Competent Professionals

a. *Misuse of Results.* Counselors do not misuse assessment results, including test results, and interpretations and take reasonable steps to prevent the misuse of such by others (See C.5.c).

b. *Release of Raw Data.* Counselors ordinarily release data (e.g., protocols, counseling or interview notes, or questionnaires) in which the client is identified only with the consent of the client or the client's legal representative. Such data are usually released only to persons recognized by counselors as competent to interpret the data (See B.1.a).

E.5. Proper Diagnosis of Mental Disorders

a. *Proper Diagnosis.* Counselors take special care to provide proper diagnosis of mental disorders. Assessment techniques (including personal interview) used to determine client care (e.g., locus of treatment, type of treatment, or recommended follow-up) are carefully selected and appropriately used (See A.3.a and C.5.c).

b. *Cultural Sensitivity.* Counselors recognize that culture affects the manner in which clients' problems are defined. Clients' socioeconomic and cultural experience is considered when diagnosing mental disorders.

E.6. Test Selection

a. *Appropriateness of Instruments.* Counselors carefully consider the validity, reliability, psychometric limitations, and appropriateness of instruments when selecting tests for use in a given situation or with a particular client.

b. *Culturally Diverse Populations.* Counselors are cautious when selecting tests for culturally diverse populations to avoid inappropriateness of testing that may be outside of socialized behavioral or cognitive patterns.

E.7. Conditions of Test Administration

a. *Administration Conditions.* Counselors administer tests under the same conditions that were established in their standardization. When tests are not administered under standard conditions or when unusual behavior or irregularities occur during the testing session, those conditions are noted in interpretation, and the results may be designated as invalid or of questionable validity.

b. *Computer Administration.* Counselors are responsible for ensuring that administration programs function properly to provide clients with accurate results when a computer or other electronic methods are used for test administration (See A.12.b).

c. *Unsupervised Test-Taking.* Counselors do not permit unsupervised or inadequately supervised use of tests or assessments unless the tests or assessments are designed, intended, and validated for self-administration and/or scoring.

d. *Disclosure of Favorable Conditions.* Prior to test administration, conditions that produce most favorable test results are made known to the examinee.

E.8. Diversity in Testing

Counselors are cautious in using assessment techniques, making evaluations, and interpreting the performance of populations not represented in the norm group on which an instrument was standardized. They recognize the effects of age, color, culture, disability, ethnic group, gender, race, religion, sexual orientation, and socioeconomic status on test administration and interpretation and place test results in proper perspective with other relevant factors (See A.2.a).

E.9. Test Scoring and Interpretation

a. *Reporting Reservations.* In reporting assessment results, counselors indicate any reservations that exist regarding validity and reliability because of the circumstances of the assessment or the inappropriateness of the norms for the person tested.

b. *Research Instruments.* Counselors exercise caution when interpreting the results of research instruments possessing insufficient technical data to support respondent results. The specific purposes for the use of such instruments are stated explicitly to the examinee.

c. *Testing Services.* Counselors who provide test scoring and test interpretation services to support the assessment process confirm the validity of such interpretations. They accurately describe the purpose, norms, validity, reliability, and applications of the procedures and any special qualifications applicable to their use. The public offering of an automated test interpretations service is considered a professional-to-professional consultation. The formal responsibility of the consultant is to the consultee, but the ultimate and overriding responsibility is to the client.

E.10. Test Security

Counselors maintain the integrity and security of tests and other assessment techniques consistent with legal and contractual obligations. Counselors do not appropriate, reproduce, or modify published tests or parts thereof without acknowledgment and permission from the publisher.

E.11. Obsolete Tests and Outdated Test Results

Counselors do not use data or test results that are obsolete or outdated for the current purpose. Counselors make every effort to prevent the misuse of obsolete measures and test data by others.

E.12. Test Construction

Counselors use established scientific procedures, relevant standards, and current professional knowledge for test design in the development, publication, and utilization of educational and psychological assessment techniques.

B

Excerpts From the Responsibilities of Users of Standardized Tests (The RUST Statement Revised)

by
The Association for Measurement and Evaluation in
Counseling and Development (AMECD) and
The American Association for Counseling and
Development (AACD)
March 1989

II. *TEST DECISIONS:* Decisions should be based on data. In general, test data improve the quality of decisions. However, deciding whether or not to test creates the possibility of three kinds of errors. First, a decision not to test can result in misjudgments that stem from inadequate or subjective data. Second, tests may produce data which could improve accuracy in decisions affecting the client but which are not used in counseling. Third, tests may be misused. The responsible practitioner will determine, in advance, the purpose for administering a given test, considering protections and benefits for the client, practitioner, and agency.

A. Define purposes for testing by developing specific objectives and limits for the use of test data in relation to the particular assessment purpose:

    1. Placement: If the purpose is selection or placement, the test user should understand the programs or institutions into which the client may be placed and be able to judge the consequences of inclusion or exclusion decisions for the client.

    2. Prediction: If the purpose is prediction, the test user should understand the need for predictive data as well as possible negative consequences (e.g., stereotyping).

    3. Description: If the purpose is diagnosis or description, the test user should understand the general domain being measured and be able to identify those aspects which are adequately measured and those which are not.

    4. Growth: If the purpose is to examine growth or change, the test user should understand the practical and theoretical difficulties associated with such measurement.

    5. Program Evaluation: If the purpose of assessment is the evaluation of an agency's programs, the test user should be aware of the various information needs for the evaluation and of the limitation of each instrument used to assess those needs, as well as how the evaluation will be used.

B. Determine Information Needs and Assessment Needs:

    1. Determine whether testing is intended to assess individuals, groups, or both.

    2. Identify the particular individual and/or group to be tested with regard to the agency's purposes and capabilities.

    3. Determine the limitations to testing created by an individual's age; racial, sexual, ethnic, and cultural background; or other characteristics.

    4. Avoid unnecessary testing by identifying decisions which can be made with existing information.

5. Assess the consequences for clients of deciding either to test or not to test.
6. Limit data gathering to the variables that are needed for the particular purpose.
7. Cross-validate test data using other available information whenever possible.

III. *QUALIFICATIONS OF TEST USERS:* While all professional counselors and personnel workers should have formal training in psychological and educational measurement and testing, this training does not necessarily make one an expert and even an expert does not have all the knowledge and skills appropriate to some particular situations or instruments. Questions of user qualifications should always be addressed when testing is being considered.

Lack of proper qualifications can lead to errors and subsequent harm to clients. Each professional is responsible for making judgments on this in each situation and cannot leave that responsibility either to the client or to others in authority. It is incumbent upon the individual test user to obtain appropriate training or arrange for proper supervision and assistance when engaged in testing.

Qualifications for test users depend on four factors:
A. Purposes of Testing: Technically proper testing for ill-understood purposes may constitute misuse. Because the purposes of testing dictate how the results are used, qualifications of test users are needed beyond general testing competencies to interpret and apply data.
B. Characteristics of Tests: Understanding the nature and limitations of each instrument used is needed by test users.
C. Settings and Conditions of Test Use: Assessment of the quality and relevance of test user knowledge and skill to the situation is needed before deciding to test or to participate in a testing program.
D. Roles of Test Selectors, Administrators, Scorers, and Interpreters: Test users must be engaged in only those testing activities for which their training and experience qualify them.

IV. *TEST SELECTION:* The selection of tests should be guided by information obtained from a careful analysis of the characteristics of the population to be tested; the knowledge, skills, abilities, or attitudes to be assessed; the purposes for teaching; and the eventual use and interpretation of the test scores. Use of tests should also be guided by criteria for technical quality recommended by measurement professionals (i.e., the APA/AERA/ NCME "Standards for Educational and Psychological Tests" and the APA/AERNNCME/AACD/ASHA "Code of Fair Testing Practices in Education").

A. Relate Validity to Usage.

B. Use Appropriate Tests.

C. Consider Technical Characteristics.

D. Employ User Participation in Test Selection: Actively involve everyone who will be using the assessments (administering, scoring, summarizing, interpreting, making decisions) as appropriate in the selection of tests so that they are congruent with local purposes, conditions, and uses.

VI. *TEST SCORING:* Accurate measurement of human performance necessitates adequate procedures for scoring the responses of examinees. These procedures must be audited as necessary to ensure consistency and accuracy of application.

A. Consider Accuracy and Interpretability: Select a test scoring process that maximizes accuracy and interpretability.

B. Rescore Samples: Routinely rescore samples of examinee responses to monitor the accuracy of the scoring process.

C. Screen Test Results: Screen reports of test results using personnel competent to recognize unreasonable or impossible scores.

D. Verify Scores and Norms: Verify the accuracy of computation of raw scores and conversion to normative scales prior to release of such information to examinees or users of test results.

E. Communicate Deviations: Report as part of the official record any deviation from normal conditions and examinee behaviors.

F. Label Results: Clearly label the date of test administration along with the scores.

VII. *TEST INTERPRETATION:* Test interpretation encompasses all the ways that meaning is assigned to the scores. Proper interpretation requires knowledge about the test which can be obtained by studying its manual and other materials along with current research literature with respect to its use; no one should undertake the interpretation of scores on any test without such study.

   A. Consider Reliability: Reliability is important because it is a prerequisite to validity and because the degree to which a score may vary due to measurement error is an important factor in its interpretation.

   1. Estimate test stability using a reliability (or other appropriate) coefficient.

   2. Use the standard error of measurement to estimate the amount of variation due to random error in individual scores and to evaluate the precision of cut-scores in selection decisions.

   3. Consider, in relationship to the uses being made of the scores, variance components attributed to error in the reliability index.

   4. Evaluate reliability estimates with regard to factors that may have artificially raised or lowered them (e.g., test speededness, biases in population sampling).

   5. Distinguish indices of objectivity (i.e., scorer reliability) from test reliability.

   B. Consider Validity: Proper test interpretation requires knowledge of the validity evidence available for the intended use of the test. Its validity for other uses is not relevant. Indeed, use of a measure for a purpose for which it was not designed may constitute misuse. The nature of the validity evidence required for a test depends upon its use.

   1. Use for Placement: Predictive validity is the usual basis for valid placement.

      a. Obtain adequate information about the programs or institutions in which the client may be placed to judge the consequences of such placement.

      b. Use all available evidence to infer the validity of an individual's score. A single test score should not be the sole basis for a placement or selection recommendation. Other items of information about an individual (e.g., teacher report, counselor opinion) frequently improve the likelihood that proper judgments and decisions will be made.

c. Consider validity for each alternative (i.e., each placement option) when interpreting test scores and other evidence.

d. Examine the possibility that a client's group membership (socioeconomic status, gender, subculture, etc.) may affect test performance and, consequently, validity.

e. Examine the probability of favorable outcomes for each possible placement before making recommendations.

f. Consider the possibility that outcomes favorable from an institutional point of view may differ from those that are favorable from the individual's point of view.

2. Use for Prediction: The relationship of the test scores to an independently developed criterion measure is the basis for predictive validity.

a. Consider the reliability and validity of the criterion measure(s) used.

b. Consider the validity of a measure in the context of other predictors available (i.e., does the test make a valid contribution to prediction beyond that provided by other measures).

c. Use cross-validation to judge the validity of prediction processes.

d. Consider the effect of labeling, stereotyping, and prejudging people (e.g., self-fulfilling prophecies that may result from labeling are usually undesirable).

e. If a statistically valid predictor lacks both construct and content validity, analyze the mechanism by which it operates to determine whether or not its predictive validity is spurious.

3. Use for Description: Comprehensiveness of information is fundamental to effective description, since no set of test scores completely describes an individual.

    a. Clearly identify the domain assessed by any measure and the adequacy of the content sampling procedures used in developing items.

    b. Clarify the dimensions being measured when multiple scores from a battery or inventory are used for description.

    c. Distinguish characteristics that can be validated only empirically and those for which content specifications exist.

4. Use for Assessment of Growth: Assessment of growth or change requires valid tests as well as valid procedures for combining them.

    a. Specifically evaluate the reliability of differences between scores as measures of change.

    b. Establish the validities of the measures used to establish change in relation to one another as well as individually.

    c. Consider comparability of intervals in scales used to assess change.

    d. Assess potential for undesirable correlations of difference scores with the measures entering into their calculations (e.g., regression toward the mean).

    e. Recognize the potential lack of comparability between norms for differences derived from norms and norms for differences derived from differences (i.e., mathematically derived norms for differences are not necessarily equivalent to norms based on distributions of actual differences).

5. Use for Program Evaluation: Assessments of group differences (between groups or within groups over time) are based on research designs, which to varying degrees admit competing interpretations of the results.

    a. Use procedures in the evaluation which ensure that no factors other than those being studied have major influence on the results (i.e., internal validity).

    b. Use statistical procedures which are appropriate and have all assumptions met by the data being analyzed.

    c. Evaluate the generalizability (external validity) of the results for different individuals, settings, tests, and variables.

C. Scores, Norms, and Related Technical Features: The result of scoring a test or subtest is usually a number called a raw score, which by itself is not interpretable. Additional steps are needed to translate the number directly into either a verbal description (e.g., pass or fail) or a derived score (e.g., a standard score). Less than full understanding of these procedures is likely to produce errors in interpretation and ultimately in counseling or other uses.

1. Examine appropriate test materials (e.g., manuals, handbooks, users' guides, and technical reports) to identify the descriptions or derived scores produced and their unique characteristics.

   a. Know the operational procedures for translating raw scores into descriptions or derived scores.

   b. Know specific psychological or educational concepts or theories before interpreting the scores of tests based on them.

   c. Consider differential validity along with equating error when different tests, different test forms, or scores on the same test administered at different times are compared.

2. Clarify arbitrary standards used in interpretation (e.g., mastery or nonmastery for criterion-referenced tests).

   a. Recognize that when a score is interpreted based on a proportion score (e.g., percent correct), its elements are being given arbitrary weights.

   b. Recognize that the difficulty of a fixed standard (e.g., 80 percent right) varies widely and thus does not have the same meaning for different content areas and for different assessment methods.

   c. Report the number (or percentage) of items right in addition to the interpretation when it will help others understand the quality of the examinee's performance.

3. Employ derived scores based on norms which fit the needs of the current use of the test.

   a. Evaluate whether available norm groups are appropriate as part of the process of interpreting the scores of clients.

   b. Choose a score based on its intended use.

D. Administration and Scoring Variation: Stated criteria for score interpretation assume standard procedures for administering and scoring the test. Departures from standard conditions and procedures modify and often invalidate these criteria.

    1. Evaluate unusual circumstances peculiar to the administration and scoring of the test.

        a. Examine reports from administrators, proctors, and scorers concerning irregularities or unusual conditions (e.g., excessive anxiety) for possible effects on test performance.

        b. Consider potential effects of examiner–examinee differences in ethnic and cultural background, attitudes, and values based on available relevant research.

        c. Consider any reports of examinee behavior indicating the responses were made on some basis other than that intended.

        d. Consider differences among clients in their reaction to instructions about guessing and scoring.

    2. Evaluate scoring irregularities (e.g., machine scoring errors) and bias and judgment effects when subjective elements enter into scoring.

VIII. *COMMUNICATING TEST RESULTS:* The responsible counselor or other practitioner reports test data with a concern for the individual's need for information and the purposes of the information. There must also be protection of the right of the person tested to be informed about how the results will be used and what safeguards exist to prevent misuse (right to information) and about who will have access to the results (right to privacy).

A. Decisions About Individuals: Where test data are used to enhance decisions about an individual, the practitioner's responsibilities include:

    1. Limitations on Communication:

        a. Inform the examinee of possible actions that may be taken by any person or agency who will be using the results.

        b. Limit access to users specifically authorized by the law or by the client.

    c. Obtain the consent of the examinee before using test results for any purpose other than those advanced prior to testing.

2. Practitioner Communication Skills:

    a. Develop the ability to interpret test results accurately before attempting to communicate them.

    b. Develop appropriate communication skills, particularly with respect to concepts that are commonly misunderstood by the intended audience, before attempting to explain test results to clients, the public, or other recipients of the information.

3. Communication of Limitations of the Assessment:

    a. Inform persons receiving test information that scores are not perfectly accurate and indicate the degree of inaccuracy in some way, such as by reporting score intervals.

    b. Inform persons receiving test information of any circumstances that could have affected the validity or reliability of the results.

    c. Inform persons receiving test information of any factors necessary to understand potential sources of bias for a given test result.

    d. Communicate clearly that test data represent just one source of information and should rarely, if ever, be used alone for decision making.

4. Communication of Client Rights:

    a. Provide test takers or their parents or guardians with information about any rights they may have to obtain test copies and/or their completed answer sheets, to retake tests, to have test rescored, or to cancel test scores.

    b. Inform test takers or their parents or guardians about how long the test scores will remain on file along with the persons to whom, and circumstances under which, they may be released.

    c. Describe the procedures test takers or their parents or guardians may use to register complaints or have problems resolved.

C

Excerpts From Standards for Educational and Psychological Testing

by
Committee to Develop Standards for Educational and
Psychological Testing
American Educational Research Association (AERA)
American Psychological Association (APA)
National Council on Measurement in Education (NCME)
1999

Standard
11.1   Prior to the adoption and use of a published test, the test user should study and evaluate the materials provided by the test developer. Of particular importance are those that summarize the test's purposes, specify the procedures for test administration, define the

intended populations of test takers, and discuss the score interpretations for which validity and reliability data are available.

11.2	When a test is to be used for a purpose for which little or no documentation is available, the user is responsible for obtaining evidence of the test's validity and reliability for this purpose.
11.3	Responsibility for test use should be assumed by or delegated only to those individuals who have the training, professional credentials, and experience necessary to handle this responsibility. Any special qualifications for test administration or interpretation specified in the test manual should be met.
11.4	The test user should have a clear rationale for the intended uses of a test or evaluation procedure in terms of its validity and contribution to the assessment and decision-making process.
11.5	Those who have a legitimate interest in an assessment should be informed about the purposes of testing, how tests will be administered, the factors considered in scoring examinee responses, how the scores are typically used, how long the records will be retained, and to whom and under what conditions the records may be released.
11.6	Unless the circumstances clearly require that the test results be withheld, the test user is obligated to provide a timely report of the results that is understandable to the test taker and others entitled to receive this information.
11.7	Test users have the responsibility to protect the security of tests, to the extent that developers enjoin users to do so.
11.8	Test users have the responsibility to respect test copyrights.

11.9   Test users should remind test takers and others who have access to test materials that the legal rights of test publishers, including copyrights, and the legal obligations of other participants in the testing process may prohibit the disclosure of test items without specific authorization.

11.10   Test users should be alert to the possibility of scoring errors; they should arrange for rescoring if individual scores or aggregated data suggest the need for it.

11.11   If the integrity of a test taker's scores is challenged, local authorities, the test developer, or the test sponsor should inform the test takers of their relevant rights, including the possibility of appeal and representation by counsel.

11.12   Test users or the sponsoring agency should explain to test takers their opportunities, if any, to retake an examination; users should also indicate whether the earlier as well as later scores will be reported to those entitled to receive the score reports.

11.13   When test-taking strategies that are unrelated to the domain being measured are found to enhance or adversely affect test performance significantly, these strategies and their implications should be explained to all test takers before the test is administered. This may be done either in an information booklet or, if the explanation can be made briefly, along with the test directions.

11.14   Test users are obligated to protect the privacy of examinees and institutions that are involved in a measurement program, unless a disclosure of private information is agreed upon, or is specifically authorized by law.

11.15   Test users should be alert to potential misinterpretations of test scores and to possible unintended consequences of test use; users should take steps to minimize or avoid foreseeable misinterpretations and unintended negative consequences.

11.16   Test users should verify periodically that their interpretations of test data continue to be appropriate, given any significant changes in their population of test takers, their modes of test administration, and their purposes in testing.

11.17   In situations where the public is entitled to receive a summary of test results, test users should formulate a policy regarding timely release of the results and apply that policy consistently over time.

11.18   When test results are released to the public or to policymakers, those responsible for the release should provide and explain any supplemental information that will minimize possible misinterpretations of the data.

11.19   When a test user contemplates an approved change in test format, mode of administration, instructions, or the language used in administering the test, the user should have a sound rationale for concluding that validity, reliability, and appropriateness of norms will not be compromised.

11.20   In educational, clinical, and counseling settings, a test taker's score should not be interpreted in isolation; collateral information that may lead to alternative explanations for the examinee's test performance should be considered.

11.21   Test users should not rely on computer-generated interpretations of test results unless they have the expertise to consider the appropriateness of these interpretations in individual cases.

11.22   When circumstances require that a test be administered in the same language to all examinees in a linguistically diverse population, the test user should investigate the validity of the score interpretations

418

for test takers believed to have limited proficiency in the language of the test.

| 11.23 | If a test is mandated for persons of a given age or all students in a particular grade, users should identify individuals whose disabilities or linguistic background indicates the need for special accommodations in test administration and ensure that these accommodations are employed. |
| 11.24 | When a major purpose of testing is to describe the status of a local, regional, or particular examinee population, the program criteria for inclusion or exclusion of individuals should be strictly adhered to. |

D

Names and Acronyms of Tests Commonly Used by Counselors and the Names and Addresses of Publishers of Those Tests

TESTS AND TEST PUBLISHERS

American College Testing Program, P.O. Box 1008, Iowa City, IA 52243-1008. Tel: 319-337-1000, fax: 319-337-1578, Internet: www.act.org

ACT Assessment (The "ACT" test)
ASSET
Career Planning Survey (CPS)
COMPASS
DISCOVER
English as a Second Language Placement Test (ESL)
EXPLORE
PLAN Program
Proficiency Examination Program (PEP)
WorkKeys

American Guidance Service, P.O. Box 99,
Circle Pines, MN 55014-1796. Tel: 800-328-2560,
fax: 800-471-8457, Internet: www.agsnet.com
  Behavior Assessment System for Children (BASC)
  Harrington–O'Shea Career Decision-Making System–Revised
    (CDM-R)
  Kaufman Adolescent and Adult Intelligence Test (KAIT)
  Kaufman Assessment Battery for Children (K-ABC)
  Kaufman Brief Intelligence Test (K-BIT)
  Kaufman Functional Academic Skills Test (K-FAST)
  Kaufman Test of Educational Achievement (K-TEA)
  Peabody Picture Vocabulary Test–III (PPVT-III)
  Vineland Adaptive Behavior Scales

The Ball Foundation, 800 Roosevelt Road C-120,
Glen Ellyn, IL 60137. Tel: 800-469-TEST,
e-mail: www.testinfo@ballfoundation.org
  Ball Aptitude Battery (BAB)

Careerware, 808 Commerce Park Drive, Ogdensburg, NY 13669.
Tel: 800-267-1544, fax: 800-636-9754
  Career Maturity Inventory
  CHOICES

Consulting Psychologists Press, 3803 East Bayshore Road,
P.O. Box 10096, Palo Alto, CA 94303-0979. Tel: 800-624-1765,
fax: 650-969-8608, Internet: www.cpp-db.com
  Adjective Check List (ACL)
  California Psychological Inventory (CPI)
  Career Beliefs Inventory (CBI)
  Career Development Inventory (CDI)
  Career Factors Inventory (CFI)
  Coopersmith Self-Esteem Inventories
  Family Environment Scale (FES)
  FIRO Awareness Scales (FIRO) [Fie-Roe]
  Guilford–Zimmerman Temperament Survey (GZTS)
  Myers–Briggs Type Indicator (MBTI)
  Problem Solving Inventory (PSI)
  Rokeach Value Survey

Skills Confidence Inventory (SCI)
Strong Interest Inventory (Strong)
Thomas–Kilman Conflict Mode Instrument (TKI)
Values Scale (VS)

CTB/McGraw-Hill, 20 Ryan Ranch Road,
Monterey, CA 93940-5703. Tel: 800-538-9547,
fax: 800-282-0266, Internet: www.ctb.com
  Primary Test of Cognitive Skills (PTCS)
  TerraNova, 2nd Ed. (TerraNova CAT)
  TerraNova Comprehensive Tests of Basic Skills
  Test of Cognitive Skills, 2nd Ed. (TCS/2)
  Tests of Adult Basic Education (TABE)

Educational and Industrial Testing Service (EdITS), P.O. Box 7234,
San Diego, CA 92167. Tel: 800-416-1666, fax: 619-226-1666,
Internet: www.edits.net
  Career Ability Placement Survey (CAPS)
  Career Occupational Preference System Interest Inventory (COPS)
  Career Orientation Placement and Evaluation Survey (COPES)
  Comrey Personality Scales (CPS)
  Eysenck Personality Questionnaire–Revised (EPQ-R)
  Personal Orientation Inventory (POI)
  Profile of Mood States (POMS) [Poms]
  Study Attitudes and Methods Survey (SAMS)

Educational and Psychological Consultants, Inc., 1715 W. Worley,
Suite A, Columbia, MO 65203-2603. Tel: 573-446-6232
  Personal Styles Inventory

Educational Testing Service (ETS), Rosedale Road,
Princeton, NJ 08541. Tel: 609-921-9000, email: www.ets.org
  Advanced Placement Program (AP)
  College Level Examination Program (CLEP)
  Graduate Management Admission Test (GMAT)
  Graduate Record Examinations (GRE)
  LearningPlus
  POWERPREP

Preliminary Scholastic Aptitude Test (PSAT)
SAT I & II (SAT)
System of Interactive Guidance and Information, Plus More (SIGI PLUS)
Test of English as a Foreign Language (TOEFL)

H&H Publishing Co., Inc., 1231 Kapp Drive,
Clearwater, FL 33765. Tel: 800-366-4079, fax: 727-442-2195,
Internet: www.hhpublishing.com
    Learning and Study Strategies Inventory (LASSI)
    Perceptions, Expectations, Emotions, and Knowledge about
        college (PEEK)
    Working

Harcourt Educational Measurement, P.O. Box 839959,
San Antonio, TX 78283-3959. Tel: 800-211-8378,
fax: 877-576-1816, Internet: www.hemweb.com
    Adult Basic Learning Examination, 2nd Ed. (ABLE-II)
    Career Interest Inventory (CII)
    Differential Aptitude Tests (DAT)
    Metropolitan Achievement Tests, 8th Ed. (METROPOLITAN8)
    Ohio Vocational Interest Survey, 2nd Ed. (OVIS-II)
    Otis–Lennon School Ability Test, 7th Ed. (OLSAT7)
    Stanford Achievement Test Scores, 9th Ed. (Stanford9)
    Survey of Study Habits and Attitudes (SSHA)
    Wechsler Individual Achievement Test (WIAT)

Hogan Assessment Systems, P.O. Box 521176, Tulsa, OK
74152-1176. Tel: 800-756-0632, fax: 918-749-0635,
Internet: www.hoganassessments.com
    Hogan Development Survey (HDS)
    Hogan Personality Inventory (HPI)
    Motives, Values, Preferences Inventory (MVPI)

Hogrefe & Huber Publishers, Inc., P.O. Box 2487,
Kirkland, WA 98083. Tel: 800-228-3749, fax: 425-823-8324,
Internet: www.hhpub.com
    Family System Test (FAST)
    Rorschach Inkblot Test

Innovative Training Systems, 199 Wells Avenue, Suite 108, Newton,
MA 02159. Tel: 617-332-6028, Internet: www.itshomepage.com
   Addiction Severity Index: Multimedia Version
   Health Habits Survey

Institute for Personality and Ability Testing Incorporated (IPAT),
P.O. Box 1188, Champaign, IL 61824-1188. Tel: 800-225-4728,
Internet: www.ipat.com
   Adult Personality Inventory
   Children's Personality Questionnaire
   Clinical Analysis Questionnaire (CAQ)
   Culture Fair Intelligence Tests
   Early School Personality Questionnaire
   High School Personality Questionnaire
   16 Personality Factor Questionnaire (16 PF)

Mind Garden, 1690 Woodside Road, Suite 202,
Redwood City, CA 94061. Tel: 650-261-3500, fax: 650-261-3505,
Internet: www.mindgarden.com
   Bem Sex-Role Inventory (BSRI)
   Older Persons Counseling Needs Survey
   State–Trait Anxiety Inventory (STAI)
   State–Trait Anxiety Inventory for Children (STAI-C)
   Test Anxiety Inventory
   University Residence Environment Scale (URES)
   Ways of Coping Questionnaire

Multi-Health Systems Inc., 908 Niagra Falls Boulevard,
North Tonawanda, NY 14120-2060. Tel: 800-456-3003,
fax: 800-540-4484, Internet: www.mhs.com
   Children's Depression Inventory (CDI)
   Conners' Adult ADHD Rating Scales (CAARS)
   Conners' Continuous Performance Test II (CDT-II)
   Conners' Rating Scales–Revised (CRS-R)
   Coping Inventory for Stressful Situation (CISS)
   Family Assessment Measure III (FAM-III)
   Hare Psychopathy Checklist–Revised (HPC-R)
   Holden Psychological Screening Inventory (HPSI)
   Parenting Stress Index (PSI)
   Social Problem Solving Inventory–Revised (SPSI–R)

National Career Assessment Services, P.O. Box 277, Adel, IA 50003.
Tel: 800-314-8972, fax: 515-993-5422, Internet: www.kuder.com
    Adult Career Concerns Inventory (ACCI)
    Iowa Career Learning Assessment (ICLA)
    Kuder Career Search With Person Match (KCS)
    Kuder General Interest Survey (KGIS)
    Kuder Occupational Interest Survey (KOIS)

NCS Assessments, P.O. Box 1416, Minneapolis, MN 55440.
Tel: 800-NCS-7271, fax 800-632-9011,
Internet: http://assessments.ncspearson.com
    Alcohol Use Inventory (AUI)
    Brief Symptom Inventory (BSI)
    Campbell–Hallam Team Development Survey
    Campbell Interest and Skill Survey (CISS)
    Campbell Leadership Index
    Campbell Organizational Survey
    Career Assessment Inventory–Enhanced Version (CAI-EV)
    Career Assessment Inventory–Vocational Version (CAI-VV)
    General Ability Measures for Adults (GAMA)
    IDEAS: Interest Determination, Exploration and Assessment
        System
    Millon Adolescent Clinical Inventory (MACI)
    Millon Adolescent Personality Inventory (MAPI)
    Millon Clinical Multiaxial Inventory–III (MCMI-III)
    Minnesota Multiphasic Personality Inventory–2 (MMPI-2)
    Minnesota Multiphasic Personality Inventory–Adolescent
        (MMPI-A)
    Quality of Life Inventory (QOLI)
    Quickview Social History
    Symptom Checklist–90–Revised (SCL-90-R)

Pro-Ed, 8700 Shoal Creek Boulevard, Austin, TX 78757-6897.
Tel: 800-897-3202, fax: 800-397-7633,
Internet: www.proedinc.com
    Comprehensive Test of Non-Verbal Intelligence (CTONI)
    Self Esteem Index (SEI)
    Test of Nonverbal Intelligence–3rd Ed. (TONI-3)

Psychological Assessment Resources (PAR), P.O. Box 998,
Odessa, FL 33556. Tel: 800-331-TEST, fax: 800-727-9329,
Internet: www.parinc.com
   Adolescent Drinking Index (ADI)
   Career Attitudes and Strategies Inventory (CASI)
   Career Decision Scale (CDS)
   Career Thoughts Inventory (CTI)
   Clinical Assessment Scales for the Elderly (CASE)
   College Adjustment Scales (CAS)
   Coping Responses Inventory (CRI)
   Eating Disorder Inventory–2 (EDI-2)
   Employee Assistance Program Inventory (EAPI)
   Hamilton Depression Inventory (HDI)
   Interpersonal Adjective Scales (IAS)
   Life Stressors and Social Resources Inventories (LISRES)
   Mental Status Checklists
   Mini-Mental State Examination (MMSE)
   My Vocational Situation
   NEO Five-Factor Inventory (NEO-FFI)
   NEO Four (NEO-4)
   NEO Personality Inventory–Revised (NEO PI-R)
   Occupational Stress Inventory–R (OSI-R)
   Personal History Checklists
   Personality Assessment Inventory (PAI)
   Personality Assessment Screener (PAS)
   Position Classification Inventory (PCI)
   Self-Directed Search (SDS)
   State–Trait Anger Expression Inventory–2 (STAXI-2)
   Suicidal Ideation Questionnaire (SIQ)
   Vocational Exploration and Insight Kit (VEIK)
   Vocational Preference Inventory (VPI)

The Psychological Corporation (Psych Corp), P.O. Box 839954,
San Antonio, TX 78283-3954. Tel: 800-872-1726,
fax: 800-232-1223, Internet: www.psychcorp.com
   Beck Anxiety Inventory (BAI)
   Beck Depression Inventory–II (BDI-II)
   Beta III
   Brown Attention-Deficit Disorder Scales

Differential Ability Scales (DAS)
Edwards Personal Preference Schedule (EPPS)
Miller Analogies Test (MAT)
Millon Index of Personality Styles (MIPS)
Mooney Problem Checklists
Naglieri Nonverbal Ability Test (NNAT)
Pharmacy College Admission Test (PCAT)
Raven's Progressive Matrices
Rotter Incomplete Sentences Blank
Thematic Apperception Test (TAT)
Watson–Glaser Critical Thinking Appraisal (WGCTA)
Wechsler Abbreviated Scale of Intelligence (WASI)
Wechsler Adult Intelligence Scale–III (WAIS-III)
Wechsler Intelligence Scale for Children–III (WISC-III)
Wechsler Preschool and Primary Scale of Intelligence–Revised (WPPSI-R)

Psychological Publications, Inc., 290 Conejo Ridge Avenue, Suite 100, Thousand Oaks, CA 91361-4928. Tel: 800-345-TEST, fax: 805-373-1753, Internet: www.TJTA.com
Family Relationship Inventory (FRI)
Taylor–Johnson Temperament Analysis (TJTA)

Riverside Publishing Company, 425 Spring Lake Drive, Itasca, IL 60143-2079. Tel: 800-323-9540, fax: 630-467-7192, Internet: www.riverside.publishing.com
Ability Explorer
Achenbach System of Empirically-Based Assessment (ASEBA)
Cognitive Abilities Test (COGAT)
Das–Naglieri Cognitive Assessment System (CAS)
Guidance Information System (GIS)
Iowa Tests of Basic Skills (ITBS)
Iowa Tests of Educational Development (ITED)
Nelson–Denny Reading Test
Scales of Independent Behavior–Revised (SIB-R)
Stanford–Binet Intelligence Scale (Stanford–Binet)
Tests of Achievement and Proficiency (TAP)
Universal Nonverbal Intelligence Test (UNIT)
Woodcock–Johnson III Tests of Achievement
Woodcock–Johnson III Tests of Cognitive Abilities

The SASSI Institute, 201 Camelot Lane, Springville, IN 47462
Tel: 800-726-0526, fax: 800-546-7995. Internet: www.sassi.com
  Adolescent SASSI (SASSI-A2)
  Substance Abuse Subtle Screening Inventory–3 (SASSI-3)

Scholastic Testing Service Incorporated, 480 Meyer Road,
Bensenville, IL 60106-1617. Tel: 800-642-6454, fax: 708-766-8054,
Internet: www.ststesting.com
  Educational Development Series
  Hall Occupational Orientation Inventories
  Kuhlman Anderson Tests (KA)
  Torrance Tests of Creative Thinking (TTCT)

Sigma Assessment Systems Inc., P.O. Box 610984,
Port Huron, MI 48061-0984. Tel: 800-265-1285,
fax: 800-361-9411, Internet: www.sigmaassessmentsystems.com
  Ashland Interest Assessment (AIA)
  Basic Personality Inventory (BPI)
  Career Directions Inventory (CDI)
  Jackson Personality Inventory–Revised (JPI-R)
  Jackson Vocational Interest Survey (JVIS)
  Multidimensional Aptitude Battery–II (MAB-II)
  Personality Research Form (PRF)
  Psychological Screening Inventory (PSI)
  Six Factor Personality Questionnaire (6PFQ)
  Survey of Work Styles (SWS)

Slosson Educational Publications, Inc., P.O. Box 280,
East Aurora, NY 14052. Tel: 888-756-7766, fax: 716-655-3840,
Internet: www.slosson.com
  Slosson Intelligence Test–Revised (SIT-R)

U.S. Department of Labor, Employment and Training
Administration, 200 Constitution Avenue, NW,
Washington, DC 20213. Tel: 202-535-0157,
Internet: www.doleta.gov
  Ability Profiler
  Interest Profiler
  Work Importance Profiler

U.S. Military Entrance Processing Command (USMEPCOM),
2500 Green Bay Road, North Chicago, IL 60064-3094.
Tel: 800-323-0513, Internet: www.dmdc.osd.mil/asvab
  Armed Services Vocational Aptitude Battery (ASVAB)

Western Psychological Services, 12031 Wilshire Boulevard,
Los Angeles, CA 90025-1251. Tel: 800-648-8857,
fax: 310-478-7838, Internet: www.wpspublish.com
  Assessment of Career Decision Making (ACDM)
  Bender Visual Motor Gestalt Test
  House–Tree–Person Prospective Drawing Technique (H-T-P)
  Learning Styles Inventory (LSI)
  Marital Satisfaction Inventory–Revised (MSI-R)
  Parent–Child Relationship Inventory (PCRI)
  Personal Experience Inventory (PEI)
  Personal Experience Screening Questionnaire (PESQ)
  Personality Inventory for Youth (PIY)
  Piers–Harris Children's Self-Concept Scale (PHCSCS)
  Shipley Institute of Living Scale
  Tennessee Self-Concept Scale–2 (TSCS:2)
  Vocational Interest Inventory–Revised (VII-R)

Wide Range, Inc., P.O. Box 3410, Wilmington, DE 19804-0250.
Tel: 800-221-9728, fax: 302-652-1644,
Internet: www.widerange.com
  Wide Range Achievement Test–Expanded (WRAT-Expanded)
  Wide Range Achievement Test 3 (WRAT3)
  Wide Range Intelligence Test (WRIT)
  Wide Range Interest–Opinion Test (WRIOT)

Wonderlic Personnel Test, Inc., 1509 N. Milwaukee Avenue,
Libertyville, IL 60048-1380. Tel: 800-323-3742,
Internet: www.wonderlic.com
  Wonderlic Basic Skills Test
  Wonderlic Personnel Test

PERMISSIONS

We are grateful to the following authors and publishers for permission to reproduce sample items from the assessment instruments named below:

Career Assessment Inventory by C. B. Johansson. Copyright © 1973, 1976, 1980, 1982, 1984, 1985, 1986 by National Computer Systems, Inc. All rights reserved. Reproduced with permission of NCS Pearson, Inc.

Career Attitudes and Strategies Inventory by J. L. Holland and G. D. Gottfredson. Adapted and reproduced by special permission of the publisher, Psychological Assessment Resources, Inc., Odessa, FL 33556. Copyright © 1994 by PAR, Inc. Further reproduction is prohibited without permission from PAR, Inc.

Career Orientation Placement and Evaluation Survey (COPES) by L. Knapp, L. Knapp-Lee, and R. Knapp. Published by Educational and Industrial Testing Service (EdITS), San Diego, CA. Copyright © 1995. Reproduced with permission.

Eating Attitudes Test by David M. Garner and Paul E. Garfinkel (1979). Published by Cambridge University Press. Copyright © 1979. Reproduced with permission.

Kuder Career Search With Person Match™ by National Career Assessment Services, Inc™. Reproduced with permission. Copyright © 1999. All rights reserved.

Minnesota Multiphasic Personality Inventory–2 (MMPI-2). Copyright © by the Regents of the University of Minnesota 1942, 1943 (renewed 1970), 1989. This booklet 1989. Reproduced with permission.

SCL-90-R by Leonard R. Derogatis. Copyright © 1975, 1983, 1990 by L. R. Derogatis, PhD, Towson, MD. Reproduced with permission. All rights reserved.

431

REFERENCES

Achenbach, T. M. (1991). *Manual for the Child Behavior Checklist.* Burlington: University of Vermont, Department of Psychiatry.

Aiken, L. R. (1999). *Personality assessment methods and practices* (3rd ed.). Seattle, WA: Hogrefe & Huber.

Aiken, L. R. (2000). *Psychological testing and assessment.* Needham Heights, MA: Allyn & Bacon.

Ambrosini, P. J., Bianchi, M. D., Metz, C., & Rabinovich, H. (1994). Evaluating clinical response of open nortriptyline pharmacotherapy in adolescent major depression. *Journal of Child and Adolescent Psychopharmacology, 4,* 233–244.

American Academy of Pediatrics. (2000). Diagnosis and evaluation of the child with attention-deficit/hyperactivity disorder (AC0002). *Pediatrics, 105,* 1158–1170.

American Association for Counseling and Development & Association for Measurement and Evaluation in Counseling and Development. (1989, May). The responsibilities of test users. *AACD Guidepost,* pp. 12–28.

American Association for Geriatric Psychiatry, Alzheimer's Association, & American Geriatrics Society. (1997). Consensus statement: Diagnosis and treatment of Alzheimer disease and related disorders. *Journal of the American Medical Association, 278,* 1363–1371.

American College Testing Program. (1985). *Proficiency Examination Program (PEP) technical handbook.* Iowa City, IA: Author.

American College Testing Program. (1995). *Technical manual: Revised unisex edition of the ACT Interest Inventory (UNIACT).* Iowa City, IA: Author.

American College Testing Program. (1998a). *ACT ESL Placement Test.* Iowa City, IA: Author.

American College Testing Program. (1998b). *Career Planning Survey technical manual.* Iowa City, IA: Author.

American College Testing Program. (1998c). *COMPASS/ESL: An ACT program for educational planning.* Iowa City, IA: Author.

American College Testing Program. (1999a). *PLAN program handbook.* Iowa City, IA: Author.

American College Testing Program. (1999b). *User handbook 1999–2000.* Iowa City, IA: Author.

433

American College Testing Program. (1999c). *Using the ACT in advising and course placement.* Iowa City, IA: Author.

American College Testing Program. (1999d). *WorkKeys: Interim technical handbook.* Iowa City, IA: Author.

American College Testing Program. (1999e). *WorkKeys: Score interpretation guide–education.* Iowa City, IA: Author.

American College Testing Program. (2000). *The World-of-Work Map (3rd ed., Counselor Version).* Iowa City, IA: Author.

American College Testing Program. (2001). *WorkKeys occupational profiles* [On-line]. Available: http://www.act.org/workkeys/profiles/occup.html.

American Counseling Association. (1995). *Code of ethics and standards of practice.* Alexandria, VA: Author.

American Educational Research Association, American Psychological Association, & National Council on Measurement in Education. (1999). *Standards for educational and psychological testing.* Washington, DC: American Educational Research Association.

American Mental Health Counselors Association. (2001). Code of ethics of the American Mental Health Counselors Association: 2000 revision. *Journal of Mental Health Counseling, 23,* 2–21.

American Psychiatric Association. (1994). *Diagnostic and statistical manual of mental disorders* (4th ed.). Washington, DC: Author.

American Psychiatric Association. (2000a). *Diagnostic and statistical manual of mental disorders* (4th ed., text revision). Washington, DC: Author.

American Psychiatric Association. (2000b). *Practice guidelines for the treatment of patients with eating disorders* (2nd ed.) [On-line]. Available: http://www.psych.org/clin_res/guide.bk.cfm

American Psychological Association. (1993). *Ethical principles of psychologists and code of conduct.* Washington, DC: Author.

American Psychological Association. (1996). Statement on the disclosure of test data. *American Psychologist, 51,* 644–648.

American Rehabilitation Counseling Association, Commission on Rehabilitation Counselor Certification, & National Rehabilitation Counseling Association. (1995). *Code of professional ethics for rehabilitation counselors.* Chicago: American Rehabilitation Counseling Association.

American School Counselor Association. (1992). *Ethical standards for school counselors.* Alexandria, VA: Author.

American School Counselor Association & Association for Assessment in Counseling. (1998). *Competencies in assessment and evaluation for school counselors.* Alexandria, VA: Author.

Americans With Disabilities Act of 1990, Pub. L. No. 101–336, § 2, 104 Stat. 328 (1991).

Anastasi, A. (1988). *Psychological testing* (6th ed.). New York: Macmillan.

Anastasi, A. (1992). What counselors should know about the use and interpretation of psychological tests. *Journal of Counseling & Development, 70,* 610–615.

Anastasi, A., & Urbina, S. (1997). *Psychological testing* (7th ed.). Upper Saddle River, NJ: Prentice Hall.

Anderson, W. (1995). Ethnic and cross-cultural differences on the MMPI-2. In J. C. Duckworth & W. P. Anderson (Eds.), *MMPI and MMPI-2 interpretation manual for clinicians* (4th ed.). Bristol, PA: Accelerated Development.

Annis, H. M., Graham, J. M., & Davis, C. S. (1987). *Inventory of Drinking Situations.* Toronto, Ontario, Canada: Addiction Research Foundation.

Anton, W. D., & Reed, J. R. (1991). *College Adjustment Scales.* Odessa, FL: Psychological Assessment Resources.

Arbona, C. (1990). Career counseling research and Hispanics: A review of the literature. *The Counseling Psychologist, 18,* 300–323.

Arbona, C. (1998). Psychological assessment: Multicultural or universal? *The Counseling Psychologist, 26,* 911–921.

Archer, R. P., Maruish, M., Imhof, E. A., & Piotrowski, C. (1991). Psychological test usage with adolescent clients: 1990 survey findings. *Professional Psychology: Research and Practice, 22,* 247–252.

Association of American Medical Colleges. (2000). *Medical College Admission Test.* Washington, DC: Author.

Azar, B. (1999, November). Fairness a challenge when developing special-needs tests. *APA Monitor, 30,* 31.

Baer, L., Jacobs, D. G., Meszler-Reizes, J., Blais, M., Fava, M., Kessler, R., Magruder, K., Murphy, J., Kopans, B., Cukor, P., Leahy, L., & O'Laughlen, J. (2000). Development of a brief screening instrument: The HANDS. *Psychotherapy and Psychosomatics, 69,* 35–41.

Bandura, A. (1986). *Social foundations of thought and action.* Englewood Cliffs, NJ: Prentice Hall.

Barker, R. G. (1968). *Ecological psychology: Concepts and methods for studying the environment of human behavior.* Stanford, CA: Stanford University Press.

Barkley, R. A. (1991). *Attention-deficit hyperactivity disorder: A clinical workbook.* New York: Guilford Press.

Barrett, G. V., & Depinet, R. L. (1991). A reconsideration of testing for competence rather than for intelligence. *American Psychologist, 46,* 1012–1024.

Barrios, B. A. (1988). On the changing nature of behavioral assessment. In A. S. Bellack & M. Hersen (Eds.), *Behavioral assessment: A practical handbook* (pp. 3–41). New York: Pergamon.

Barrons Educational Series. (2000). *Profiles of American colleges 2001.* Hauppauge, NY: Author.

Barthlow, D. L., Graham, J. R., Ben-Porath, Y. S., & McNulty, J. L. (1999). Incremental validity of the MMPI-2 content scales in an outpatient mental health setting. *Psychological Assessment, 11,* 39–47.

Bartling, H. C., & Hood, A. B. (1981). An 11-year follow-up of measured interest and vocational choice. *Journal of Counseling Psychology, 28,* 27–35.

Baxter-Magolda, M. B. (1992). *Knowing and reasoning in college: Gender related patterns in students' intellectual development.* San Francisco: Jossey-Bass.

Beck, A. T. (1996). *Beck Depression Inventory: Second Edition.* San Antonio, TX: Psychological Corporation.

Beck, A. T., & Steer, R. A. (1993). *Beck Anxiety Inventory manual.* San Antonio, TX: Psychological Corporation.

Beck, A. T., Steer, R. A., & Brown, G. K. (1996). *Beck Depression Inventory–II manual.* San Antonio, TX: Psychological Corporation.

Benbow, C. P. (1988). Sex differences in mathematical reasoning ability in intellectually talented preadolescents: Their nature, effects and probable causes. *Behavioral and Brain Sciences, 11,* 169–232.

Bennett, G. K., Seashore, H. G., & Wesman, A. G. (1989). *Differential aptitude tests for personnel and career assessment.* San Antonio, TX: Psychological Corporation.

Bennett, R. E., Rock, D. A., Kaplan, B. A., & Jirele, T. (1988). Psychometric characteristics. In W. W. Williamham, M. Ragosta, R. Bennett, H. Braun, D. A. Rock, & D. E. Powers (Eds.), *Testing handicapped people* (pp. 83–97). Needham Heights, MA: Allyn & Bacon.

Benson, P. G. (1988). Review of the Minnesota Importance Questionnaire (MIQ). In J. T. Kapes & M. M. Mastie (Eds.), *A counselor's guide to career assessment instruments* (2nd ed., pp. 144–149). Alexandria, VA: National Career Development Association.

Berven, N. L. (1980). Psychometric assessment in rehabilitation. In B. Bolton & D. W. Cook (Eds.), *Rehabilitation client assessment* (pp. 46–64). Baltimore: University Park Press.

Betz, N. E., Borgen, F. H., & Harmon, L. W. (1996). *Skills Confidence Inventory applications and technical guide.* Palo Alto, CA: Consulting Psychologists Press.

Betz, N. E., Klein, K. L., & Taylor, K. M. (1996). Evaluation of a short form of the Career Decision-Making Self-Efficacy Scale. *Journal of Career Assessment, 4,* 47–57.

Betz, N. E., & Luzzo, D. A. (1996). Career assessment and the Career Decision-Making Self-Efficacy Scale. *Journal of Career Assessment, 4,* 413–428.

Betz, N. E., & Taylor, K. M. (1994). *Manual for the Career Decision-Making Self-Efficacy Scale.* Columbus: Ohio State University, Department of Psychology.

Beutler, L. E. (2000). David and Goliath: When empirical and clinical standards of practice meet. *American Psychologist, 55,* 997–1007.

Block, J. (1961). *The Q-sort method in personality assessment and psychiatric research.* Palo Alto, CA: Consulting Psychologists Press.

Bolles, R. N. (1990). *The Quick Job-Hunting Map for Beginners* (Advanced version). Berkeley, CA: Ten Speed Press.

Bolles, R. N. (1991). *How to create a picture of your ideal job or next career: Advanced version (revised) of the Quick Job Hunting (and Career-Changing) Map.* Berkeley, CA: Ten Speed Press.

Bolles, R. N. (2001). *The 2001 what color is your parachute?: A practical manual for job-hunters and career-changers.* Berkeley, CA: Ten Speed Press.

Boughner, S. R., Hayes, S. F., Bubenzer, D. L., & West, J. D. (1994). Use of standardized assessment instruments by marital and family therapists: A survey. *Journal of Marital and Family Therapy, 20,* 69–75.

Bowman, S. L. (1995). Career strategies and assessment issues for African-Americans. In F. T. L. Leong (Ed.), *Career development and vocational behavior of racial and ethnic minorities* (pp. 137–164). Mahwah, NJ: Erlbaum.

Braden, J. P., & Hannah, J. M. (1998). Assessment of hearing-impaired and deaf children with the WISC-III. In A. Prifitera & D. H. Saklofske (Eds.), *WISC-III clinical use and interpretation* (pp. 175–201). San Diego, CA: Academic Press.

Bradley-Johnson, S., & Ekstrom, R. (1998). Visual impairments. In J. Sandoval, C. L. Frisby, K. F. Geisinger, J. D. Scheuneman, & J. R. Grenier (Eds.), *Test interpretation and diversity* (pp. 271–296). Washington, DC: American Psychological Association.

Brauer, B. A., Braden, J. P., Pollard, R. Q., & Hardy-Braz, S. T. (1998). Deaf and hard of hearing people. In J. Sandoval, C. L. Frisby, K. F. Geisinger, J. D. Scheuneman, & J. R. Grenier (Eds.), *Test interpretation and diversity* (pp. 297–315). Washington, DC: American Psychological Association.

Brener, N. D., Hassan, S. S., & Barrios, L. C. (2000). Suicidal ideation among college students in the United States. *Journal of Consulting and Clinical Psychology, 67,* 1004–1008.

Brescia, W., & Fortune, J. C. (1989). Standardized testing of American Indian students. *The College Student Journal, 23,* 98–104.

Brickman, P., Rabinowitz, V. C., Karuza, J., Coates, D., Cohn, E., & Kidder, L. (1982). Models of helping and coping. *American Psychologist, 37,* 368–384.

Brookhart, S. M. (1995). Review of the Rokeach Value Survey. In J. D. Conoley & J. D. Impara (Eds.), *The twelfth mental measurements yearbook* (pp. 878–879). Lincoln, NE: Buros Institute of Mental Measurements.

Brookhart, S. M. (1998). Review of the Iowa Tests of Basic Skills Forms K, L, & M. In J. C. Impara & B. S. Plake (Eds.), *The thirteenth mental measurements yearbook* (pp. 539–542). Lincoln, NE: Buros Institute of Mental Measurements.

Brown, D. (1995). A values-based approach to facilitating career transitions. *Career Development Quarterly, 44,* 4–11.

Brown, L., Sherbenou, R. J., & Johnsen, S. K. (1997). *Test of Nonverbal Intelligence–Third Edition.* Austin, TX: Pro-Ed.

Brown, M. B. (1998). Review of the Career Attitudes and Strategies Inventory. In J. C. Impara & B. S. Plake (Eds.), *The thirteenth mental measurements yearbook* (pp. 182–183). Lincoln, NE: Buros Institute of Mental Measurements.

Brown, M. B. (2000). Diagnosis and treatment of children and adolescents with attention-deficit/hyperactivity disorder. *Journal of Counseling & Development, 78,* 195–203.

Brown, T. E. (1996). *The Brown Attention-Deficit Disorder Scales.* San Antonio, TX: Psychological Corporation.

Brown, W. F., & Holtzman, W. H. (1984). *Survey of Study Habits and Attitudes manual.* San Antonio, TX: Psychological Corporation.

Bubenzer, D. L., Zimpfer, D. G., & Mahrle, C. L. (1990). Standardized individual appraisal in agency and private practice: A survey. *Journal of Mental Health Counseling, 12,* 51–66.

Buck, J. N. (1992). House-Tree-Person Projective Drawing Technique H-T-P: Manual and interpretive guide. Los Angeles: Western Psychological Services.

Buck, J. N., & Daniels, M. H. (1985). *Assessment of Career Decision Making manual.* Los Angeles: Western Psychological Services.

Budman, S. H. (2000). Behavioral health care dot.com and beyond: Computer-mediated communications in mental health and substance abuse treatment. *American Psychologist, 55,* 1290–1300.

Butcher, J. N. (Ed.). (1997). *Personality assessment in managed health care: Using the MMPI-2 in treatment planning.* New York: Oxford University Press.

Butcher, J. N. (1999). *A beginner's guide to the MMPI-2*. Washington, DC: American Psychological Association.

Butcher, J. N., Ben-Porath, Y. S., Shondrick, D. D., Stafford, K. P., McNulty, J. L., Graham, J. R., Stein, L. A. R., Whitworth, R. H., & McBlaine, D. D. (2000). Cultural and subcultural factors in MMPI-2 interpretation. In J. N. Butcher (Ed.), *Basic sources on the MMPI-2* (pp. 501–536). Minneapolis: University of Minnesota Press.

Butcher, J. N., Dahlstrom, W. G., Graham, J. R., Tellegen, A., & Kaemmer, B. (1989). *Minnesota Multiphasic Personality Inventory–2: Manual for administration and scoring*. Minneapolis: University of Minnesota Press.

Butcher, J. N., Graham, J. R., Williams, C. L., & Ben-Porath, Y. (1990). *Development and use of the MMPI-2 content scales*. Minneapolis: University of Minnesota Press.

Butcher, J. N., Perry, J. N., & Atlis, M. M. (2000). Validity and utility of computer-based test interpretation. *Psychological Assessment, 12*, 6–18.

Butcher, J. N., Williams, C. L., & Fowler, R. D. (2000). *Essentials of MMPI-2 and MMPI-A interpretation* (2nd ed.). Minneapolis: University of Minnesota Press.

Butcher, J. N., Williams, C. L., Graham, J. R., Archer, R. P., Tellegen, A., Ben-Porath, Y. S., & Kaemmer, B. (1992). *Minnesota Multiphasic Personality Inventory–Adolescent (MMPI-A): Manual for administration, scoring, and interpretation*. Minneapolis: University of Minnesota Press.

Cairo, P. C., Kritis, K. J., & Myers, R. M. (1996). Career assessment and the Adult Career Concerns Inventory. *Journal of Career Assessment, 4*, 189–204.

Camera, W., Nathan, J., & Puente, A. (1998). *Psychological test usage in professional psychology: Report to the APA Practice and Science Directorates*. Washington, DC: American Psychological Association.

Campbell, C. A., & Ashmore, R. J. (1995). The Slossan Intelligence Test–Revised (SIT-R). *Measurement and Evaluation in Counseling and Development, 28*, 116–118.

Campbell, D. P. (1992). A reaction to McArthur. *Journal of Counseling & Development, 70*, 522–523.

Campbell, D. P. (1993). A new integrated battery of psychological surveys. *Journal of Counseling & Development, 71*, 575–587.

Campbell, D. P. (2000). Forty years of psychological assessment: Some observations. In Minnesota Career Development Association (Ed.), *Past reflections, future vision* (pp. 13–28). St. Paul, MN: Author.

Campbell, D. P., & Borgen, F. H. (1999). Holland's theory and the development of interest inventories. *Journal of Vocational Behavior, 55*, 86–101.

Campbell, D. P., Hyne, S. A., & Nilsen, D. L. (1992). *Manual for the Campbell Interest and Skill Survey*. Minneapolis, MN: National Computer System.

Canfield, A. A., & Canfield, J. S. (1988). *Canfield Learning Styles Inventory*. Los Angeles: Western Psychological Services.

Carroll, J. B. (1993a). *Human cognitive abilities*. New York: Cambridge University Press.

Carroll, J. B. (1993b). *Human cognitive abilities: A survey of factor-analytic studies*. Cambridge, UK: Cambridge University Press.

Cass-Liepmann, J. (Ed.). (2000). *Cass and Birnbaum's guide to American colleges*. New York: Harper-Collins.

Cattell, R. B. (1973). *Measuring intelligence with the Culture Fair Test*. Champaign, IL: Institute for Personality and Ability Testing.

Cattell, R. B., Cattell, A. K., & Cattell, H. E. (1993). *The 16 PF test booklet*. Champaign, IL: Institute for Personality and Ability Testing.

Center on Education and Work. (1999). *Career skills workbook*. Madison: University of Wisconsin System Board of Regents.

Cesnik, B. I., & Nixon, S. K. (1977). Counseling suicidal persons. In C. Zastrow & D. H. Chang (Eds.), *Personal problem solver* (pp. 275–289). Englewood Cliffs, NJ: Prentice Hall.

Chaplin, W. F. (1985). Review of State–Trait Anxiety Inventory. In D. J. Keyser & R. C. Sweetland (Eds.), *Test critiques* (Vol. 2, pp. 626–632). Kansas City, MO: Test Corporation of America.

Chartrand, J. M. (1991). The evolution of trait-and-factor career counseling: A Person × Environment fit approach. *Journal of Counseling & Development, 69,* 518–524.

Chartrand, J. M., Robbins, S. B., & Morrill, W. H. (1997). *Career Factors Inventory*. Palo Alto, CA: Consulting Psychologists Press.

Cherpitel, C. J. (2000). A brief screening instrument for problem drinking in the emergency room: The RAPS4. *Journal of Studies on Alcohol, 61,* 447–449.

Chickering, A. W., & Reisser, L. (1993). *Education and identity* (2nd ed.). San Francisco: Jossey-Bass.

Choca, J. P. (1998). Review of the Millon Index of Personality Styles. In J. C. Impara & B. S. Plake (Eds.), *The thirteenth mental measurements yearbook* (pp. 668–670). Lincoln, NE: Buros Institute of Mental Measurements.

Choca, J. P., & VanDenburg, E. J. (1997). *Interpretive guide to the Millon Clinical Multiaxial Inventory* (2nd ed.). Washington, DC: American Psychological Association.

Cicchetti, D. V. (1994). Guidelines, criteria, and rules of thumb for evaluating normed and standardized assessment interests in psychology. *Psychological Assessment, 6,* 284–290.

Claiborn, C. D., & Hanson, W. E. (1999). Test interpretation: A social influence perspective. In J. W. Lichtenberg & R. K. Goodyear (Eds.), *Scientist–practitioner perspectives on test interpretation* (pp. 151–166). Needham Heights, MA: Allyn & Bacon.

Clark, L. A., Watson, D., & Reynolds, S. (1995). Diagnosis and classification of psychopathology: Challenges to the current system and future directions. *Annual Review of Psychology, 46,* 121–153.

Cochran, L. (1983). Implicit versus explicit importance of career values in making a career decision. *Journal of Counseling Psychology, 30,* 188–193.

Code of Fair Testing Practices in Education. (1988). Washington, DC: American Psychological Association, Joint Committee on Testing Practices.

Cohen, R. J., Swerdlik, M. E., & Smith, D. K. (1992). *Psychological testing and assessment.* Mountain View, CA: Mayfield.

College Board. (1992a). *The new PSAT/NSQT.* New York: Author.

College Board. (1992b). *The official handbook for the CLEP examinations.* New York: Author.

College Board. (1994a). *Balancing the SAT scales.* New York: Author.

College Board. (1994b). *A guide to the advanced placement program.* New York: Author.

College Board. (2000a). *PSAT/NMSQT student bulletin.* New York: Author.

College Board. (2000b). *Registration bulletin, SAT I and SAT II.* New York: Author.

College Board. (2000c). *Taking the SAT I: Reasoning test.* New York: Author.

College Board. (2001). *Career Questionnaire* [On-line]. Available: http://cbweb9p.collegeboard.org/career/html/searchQues.html

College Entrance Examination Board. (1988). *Working with the PSAT/NMSQT: Preparation, administration, interpretation.* New York: Author.

College Entrance Examination Board. (2000). *The college handbook.* New York: Author.

Comas-Díaz, L., & Grenier, J. R. (1998). Migration and acculturation. In J. Sandoval, C. L. Frisby, K. F. Geisinger, J. D. Scheuneman, & J. R. Grenier (Eds.), *Test interpretation and diversity* (pp. 213–239). Washington, DC: American Psychological Association.

Conn, S. R., & Rieke, M. (1997). *16PF fifth edition technical manual.* Champaign, IL: Institute for Personality and Ability Testing.

Conners, C. K. (1997). *Conners' Rating Scales–Revised.* North Tonawanda, NY: Multi-Health Systems.

Conners, C. K., Erhardt, D., & Sparrow, E. (1998). *Conners' Adult ADHD Rating Scales.* North Tonawanda, NY: Multi-Health Systems.

Controversy follows psychological testing. (1999, December). *APA Monitor, 30,* 17.

Cooper-Patrick, L., Crum, R. M., & Ford, D. E. (1994). Identifying suicidal ideation in general medical patients. *Journal of the American Medical Association, 272,* 1757–1762.

Coopersmith, S. (1993). *Self Esteem Inventories (SEI).* Palo Alto, CA: Consulting Psychologists Press.

Coopersmith, S., & Gilberts, R. (1982). *Professional manual: Behavioral Academic Self-Esteem (BASE), a rating scale.* Palo Alto, CA: Consulting Psychologists Press.

Corcoran, K., & Fischer, J. (2000). *Measures for clinical practice: A sourcebook—Vol. 2: Adults* (3rd ed.). New York: Free Press.

Costa, P. T., & McCrae, R. (1992). *NEO-PI-R professional manual.* Odessa, FL: Psychological Assessment Resources.

Costa, P. T., Jr., & Widiger, T. A. (Eds.). (1994). *Personality disorders and the five-factor model of personality.* Washington, DC: American Psychological Association.

Crace, R. K., & Brown, D. (1992). *The Life Values Inventory.* Minneapolis, MN: National Computer Systems.

Craig, R. J. (1999). *Interpreting personality tests.* New York: Wiley.

Craighead, W. E., Curry, J. F., & Ilardi, S. S. (1995). Relationship of Children's Depression Inventory factors to major depression among adolescents. *Psychological Assessment, 7,* 171–176.

Crites, J. O. (1978). *Career Maturity Inventory: Theory and research handbook* (2nd ed.). Monterey, CA: CTB/McGraw-Hill.

Crites, J. O. (1993). *Career Mastery Inventory sourcebook.* Boulder, CO: Crites Career Consultants.

Crites, J. O., & Savickas, M. L. (1996). Revision of the Career Maturity Inventory. *Journal of Career Assessment, 4,* 131–138.

Cronbach, L. J. (1990). *Essentials of psychological testing* (5th ed.). New York: Harper Collins.

Cronbach, L. J., & Gleser, G. C. (1965). *Psychological tests and personnel decisions* (2nd ed.). Urbana: University of Illinois Press.

CTB/Macmillan/McGraw-Hill. (1993). *Test of Cognitive Skills test coordinator's handbook and guide to interpretation.* Monterey, CA: Author.

CTB/Macmillan/McGraw-Hill. (1994). *TABE examiner's manual.* Monterey, CA: Author.

CTB/Macmillan/McGraw-Hill. (1996). *TerraNova Comprehensive Tests of Basic Skills.* Monterey, CA: Author.

CTB/Macmillan/McGraw-Hill. (2001). *TerraNova CAT.* Monterey, CA: Author.

Cummings, W. H. (1995). Age group differences and estimated frequencies of the Myers–Briggs Type Indicator preferences. *Measurement and Evaluation in Counseling and Development, 2,* 69–77.

REFERENCES

Dahlstrom, W. G. (1993). Tests: Small samples, large consequences. *American Psychologist, 48,* 393–399.

Dana, R. H. (1993). *Multicultural assessment perspectives in professional psychology.* Boston: Allyn & Bacon.

Dana, R. H. (1998). *Understanding cultural identity in intervention and assessment.* Thousand Oaks, CA: Sage.

Dana, R. H. (2000). *Handbook of cross cultural and multicultural personality assessment.* Mahwah, NJ: Erlbaum.

Dawis, R. V., & Lofquist, L. H. (1984). *A psychological theory of work adjustment: An individual-differences model and its applications.* Minneapolis: University of Minnesota Press.

Day, S. X., & Rounds, J. (1998). Universality of vocational interest structure among racial and ethnic minorities. *American Psychologist, 53,* 728–736.

Dejong, P., & Berg, I. S. (1998). *Interviewing for solutions.* Pacific Grove, CA: Brooks/Cole.

Denzine, G. (1995). Psychometric resources for student affairs professionals. *Journal of College Student Development, 36,* 495–496.

Department of Education Office of Civil Rights. (2000). *The use of tests as part of high-stakes decision-making for students: A resource guide for educators and policymakers* [On-line]. Washington, DC: U.S. Department of Education. Available: www.ed.gov/offices/OCR/testing.

Derogatis, L. R. (1979). *Sexual Functioning Inventory manual.* Riderwood, MD: Clinical Psychometric Research.

Derogatis, L. R. (1994). *Administration, scoring, and procedures manual for the SCL-90-R.* Minneapolis, MN: National Computer Systems.

Derogatis, L. R., & Melisaratos, N. (1983). The Brief Symptom Inventory: An introductory report. *Psychological Medicine, 13,* 595–605.

Derogatis, L. R., & Savitz, K. L. (1999). The SCL-90-R, Brief Symptom Inventory, and Matching Clinical Rating Scales. In M. E. Maruish (Ed.), *The use of psychological testing for treatment planning and outcomes assessment* (2nd ed., pp. 679–724). Mahwah, NJ: Erlbaum.

Derogatis, L. R., & Savitz, K. L. (2000). The SCL-90-R and Brief Symptom Inventory in primary care. In M. E. Maruish (Ed.), *Handbook of psychological assessment in primary care settings* (pp. 297–334). Mahwah, NJ: Erlbaum.

Diamond, R. J. (1989). *Psychiatric presentations of medical illness: An introduction for non-medical mental health professionals.* Unpublished manuscript, University of Wisconsin–Madison, Department of Psychiatry.

Dickens, W. T., & Flynn, S. R. (2001). Heritability estimates versus large environmental effects: The IQ paradox resolved. *Psychological Review, 108,* 346–369.

Division of Educational Measurements, Council on Dental Education. (1994). *Dental Admission Testing Program (DATP) overview.* Chicago: American Dental Association.

Dolliver, R. H., & Worthington, E. L., Jr. (1981). Concurrent validity of other-sex and same-sex twin Strong–Campbell Interest Inventory Occupational scales. *Journal of Counseling Psychology, 28,* 126–134.

Donnay, D. A. C. (1997). E. K. Strong's legacy and beyond: 70 years of the Strong Interest Inventory. *Career Development Quarterly, 46,* 2–22.

Donnay, D. A. C., & Borgen, F. H. (1996). Validity, structure, and content of the 1994 Strong Interest Inventory. *Journal of Counseling Psychology, 43,* 275–291.

Donnay, D. A. C., & Borgen, F. H. (1999). The incremental validity of vocational self-efficacy: An examination of interest, self-efficacy, and occupation. *Journal of Counseling Psychology, 46,* 432–447.

Dorn, F. J. (1988). Utilizing social influence in career counseling: A case study. *Career Development Quarterly, 36,* 269–280.

Drummond, P. J. (1996). *Appraisal procedures for counselors and helping professionals.* Englewood Cliffs, NJ: Prentice Hall.

Duckworth, J. (1990). The counseling approach to the use of testing. *The Counseling Psychologist, 18,* 198–204.

Duckworth, J. C., & Anderson, W. P. (1995). *MMPI and MMPI-2 interpretation manual for counselors and clinicians* (4th ed.). Bristol, PA: Accelerated Development.

Dunn, L. M., & Dunn, L. M. (1997). *The Peabody Picture Vocabulary Test–Third edition: Examiner's manual.* Circle Pines, MN: American Guidance Service.

Dunn, R., Dunn, K., & Price, G. E. (1987). *Manual for the Learning Style Inventory (LSI).* Lawrence, KS: Price Systems.

DuPaul, G. J. (1991). Parent and teacher ratings of ADHD symptoms: Psychometric properties in a community-based sample. *Journal of Clinical Child Psychology, 20,* 245–253.

D'Zurilla, T. J., & Goldfried, M. R. (1971). Problem solving and behavior modification. *Journal of Abnormal Psychology, 78,* 107–126.

Eagly, A. H. (1995). The science and politics of comparing women and men. *American Psychologist, 50,* 145–158.

Eby, L. T., Johnson, C. D., & Russell, J. E. A. (1998). A psychometric review of career assessment tools for use with diverse individuals. *Journal of Career Assessment, 6,* 269–310.

EdITS (Educational and Industrial Testing Service). (1995). *COPSystem: A career awareness unit.* San Diego, CA: Author.

Education of All Handicapped Children Act of 1975, Pub. L. No. 94-142, 20 U.S.C. 89 Stat. 773.

Educational Testing Service. (1990). *Validity of the GRE: 1988–89 summary report*. Princeton, NJ: Author.

Educational Testing Service. (1995). *Graduate Management Admission Test bulletin*. Princeton, NJ: Author.

Educational Testing Service. (1998). *TOEFL on computer*. Princeton, NJ: Author.

Educational Testing Service. (2000a). *Graduate Record Examinations: Information bulletin*. Princeton, NJ: Author.

Educational Testing Service. (2000b). *TOEFL information bulletin*. Princeton, NJ: Author.

Elizur, D., Borg, I., Hunt, R., & Beck, I. M. (1991). The structure of work values: A cross cultural comparison. *Journal of Organizational Behavior, 12*, 21–38.

Elizur, D., & Tziner, A. (1977). Vocational needs, job rewards, and satisfaction: A canonical analysis. *Journal of Vocational Behavior, 10*, 205–211.

Elmore, P. B., & Bradley, R. W. (1994). Review of Armed Services Vocational Aptitude Battery (ASVAB) career exploration program. In J. T. Kapes, M. M. Mastie, & E. A. Whitfield (Eds.), *A counselor's guide to career assessment instruments* (3rd ed., pp. 71–77). Alexandria, VA: National Career Development Association.

Elmore, P. B., Ekstrom, R. B., & Diamond, E. E. (1993). Counselors' test use practices: Indicators of the adequacy of measurement training. *Measurement and Evaluation in Counseling and Development, 26*, 116–124.

Elmore, P. B., Ekstrom, R. B., Diamond, E. E., & Whittaker, S. (1993). School counselors' test use patterns and practices. *The School Counselor, 41*, 73–80.

Embertson, S. E. (1996). The new rules of measurement. *Psychological Assessment, 8*, 341–349.

Endler, N. S., & Parker, J. D. A. (1994). Assessment of multidimensional coping task, emotion, and avoidance strategies. *Psychological Assessment, 6*, 50–60.

Epperson, D. L., Bushway, D. J., & Warman, R. E. (1983). Client self-terminations after one counseling session: Effects of problem recognition, counselor gender, and counselor experience. *Journal of Counseling Psychology, 30*, 307–315.

ERIC Clearinghouse on Assessment and Evaluation. (1999). *ERIC/AE test locator* [On-line]. Available: http://ericae.net/testcol.htm.

Erikson, E. H. (1968). *Identity, youth and crisis*. New York: Norton.

Erwin, T. D. (1983). The Scale of Intellectual Development: Measuring Perry's scheme. *Journal of College Student Personnel, 24*, 6–12.

Evans, W. N. (1998). Assessment and diagnosis of the substance use disorders (SUDs). *Journal of Counseling & Development, 76*, 325–333.

Eveland, A. P., Conyne, R. K., & Blakney, V. L. (1998). University students and career decidedness: Effects of two computer-based career guidance interventions. *Computers in Human Behavior, 14,* 531–541.

Ewing, J. A. (1984). Detecting alcoholism: The CAGE Questionnaire. *Journal of the American Medical Association, 252,* 1905–1907.

Exner, J. E. (1993). *The Rorschach: A comprehensive system: Vol. 1. Basic foundations* (3rd ed.). New York: Wiley.

Exner, J. E. (2001). *A Rorschach workbook for the comprehensive system* (5th ed.). Odessa, FL: Psychological Assessment Resources.

Eyde, L. D., Moreland, K. L., Robertson, G. J., Primoff, E. S., & Most, R. B. (1988). *Executive summary—Test user qualifications: A data-based approach to promoting good test use. Issues in Scientific Psychology* (Report of the Test User Qualifications Working Group of the Joint Committee on Testing Practices). Washington, DC: American Psychological Association.

Eyde, L. D., Robertson, G. J., Krug, S. E., Moreland, K. L., Robertson, A. G., Shewan, C. M., Harrison, P. L., Porch, B. E., Hammer, A. L., & Primoff, E. S. (1993). *Responsible test use: Case studies for assessing human behavior.* Washington, DC: American Psychological Association.

Eysenck, H. J., & Eysenck, S. B. G. (1993). *Manual: Eysenck Personality Questionnaire (Junior & Adult).* San Diego, CA: Educational and Industrial Testing Service.

Fals-Stewart, W., O'Farrell, T. J., Feitas, T. T., McFarlin, S. K., & Rutigliano, P. (2000). The Timeline Followback reports of psychoactive substance use by drug-abusing patients: Psychometric properties. *Journal of Consulting and Clinical Psychology, 68,* 134–144.

Family Education Rights and Privacy Act of 1974 (FERPA). Pub. L. No. 93-380 20 U.S.C. § 241.

Fico, J. M., & Hogan, R. (2000). *Interpersonal compass manual.* Tulsa, OH: Hogan Assessment Systems.

Figler, H. E. (1993). *PATH: A career workbook for liberal arts students* (3rd ed.). New York: Sulzburger & Graham.

Finger, M. S., & Ones, D. S. (1999). Psychometric equivalence of the computer and booklet forms of the MMPI: A meta-analysis. *Psychological Assessment, 11,* 58–66.

Finn, S. E., & Tonsager, M. E. (1992). Therapeutic effects of providing MMPI-2 test feedback to college students awaiting therapy. *Psychological Assessment, 4,* 278–287.

Finn, S. E., & Tonsager, M. E. (1997). Information-gathering and therapeutic models of assessment: Complementary paradigms. *Psychological Assessment, 9,* 374–385.

Fischer, J., & Corcoran, K. (2000). *Measures for clinical practice: A sourcebook: Vol. 1. Couples, families, and children* (3rd ed.). New York: Free Press.

Fitts, W. H. (1996). *Manual Tennessee Self-Concept Scale* (2nd ed.). Los Angeles: Western Psychological Services.

Flowers, J. V., Booream, C. D., & Schwartz, B. (1993). Impact of computerized rapid assessment instruments on counselors and client outcome. *Computers in Human Services, 10,* 9–18.

Foa, E. B., Riggs, D. S., Dancu, C. V., & Rothbaum, B. O. (1993). Reliability and validity of a brief instrument for assessing post-traumatic stress disorder. *Journal of Traumatic Stress, 6,* 459–473.

Folkman, S., & Lazarus, R. S. (1988). *Manual for the Ways of Coping Questionnaire: Research edition.* Palo Alto, CA: Consulting Psychologists Press.

Folstein, M. F., Folstein, S. E., & McHugh, P. R. (1975). Mini-mental state: A practical method for grading the state of patients for the clinician. *Journal of Psychiatric Research, 12,* 189–198.

Folstein, M. F., Folstein, S. E., McHugh, P. R., & Fanjiang, G. (2001). *Mini-Mental State Examination user's guide.* Odessa, FL: Psychological Assessment Resources.

Fong, M. L. (1993). Teaching assessment and diagnosis within a DSM-III-R framework. *Counselor Education and Supervision, 32,* 276–287.

Fong, M. L. (1995). Assessment and DSM-IV diagnosis of personality disorders: A primer for counselors. *Journal of Counseling & Development, 73,* 635–639.

Fong, M. L., & Silien, K. A. (1999). Assessment and diagnosis of DSM-IV anxiety disorders. *Journal of Counseling & Development, 77,* 209–217.

Forgays, D. G., Forgays, D. K., & Spielberger, C. D. (1997). Factor structure of the State–Trait Anger Expression Inventory. *Journal of Personality Assessment, 69,* 497–507.

Forsyth, R. A., Ansley, T. N., Feldt, L. S., & Alnot, S. D. (2001). *Teacher, administrator, and counselor manual, Iowa Tests of Educational Development.* Chicago: Riverside.

Fouad, N. A., & Chan, P. M. (1999). Gender and ethnicity: Influence on test interpretation and reception. In J. W. Lichtenberg & R. K. Goodyear (Eds.), *Scientist–practitioner perspectives on test interpretation* (pp. 31–58). Needham Heights, MA: Allyn & Bacon.

Fouad, N. A., Harmon, L. W., & Borgen, F. H. (1997). Structure of interests in employed male and female members of U.S. racial–ethnic minority and nonminority groups. *Journal of Counseling Psychology, 44,* 339–345.

Fouad, N. A., Harmon, L. W., & Hansen, J. C. (1994). Cross-cultural use of the Strong. In L. W. Harmon, J. C. Hansen, F. H. Borgen, & A. L.

Hammer (Eds.), *Strong Interest Inventory applications and technical guide* (pp. 255–280). Stanford, CA: Stanford University Press.

Frank, R. G., & Elliott, T. R. (Eds.). (2000). *Handbook of rehabilitation psychology.* Washington, DC: American Psychological Association.

Frauenhoffer, D., Ross, M. J., Gfeller, J., Searight, H. R., & Piotrowski, C. (1998). Psychological test usage among licensed mental health practitioners: A multidisciplinary survey. *Journal of Psychological Practice, 4,* 28–33.

Fremer, J. (1992, August). *One hundred years of psychological testing.* Paper presented at the 100th Annual Convention of the American Psychological Association, Washington, DC.

French, J. W. (1962). Effective anxiety on verbal and mathematical examination scores. *Educational and Psychological Measurement, 22,* 553–564.

Friedenberg, L. (1995). *Psychological testing: Design, analysis, and use.* Needham Heights, MA: Allyn & Bacon.

Friedman, A. F., Lewak, R., Nichols, D. S., & Webb, J. T. (2001). *Psychological assessment with the MMPI-2.* Mahwah, NJ: Erlbaum.

Friedman, S. L., & Wachs, T. D. (Eds.). (1999). *Measuring environment across the life span: Emerging methods and concepts.* Washington, DC: American Psychological Association.

Frisby, C. L. (1998). Culture and cultural differences. In J. Sandoval, C. L. Frisby, K. F. Geisinger, J. D. Scheuneman, & J. R. Grenier (Eds.), *Test interpretation and diversity* (pp. 51–74). Washington, DC: American Psychological Association.

Frisch, M. B. (1994). *Manual and treatment guide for the Quality of Life Inventory.* Minneapolis, MN: National Computer Systems.

Fuqua, D. R., & Newman, J. L. (1994). Review of Campbell Interest and Skill Survey. In J. T. Kapes, M. M. Mastie, & E. A. Whitfield (Eds.), *A counselor's guide to career assessment instruments* (pp. 138–143). Alexandria, VA: National Career Development Association.

Galassi, J. P., & Perot, A. R. (1992). What you should know about behavioral assessment. *Journal of Counseling & Development, 70,* 624–631.

Garb, H. N. (1997). Race bias, social class bias, and gender bias in clinical judgment. *Clinical Psychology: Science and Practice, 4,* 99–120.

Garb, H. N. (1998). *Studying the clinician: Judgment research and psychological assessment.* Washington, DC: American Psychological Association.

Gardner, H. (1993). *Multiple intelligences: The theory in practice.* New York: Basic Books.

Garner, D. M. (1991). *Eating Disorder Inventory-2: Professional manual.* Odessa, FL: Psychological Assessment Resources.

Garner, D. M., & Garfinkel, P. E. (1979). The Eating Attitudes Test: An index of the symptoms of anorexia nervosa. *Psychological Medicine, 9,* 273–279.

Garrett, M. T., & Pichette, E. F. (2000). Red as an apple: Native American acculturation and counseling with or without reservation. *Journal of Counseling & Development, 78,* 3–13.

Gay, G. H. (1990). Standardized tests: Irregularities in administration of tests affect test results. *Journal of Instructional Psychology, 17,* 93–103.

Geisinger, K. F. (1998). Psychometric issues in test interpretation. In J. Sandoval, C. L. Frisby, K. F. Geisinger, J. D. Scheuneman, & J. R. Grenier (Eds.), *Test interpretation and diversity* (pp. 17–30). Washington, DC: American Psychological Association.

Geroski, A. M., Rodgers, K. A., & Breen, D. T. (1997). Using the DSM-IV to enhance collaboration among school counselors, clinical counselors, and primary care physicians. *Journal of Counseling & Development, 75,* 231–239.

Giannetti, R. A. (1992). *User's guide for Quickview Social History–Clinical version.* Minneapolis, MN: National Computer Systems.

Goldberg, L. R. (1993). The structure of phenotypic personality traits. *American Psychologist, 48,* 26–34.

Goldenson, R. M. (Ed.). (1984). *Longman dictionary of psychology and psychiatry.* New York: Longman.

Goldfried, M. R. (1997). Considerations in developing a core assessment battery. In H. H. Strupp, L. M. Horowitz, & M. J. Lambert (Eds.), *Measuring patient changes in mood, anxiety, and personality disorders: Toward a core battery* (pp. 99–114). Washington, DC: American Psychological Association.

Goldfried, M. R., Stricker, G., & Weiner, I. R. (1971). *Rorschach handbook of clinical and research applications.* Englewood Cliffs, NJ: Prentice Hall.

Goldman, L. (1972). Tests and counseling: The marriage that failed. *Measurement and Evaluation in Guidance, 4,* 197–205.

Goldman, L. (1992). Qualitative assessment: An approach for counselors. *Journal of Counseling & Development, 70,* 616–621.

Goldman, L. (1994). The marriage is over . . . for most of us. *Measurement and Evaluation in Counseling and Development, 26,* 217–218.

Goodyear, R. K. (1990). Research on the effects of test interpretation: A review. *The Counseling Psychologist, 18,* 240–257.

Gottfredson, G. D., & Holland, J. L. (1991). *Manual for Position Classification Inventory.* Odessa, FL: Psychological Assessment Resources.

Gottfredson, G. D., & Holland, J. L. (1996). *Dictionary of Holland occupational codes* (3rd ed.). Odessa, FL: Psychological Assessment Resources.

Gottfredson, L. S. (1982). The sex fairness of unnormed interest inventories. *Vocational Guidance Quarterly, 31,* 128–132.

Gough, H. G. (1987). *California Psychological Inventory administrator's guide.* Palo Alto, CA: Consulting Psychologists Press.

Gough, H. G. (1999). *CPI: Introduction to Form 434*. Palo Alto, CA: Consulting Psychologists Press.

Gough, H. G. (2000). The California Psychological Inventory. In C. E. Watkins & V. L. Campbell (Eds.), *Testing and assessment in counseling practice* (pp. 45–71). Mahwah, NJ: Erlbaum.

Gough, H. G., & Bradley, P. (1996). *CPI manual*. Palo Alto, CA: Consulting Psychologists Press.

Graham, J. R. (2000). *MMPI-2: Assessing personality and psychopathology* (3rd ed.). New York: Oxford University Press.

Graham, J. R., & Strenger, V. E. (1988). MMPI characteristics of alcoholics: A review. *Journal of Consulting and Clinical Psychology, 56,* 197–205.

Gray-Little, B., & Kaplan, D. A. (1998). Interpretation of psychological tests in clinical and forensic evaluations. In J. Sandoval, C. L. Frisby, K. F. Geisinger, J. D. Scheuneman, & J. R. Grenier (Eds.), *Test interpretation and diversity* (pp. 141–178). Washington, DC: American Psychological Association.

Green, K. E. (1998). Review of the Values Scale, Second Edition. In J. C. Impara & B. S. Plake (Eds.), *The thirteenth mental measurements yearbook* (pp. 1112–1114). Lincoln, NE: Buros Institute of Mental Measurements.

Greenberg, L. (1994). *Interpretation manual for Test of Variables of Attention*. Circle Pines, MN: American Guidance Service.

Greene, R. L. (1987). Ethnicity and MMPI performance: A review. *Journal of Consulting and Clinical Psychology, 35,* 497–512.

Greene, R. L. (1999). *The MMPI-2: An interpretive manual*. Boston: Allyn & Bacon.

Gross, M. L. (1962). *The brain watchers*. New York: New American Library.

Groth-Marnat, G. (1997). *Handbook of psychological assessment* (3rd ed.). New York: Wiley.

Grove, W. M., Zald, D. H., Lebow, B. S., Snitz, B. E., & Nelson, C. (2000). Clinical versus mechanical prediction: A meta-analysis. *Psychological Assessment, 12,* 19–30.

Guilford, J. P. (1959). *Personality*. New York: McGraw-Hill.

Guion, R. M. (1995). Review of the Career Beliefs Inventory. In J. D. Conoley & J. C. Impara (Eds.), *Twelfth mental measurements yearbook* (pp. 160–161). Lincoln, NE: Buros Institute of Mental Measurements.

Hahn, W. K., & Marks, L. I. (1996). Client receptiveness to the routine assessment of past suicide attempts. *Professional Psychology: Research and Practice, 27,* 592–594.

Hammen, C. L. (1980). Depression in college students: Beyond the Beck Depression Inventory. *Journal of Consulting and Clinical Psychology, 45,* 126–128.

Hammer, A. L. (Ed.). (1996). *MBTI applications: A decade of research on the Myers–Briggs Type Indicator*. Palo Alto, CA: Consulting Psychologists Press.

Han, L., & Hoover, H. D. (1994, April). *Gender differences in achievement test scores*. Paper presented at the annual meeting of the National Council on Measurement in Education, New Orleans, LA.

Handel, R. W., Ben-Porath, Y. S., & Watt, M. (1999). Computerized adaptive assessment with the MMPI-2 in a clinical setting. *Psychological Assessment, 11*, 369–380.

Haney, W. (1981). Validity, vaudeville, and values: A short history of social concerns over standardized testing. *American Psychologist, 36*, 1021–1034.

Hansen, J. C. (1999). Test psychometrics. In J. W. Lichtenberg & R. K. Goodyear (Eds.), *Scientist–practitioner perspectives on test interpretation* (pp. 15–30). Needham Heights, MA: Allyn & Bacon.

Hansen, J. C. (2000). Interpretation of the Strong Interest Inventory. In C. E. Watkins, Jr. & V. L. Campbell (Eds.), *Testing and assessment in counseling practice* (2nd ed., pp. 227–262). Mahwah, NJ: Erlbaum.

Hansen, J. C., Neuman, J. L., Haverkamp, B. E., & Lubinski, B. R. (1997). Comparison of user reaction to two methods of Strong Interest Inventory administration and report feedback. *Measurement and Evaluation in Counseling and Development, 30*, 115–127.

Hansen, L. S. S. (1999). Integrative life planning: An interdisciplinary framework for aligning personal growth and organizational and social development in the 21st century. *International Medical Journal, 6*, 87–93.

Harcourt Brace. (1996). *Stanford 9 technical data report*. San Antonio, TX: Author.

Harcourt Brace. (2000). *MAT8 technical manual*. San Antonio, TX: Author.

Harmon, L. W. (1994). Review of the Career Decision Scale. In J. T. Kapes, M. M. Mastie, & E. A. Whitfield (Eds.), *A counselor's guide to career assessment instruments* (pp. 258–262). Alexandria, VA: National Career Development Association.

Harmon, L. W., & Borgen, F. H. (1995). Advances in career assessment and the 1994 Strong Interest Inventory. *Journal of Career Assessment, 3*, 347–372.

Harmon, L. W., Hansen, J. C., Borgen, F. H., & Hammer, A. L. (1994). *Strong Interest Inventory applications and technical guide*. Stanford, CA: Stanford University Press.

Harrell, A. V., & Wirtz, P. W. (1989). *Adolescent Drinking Index: Professional manual*. Odessa, FL: Psychological Assessment Resources.

Harren, V. A. (1979). A model of career decision making for college students. *Journal of Vocational Behavior, 14*, 119–133.

Harrington, T. F. (1991). The cross-cultural applicability of the Career Decision-Making System. *Career Development Quarterly, 39,* 209–220.

Harrington, T. F., & O'Shea, A. J. (1992). *Career Decision-Making System Revised.* Circle Pines, MN: American Guidance Service.

Hay, R. G. (1988). Screening counseling center clients for drinking problems. *Journal of College Student Development, 29,* 79–81.

Hayes, J. A., Wall, T. N., & Shea, A. (1998, August). *The relationship of client–therapist attribution congruence to the working alliance and psychotherapy outcome.* Paper presented at the 106th Annual Convention of the American Psychological Association, San Francisco.

Healy, C. C. (1990). Reforming career appraisals to meet the needs of clients in the 1990s. *The Counseling Psychologist, 18,* 214–226.

Healy, C. C. (1994). Review of Career Maturity Inventory. In J. T. Kapes, M. M. Mastie, & E. A. Whitfield (Eds.), *A counselor's guide to career assessment instruments* (pp. 268–272). Alexandria, VA: National Career Development Association.

Heck, E. J. (1991). Developing a screening questionnaire for problem drinking in college students. *Journal of American College Health, 39,* 227–234.

Heiligenstein, E., Guenther, G., Levy, A., Savino, F., & Fulwiler, J. (1999). Psychological and academic functioning in college students with attention deficit hyperactivity disorder. *Journal of American College Health, 47,* 181–185.

Helmes, E., & Reddon, J. R. (1993). A perspective on developments in assessing psychopathology: A critical review of the MMPI and MMPI-2. *Psychological Bulletin, 113,* 453–471.

Heppner, M. J., Multon, K. D., & Johnston, J. A. (1994). Assessing psychological resources during career change: Development of the Career Transitions Inventory. *Journal of Vocational Behavior, 44,* 55–74.

Heppner, P. P. (1988). *The Problem-Solving Inventory: Manual.* Palo Alto, CA: Consulting Psychologists Press.

Heppner, P. P., Cook, S. W., Wright, D. M., & Johnson, W. C., Jr. (1995). Progress in resolving problems: A problem-focused style of coping. *Journal of Counseling Psychology, 42,* 279–293.

Hess, A. K. (2001). Review of the Wechsler Adult Intelligence Scale–Third Edition. In B. S. Plake & J. C. Impara (Eds.), *The fourteenth mental measurements yearbook* (pp. 1332–1336). Lincoln, NE: Buros Institute of Mental Measurements.

Higgins, R. W. (1997). ADHD: The role of the family physician. *American Family Physician, 56,* 42–43.

Hiller, J. B., Rosenthal, R., Bornstein, R. F., Barry, D. R., & Brunell-Neuleib, T. (1999). A comparative meta-analysis of Rorschach and MMPI validity. *Psychological Assessment, 11,* 278–296.

Hinkle, J. S. (1994). Practitioners and cross-cultural assessment: A practical guide to information and training. *Measurement and Evaluation in Counseling and Development, 27,* 103–115.

Hinkle, J. S. (1999). A voice from the trenches: A reaction to Ivey and Ivey (1998). *Journal of Counseling & Development, 77,* 474–483.

Hodgson, R. J., & Rachman, S. (1977). Obsessional–compulsive complaints. *Behaviour Research and Therapy, 15,* 389–395.

Hoffman, J. A., & Weiss, B. (1986). A new system for conceptualizing college students' problems: Types of crises and the Inventory of Common Problems. *Journal of American College Health, 34,* 259–266.

Hogan, R. (1997). *Hogan Development Survey.* Tulsa, OK: Hogan Assessment Systems.

Hohenshil, T. H. (1996). Editorial: Role of assessment and diagnosis in counseling. *Journal of Counseling & Development, 75,* 64–67.

Holden, R. R. (1996). *Holden Psychological Screening Inventory.* Tonawanda, NY: Multi-Health Systems.

Holland, J. L. (1992). *Vocational exploration and insight kit.* Odessa, FL: Psychological Assessment Resources.

Holland, J. L. (1997). *Making vocational choices: A theory of vocational personalities and work environments* (3rd ed.). Odessa, FL: Psychological Assessment Resources.

Holland, J. L., Daiger, D. C., & Power, P. G. (1980). *My Vocational Situation.* Palo Alto, CA: Consulting Psychologists Press.

Holland, J. L., Fritzsche, B. A., & Powell, A. B. (1994). *The Self-Directed Search technical manual.* Odessa, FL: Psychological Assessment Resources.

Holland, J. L., & Gottfredson, G. D. (1976). Using a typology of persons and environments to explain careers: Some extensions and clarifications. *The Counseling Psychologist, 6,* 20–29.

Holland, J. L., & Gottfredson, G. D. (1994a, April). *Career Attitudes and Strategies Inventory: A new tool for counseling adults.* Paper presented at the annual convention of the American Counseling Association, Minneapolis, MN.

Holland, J. L., & Gottfredson, G. D. (1994b). *CASI: Career Attitudes and Strategies Inventory.* Odessa, FL: Psychological Assessment Resources.

Holland, J. L., Powell, A. B., & Fritzsche, B. A. (1994). *Self-Directed Search professional user's guide.* Odessa, FL: Psychological Assessment Resources.

Holmberg, K., Rosen, D., & Holland, J. L. (1990). *The leisure activities finder.* Odessa, FL: Psychological Assessment Resources.

Holroyd, S., & Clayton, A. H. (2000). Measuring depression in the elderly: Which scale is best? *Medscape Mental Health* [On-line], *5*(5). Available: http://www.medscape.com/Medscape/psychiatry/journal/2000/v05.n05/ mh3033.holr/mh3033.holr-01.html

Hood, A. B. (1968). *What type of college for what type of student?* Minneapolis: University of Minnesota Press.

Hood, A. B. (1997). *The Iowa Student Development Inventories, 2nd edition.* Iowa City, IA: Hitech Press.

Hoover, H. D., Dunbar, S. B., & Frisbie, D. A. (2001). *Iowa Tests of Basic Skills: Spring norms and score conversions with technical information.* Chicago: Riverside.

Hoover, H. D., & Han, L. (1995, April). *The effect of differential selection on gender differences in college admission test scores.* Paper presented at the annual meeting of the American Educational Research Association, San Francisco.

Horan, J. J. (1979). *Counseling for effective decision-making: A cognitive–behavioral perspective.* North Scituate, MA: Duxbury Press.

Horn, J. L., Wanberg, K. W., & Foster, F. M. (1986). *Alcohol Use Inventory.* Minneapolis, MN: National Computer Systems.

Hoyt, D. P. (1960). Measurement and prediction of the permanence of interests. In W. L. Layton (Ed.), *The Strong Vocational Interest Blank: Research and uses* (pp. 93–103). Minneapolis: University of Minnesota Press.

Huszczo, G. E. (1996). *Tools for team excellence.* Palo Alto, CA: Davies-Black.

Impara, J. C., & Plake, B. S. (1995). Comparing counselors', school administrators', and teachers' knowledge in student assessment. *Measurement and Evaluation in Counseling and Development, 28,* 78–87.

Individuals With Disabilities Education Act (1997 Revision). 20 U.S.C. 1400, Pub. L. No. 105-17 111 Stat. 37 (1997).

Ivey, A. E., & Ivey, M. B. (1998). Reframing DSM-IV: Positive strategies from developmental counseling and therapy. *Journal of Counseling & Development, 68,* 334–350.

Ivey, A. E., & Ivey, M. B. (1999). Toward a developmental diagnostic and statistical manual: The vitality of a contextual framework. *Journal of Counseling & Development, 77,* 484–490.

Jackson, B., & Farrugia, D. (1997). Diagnosis and treatment of adults with attention deficit hyperactivity disorder. *Journal of Counseling & Development, 75,* 312–319.

Jackson, D. N. (1989). *Basic Personality Inventory manual.* Port Huron, MI: Sigma Assessment Systems.

Jackson, D. N. (1997a). *Jackson Personality Inventory–Revised manual.* Port Huron, MI: Sigma Assessment Systems.

Jackson, D. N. (1997b). *Personality Research Form manual.* Port Huron, MI: Research Psychologists Press.

Jackson, D. N. (1998). *Multidimensional Aptitude Battery–II manual.* Port Huron, MI: Sigma Assessment Systems.

Jackson, D. N. (1999). *Jackson Vocational Interest Survey manual* (2nd ed., rev.). Port Huron, MI: Sigma Assessment Systems.

Jaeger, R. M. (1985). Graduate Record Examination: General test. In J. D. Mitchell, Jr. (Ed.), *The ninth mental measurements yearbook* (pp. 624–626). Lincoln, NE: Buros Institute of Mental Measurements.

Jenkins, J. O., & Ramsey, G. A. (1991). Minorities. In M. Herson, A. E. Kazdin, & A. S. Bellack (Eds.), *The clinical psychology handbook* (2nd ed., pp. 683–696). New York: Pergamon.

Jepsen, D. A. (1994). Review of Jackson Vocational Interest Survey. In J. T. Kapes, M. M. Mastie, & E. A. Whitfield (Eds.), *A counselor's guide to career assessment instruments* (pp. 183–188). Alexandria, VA: National Career Development Association.

Johansson, C. B. (1984). *Manual for Career Assessment Inventory* (2nd ed.). Minneapolis, MN: National Computer Systems.

Johansson, C. B. (1986). *Manual for Career Assessment Inventory: The enhanced version.* Minneapolis, MN: National Computer Systems.

Johnson, A. K. (1997). Conflict-handling intentions and the MBTI: A construct validation study. *Journal of Psychological Types, 43,* 29–39.

Johnson, R. W. (2001). Review of the Quality of Life Inventory. In B. S. Plake & J. C. Impara (Eds.), *The fourteenth mental measurements yearbook* (pp. 975–977). Lincoln, NE: Buros Institute of Mental Measurements.

Johnson, R. W., Ellison, R. A., & Heikkinen, C. A. (1989). Psychological symptoms of counseling center clients. *Journal of Counseling Psychology, 36,* 110–114.

Johnson, R. W., Heikkinen, C. A., & Ellison, R. A. (1988). [Frequency of symptoms indicating depression among counseling service clients]. Unpublished raw data.

Johnson, S. L. (1997). *Therapist's guide to clinical intervention: The 1-2-3's of treatment planning.* San Diego, CA: Academic Press.

Joiner, T. E., Jr., Walker, R. L., Rudd, M. D., & Jobes, D. A. (1999). Scientizing and routinizing the assessment of suicidality in outpatient practice. *Professional Psychology: Research and Practice, 30,* 447–453.

Joint Committee on Testing Practices. (1998). *Rights and responsibilities of test takers: Guidelines and expectations* [On-line]. Available: www.apa.org/science/jctpweb.

Jones, L. K. (2000). *The Career Key* [On-line]. Available: http://www.ncsu.edu/careerkey/

Juhnke, G. A. (1996). The adapted–SAD PERSONS: A suicide assessment scale designed for use with children. *Elementary School Guidance and Counseling, 30,* 252–258.

Juhnke, G. A., & Hovestadt, A. J. (1995). Using the SAD PERSONS Scale to promote supervisee suicide assessment knowledge. *Clinical Supervisor, 13,* 31–40.

Jung, C. G. (1960). *The structure and dynamics of the psyche.* New York: Bollingan Foundation.

Kapes, J. T., Borman, C. A., & Frazier, N. (1989). An evaluation of the SIGI and DISCOVER microcomputer-based career guidance systems. *Measurement and Evaluation in Counseling and Development, 22,* 126–136.

Kapes, J. T., & Vansickle, T. R. (1992). Comparing paper-and-pencil and computer-based versions of the Harrington–O'Shea Career Decision-Making System. *Measurement and Evaluation in Counseling and Development, 25,* 5–13.

Kapes, J. T., & Whitfield, E. A. (Eds.). (2001). *A counselor's guide to career assessment instruments* (4th ed.). Columbus, OH: National Career Development Association.

Karlsen, B., & Gardner, F. E. (1986). *Adult Basic Learning Examination, 2nd Edition.* San Antonio, TX: Psychological Corporation.

Karson, M., Karson, S., & O'Dell, J. (1997). *16PF interpretation in clinical practice: A guide to the fifth edition.* Champaign, IL: IPAT.

Katz, L., Joyner, J. W., & Seaman, N. (1999). Effects of joint interpretation of the Strong Interest Inventory and the Myers–Briggs Type Indicator in career choice. *Journal of Career Assessment, 7,* 281–297.

Kaufman, A. S., & Kaufman, N. L. (1983). *KABC: Kaufman Assessment Battery for Children, administration and scoring manual.* Circle Pines, MN: American Guidance Service.

Kaufman, A. S., & Kaufman, N. L. (1990). *Kaufman Brief Intelligence Test manual.* Circle Pines, MN: American Guidance Service.

Kaufman, A. S., & Kaufman, N. L. (1993). *Manual: Kaufman Adolescent and Adult Intelligence Test.* Circle Pines, MN: American Guidance Service.

Kaufman, A. S., & Kaufman, N. L. (1997). *K-TEA normative update.* Circle Pines, MN: American Guidance Service.

Kaufman, A. S., & Lichtenberger, E. O. (1999). *Essentials of WAIS-III.* New York: Wiley.

Keirsey, D. M. (2000). *Personality: Character and temperament* [On-line]. Available: http://www.keirsey.com.

Keirsey, D., & Choiniere, R. (1998). *Please understand me II: Temperament, character, intelligence.* Del Mar, CA: Prometheus Nemisis.

Kellogg, C. E., & Morton, N. W. (1999). *Beta III manual.* San Antonio, TX: Harcourt Educational Measurement.

Kenrick, D. T., & Funder, D. C. (1988). Profiting from controversy: Lessons from the person–situation debate. *American Psychologist, 43,* 23–34.

Kessler, R. C., McGonagle, K. A., Zhao, S., Nelson, C. B., Hughes, M., Eshleman, S., Wittchen, H., & Kendler, K. S. (1994). Lifetime and 12-month prevalence of DSM-III-R psychiatric disorders in the United States. *Archives of General Psychiatry, 51,* 8–19.

Keutzer, C. S., Morrill, W. H., Holmes, R. H., Sherman, L., Davenport, E., Tistadt, G., Francisco, R., & Murphy, M. J. (1998). Precipitating events and presenting problems of university counseling center clients: Some demographic differences. *Journal of College Student Psychotherapy, 12,* 3–23.

Keyser, D. J., & Sweetland, R. C. (Eds.). (1984–1994). *Test critiques: Vols. I–X.* Kansas City, MO: Test Corporation of America.

Kiesler, D. J. (1987). *Checklist of Psychotherapy Transactions–Revised (CLOPT-R) and Checklist of Interpersonal Transactions–Revised (CLOIT-R).* Richmond: Virginia Commonwealth University Press.

Kiesler, D. J., Schmidt, J. A., & Wagner, C. C. (1997). A circumplex inventory of impact messages: An operational bridge between emotion and interpersonal behavior. In R. Plutchik & H. R. Conte (Eds.), *Circumplex models of personality and emotions* (pp. 221–224). Washington, DC: American Psychological Association.

King, P. M., & Kitchener, K. S. (1994). *Developing reflective judgment: Understanding and promoting intellectual growth and critical thinking in adolescents and adults.* San Francisco: Jossey-Bass.

Kinnier, R. T. (1987). Development of a values conflict resolution assessment. *Journal of Counseling Psychology, 34,* 31–37.

Kinnier, R. T. (1995). A reconceptualization of values clarification: Values conflict resolution. *Journal of Counseling & Development, 74,* 18–24.

Kiresuk, T. J., Smith, A., & Cardillo, J. E. (Ed.). (1994). *Goal attainment scaling: Applications, theory, and measurement.* Hillsdale, NJ: Erlbaum.

Kishline, A. (1994). *Moderate drinking: The moderation management guide for people who want to reduce their drinking.* New York: Crown Trade.

Kitchens, J. M. (1994). Does this patient have an alcohol problem? *Journal of the American Medical Association, 272,* 1782–1787.

Klerman, G. (1987). Clinical epidemiology of suicide. *Journal of Clinical Psychiatry, 48,* 33–38.

Knapp, L., Knapp, R. R., & Knapp-Lee, L. (1992). *Career Ability Placement Survey technical manual.* San Diego, CA: Educational and Industrial Testing Service.

Knapp, L., Knapp-Lee, L., & Knapp, R. (1995). *Career Orientation Placement and Evaluation Survey.* San Diego, CA: Educational and Industrial Testing Service.

Knapp-Lee, L. J. (1996). Use of the COPES, a measure of work values, in career assessment. *Journal of Career Assessment, 4,* 429–443.

Knapp-Lee, L. (2000). A complete career guidance program: The COPSystem. In C. E. Watkins, Jr. & V. L. Campbell (Eds.), *Testing and assessment in counseling practice* (2nd ed., pp. 295–338). Mahwah, NJ: Erlbaum.

Kobak, K. A., Greist, J. H., Jefferson, J. W., & Katzelnick, D. J. (1996). Computer-administered clinical rating scales: A review. *Psychopharmacology, 127,* 291–301.

Kohlberg, L. (1969). Stage and sequence: The cognitive developmental approach to socialization. In D. Goslin (Ed.), *Handbook of socialization theory and research* (pp. 347–480). Chicago: Rand McNally.

Kohlberg, L. (1971). Stages of moral development. In C. M. Beck, V. S. Crittenden, & E. B. Sullivan (Eds.), *Moral education* (pp. 23–92). Toronto, Ontario, Canada: University of Toronto Press.

Kolb, D. A. (1985). *Learning Style Inventory.* Boston: McBer.

Korotitsch, W. J., & Nelson-Gray, R. O. (1999). An overview of self-monitoring research in assessment and treatment. *Psychological Assessment, 11,* 415–425.

Kovacs, M. (1992). *Children's Depression Inventory manual.* North Tonawanda, NY: Mental Health Systems.

Kramer, J. J., & Conoley, J. C. (Eds.). (1992). *Eleventh mental measurements yearbook.* Lincoln, NE: Buros Institute of Mental Measurements.

Krumboltz, J. D. (1991). *Manual for the Career Beliefs Inventory.* Palo Alto, CA: Consulting Psychologists Press.

Krumboltz, J. D. (1994). The Career Beliefs Inventory. *Journal of Counseling & Development, 72,* 424–428.

Krumboltz, J. D., Blando, J. A., Kim, H., & Reikowski, D. J. (1994). Embedding work values in stories. *Journal of Counseling & Development, 73,* 57–62.

Krumboltz, J. D., & Worthington, R. L. (1999). The school-to-work transition from a learning theory perspective. *Career Development Quarterly, 47,* 312–325.

Kuder, F. (1988). *General manual for Kuder General Interest Survey, Form E.* Monterey, CA: CTB/McGraw-Hill.

Kuder, F., & Zytowski, D. G. (1991). *Kuder Occupational Interest Survey general manual.* Monterey, CA: CTB/McGraw-Hill.

Kuncel, N. R., & Hezlett, S. A. (2001). A comprehensive meta-analysis of the predictive validity of the Graduate Record Examinations: Implications for graduate student selection and performance. *Psychological Bulletin, 127,* 162–181.

LaBruzza, A. L., & Mendez-Villarrubia, J. M. (1994). *Using DSM-IV: A clinician's guide to psychiatric diagnosis.* Northvale, NJ: Jason Aronson.

Lachar, B. (1992). Review of Minnesota Importance Questionnaire. In J. J. Kramer & J. C. Conoley (Eds.), *Eleventh mental measurements yearbook* (pp. 542–544). Lincoln, NE: Buros Institute of Mental Measurements.

Laing, J., & Farmer, M. (1984). *Use of the ACT assessment by examinees with disabilities* (Research Report No. 84). Iowa City, IA: American College Testing Program.

Lamb, R. R. (1974). *Concurrent validity of the American College Testing Interest Inventory for minority group members.* Unpublished doctoral dissertation, University of Iowa.

Lampe, R. E. (1985). Self-scoring accuracy of the Kuder General Interest Survey. *The School Counselor, 32,* 319–324.

Lanier, C. W. (1994). *ACT composite scores of re-tested students.* Iowa City, IA: American College Testing Program.

Lanyon, R. I. (1978). *Manual for Psychological Screening Inventory.* Port Huron, MI: Research Psychologists Press.

Lattimore, R. R., & Borgen, F. H. (1999). Validity of the 1994 Strong Interest Inventory with racial and ethnic groups in the United States. *Journal of Counseling Psychology, 46,* 185–195.

Law School Admission Council. (2000). *LSAT/LSDAS registration and information book.* Newton, PA: Author.

Lawrence, G. (1992). *People types and tiger stripes* (3rd ed.). Gainesville, FL: Center for the Application of Type.

Layton, W. L. (1992). Review of Minnesota Importance Questionnaire. In J. J. Kramer & J. C. Conoley (Eds.), *Eleventh mental measurements yearbook* (pp. 544–546). Lincoln, NE: Buros Institute of Mental Measurements.

Lazowksi, L. E., Miller, F. G., Boye, M. W., & Miller, G. A. (1998). Efficacy of the Substance Abuse Subtle Screening Inventory–3 (SASSI-3) in identifying substance dependence disorders in clinical settings. *Journal of Personality Assessment, 71,* 114–128.

LeBold, W. K., & Shell, K. D. (1986). *Purdue Interest Questionnaire: A brief interpretive guide for the revision.* West Lafayette, IN: Purdue University, Department of Freshman Engineering.

Lehman, N. (1999). *The big test: The secret history of American meritocracy.* New York: Farrar, Straus, & Giroux.

Leong, F. T. L., & Gim-Chung, R. H. (1995). Career assessment and intervention with Asian Americans. In F. T. L. Leong (Ed.), *Career development and vocational behavior of racial and ethnic minorities* (pp. 193–226). Mahwah, NJ: Erlbaum.

Leonhard, C., Mulvey, K., Gastfriend, D. R., & Schwartz, M. (2000). The Addiction Severity Index: A field study of internal consistency and validity. *Journal of Substance Abuse Treatment, 18,* 129–135.

Levinson, E. M., Ohler, D. L., Caswell, S., & Kiewra, K. (1998). Six approaches to the assessment of career maturity. *Journal of Counseling & Development, 76*, 475–482.

Lewin, K. (1935). *A dynamic theory of personality: Selected papers.* New York: McGraw-Hill.

Lichtenberger, E. O., & Kaufman, A. S. (1998). Assessment Battery for Children (K-ABC). In R. J. Samuda, R. Feuerstein, A. S. Kaufman, J. E. Lewis, R. J. Sternberg, & Associates (Eds.), *Advances in cross-cultural assessment* (pp. 56–99). Thousand Oaks, CA: Sage.

Loesch, L. C., & Vacc, N. A. (1993). *A work behavior analysis of professional counselors.* Greensboro, NC: National Board for Certified Counselors.

Lonner, W. J., & Ibrahim, F. A. (1996). Assessment in cross-cultural counseling. In P. Pederson & J. G. Draguns (Eds.), *Counseling across cultures* (pp. 293–322). Thousand Oaks, CA: Sage.

Lonner, W. J., & Sundberg, N. D. (1987). Assessment in cross-cultural counseling and therapy. In P. Pederson (Ed.), *Handbook of cross-cultural counseling and therapy* (pp. 199–205). New York: Praeger.

LoVerde, M., McMahon, B. T., & Morris, G. W. (1992). Employment testing and evaluation. In N. Hablutzel & B. T. McMahon (Eds.), *The Americans With Disabilities Act: Access and accommodations* (pp. 79–88). Orlando, FL: Paul M. Deutsch Press.

Lovitt, R. (1998). Teaching assessment skills in internship settings. In L. Handler & M. J. Hilsenroth (Eds.), *Teaching and learning personality assessment* (pp. 471–484). Mahwah, NJ: Erlbaum.

Lubinski, D., Benbow, C. P., & Ryan, J. (1995). Stability of vocational interests among the intellectually gifted from adolescence to adulthood: A 15-year longitudinal study. *Journal of Applied Psychology, 80*, 196–200.

Lucas, J. L., Wanberg, C. R., & Zytowski, D. G. (1997). Development of a career task self-efficacy scale: The Kuder Task Self-Efficacy Scale. *Journal of Vocational Behavior, 50*, 432–459.

Luria, A. R. (1980). *Higher cortical functions in man* (2nd ed.). New York: Basic Books.

Lustman, P. J., Sowa, C. J., & O'Hara, D. J. (1984). Factors influencing college student health: Development of the Psychological Distress Inventory. *Journal of Counseling Psychology, 31*, 28–35.

Luzzo, D. A. (1996). A psychometric evaluation of the Career Decision-Making Self-Efficacy Scale. *Journal of Counseling & Development, 74*, 276–279.

Maccoby, E. E., & Jacklin, C. N. (1974). *The psychology of sex differences.* Stanford, CA: United Press.

REFERENCES

Maddox, T. (Ed.). (1997). *Tests: A comprehensive reference for assessments in psychology, education, and business* (4th ed.). Kansas City, MO: Test Corporation of America.

Maloney, M. P., & Ward, M. P. (1976). *Psychological assessment: A conceptual approach.* New York: Oxford University Press.

Marchetti-Mercer, M. C., & Cleaver, G. (2000). Genograms and family sculpting: An aid to cross-cultural understanding in the training of psychology students in South Africa. *Counseling Psychologist, 28,* 61–80.

Mariani, M. (1999). Replace with a database: O*NET replaces the Dictionary of Occupational Titles. *Occupational Outlook Quarterly, 43*(1), 3–9.

Marks, I. M., & Mathews, A. M. (1978). Brief standard self-rating for phobic patients. *Behavior Research and Therapy, 17,* 263–267.

Marlatt, G. A., & Miller, W. R. (1984). *Comprehensive Drinking Profile.* Odessa, FL: Psychological Assessment Resources.

Maslow, A. H. (1987). *Motivation and personality* (3rd ed.). New York: Harper & Row.

McAllister, L. W. (1996). *A practical guide to CPI interpretation* (3rd ed.). Palo Alto, CA: Consulting Psychologists Press.

McCarney, S. B., & Anderson, P. D. (1996). *Adult Attention Deficit Disorders Evaluation Scale.* Columbia, MO: Hawthorne Educational Services.

McCloy, R., Waugh, G., Medsker, G., Wall, J., Rivkin, D., & Lewis, P. (1999). *Determining the occupational reinforcer patterns for O*NET occupational units* (Vol. I). Raleigh, NC: National Center for O*NET Development.

McCrae, R. R., & Costa, P. T. (1986). Clinical assessment can benefit from recent advances in personality psychology. *American Psychologist, 41,* 1001–1003.

McCrae, R. R., & Costa, P. T. (1997). Personality trait structure as a human universal. *American Psychologist, 52,* 509–516.

McDivitt, P. J. (1994). Using portfolios for career assessment. In J. T. Kapes, M. M. Mastie, & E. A. Whitfield (Eds.), *A counselor's guide to career assessment instruments* (pp. 423–434). Alexandria, VA: National Career Development Association.

McGoldrick, M., & Gerson, R. (1985). *Genograms in family assessment.* New York: Norton.

McLellan, A. T., Kushner, H., Metzger, D., Peters, R., Smith, I., Grissom, G., Pettinati, H., & Argeriou, M. (1992). The fifth edition of the Addiction Severity Index: Reliability and validity in three centers. *Journal of Nervous and Mental Disease, 173,* 412–423.

McNulty, J. L., Graham, J. R., Ben-Porath, Y. S., & Stein, L. A. R. (1997). Comparative validity of MMPI-2 scores of African American and

Caucasian mental health center clients. *Psychological Assessment, 9*, 464–470.

Mehrens, W. A. (1994). Review of Kuder General Interest Survey, Form E (KGIS). In J. T. Kapes, M. M. Mastie, & E. A. Whitfield (Eds.), *A counselor's guide to career assessment instruments* (pp. 189–193). Alexandria, VA: National Career Development Association.

Mehrens, W. A. (1998). Review of the Iowa Tests of Educational Development. In J. C. Impara & B. S. Plake (Eds.), *The thirteenth mental measurements yearbook* (pp. 547–550). Lincoln, NE: Buros Institute of Mental Measurements.

Mendelsohn, G. A., & Kirk, B. A. (1962). Personality differences not used. *Journal of Counseling Psychology, 9*, 341–346.

Messick, S. (1980). Test validity and the ethics of assessment. *American Psychologist, 35*, 1012–1027.

Messick, S. (1995). Validity of psychological assessment: Validation of inferences from person's responses and performances as scientific inquiry into score meaning. *American Psychologist, 50*, 741–749.

Meyer, G. J., Finn, S. E., Eyde, L. D., Kay, G. G., Moreland, K. L., Dies, R. R., Eisman, E. J., Kubiszyn, T. W., & Reed, G. M. (2001). Psychological testing and psychological assessment: A review of evidence and issues. *American Psychologist, 56*, 128–165.

Meyer, P., & Davis, S. (1992). *The CPI applications guide: An essential tool for individual, group, and organizational development*. Palo Alto, CA: Consulting Psychologists Press.

Michael, W. B., Michael, J. J., & Zimmerman, W. S. (1988). *Study Attitudes and Methods Survey, manual of instructions and interpretations*. San Diego, CA: EdITS.

Miller, W. R., & Munoz, R. F. (1982). *How to control your drinking: A practical guide to responsible drinking* (Rev. ed.). Albuquerque: University of New Mexico Press.

Millon, T. (1990). *Toward a new personology: An evolutionary model*. New York: Wiley-Interscience.

Millon, T. (1995). *Millon Index of Personality Styles manual*. San Antonio, TX: Psychological Corporation.

Millon, T., & Davis, R. D. (1993). The Millon Adolescent Personality Inventory and the Millon Adolescent Clinical Inventory. *Journal of Counseling & Development, 71*, 570–574.

Millon, T., Millon, C., & Davis, R. (1994). *Millon Clinical Multiaxial Inventory–III: Manual for MCMI-III*. Minneapolis, MN: National Computer Systems.

Mintz, L. B., & O'Halloran, M. S. (2000). The Eating Attitudes Test: Validation with DSM-IV eating disorder criteria. *Journal of Personality Assessment, 74*, 489–503.

Mintz, L. B., O'Halloran, M. S., Mulholland, A. M., & Schneider, P. A. (1997). Questionnaire for Eating Disorder Diagnoses: Reliability and validity of operationalizing DSM-IV criteria into a self-report format. *Journal of Counseling Psychology, 44,* 63–79.

Mitchell, L. K., & Krumboltz, J. D. (1987). The effects of cognitive restructuring and decision-making training on career indecision. *Journal of Counseling & Development, 66,* 171–174.

Moore, W. S. (1988). *The Measure of Intellectual Development: An instrument manual.* Farmville, VA: Center for the Study of Intellectual Development.

Moos, R. H. (1974). *The social climate scales: An overview.* Palo Alto, CA: Consulting Psychologists Press.

Moos, R. H. (1976). *The human context: Environmental determinants of behavior.* New York: Wiley.

Moos, R. H., & Moos, B. S. (1994a). *Family Environment Scale manual: Development, application and research.* Palo Alto, CA: Consulting Psychologists Press.

Moos, R. H., & Moos, B. S. (1994b). *Life Stressors and Social Resources Inventory–Adult Form.* Odessa, FL: Psychological Assessment Resources.

Moos, R. H., & Moos, B. S. (1994c). *Life Stressors and Social Resources Inventory–Youth Form.* Odessa, FL: Psychological Assessment Resources.

Moreland, K. L., Eyde, L. D., Robertson, G. J., Primoff, E. S., & Most, R. B. (1995). Assessment of test user qualifications: A research-based measurement procedure. *American Psychologist, 50,* 14–23.

Morey, L. (1991). *Personality Assessment Inventory: Professional manual.* Odessa, FL: Psychological Assessment Resources.

Morey, L. (1998). *A user's guide: Personality Assessment Screener.* Odessa, FL: Psychological Assessment Resources.

Morrison, J. (1995a). *DSM-IV made easy: The clinician's guide to diagnosis.* New York: Guilford Press.

Morrison, J. (1995b). *The first interview: Revised for DSM-IV.* New York: Guilford Press.

Muhs, W. F., Popp, G. E., & Patterson, H. F. (1979). The Mexican-American in higher education: Implications for educators. *Personnel and Guidance Journal, 58,* 20–24.

Mulholland, A. M., & Mintz, L. B. (2001). Prevalence of eating disorders among African American women. *Journal of Counseling Psychology, 48,* 111–116.

Murphy, L. L., Impara, J. C., & Plake, B. S. (1999). *Tests in print V* (Vols. 1–2). Lincoln, NE: Buros Institute of Mental Measurements.

Murray, B. (1998, April). Getting smart about learning is her lesson. *APA Monitor, 29,* 36.

Murray, H. A. (1938). *Explorations in personality.* New York: Oxford University Press.

Murray, H. A. (1943). *Thematic Apperception Test manual*. Cambridge, MA: Harvard University Press.

Myers, I. B., Kirby, L. K., & Myers, K. D. (1998). *Introduction to type*. Palo Alto, CA: Consulting Psychologists Press.

Myers, I. B., McCaulley, M. H., Quenk, N. L., & Hammer, A. L. (1998). *MBTI manual: A guide to the development and use of the Myers–Briggs Type Indicator* (3rd ed.). Palo Alto, CA: Consulting Psychologists Press.

Myers, I. B., & Myers, P. B. (1995). *Gifts differing*. Palo Alto, CA: Davies-Black.

Nagayama Hall, G. C., Bansal, A., & Lopez, I. R. (1999). Ethnicity and psychopathology: A meta-analytic review of 31 years of comparative MMPI/MMPI-2 research. *Psychological Assessment, 11*, 186–197.

Naglieri, J. A. (1996). *Naglieri Nonverbal Ability Test–Multilevel Form*. San Antonio, TX: Psychological Corporation.

Naglieri, J. A. (1999). *Essentials of CAS assessment*. Odessa, FL: Psychological Assessment Resources.

Naglieri, J. A. (2000). *Naglieri Nonverbal Ability Test: Individual administration*. San Antonio, TX: Psychological Corporation.

Naglieri, J. A., & Ronning, M. W. (2000). Comparison of White, African American, Hispanic, and Asian children on the Naglieri Nonverbal Ability Test. *Psychological Assessment, 12*, 328–334.

National Board of Certified Counselors. (1997a). *Ethical standards for National Board of Certified Counselors*. Alexandria, VA: Author.

National Board of Certified Counselors. (1997b). National Board of Certified Counselors Code of Ethics. [On-line]. Available: www.nbcc.org.

National Career Assessment Services. (2000). *Kuder tutor: Administration and interpretation of the Kuder Career Search with Person Match* [On-line]. Available: www.kuder.com/KuderTutor/

National Career Assessment Services. (2001). *Kuder Electronic Career Portfolio* [On-line]. Available: www.ncasi.com/kcps.asp

National Career Development Association. (1997). *NCDA guidelines for the use of the Internet for provision of career information and planning services* [On-line]. Available: www.ncda.org.

National Center for O*NET Development. (2001). *O*NET online* [On-line]. Available: http://online.onetcenter.org/

National Consortium of State Career Guidance Supervisors. (1999, Fall). Career planning and the Internet: Picking your path through the World Wide Web. *National Career Guidance News*, pp. 9–13.

National Institute of Mental Health. (1999, December). *Suicide facts* [On-line]. Available: http://www.nimh.nih.gov/research/suifact.htm

National Mental Health Association. (1999). *Depression-screening.org* [On-line]. Available: http://www.depression-screening.org/

Naugle, R. I., Chelune, G. J., & Tucker, G. D. (1993). Validity of the Kaufman Brief Intelligence Test. *Psychological Assessment, 5,* 182–186.

Naylor, F. D., & Krumboltz, J. D. (1994). The independence of aptitudes, interests, and beliefs. *Career Development Quarterly, 43,* 152–160.

Neimeyer, G. J. (1989). Applications of repertory grid technique to vocational assessment. *Journal of Counseling & Development, 67,* 585–589.

Neisser, V. (1998). *The rising curve: Long-term gains in IQ and related measures.* Washington, DC: American Psychological Association.

Neisser, V., Boodoo, G., Bouchardt, T. J., Boykin, A. W., Brody, N., Ceci, S. J., Halpern, D. F., Loehlin, J. C., Perloff, R., Sternberg, R. J., & Urbina, S. (1996). Intelligence: Knowns and unknowns. *American Psychologist, 51,* 77–101.

Nevill, D. D., & Calvert, P. D. (1996). Career assessment and the Salience Inventory. *Journal of Career Assessment, 4,* 312–399.

Nevill, D. D., & Kruse, S. J. (1996). Career assessment and the Values Scale. *Journal of Career Assessment, 4,* 383–397.

Nevill, D. D., & Super, D. E. (1986a). *Manual for the Salience Inventory.* Palo Alto, CA: Consulting Psychologists Press.

Nevill, D. D., & Super, D. E. (1986b). *Manual for the Values Scale.* Palo Alto, CA: Consulting Psychologists Press.

New England Medical Center. (2000). *The Mini Mental State Examination* [On-line]. Available: http://www.nemc.org/psych/mmsc.asp.

Nezu, A. M., & Nezu, C. M. (1993). Identifying and selecting target problems for clinical interventions: A problem-solving model. *Psychological Assessment, 5,* 254–263.

Nezu, A. M., Ronan, G. F., Meadows, E. A., & McClure, K. S. (Eds.). (2000). *Practitioner's guide to empirically based measures of depression.* New York: Kluwer Academic/Plenum.

Nicholson, C. L., & Hibpshman, T. L. (1998). *Manual, Slosson Intelligence Test–Revised.* East Aurora, NY: Slosson Educational.

Niv, N., Kaplan, Z., Mitrani, E., & Shiang, J. (1998). Validity study of the EDI-2 in Israeli population. *Israel Journal of Psychiatry and Related Sciences, 35,* 287–292.

Noble, J., Davenport, M., Schiel, J., & Pommerich, M. (1999). *High school academic and noncognitive variables related to the ACT scores of racial/ethnic groups.* Iowa City, IA: American College Testing Program.

Norris, L., & Cochran, D. J. (1977). The SIGI prediction system: Predicting college grades with and without tests. *Measurement and Evaluation in Guidance, 10,* 134–140.

Novy, D. M., Nelson, D. V., Goodwin, J., & Rowzee, R. D. (1993). Psychometric comparability of the State–Trait Anxiety Inventory for different ethnic populations. *Psychological Assessment, 5,* 343–349.

REFERENCES

Okocha, A. A. G. (1998). Using qualitative appraisal strategies in career counseling. *Journal of Employment Counseling, 35,* 151–159.

Osborne, W. L., Brown, S., Niles, S., & Miner, C. U. (1997). *Career development, assessment, and counseling: Applications of the Donald E. Super C-DAC approach.* Alexandria, VA: American Counseling Association.

Osgood, C. E., & Tzeng, O. C. S. (Eds.). (1990). *Language, meaning, and culture: The selected papers of C. E. Osgood.* New York: Praeger.

Osipow, S. H. (1987). *Manual for the Career Decision Scale* (Rev. ed.). Odessa, FL: Psychological Assessment Resources.

Osipow, S. H., & Gati, I. (1998). Construct and concurrent validity of the Career Decision-Making Difficulties Questionnaire. *Journal of Career Assessment, 6,* 347–364.

Osipow, S. H., & Winer, J. L. (1996). The use of the Career Decision Scale in career assessment. *Journal of Career Assessment, 4,* 117–130.

Othmer, E., & Othmer, S. C. (1994). *The clinical interview using DSM-IV: Vol. 1. Fundamentals.* Washington, DC: American Psychiatric Press.

Otis, A. S., & Lennon, R. T. (1996). *Otis–Lennon School Ability Test, Seventh Edition: Preliminary technical manual.* San Antonio, TX: Psychological Corporation.

Owens, W. A. (1983). Background data. In M. D. Dunnette (Ed.), *Handbook of industrial and organizational psychology* (pp. 609–644). New York: Wiley.

Pace, C. R. (1987). *CSEQ: Test manual and norms.* Los Angeles: University of California, Los Angeles, Center for the Study of Evaluations.

Pace, C. R., & Kuh, G. D. (1998). *College Student Experiences Questionnaire.* Bloomington: Indiana University Center for Postsecondary Research and Planning.

Paniagua, F. A. (1998). *Assessing and treating culturally diverse clients.* Thousand Oaks, CA: Sage.

Panksepp, J. (1998). Attention deficit hyperactivity disorders, psychostimulants, and intolerance of childhood playfulness: A tragedy in the making? *Current Directions in Psychological Science, 7,* 91–98.

Parker, J., & Hood, A. B. (1997). The Parker Cognitive Development Inventory. In A. B. Hood (Ed.), *The Iowa student development inventories* (2nd ed., pp. 109–133). Iowa City, IA: Hitech Press.

Parks, C. W., Jr., & Hollon, S. D. (1988). Cognitive assessment. In A. S. Bellack & M. Hersen (Eds.), *Behavioral assessment: A practical handbook* (pp. 161–212). New York: Pergamon.

Parsons, F. (1909). *Choosing a vocation.* Boston: Houghton-Mifflin.

Patterson, W. M., Dohn, H. H., Bird, J., & Patterson, G. A. (1983). Evaluation of suicidal patients: The SAD PERSONS Scale. *Psychosomatics, 24,* 343–349.

Pearman, R. P., & Albritton, S. C. (1997). *I'm not crazy, I'm just not you.* Palo Alto, CA: Davies-Black.

Pekarik, G. (1988). Relation of counselor identification of client problem description to continuance in a behavioral weight loss program. *Journal of Counseling Psychology, 35,* 66–70.

Penick, N. (2000). The genogram technique. In N. Peterson & R. C. Gonzales (Eds.), *Career counseling models for diverse populations* (pp. 137–149). Pacific Grove, CA: Brooks/Cole.

Perry, W. (1970). *Forms of intellectual and ethical development in college years: A scheme.* New York: Holt, Rinehart & Winston.

Peruzzi, N., & Bongar, B. (1999). Assessing risk for completed suicide in patients with major depression: Psychologists' views of critical factors. *Professional Psychology: Research and Practice, 30,* 576–580.

Peterson, C., & Austin, J. T. (1985). Review of Coopersmith Self-Esteem Inventories. In J. V. Mitchell, Jr. (Ed.), *The ninth mental measurements yearbook* (pp. 396–397). Lincoln, NE: Buros Institute of Mental Measurements.

Peterson, G. W. (1998). Using a vocational card sort as an assessment of occupational knowledge. *Journal of Career Assessment, 6,* 49–67.

Peterson, N. G., Mumford, M. D., Borman, W. C., Jeanneret, P. R., & Fleishman, E. A. (Eds.). (1999). *An occupational information system for the 21st century: The development of O*NET.* Washington, DC: American Psychological Association.

Piaget, J. (1965). *The moral judgment of the child.* New York: Free Press.

Pickering, J. W. (1998). Test review: Career Thoughts Inventory (CTI). *AAC Newsnotes, 33*(1), 5–6.

Piers, E. B., & Harris, D. B. (1996). *Piers–Harris Children's Self-Concept Scale, Revised manual.* Los Angeles: Western Psychological Services.

Piotrowski, C. (2000). How popular is the Personality Assessment Inventory in practice and training? *Psychological Reports, 86,* 65–66.

Pittenger, D. J. (1993). The utility of the Myers–Briggs Type Indicator. *Review of Educational Research, 63,* 467–488.

Plake, B. S., & Impara, J. C. (Eds.). (2001). *The fourteenth mental measurements yearbook.* Lincoln, NE: Buros Institute of Mental Measurements.

Plake, B. S., & Parker, C. S. (1982). The development and validation of a revised version of the Mathematics Anxiety Rating Scale. *Educational and Psychological Measurement, 42,* 551–557.

Pledge, D. S., Lapan, R. T., Heppner, P. P., Kivlighan, D., & Roehlke, H. J. (1998). Stability and severity of presenting problems at a university counseling center: A 6-year analysis. *Professional Psychology: Research and Practice, 29,* 386–389.

Podar, I., Hannus, A., & Allik, J. (1999). Personality and affectivity characteristics associated with eating disorders: A comparison of eating disor-
dered, weight-preoccupied, and normal samples. *Journal of Personality
Assessment, 73*, 133–147.

Polanski, P. J., & Hinkle, J. S. (2000). The mental status examination: Its use
by professional counselors. *Journal of Counseling & Development, 78*,
357–364.

Pollak, J., Levy, S., & Breitholtz, T. (1999). Screening for medical and neu-
rodevelopmental disorders for the professional counselor. *Journal of Counseling & Development, 77*, 350–358.

Ponterotto, J. G., Pace, T. M., & Kavan, M. G. (1989). A counselor's guide
to the assessment of depression. *Journal of Counseling & Development,
67*, 301–309.

Ponterotto, J. G., Rivera, L., & Sueyoshi, L. A. (2000). The career-in-culture
interview: A semi-structured protocol for the cross-cultural intake interview. *Career Development Quarterly, 49*, 85–96.

Powers, D. E., & Rock, D. A. (1998). *Effects of coaching on SAT-I: Reasoning scores* (Report No. 988-6). New York: College Board.

Prediger, D. (Ed.). (1972). Symposium: Tests and counseling—The marriage
that failed? *Measurement and Evaluation in Guidance, 5*, 395–429.

Prediger, D. J. (1988). Review of Assessment of Career Decision Making. In
J. T. Kapes & M. M. Mastie (Eds.), *A counselor's guide to career assess-
ment instruments* (2nd ed., pp. 165–169). Alexandria, VA: National
Career Development Association.

Prediger, D. J. (1994a). Multicultural assessment standards: A compilation
for counselors. *Measurement and Evaluation in Counseling and Development, 27*, 68–73.

Prediger, D. J. (1994b). Tests and counseling: The marriage that prevailed.
Measurement and Evaluation in Counseling and Development, 26,
227–234.

Prediger, D. J., & Swaney, K. B. (1992). *Career counseling validity of
DISCOVER's job cluster scales for the revised ASVAB score report*
(Report No. 92-2). Iowa City, IA: American College Testing Program.

Prieto, L. R., McNeill, B. W., Walls, R. G., & Gomez, S. P. (2001). Chicanas/os
and mental health services: An overview of utilization, counselor preference and assessment issues. *The Counseling Psychologist, 29*, 18–54.

Prince, J. P. (1998). Interpreting the Strong Interest Inventory: A case study.
Career Development Quarterly, 46, 339–346.

Prochaska, J. O., DiClemente, C. C., & Norcross, J. C. (1992). In search of
how people change: Applications to addictive behaviors. *American Psychologist, 47*, 1102–1114.

Provost, J. A., & Anchors, S. (1987). *Applications of the Myers–Briggs Type Indicator in higher education*. Palo Alto, CA: Consulting Psychologists Press.

Pryor, R. G., & Taylor, N. B. (1986). On combining scores from interest and value measures for counseling. *Vocational Guidance Quarterly, 34*, 178–187.

Psychological Assessment Resources. (1998). *Self-Directed Search* [On-line]. Available: http://www.self-directed-search.com/

Psychological Corporation. (1991). *Miller Analogies Test technical manual*. San Antonio, TX: Author.

Psychological Corporation. (1992). *Differential Aptitude Tests manual* (5th ed.). San Antonio, TX: Author.

Psychological Corporation. (1994). *Miller Analogies Test candidate information booklet*. San Antonio: TX: Author.

Pyle, K. R. (1984). Career counseling and computers: Where is the creativity? *Journal of Counseling & Development, 63*, 141–144.

Quinn, M. T., Lewis, R. J., & Fischer, K. L. (1992). A cross-correlation of the Myers–Briggs and Keirsey instruments. *Journal of College Student Development, 33*, 279–280.

Randahl, G. J., Hansen, J. C., & Haverkamp, B. E. (1993). Instrumental behaviors following test administration and interpretation: Exploration validity of the Strong Interest Inventory. *Journal of Counseling & Development, 71*, 435–439.

Raths, L., Harmin, M., & Simon, S. (1978). *Values and teaching: Working with values in the classroom* (2nd ed.). Columbus, OH: Charles E. Merrill.

Raven, J. C., Court, J. H., & Raven, J. (1993). *Manual for Raven's Progressive Matrices and Vocabulary Scales*. San Antonio, TX: Psychological Corporation.

Rayman, J. R. (1976). Sex and the Single Interest Inventory: The empirical validation of sex-balanced interest inventory items. *Journal of Counseling Psychology, 23*, 239–246.

Reardon, R. C., Lenz, J. G., Sampson, J. P., & Peterson, G. W. (2000). *Career development and planning: A comprehensive approach*. Belmont, CA: Wadsworth.

Reardon, R. C., & Wright, L. K. (1999). The case of Mandy: Applying Holland's theory and cognitive information processing theory. *Career Development Quarterly, 47*, 195–203.

Regier, D. A., Boyd, J. H., Burke, J. D., Rae, D. S., Myers, J. K., Kramer, M., Robins, L. N., George, L. K., Karno, M., & Locke, B. Z. (1988). One-month prevalence of mental disorders in the United States. *Archives of General Psychiatry, 45*, 977–986.

REFERENCES

Rehabilitation Act of 1973, 29 U.S.C. Pub. L. No. 93-112 87 Stat 355.

Renzulli, J. S., & Smith, L. H. (1978). *Learning Styles Inventory: A measure of student preference for instructional techniques*. Mansfield Center, CT: Creative Learning Press.

Rest, J. R. (1974). *Manual for the Defining Issues Test*. (Available from J. R. Rest, 330 Burton Hall, University of Minnesota, Minneapolis, MN 55455)

Rest, J. R. (1979). *Development in judging moral issues*. Minneapolis: University of Minnesota Press.

Reynolds, C. R., & Bigler, E. D. (2000). *CASE/CASE–SF professional manual*. Odessa, FL: Psychological Assessment Resources.

Reynolds, C. R., & Kamphaus, R. W. (1992). *Behavior Assessment System for Children*. Circle Pines, MN: American Guidance Services.

Reynolds, W. M., & Kobak, K. A. (1995). *Professional manual for Hamilton Depression Inventory: A self-report version of the Hamilton Depression Rating Scale*. Odessa, FL: Psychological Assessment Resources.

Ridley, C. S., Li, L. C., & Hill, C. L. (1998). Multicultural assessment: Reexamination, reconceptualization, and practical application. *The Counseling Psychologist, 26*, 827–910.

Riverside Publishing Co. (1994). *Technical summary I, Riverside 2000 Cognitive Abilities Test*. Chicago: Author.

Robins, L. N., Heizer, J. E., Weissman, M. M., Orvaschel, H., Gruenberg, E., Burke, J. D., & Regier, D. A. (1984). Lifetime prevalence of specific psychiatric disorders in three sites. *Archives of General Psychiatry, 41*, 949–958.

Robinson, J. P., Shaver, P. R., & Wrightsman, L. S. (Eds.). (1991). *Measures of personality and social psychological attitudes: Vol. 1. Measures of social psychological attitudes series*. San Diego, CA: Academic Press.

Rogers, J. R., Alexander, R. A., & Subich, L. M. (1994). Development and psychometric analysis of the Suicide Assessment Checklist. *Journal of Mental Health Counseling, 16*, 352–368.

Rokeach, M. (1973). *The nature of human values*. New York: Free Press.

Rollock, D., & Terrell, M. D. (1996). Multicultural issues in assessment: Toward an inclusive model. In J. L. DeLucia-Waack (Ed.), *Multicultural counseling competencies: Implications for training and practice* (pp. 113–153). Alexandria, VA: Association for Counselor Education and Supervision.

Rosen, D., Holmberg, K., & Holland, J. L. (1994). *The educational opportunities finder*. Odessa, FL: Psychological Assessment Resources.

Rosen, J. C., Silberg, N. T., & Gross, J. (1988). Eating Attitudes Test and Eating Disorders Inventory: Norms for adolescent girls and boys. *Journal of Consulting and Clinical Psychology, 56*, 305–308.

Rosenthal, R. (1990). How are we doing in soft psychology? *American Psychologist, 45,* 775–776.

Rosnow, R. L., & Rosenthal, R. (1988). Focused tests of significance and effect size estimation in counseling psychology. *Journal of Counseling Psychology, 35,* 203–208.

Rotter, J. B., Lah, M. I., & Rafferty, J. E. (1992). *Manual for the Rotter Incomplete Sentence Blank, Second Edition.* San Antonio, TX: Psychological Corporation.

Rounds, J. B. (1989). Review of the Career Assessment Inventory. In J. C. Conoley & J. J. Kramer (Eds.), *Tenth mental measurements yearbook* (pp. 139–141). Lincoln, NE: Buros Institute of Mental Measurements.

Rounds, J. B. (1990). The comparative and combined utility of work value and interest data in career counseling with adults. *Journal of Vocational Behavior, 37,* 32–45.

Rounds, J. B., Jr., Henly, G. A., Dawis, R. V., Lofquist, L. H., & Weiss, D. J. (1981). *Manual for the Minnesota Importance Questionnaire: A measure of vocational needs and values.* Minneapolis: University of Minnesota, Department of Psychology.

Rounds, J., Smith, T., Hubert, L., Lewis, P., & Rivkin, D. (1999). *Development of Occupational Interest Profiles for O*NET.* Raleigh, NC: National Center for O*NET Development.

Russell, M., & Karol, D. (1993). *16-PF, Fifth Edition, administrator's manual.* Champaign, IL: Institute for Personality and Ability Testing.

Sackett, P. R., Schmitt, N., Ellingson, J. E., & Kabin, M. B. (2001). High-stakes testing in employment, credentialing, and higher education. *American Psychologist, 56,* 302–318.

Sackett, S. A., & Hansen, J. C. (1995). Vocational outcomes of college freshmen with flat profiles on the Strong Interest Inventory. *Measurement and Evaluation in Counseling and Development, 28,* 9–24.

Sampson, J. P. (1990). Computer-assisted testing and the goals of counseling psychology. *The Counseling Psychologist, 18,* 227–239.

Sampson, J. P., Jr. (2000). Computer applications. In C. E. Watkins, Jr. & V. L. Campbell (Eds.), *Using tests and assessment procedures in counseling* (2nd ed., pp. 517–544). Hillsdale, NJ: Erlbaum.

Sampson, J. P., Jr., Peterson, G. W., Lenz, J. G., Reardon, R. C., & Saunders, D. E. (1996). *Career Thoughts Inventory: Professional manual.* Odessa, FL: Psychological Assessment Resources.

Sampson, J. P., Jr., Peterson, G. W., Reardon, R. C., & Lenz, J. G. (2000). Using readiness assessment to improve career services: A cognitive information-processing approach. *Career Development Quarterly, 49,* 146–174.

Samuda, R. J. (1998a). Cross-cultural assessment: Issues and alternatives. In R. J. Samuda, R. Feuerstein, A. S. Kaufman, J. E. Lewis, R. J. Sternberg, & Associates (Eds.), *Advances in cross-cultural assessment* (pp. 1–19). Thousand Oaks, CA: Sage.

Samuda, R. J. (1998b). *Psychological testing of American minorities: Issues and consequences* (2nd ed.). Thousand Oaks, CA: Sage.

Sandoval, J. (1998). Testing in a changing world. In J. Sandoval, C. L. Frisby, K. F. Geisinger, J. D. Scheuneman, & J. R. Grenier (Eds.), *Test interpretation and diversity* (pp. 3–16). Washington, DC: American Psychological Association.

Sandoval, J., Frisby, C. L., Geisinger, K. F., Scheuneman, J. D., & Grenier, J. R. (Eds.). (1998). *Test interpretation and diversity*. Washington, DC: American Psychological Association.

Sanford, E. E. (1995). Review of the Rokeach Value Survey. In J. C. Conoley & J. C. Impara (Eds.), *Twelfth mental measurements yearbook* (pp. 879–880). Lincoln, NE: Buros Institute of Mental Measurements.

Sarason, L. G. (Ed.). (1980). *Test anxiety: Theory, research, and applications.* Hillsdale, NJ: Erlbaum.

Sarason, I. G., Johnson, J. H., & Siegel, J. M. (1978). Assessing the impact of life changes: Development of the Life Experiences Survey. *Journal of Consulting and Clinical Psychology, 46,* 932–946.

Sattler, J. M. (1989). Vineland Adaptive Behavior Scales. In J. C. Conoley & J. J. Kramer (Eds.), *Tenth mental measurements yearbook* (pp. 878–881). Lincoln, NE: Buros Institute of Mental Measurements.

Saunders, J. B., Aasland, O. G., Amundsen, A., & Grant, M. (1993). Alcohol consumption and related problems among primary health care patients: WHO collaborative project on early detection of persons with harmful alcohol consumption, I. *Addiction, 88,* 349–362.

Savickas, M. L. (1990). The use of career choice process scales in counseling practice. In C. E. Watkins, Jr. & V. L. Campbell (Eds.), *Testing in counseling practice* (pp. 373–418). Hillsdale, NJ: Erlbaum.

Savickas, M. L. (1993). Career counseling in the postmodern era. *Journal of Cognitive Psychotherapy, 7,* 205–215.

Savickas, M. L. (1997). Career adaptability: An integrative construct for life-span, life-space theory. *Career Development Quarterly, 45,* 247–259.

Savickas, M. L. (2000). Assessing career decision making. In C. E. Watkins, Jr. & V. L. Campbell (Eds.), *Testing and assessment in counseling practice* (2nd ed., pp. 429–477). Mahwah, NJ: Erlbaum.

Savickas, M. L., Brizzi, J. S., Brisbin, L. A., & Pethtel, L. L. (1988). Predictive validity of two medical specialty preference inventories. *Measurement and Evaluation in Counseling and Development, 21,* 106–112.

Savickas, M. L., & Hartung, P. J. (1996). The Career Development Inventory in review: Psychometric and research findings. *Journal of Career Assessment, 4,* 171–188.

Schafer, W. D. (1998, January). *Survey of assessment and evaluation activities of school counselors: Assessment for change—Changes in assessment.* Symposium sponsored by Educational Resources Information Center, Association for Assessment in Counseling, and National Board for Certified Counselors, St. Petersburg, FL.

Scheuneman, J. D., & Oakland, T. (1998). High stakes testing in education. In J. Sandoval, C. L. Frisby, K. F. Geisinger, J. D. Scheuneman, & J. R. Grenier (Eds.), *Test interpretation and diversity* (pp. 77–104). Washington, DC: American Psychological Association.

Schinka, J. A. (1984). *Personal Problems Checklist–Adult.* Odessa, FL: Psychological Assessment Resources.

Schinka, J. A. (1985). *Personal Problems Checklist–Adolescent.* Odessa, FL: Psychological Assessment Resources.

Schmidt, F. L., & Hunter, J. E. (1998). The validity and utility of selection methods in personnel psychology. *Psychological Bulletin, 124,* 262–274.

Schoemaker, C., Verbraak, M., Breteler, R., & vanderStaak, C. (1997). The discriminant validity of the Eating Disorder Inventory–2. *British Journal of Clinical Psychology, 36,* 627–629.

Schoenrade, P. (1998). Review of the Values Scale, Second Edition. In J. C. Impara & B. S. Plake (Eds.), *The thirteenth mental measurements yearbook* (pp. 1114–1115). Lincoln, NE: Buros Institute of Mental Measurements.

Scholastic Testing Service. (1997). *Kuhlmann–Anderson tests manual of directions.* Bensenville, IL: Author.

Schuerger, J. M. (1992). The Sixteen Personality Factor Questionnaire and its junior versions. *Journal of Counseling & Development, 71,* 231–244.

Schuerger, J. M. (2000). The Sixteen Personality Factor Questionnaire (16PF). In C. E. Watkins, Jr. & V. L. Campbell (Eds.), *Testing and assessment in counseling practice* (2nd ed., pp. 73–110). Mahwah, NJ: Erlbaum.

Schutte, N. S., & Malouff, J. M. (1995). *Sourcebook of adult assessment strategies.* New York: Plenum.

Seligman, L. (1998). *Selecting effective treatments: A comprehensive, systematic guide to treating adult mental disorders* (Rev. ed.). San Francisco: Jossey-Bass.

Selzer, M. L. (1971). The Michigan Alcoholism Screening Test: The quest for a new diagnostic instrument. *American Journal of Psychiatry, 127,* 1653–1658.

Sewell, T. E. (1985). Review of Coopersmith Self-Esteem Inventories. In J. V. Mitchell, Jr. (Ed.), *The ninth mental measurements yearbook* (pp. 397–398). Lincoln, NE: Buros Institute of Mental Measurements.

473

Sharf, R. S. (1994). Review of the Assessment of Career Decision Making. In J. T. Kapes, M. M. Mastie, & E. A. Whitfields (Eds.), *A counselor's guide to career assessment instruments* (3rd ed., pp. 248–252). Alexandria, VA: National Career Development Association.

Shimizu, K., Vondracek, F. W., Schulenberg, J. E., & Hostetler, M. (1988). The factor structure of the Career Decision Scale: Similarities across selected studies. *Journal of Vocational Behavior, 32,* 213–225.

Shinn, M. R., & Shinn, M. M. (2000). Writing and evaluating IEP goals and making appropriate revisions to ensure participation and progress in the general curriculum. In C. F. Telzrow & M. Tankersley (Eds.), *IDEA Amendments of 1997: Practice guidelines for school-based teams* (pp. 351–382). Bethesda, MD: National Association of School Psychologists.

Shrauger, J. S., & Osberg, R. M. (1981). The relative accuracy of self-predictions and judgments by others in psychological assessment. *Psychological Bulletin, 90,* 322–351.

Singelis, T. M. (Ed.). (1998). *Teaching about culture, ethnicity, and diversity: Exercises and planned activities.* Thousand Oaks, CA: Sage.

Skinner, H. A., Steinhauer, P. D., & Santa-Barbara, J. (1995). *The Family Assessment Measure.* North Tonawanda, NY: Multi-Health Systems.

Slaney, R. B., & MacKinnon-Slaney, F. (2000). Using vocational card sorts in career counseling. In C. E. Watkins, Jr. & V. L. Campbell (Eds.), *Testing and assessment in counseling practice* (2nd ed., pp. 371–428). Mahwah, NJ: Erlbaum.

Smart, D. W., & Smart, J. F. (1997). DSM-IV and culturally sensitive diagnosis: Some observations for counselors. *Journal of Counseling & Development, 75,* 392–398.

Smart, R. M., & Peterson, C. C. (1994). Super's stages and the four-factor structure of the Adult Career Concerns Inventory in an Australian sample. *Measurement and Evaluation in Counseling and Development, 26,* 243–257.

Snyder, D. K. (1997). *Marriage Satisfaction Inventory manual.* Los Angeles: Western Psychological Services.

Sobell, M. B., Maisto, S. A., Sobell, L. C., Cooper, A. M., Cooper, T. C., & Sanders, B. (1980). Developing a prototype for evaluating alcohol treatment effectiveness. In L. C. Sobell, M. B. Sobell, & E. Ward (Eds.), *Evaluating alcohol and drug abuse treatment effectiveness: Recent advances* (pp. 129–150). New York: Pergamon.

Sparrow, S. S., Balla, D. A., & Cicchetti, D. V. (1985). *Vineland Adaptive Behavior Scales: Classroom edition manual.* Circle Pines, MN: American Guidance Service.

Spengler, P. M., Strohmer, D. C., Dixon, D. N., & Shivy, V. A. (1995). A scientist–practitioner model of psychological assessment: Implications for training, practice, and research. *The Counseling Psychologist, 23,* 506–534.

Spielberger, C. D. (1999). *State–Trait Anger Expression Inventory–2.* Odessa, FL: Psychological Assessment Resources.

Spielberger, C. D., Gorsuch, R. L., Lushene, R., Vagg, P. R., & Jacobs, G. A. (1983). *Manual for State–Trait Anxiety Inventory.* Palo Alto, CA: Consulting Psychologists Press.

Spielberger, C. D., Sydeman, S. J., Ritterband, L. M., Reheiser, E. C., & Unger, K. K. (1995). Assessment of emotional states and personality traits: Measuring psychological vital signs. In J. N. Butcher (Ed.), *Clinical personality assessment: Practical approaches* (pp. 42–58). New York: Oxford University Press.

Spitzer, R. L., Gibbon, M., Skodol, A. E., Williams, J. B. W., & First, M. B. (Eds.). (1994). *DSM-IV casebook: A learning companion to the Diagnostic and Statistical Manual of Mental Disorders, Fourth edition.* Washington, DC: American Psychiatric Association.

Spitzer, R. L., Williams, J. B. W., Kroenke, K., Linzer, M., de Gruy, F. V., III, Hahn, S. R., Brody, D., & Johnson, J. G. (1994). Utility of a new procedure for diagnosing mental disorders in primary care: The PRIME-MD 1000 study. *Journal of the American Medical Association, 272,* 1749–1756.

Spokane, A. R., & Catalano, M. (2000). The Self-Directed Search: A theory-driven array of self-guided career interventions. In C. E. Watkins, Jr. & V. L. Campbell (Eds.), *Testing and assessment in counseling practice* (2nd ed., pp. 339–370). Mahwah, NJ: Erlbaum.

Steenbarger, B. N., & Smith, H. B. (1996). Assessing the quality of counseling services: Developing accountable helping systems. *Journal of Counseling & Development, 75,* 145–150.

Stelmachers, Z. T. (1995). Assessing suicidal clients. In J. N. Butcher (Ed.), *Clinical personality assessment: Practical approaches* (pp. 367–379). New York: Oxford University Press.

Sternberg, R. J. (1985). *Beyond IQ.* Cambridge, England: Cambridge University Press.

Sternberg, R. J. (1987). *The triangle of love: Intimacy, passion, commitment.* New York: Basic Books.

Sternberg, R. J. (1988). *The triarchic mind.* New York: Viking Penguin.

Sternberg, R. J. (1998). All intelligence testing is "cross-cultural": Constructing intelligence tests to meet the demands of Person × Task × Situation interactions. In R. J. Samuda, R. Feuerstein, A. S. Kaufman, J. E. Lewis, R. J. Sternberg, & Associates (Eds.), *Advances in cross-cultural assessment* (pp. 192–217). Thousand Oaks, CA: Sage.

REFERENCES

Sternberg, R. J., Wagner, R. K., Williams, W. M., & Horvath, J. A. (1995). Testing common sense. *American Psychologist, 50,* 912–927.

Stewart, E. S., Greenstein, S. M., Holt, N. C., Henly, G. A., Engdahl, B. E., Dawis, R. V., Lofquist, L. H., & Weiss, D. J. (1986). *Occupational reinforcer patterns* (Rev. ed.). Minneapolis: University of Minnesota, Department of Psychology, Vocational Psychology Research.

Stuart, R. B., & Jacobson, B. (1987). *Couple's Precounseling Inventory, Revised edition.* Champaign, IL: Research Press.

Sturgis, E. T., & Gramling, S. (1988). Psychophysiological assessment. In A. S. Bellack & M. Hersen (Eds.), *Behavioral assessment: A practical handbook* (pp. 213–251). New York: Pergamon.

Sue, D. W. (1978). Work views and counseling. *Personnel and Guidance Journal, 56,* 458–462.

Sue, D. W. (1990). Barriers to effective cross-cultural counseling. In D. W. Sue & D. Sue (Eds.), *Counseling the culturally different: Theory and practice* (pp. 27–48). New York: Wiley.

Suicide Risk Advisory Committee, Risk Management Foundation, Harvard Medical Institutions. (1996). *Guidelines for identification, assessment, and treatment planning for suicidality* [On-line]. Available: http://www.rmf.harvard.edu/rmLibrary/clinical-guidelines/suicide/index.html.

Super, D. E. (1970). *Manual for the Work Values Inventory.* Boston: Houghton-Mifflin.

Super, D. E. (1990). A life-span, life-space approach to career development. In D. Brown & L. Brooks (Eds.), *Career choice and development: Applying contemporary theories to practice* (2nd ed., pp. 197–261). San Francisco: Jossey-Bass.

Super, D. E., & Thompson, A. S. (1979). A six-scale, two-factor measure of adolescent career or vocational maturity. *Vocational Guidance Quarterly, 28,* 6–15.

Super, D. E., Thompson, A. S., & Lindeman, R. H. (1988). *Adult Career Concerns Inventory: Manual for research and exploratory use in counseling.* Palo Alto, CA: Consulting Psychologists Press.

Sverko, B. (1995). The structure and hierarchy of values cross-nationally. In D. E. Super & B. Sverko (Eds.), *Life roles, values, and careers: International findings of the Work Importance Study* (pp. 225–240). San Francisco: Jossey-Bass.

Taber, B. J., & Luzzo, D. A. (1999). *A comprehensive review of research evaluating the effectiveness of DISCOVER in promoting career development* (Report No. 99-3). Iowa City, IA: ACT.

Taylor, R. M., & Morrison, W. L. (1996). *Taylor–Johnson Temperament Analysis test manual.* Los Angeles: Western Psychological Services.

476

REFERENCES

Technical Education Research Centers. (1977). *Guidance, counseling, and support services for high school students with physical disabilities.* Cambridge, MA: Author.

Teitelbaum, L., & Mullen, B. (2000). The validity of the MAST in psychiatric settings: A meta-analytic investigation. *Journal of Studies on Alcohol, 61,* 254–261.

Thomas, K. W., & Kilman, R. H. (1974). *Thomas–Kilman Conflict Mode Instrument.* Palo Alto, CA: Consulting Psychologists Press.

Thompson, A. S., Lindeman, R. H., Super, D. E., Jordaan, J. P., & Myers, R. A. (1981). *Career Development Inventory: Vol. 1. User's manual.* Palo Alto, CA: Consulting Psychologists Press.

Thompson, A. S., Lindeman, R. H., Super, D. E., Jordaan, J. P., & Myers, R. A. (1982). *Career Development Inventory: College and University Form. Supplement to user's manual.* Palo Alto, CA: Consulting Psychologists Press.

Thorndike, R. L., Hagen, E. P., & Sattler, J. M. (1986a). *The Stanford–Binet Intelligence Scale: Fourth edition, Guide for administering and scoring.* Chicago: Riverside.

Thorndike, R. L., Hagen, E. P., & Sattler, J. M. (1986b). *The Stanford–Binet Intelligence Scale: Fourth edition, Technical manual.* Chicago: Riverside.

Tieger, P. D., & Barron-Tieger, B. (2001). *Do what you are: Discover the perfect career through the secrets of personality type* (3rd ed.). Boston: Little-Brown.

Timbrook, R. E, & Graham, J. R. (1994). Ethnic differences on the MMPI-2? *Psychological Assessment, 6,* 212–217.

Todd, D. M., Deane, F. P., & McKenna, P. A. (1997). Appropriateness of SCL-90-R adolescent and adult norms for outpatient and nonpatient college students. *Journal of Counseling Psychology, 44,* 294–301.

Toman, S. M., & Savickas, M. L. (1997). Career choice readiness moderates the effects of interest inventory interpretation. *Journal of Career Assessment, 5,* 275–291.

Touliatos, J., Perlmutter, B. F., & Holdon, G. W. (Eds.). (2001). *Handbook of family measurement techniques.* Thousand Oaks, CA: Sage.

Tracey, T. J., & Rounds, J. (1999). Inference and attribution errors in test interpretation. In J. W. Lichtenberg & R. K. Goodyear (Eds.). *Scientist–practitioner perspectives on test interpretation* (pp. 113–131). Boston: Allyn & Bacon.

Tracey, T. J. G., & Schneider, P. L. (1995). An evaluation of the circular structure of the checklist of interpersonal transactions and the checklist of psychotherapy transactions. *Journal of Counseling Psychology, 42,* 496–507.

Tsai, D. C., & Pike, P. L. (2000). Effects of acculturation on the MMPI-2 scores of Asian American students. *Journal of Personality Assessment, 74,* 216–230.

Tucker, I. F., & Gillespie, B. V. (1993). Correlations among three measures of personality type. *Perceptual and Motor Skills, 77,* 650.

Ulett, G. (1994). *Rorschach introductory guide.* Los Angeles: Western Psychological Services.

Urbina, S. (1995). Review of Basic Personality Inventory. In J. C. Conoley & J. C. Impara (Eds.), *Twelfth mental measurements yearbook* (pp. 105–106). Lincoln, NE: Buros Institute of Mental Measurements.

U.S. Department of Defense, Defense Manpower Data Center. (1992). *Armed Services Vocational Aptitude Battery 18/19 counselor manual.* Monterey, CA: Author.

U.S. Department of Defense, Defense Manpower Data Center. (1994). *Technical manual for the ASVAB 18/19 Career Exploration Program.* Monterey, CA: Author.

U.S. Department of Defense, Defense Manpower Data Center. (1997). *Basic skills of career exploration: ASVAB Career Exploration Program* [On-line]. Available: http://www.dmdc.osd.mil/asvab/CareerExploration Program/

U.S. Department of Labor, Bureau of Labor Statistics. (2000). *Occupational outlook handbook: 2000–01 edition* [On-line]. Available: http://stats.bls.gov/ocohome.htm

U.S. Department of Labor, Employment and Training Administration. (2001). *O*NET career exploration tools* [On-line]. Available: http://www.doleta.gov/programs/onet/tools.asp

U.S. Public Health Service. (1999). *Mental health: A report of the Surgeon General* [On-line]. Available: http://www.mentalhealth.org/features/surgeongeneralreport/home.asp

Vacc, N. A., & Hinkle, J. S. (1994). Review of Career Assessment Inventory–Enhanced Version and Vocational Version (CAI-EV/CAI-VV). In J. T. Kapes, M. M. Mastie, & E. A. Whitfield (Eds.), *A counselor's guide to career assessment instruments* (pp. 145–150). Alexandria, VA: National Career Development Association.

Vacc, N. A., & Juhnke, G. A. (1997). The use of structured clinical interviews for assessment in counseling. *Journal of Counseling & Development, 75,* 470–480.

Vacc, N. A., Juhnke, G. A., & Nilsen, K. A. (2001). Community mental health service providers' codes of ethics and the standards for educational and psychological testing. *Journal of Counseling & Development, 79,* 217–224.

VanDenberg, T. F., Schmidt, J. A., & Kiesler, D. J. (1992). Interpersonal assessment in counseling and psychotherapy. *Journal of Counseling & Development, 71,* 84–90.

Vansickle, T. R. (1994). Review of Harrington–O'Shea Career Decision-Making System–Revised (CDM-R). In J. T. Kapes, M. M. Mastie, & E. A. Whitfield (Eds.), *A counselor's guide to career assessment instruments* (3rd ed., pp. 172–177). Alexandra, VA: National Career Development Association.

Vansickle, T. R., & Kapes, J. T. (1993). Comparing paper-pencil and computer-based versions of the Strong–Campbell Interest Inventory. *Computers in Human Behavior, 9,* 441–449.

Vernon, P. E. (1961). *The structure of human abilities* (Rev. ed.). London: Methuen.

Vilas, R. C. (1988). *Counseling outcome as related to MBTI client type, counselor type and counselor–client type similarity.* Unpublished doctoral dissertation, University of Iowa, Iowa City.

Vondracek, F. W., & Reitzle, M. (1998). The viability of career maturity theory: A developmental–contextual perspective. *Career Development Quarterly, 47,* 6–15.

Vonk, M. E., & Thyer, B. A. (1999). Evaluating the effectiveness of short-term treatment at a university counseling center. *Journal of Clinical Psychology, 55,* 1095–1106.

Vuchinich, R. E., Tucker, J. A., & Harllee, L. N. (1988). Behavioral assessment. In D. M. Dononvan & G. A. Marlart (Eds.), *Assessment of addictive behaviors* (pp. 51–83). New York: Guilford Press.

Waldinger, R. J. (1986). *Fundamentals of psychiatry.* Washington, DC: American Psychiatric Press.

Walker, C. E., & Kaufman, K. (1984). Review of State–Trait Anxiety Inventory for Children. In D. J. Keyser & R. C. Sweetland (Eds.), *Test critiques* (Vol. 2, pp. 633–640). Kansas City, MO: Test Corporation of America.

Walsh, W. B., & Betz, N. E. (2000). *Tests and assessment* (4th ed.). Englewood Cliffs, NJ: Prentice Hall.

Wang, L. (1995). Review of Differential Aptitude Tests (DAT). *Measurement and Evaluation in Counseling and Development, 28,* 168–170.

Watkins, C. E., Jr., Campbell, V. L., & Nieberding, R. (1994). The practice of vocational assessment by counseling psychologists. *The Counseling Psychologist, 22,* 115–128.

Watkins, C. E., Jr., Campbell, V. L., Nieberding, R., & Hallmark, R. (1995). Contemporary practice of psychological assessment by clinical psychologists. *Professional Psychology: Research and Practice, 26,* 54–60.

Wechsler, D. (1974). *Manual for the Wechsler Intelligence Scale for Children–Revised manual.* San Antonio, TX: Psychological Corporation.

Wechsler, D. (1981). *WAIS-R manual: Wechsler Adult Intelligence Scale–Revised manual.* San Antonio, TX: Psychological Corporation.

Wechsler, D. (1989). *Manual: Wechsler Preschool and Primary Scale of Intelligence.* San Antonio, TX: Psychological Corporation.

Wechsler, D. (1991). *Manual for the Wechsler Intelligence Scale for Children.* San Antonio, TX: Psychological Corporation.

Wechsler, D. (1997). *Wechsler Adult Intelligence Scale–Third Edition.* San Antonio, TX: Psychological Corporation.

Wechsler, D. (1999). *Wechsler Abbreviated Scale of Intelligence manual.* San Antonio, TX: Psychological Corporation.

Wechsler, D. (2001). *WIAT II examiner's manual.* San Antonio, TX: Psychological Corporation.

Wechsler, H., Davenport, A., Dowdall, G., Moeykens, B., & Castillo, S. (1994). Health and behavioral consequences of binge drinking in college: A national survey of students at 140 campuses. *Journal of the American Medical Association, 272,* 1672–1677.

Weinstein, C. E. (1987). *LASSI user's manual.* Clearwater, FL: H & H.

Weinstein, C. E., Palmer, D. R., & Schulte, A. C. (1987). *Learning and Study Strategies Inventory.* Clearwater, FL: H & H.

Weinstein, C. E., Palmer, D. R., & Schulte, A. C. (1997). *The E-LASSI for Windows.* Clearwater, FL: H & H.

Wells, C. F., & Carney, C. G. (1998). *Working well, living well: Discover the career within you* (5th ed.). Monterey, CA: Brooks/Cole.

Wells, M. G., Burlingame, G. M., Lambert, M. J., & Hoag, M. J. (1996). Conceptualization and measurement of patient change during psychotherapy: Development of the Outcome Questionnaire and Youth Outcome Questionnaire. *Psychotherapy, 33,* 275–283.

Werts, C. E., & Watley, D. J. (1969). A student's dilemma: Big fish–little pond or little fish–big pond. *Journal of Counseling Psychology, 16,* 14–19.

Westbrook, B. W. (1995). *Cognitive Vocational Maturity Test* (Rev. research ed.). Raleigh: North Carolina State University, Department of Psychology.

Westbrook, B. W., Elrod, T., & Wynne, C. (1996). Career assessment and the Cognitive Vocational Maturity Test. *Journal of Career Assessment, 4,* 139–170.

Westbrook, B. W., Sanford, E. E., Merwin, G. A., Fleenor, J., & Renzi, D. A. (1987). Reliability and construct validity of new measures of career maturity for 11th grade students. *Measurement and Evaluation in Counseling and Development, 20,* 18–26.

Westefeld, J. S., Range, L. M., Rogers, J. R., Maples, M. R., Bromley, J. L., & Alcorn, J. (2000). Suicide: An overview. *The Counseling Psychologist, 28,* 445–510.

Whiston, S. C. (2000). *Principles and applications of assessment in counseling.* Belmont, CA: Brooks/Cole.

Wickwire, P. N., & Faldet, B. (1994). Review of Career Occupational Preference System Interest Inventory (COPS). In J. T. Kapes, M. M. Mastie, & E. A. Whitfield (Eds.), *A counselor's guide to career assessment instruments* (pp. 156–161). Alexandria, VA: National Career Development Association.

Widiger, T. A., & Clark, L. A. (2000). Toward DSM-V and the classification of psychopathology. *Psychological Bulletin, 126,* 946–963.

Widiger, T. A., Mangine, S., Corbitt, E. M., Ellis, C. G., & Thomas, G. V. (1995). *Personality Disorder Interview–IV.* Odessa: FL: Psychological Assessment Resources.

Wiggins, J. S. (1993). *Interpersonal adjective scales professional manual.* Odessa, FL: Psychological Assessment Resources.

Wilkinson, G. S. (1993). *WRAT3 manual.* Wilmingotn, DE: Wide Range.

Williams, C. L., Butcher, J. N., Ben-Porath, Y. S., & Graham, J. R. (1992). *MMPI-A content scales: Assessing psychopathology in adolescents.* Minneapolis: University of Minnesota Press.

Williamson, E. G. (1939). *How to counsel students.* New York: McGraw Hill.

Willson, V. L. (1995). Review of Differential Aptitude Tests for Personnel and Career Assessment. In J. C. Conoley & J. C. Impara (Eds.), *The twelfth mental measurements yearbook* (pp. 305–307). Lincoln, NE: Buros Institute of Mental Measurements.

Winston, R. B., Miller, T. K., & Cooper, D. L. (1999). *Student developmental task and lifestyle assessment.* Athens, GA: Student Development Associates.

Winters, K. C. (1991). *Personal Experience Screening Questionnaire (PESQ) manual.* Los Angeles: Western Psychological Services.

Winters, K. C. (1996). *Personal Experience Inventory for Adults manual.* Los Angeles: Western Psychological Services.

Winters, K. C. (1999). *Screening and assessing adolescents for substance use disorders: Treatment Improvement Protocol (TIP) Series No. 31.* Rockville, MD: U.S. Department of Health and Human Services.

Winters, K. C., & Henley, G. A. (1989). *The Personal Experience Inventory.* Los Angeles: Western Psychological Services.

Wisconsin Clearinghouse. (1996). *Alcohol and other drugs: A self test.* Madison, WI: Author.

Wise, L., Welsh, J., Grafton, F., Foley, P., Earles, J., Sawin, L., & Divgi, D. R. (1992, December). *Sensitivity and fairness of the Armed Services Vocational Aptitude Battery (ASVAB) technical composites* (DMOC Tech. Rep. No. 92-002). Monterey, CA: Defense Manpower Data Center.

Wise, S. L., & Plake, B. S. (1990). Computer-based testing in higher education. *Measurement and Evaluation in Counseling and Development, 23,* 3–10.

REFERENCES

Wonderlic, E. F. (1999). *WPT user's manual*. Libertyville, IL: Author.

Worthington, E. L., McCullough, M. E., Shortz, J. L., Mindes, E. J., Sandage, S. J., & Chartrand, J. M. (1995). Can couples assessment and feedback improve relationships? Assessment as a brief relationship enrichment procedure. *Journal of Counseling Psychology, 42,* 466–475.

Yell, M. L., Drasgow, E., & Ford, L. (2000). The Individuals With Disabilities Education Act Amendments of 1997: Implications for school-based teams. In C. F. Telzrow & M. Tankersley (Eds.), *IDEA Amendments of 1997: Practice guidelines for school-based teams* (pp. 1–27). Bethesda, MD: National Association of School Psychologists.

Yelland, T. (1995). Review of Basic Personality Inventory. In J. C. Conoley & J. C. Impara (Eds.), *Twelfth mental measurements yearbook* (pp. 106–107). Lincoln, NE: Buros Institute of Mental Measurements.

Yesavage, J. A., Brink, T. I., Rose, T. L., Lum, O., Huang, V., Adey, M., & Leirer, V. O. (1983). Development and validation of a geriatric depression screening scale: A preliminary report. *Journal of Psychiatric Research, 17,* 37–49.

Zachary, R. A. (1986). *Shipley Institute of Living Scale: Revised manual*. Los Angeles: Western Psychological Services.

Zaske, K. K., Hegstrom, K. J., & Smith, D. K. (1999, August). *Survey of test usage among clinical and school psychologists*. Paper presented at the 107th Annual Convention of the American Psychological Association, Boston.

Zeidner, M. (1998). *Test anxiety: The state of the art*. New York: Plenum

Zeidner, M. (1999). The big-fish–little-pond effect for academic self-concept, test anxiety, and school grades in gifted children. *Contemporary Educational Psychology, 24,* 305–329.

Zhang, L. F., & Sternberg, R. J. (2001). Thinking styles across cultures: Their relationships with student learning. In R. J. Sternberg & L. F. Zhang (Eds.), *Perspectives on thinking, learning and cognitive styles* (pp. 197–226). Mahwah, NJ: Erlbaum.

Ziemelis, A. (1988). *Report of University of Wisconsin–La Crosse alcohol and drug issues survey*. La Crosse: University of Wisconsin, Counseling and Testing Center.

Zimet, G. D., Dahlem, N. W., Zimet, S. G., & Farley, G. K. (1988). The Multidimensional Scale of Perceived Social Support. *Journal of Personality Assessment, 52,* 30–41.

Zwi, M., Ramchandani, P., & Joughin, C. (2000). Evidence and belief in ADHD. *British Medical Journal, 321,* 975–976.

Zytowski, D. G. (1992). Three generations: The continuing evolution of Frederic Kuder's interest inventories. *Journal of Counseling & Development, 71,* 245–248.

Zytowski, D. G. (1994a). A super contribution to vocational theory: Work values. *Career Development Quarterly, 43,* 25–31.

Zytowski, D. G. (1994b). Test and counseling: We are still married and living in discriminant analysis. *Measurement and Evaluation in Counseling and Development, 26,* 219–223.

Zytowski, D. G. (1997). *How to talk with people about their interest inventory results.* Paper presented at the conference of the Society of Vocational Psychology, Bethlehem, PA.

Zytowski, D. G. (2001). Changes in the activity preference scales [Online]. *Kuder User News, 1*(4). Available: www.NationalCareerAssessment Services@lh.net.

Zytowski, D. G., & England, R. J. L. (1994). Indices of interest maturity in the Kuder Occupational Interest Survey. *Measurement and Evaluation in Counseling and Development, 28,* 148–151.

INDEX

INDEX

495